Fiscal Policy Formulation and Implementation in Oil-Producing Countries

Editors

J.M. Davis, R. Ossowski, and A. Fedelino

INTERNATIONAL MONETARY FUND

Production: IMF Graphics Section
Cover design: Lai Oy
Figures: Theodore Peters
Composition: Julio R. Prego

Cataloging-in-Publication Data

Fiscal policy formulation and implementation in oil-producing
   countries / edited by J.M. Davis, R. Ossowski, A. Fedelino—
   Washington, D.C. : International Monetary Fund,
   c2003.

   p. cm.

   ISBN 1-58906-175-6

   1. Petroleum industry and trade. 2. Petroleum products. Prices. 3. Pe-
troleum. Taxation. 4. Fiscal policy. I. Davis, Jeffrey M., 1946- II. Ossowski,
Rolando. III. Fedelino, Annalisa. IV. International Monetary Fund.
HD9560.5.F36 2003

Price: $37.00

Please send orders to:
International Monetary Fund, Publication Services
700 19th Street, N.W., Washington, D.C. 20431, U.S.A.
Tel.: (202) 623-7430   Telefax: (202) 623-7201
E-mail: publications@imf.org
Internet: http://www.imf.org

recycled paper

Contents

Foreword

Oil is a vital element of the world economy, and oil-producing countries represent an important group of IMF members. The Fund's surveillance and program work with oil producers has highlighted the difficult fiscal and macroeconomic challenges that reliance on oil revenues poses for policymakers.

It is clear that many countries have had difficulties in addressing the challenges posed by oil dependence. Notably, the growth performance of many oil producers has been disappointing; despite their huge natural resources, many of these countries still face widespread poverty; and the volatility of oil prices has often been associated with a stop-go pattern of expenditures that has proved costly in economic and social terms.

When considering these issues, it is necessary to recognize that not all producers are the same, and that key factors vary from country to country. Lessons should be distilled from the varied experiences, but they should be applied with due regard for each country's particular circumstances. In considering what worked and what did not, a key focus should be on how to manage oil resources in a way that contributes to a stable macroeconomic environment, broad-based sustainable growth, and durable poverty reduction.

In my view, it is critical to broaden the discussion to encompass political and institutional factors, since the management of oil resources does not take place in a vacuum. At the IMF, we are also attaching growing importance to the transparency with which oil revenues are collected and used. These are difficult and often sensitive topics, but they need to be addressed.

I welcome this book that, in exploring a wide range of critically important issues, brings together the IMF's operational experience with oil-producing countries—including work carried out in the Fiscal Affairs Department over the past few years—and significant contributions from outside experts. The IMF strives to be an open institution that learns from experience and dialogue, because we do not have all the answers. I hope that the publication of this volume will stimulate further dialogue with member countries and, more generally, promote further policy research and debate on these difficult but important issues.

Horst Köhler
Managing Director
International Monetary Fund

Acknowledgments

This book is the result of collective efforts from many individuals. Many of the papers were presented at the Conference on Fiscal Policy Formulation and Implementation in Oil-Producing Countries organized by the IMF's Fiscal Affairs Department (FAD) during June 5–6, 2002, and benefited from comments of participants in the conference. Some of them were originally issued as IMF Working Papers, and reflect comments from many colleagues in the Fund.[1]

We are grateful to colleagues in the Fiscal Operations I division of FAD, both for their comments on these papers and their contribution to our operational work on fiscal policy issues in oil-producing countries over the past several years. We would also like to acknowledge the papers and comments contributed by other colleagues in the IMF, the World Bank, and other international financial institutions, government officials, academics and experts, and representatives of the oil industry.

Special thanks are due to Steven Barnett, who provided constructive views on the issues covered in this volume. We appreciate the excellent research assistance provided by Alvaro Vivanco. Particular thanks are due to Heather Huckstep for her exceptional effort in managing the correspondence with authors and preparing the manuscript for publication. We also gratefully acknowledge the valuable assistance of Eva Farrugia in organizing the conference. Sean M. Culhane of the External Relations Department edited the manuscript and coordinated its production.

Finally, we would like to thank Teresa Ter-Minassian, Director of FAD, for her support for this project.

The views expressed throughout this publication are those of the contributing authors only and do not necessarily represent the posi-

---

[1] One paper was presented at an earlier conference and published in its proceedings, and thanks are due to the International Research Center for Energy and Economic Development (ICEED) in Boulder, Colorado, for allowing us to reprint it.

tion or policies of either their own national governments or any organization, government, or entity mentioned anywhere in this publication.

Jeffrey Davis
Rolando Ossowski
Annalisa Fedelino
Editors

1

Fiscal Challenges in Oil-Producing Countries: An Overview

JEFFREY DAVIS, ROLANDO OSSOWSKI, AND ANNALISA FEDELINO

This volume brings together papers that deal with a wide range of macroeconomic and fiscal issues in oil-producing countries, and aims at providing policy recommendations drawing on theory and country experience. The scope of the essays reflects the significant operational involvement of the IMF with oil producers, particularly in terms of surveillance, program work, and technical assistance. This work has highlighted the difficult challenges that confront policymakers in these countries, and the possibilities in several areas for improved practice.

The volatility of oil prices in recent years has brought these major challenges into sharper focus. Over a period of just a few years, oil prices plunged to around US$12 per barrel in late 1998, surged to US$30 per barrel in late 2000—only to fall back to US$20 per barrel in early 2002 (Figure 1.1). This volatility can translate into significant fluctuations in fiscal revenue. A case in point is Venezuela, where public sector oil revenues fell from 27 percent of GDP in 1996 to less than 13 percent of GDP in 1998 before rising again to more than 22 percent of GDP in 2000. At the same time, oil is an exhaustible resource, which poses difficult intergenerational equity questions. While it may be a distant concern for some producers, for others the reality of a post-oil period is approaching. And, since oil revenue largely originates from abroad, its fiscal use can have significant effects on the domestic economy.

Many oil producers have had difficulties designing and implementing policies in this context. Studies have shown that resource-dependent economies tend to grow more slowly than nonresource-

Figure 1.1. *Crude Oil Spot Prices*[1]
(In U.S. dollars per barrel)

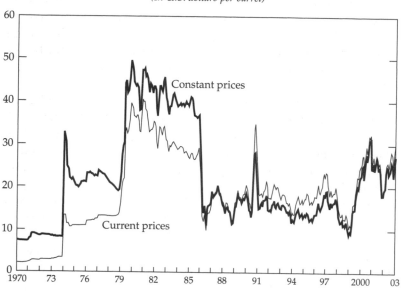

Sources: IMF, *International Financial Statistics* (Washington, various issues); and IMF staff estimates.

[1]Average of U.K. Brent, Dubai, and West Texas Intermediate. Constant prices deflated by the manufacturing unit value at January 2002 prices.

dependent ones at comparable levels of development. Poverty is still widespread in a number of oil-producing countries. Downturns in oil prices have in a number of cases led to external and fiscal crises. And a pattern of fluctuating fiscal expenditures associated with oil volatility has entailed significant economic and social costs for a number of oil producers.

Oil-producing countries, however, do not form a homogenous group. First, there is significant variation in the extent of oil dependence. In some countries, oil accounts for the vast majority of fiscal revenue and exports, while in others it is less significant for the economy. Second, oil sectors are at different stages of development. There are several new or soon-to-be producers where the oil sector is being developed, and oil revenues can be expected to grow substantially over the next few years. At the other end of the spectrum, some oil producers like Yemen face the prospect of depleting their oil resources in the not-too-distant future. Third, governments' financial positions also vary substantially. Some governments have accumulated sizable financial assets, while for others public debt is a major concern. This has implications for the options and constraints in responding to fluctuations in oil prices. And finally, the ownership of the oil sector also differs across countries. In countries such as Venezuela and Mexico, the oil sector is dominated by a state-owned producer. In other countries, the oil industry is largely in private hands.

Moreover, the way oil revenues are collected and used is not just an economic issue. Importantly, policies are framed within specific political and institutional frameworks. These frameworks—including their governance, transparency, and accountability characteristics—tend to vary among countries. Several papers in this volume incorporate wider institutional issues specifically into their analysis.

This book is structured around four broad sets of topics. The papers included in Part I examine fundamental macroeconomic and fiscal issues and institutional factors associated with the formulation and implementation of fiscal policy in oil-producing countries. Part II looks at more specific oil revenue issues, in particular the taxation and organization of the oil sector, national oil companies, and oil revenue and fiscal federalism. Institutional arrangements to deal with oil revenue instability, including oil funds and the use of oil risk markets, are the focus of the papers in Part III. Finally, the papers included in Part IV discuss domestic petroleum and energy-pricing issues.

Determining Fiscal Policy in Oil-Producing Countries

Countries with large oil resources can benefit substantially from them, and the government has an important role to play in how these resources are used. At the same time, the economic performance of many oil exporters has been disappointing, even to the extent of prompting some observers to ask whether oil is a blessing or a curse. The papers in this section address analytical and operational issues in the formulation of fiscal policy in oil-producing countries, as well as the political and institutional factors that may affect the design and execution of policy.

In Chapter 2, Hausmann and Rigobon introduce an innovative analytical approach to explain the "resource curse." Their model relates the poor growth performance of many oil-dependent countries to the interaction of government spending of oil income, specialization in nontradables, and financial market imperfections. Both the level and volatility of government expenditure contribute to lack of diversification, which, according to empirical evidence, exacerbates the resource curse. The main policy conclusions are that welfare and macroeconomic performance can be improved by reducing the volatility, and in some cases the level, of government spending; improving budget institutions, debt management, and policy credibility; and enhancing the efficiency of domestic financial markets.

Barnett and Ossowski address operational issues in formulating and assessing fiscal policy in oil-producing countries in Chapter 3. They put forward operational guidelines based on lessons drawn from the experience of many oil producers. First, the non-oil fiscal balance should be given greater attention as an indicator of fiscal policy, and should figure prominently in the budget and in fiscal analysis. Second, the non-oil balance, and expenditure in particular, should be adjusted gradually, which requires decoupling, to the extent possible, government spending from oil revenue volatility. Third, the government should strive to accumulate substantial financial assets over the period of oil production, on both sustainability and intergenerational equity grounds. Fourth, while many oil producers can afford to run sizable non-oil deficits, there are strong precautionary motives that would justify fiscal prudence. Fifth, in setting fiscal policy, consideration needs to be given to supporting the broader macroeconomic objectives. Finally, a number of oil producers should pursue strategies aimed at breaking procyclical fiscal responses to volatile oil prices and ensuring that the government's financial position is strong enough to weather downturns in oil prices.

Eifert, Gelb, and Tallroth (Chapter 4) provide an analysis of the underlying political and institutional determinants of the economic performance of oil exporters. Drawing on concepts from the comparative institutionalist tradition in political science, their paper develops a generalized typology of political states, which is used to analyze the political economy of fiscal and economic management in oil-exporting countries with widely differing political systems. Country experiences point to the key role played by constituencies for the sound use of oil rents, the importance of transparent political processes and financial management, and the value of getting the political debate to span longer time horizons.

Understanding the statistical properties of oil prices is important for fiscal policy formulation in oil-producing countries. In particular, whether oil price shocks are deemed to be temporary or persistent has implications for government wealth (including oil wealth)—a key input for assessing the sustainability of fiscal policy. In Chapter 5, Barnett and Vivanco test empirically the statistical properties of oil prices. Accepting that there are periodic permanent oil shocks (such as in 1973), their evidence suggests that most oil price movements are transitory. This implies that many year-to-year oil price fluctuations have only a minor impact on government wealth. For the most part, therefore—and looking only at sustainability considerations—governments should not adjust expenditure significantly in response to oil price changes.

Dealing with Oil Revenue

The papers included in Part II of this book address three sets of oil revenue issues. First, oil extraction plays a crucial fiscal role in generating tax and other revenue for the government in oil-producing countries. Therefore, the proper design of the fiscal regime for the oil sector is of key fiscal importance. Second, there is a need to look at the performance of national oil companies—including transparency and governance issues—since in many cases these enterprises play a major macroeconomic and fiscal role. Finally, three papers are devoted to fiscal federalism topics, as important questions arise over the assignment of oil revenues to various levels of government.

Sunley, Baunsgaard, and Simard argue in Chapter 6 that the fiscal regime must be properly designed to ensure that the state, as resource owner, receives an appropriate share of oil rent. Competing demands arise between the government and oil companies over sharing risk and reward from oil investments—where both aim at maximizing reward while shifting risk as much as possible to the other party. A balance also needs to be struck between the desire to maximize short-term revenue against any deterrent effects this may have on investment in the oil sector. The paper surveys various fiscal regimes to collect revenue from the oil sector; cross-country evidence suggests that good fiscal regimes should guarantee some up-front revenue with sufficient progressivity to provide the government with an adequate share of economic rent.

In Chapter 7, a paper by McPherson on national oil companies covers an important area where previous work has been limited. The author argues that the performance of national oil companies is generally poor, as these enterprises are often plagued by lack of competition, the assignment of noncommercial objectives, weak governance, limited transparency and accountability, lack of oversight, and conflicts of interest. These ills may be addressed by setting performance standards, increasing competition in the oil sector, divesting noncore assets, transferring noncommercial activities to the government, and conducting (and publishing) independent audits on a regular basis. The reform of national oil companies, however, faces formidable obstacles, including political opposition and entrenched vested interests. To be successful, reform programs need support from the highest political levels as well as from a wide range of public opinion.

The assignment of oil revenues to various levels of government raises a number of extremely complex issues in oil-producing countries. These include whether subnational regions should have the right to raise revenues from natural resources; the ability of subnational governments to cope with oil revenue volatility given their expenditure assignments; the implications of various intergovernmental fiscal frameworks for the maintenance of overall fiscal control by central governments; interjurisdictional equity and redistribution issues; and environmental and social concerns.

In Chapter 8, McLure provides a conceptual framework for analyzing the assignment of revenues from the taxation of oil to various levels of government in multilayer systems. The paper focuses, in particular, on whether subnational governments should have the power to tax oil, why, and (if so) how. Most of the considerations examined in the paper suggest that revenues from oil should be reserved for national governments. There may be overriding legal and political economy considerations, however, that may lead to the assignment of power to tax oil to subnational governments.

The next two papers also see the centralization of revenues as the best solution. Reflecting the complexity of the issues, however, their authors reach different conclusions regarding second-best policies.

Ahmad and Mottu present a topology of existing oil revenue assignments in Chapter 9. While recognizing that the centralization of oil revenue is preferable, they conclude that a second-best solution would be to assign oil taxation bases with stable elements (such as production excises) to subnational governments, supplemented by stable transfers from the central government. This would allow subnational governments to finance a stable level of public services. The least preferred solution would be oil revenue sharing, which complicates macroeconomic management, does not provide stable financing of local public services, and may not diffuse separatist tendencies (oil-producing regions would still be better off by keeping their oil revenues in full).

Brosio also notes that a growing trend toward sharing of oil revenue with subnational governments bears out the principle that optimal policies (oil revenue centralization) often have to give way to second-best solutions (Chapter 10). Based on a review of various types of tax assignments and equalization mechanisms, he concludes that revenue sharing (including an equalization mechanism to limit regional disparities in revenues) should be preferred over the assignment of local taxes on oil. The main reasons are that oil is typically concentrated in a few regions; oil revenue is highly volatile and thus difficult for subnational governments to manage; oil taxes are complex and difficult to administer; and energy policy is a national responsibility.

Institutional Arrangements for Dealing with Oil Revenue Instability

Fiscal policymakers in oil-producing countries need to decide how expenditure can be insulated from oil revenue shocks, and the extent to which resources should be saved for future generations. The papers in this section discuss two institutional mechanisms that have been proposed to promote better fiscal management. First, oil funds have been suggested as an institutional response to stabilization and savings concerns, particularly when there are strong political pressures to increase spending. This is a topic where judgments on political economy issues can lead to different views, as reflected in the papers included in this section. Second, a potential way to deal with the oil price risks that affect the public finances of oil producers is to use oil risk markets.

Davis, Ossowski, Daniel, and Barnett look at the effectiveness of oil funds from both a theoretical and an empirical perspective (Chapter 11). The main types of funds include stabilization funds, savings funds, and financing ("Norwegian") funds. The objective of stabilization funds is to minimize the transmission of oil price volatility to fiscal policy by smoothing budgetary oil revenue. Savings funds aim at addressing intergenerational concerns. Oil funds other than financing funds, however, ignore the fungibility of resources, and therefore do not effectively constrain expenditure. Moreover, these funds often do little to improve the conduct of fiscal policy and entail certain risks, including fragmenting fiscal policy and asset management, creating a dual budget, and reducing transparency and accountability. Econometric evidence and country experiences generally raise questions as to the effectiveness of oil funds.

In Chapter 12, Skancke describes the Norwegian Petroleum Fund. The fund, which is viewed as a tool to enhance transparency in the use of oil wealth, is fully integrated into the budget and has flexible operating rules, thereby avoiding the problems discussed in the previous paper. Since the budget targets a non-oil deficit that is financed from the fund, the accumulation of resources in the fund corresponds to net financial public savings. A large-scale buildup of public financial resources, however, requires a high degree of consensus, transparency, and accountability—traditionally present in Norway—and therefore the Norwegian model may not be easily "exported" to many other oil-producing countries.

Wakeman-Linn, Mathieu, and van Selm note in Chapter 13 that despite the ambiguous track record of oil funds in other countries, Azerbaijan and Kazakhstan have created funds to assist them in managing their new petroleum wealth. The decision to establish funds in these countries was motivated by the serious challenge posed by an unfinished transition from planned to market economy in the context of an oil boom, which in the view of the authorities argued for the separation of oil revenues from other revenues. Given the recent history of these countries' oil funds, only preliminary conclusions can be drawn on how they have performed relative to their stated objectives. According to the authors, on balance these funds, if operated in accordance with existing rules, should contribute to better management of oil wealth and improved transparency. However, a further strengthening of these funds is urgently needed for their potential to be fully realized.

Hedging represents a possible way to reduce oil revenue volatility and limit oil price risk, as Daniel argues in Chapter 14. Hedging may allow for more realistic and certain budgeting, provide insurance against declines in oil prices, and lessen the chances of oil price falls forcing costly fiscal adjustments. As oil risk markets have matured in the last decade, their range and depth could allow many oil producers to hedge oil price risk. At the same time, concerns about the potential political costs of hedging (particularly the failure to benefit from upturns in prices), institutional capacity constraints, financial costs, and the depth of the market have discouraged many governments from actively using hedging. In many cases these concerns could be overcome, however, and the author encourages governments to explore the scope for hedging oil price risk.

Designing Policies for Domestic Petroleum Pricing

In oil-producing as well as oil-importing countries, domestic petroleum product prices are often heavily regulated. Many governments keep prices below international levels, resulting in the implicit or explicit subsidization of oil consumption. The quasi-fiscal costs and appropriateness of setting domestic prices at below-market rates, as well as the potential social consequences of price reform, are contentious and deeply political issues in many countries.

Gupta, Clements, Fletcher, and Inchauste (Chapter 15) argue that the subsidization of petroleum products in oil-producing countries does not appear to be a wise use of resources. Petroleum subsidies are inefficient and inequitable, implying substantial opportunity costs in terms of foregone revenue or productive expenditure, and procyclical, thus complicating macroeconomic management. Moreover, as these subsidies are typically not recorded in government budgets as expenditures, their economic cost, as well as the incidence on different income classes, is often poorly understood. Despite the substantial costs of implicit petroleum subsidies, reform is often difficult, as there is typically strong popular opposition to their elimination. Support for subsidy reform can be promoted through countervailing measures and publicity campaigns. Undertaking poverty and social impact analyses and establishing social safety nets can mitigate the adverse social and political effects of reforming energy subsidies.

In Chapter 16, Espinasa provides a simple accounting model to analyze the distribution of the cost of domestic petroleum subsidies between the government and the national oil company. It is found that the fiscal incidence of this cost depends on the fiscal regime in place. Some tax regimes shift the burden of subsidies to the state oil company, thus hampering its ability to invest and hence to provide the government with revenues over the medium term. In addition, estimates of the implicit subsidies should take into account domestic distribution and retail costs, which typically represent a sizable share of the final retail price.

In Chapter 17, Federico, Daniel, and Bingham examine the case for smoothing retail petroleum prices in countries where these prices are regulated by the government. The authors contend that full and automatic pass-through of international price changes to domestic retail prices is the first-best solution in a competitive market economy, as it allows for correct price signals and does not expose the government to undue fiscal risk as a result of volatile oil prices. However, most developing countries that regulate petroleum prices follow a discretionary approach to adjusting them, which suggests that from a political economy perspective full-cost pass-through is not a robust policy option. The paper therefore explores the case for government-managed retail price smoothing. It concludes that there is a sharp trade-off between the degree of price smoothing and government fiscal stability. Since many pricing rules would leave the government overexposed to oil price risk, only limited price smoothing is likely to be fiscally sustainable.

Energy sector operations often lead to quasi-fiscal activities. Petri, Taube, and Tsyvinski stress in Chapter 18 that this is the case in many of the countries of the former Soviet Union. Their study provides an analysis of quasi-fiscal activities arising from the mispricing of energy and the toleration of payment arrears. In addition to information on various countries of the former Soviet Union, the paper presents detailed case studies on Ukraine (a net energy importer) and Azerbaijan (an energy-rich country). The main policy recommendations in the paper focus on the need to adjust inappropriately low energy tariffs and improve financial discipline in order to reduce energy consumption and waste and streamline untargeted energy subsidies; to supplement these reforms with the provision of explicit and better targeted subsidies to needy population groups; to include estimates of quasi-fiscal activities in the reported fiscal positions; and to enhance the scrutiny of these activities and promote fiscal transparency.

Part I.
Determining Fiscal Policy in Oil-Producing Countries

2

An Alternative Interpretation of the "Resource Curse": Theory and Policy Implications

RICARDO HAUSMANN AND ROBERTO RIGOBON[1]

I. Introduction

It is often said that most people when reading about a theory wonder if it works in practice. Economists, when seeing things working in practice, wonder if they work in theory. The natural resource curse is a case in point. Countries highly dependent on oil or other natural resources have performed very poorly since 1980. Figure 2.1 shows GDP per capita at purchasing power parity for highly resource-intensive countries such as Saudi Arabia, Nigeria, Venezuela, and Zaïre, and for less intensive countries such as Indonesia and Mexico. The pattern is clear: the more dependent performed remarkably poorly. The less oil-dependent did better.

The concern that natural resource wealth may somehow be inmiserating is a recurring theme in both policy discussions and empirical analysis. The empirical regularity seems to be in the data,[2] but understanding its causes has been a much harder task.[3] Theorists have been hard at

---

[1]We are indebted to Dani Rodrik and Andrés Velasco for useful comments.

[2]For example, Sachs and Warner (1995b) estimated that countries fully dependent on the export of primary products grew about 2.5 percent per year more slowly in the 1970–1989 period. Gavin and Hausmann (1998) and Higgins and Williamson (1999) find a strong relationship between resource intensity and inequality.

[3]For example, Manzano and Rigobon (2001) attribute the low growth to a debt overhang associated with overborrowing during the boom of the 1970s.

Figure 2.1. *GDP Per Capita at Purchasing Power Parity for Different Countries*
(In constant U.S. dollar prices)

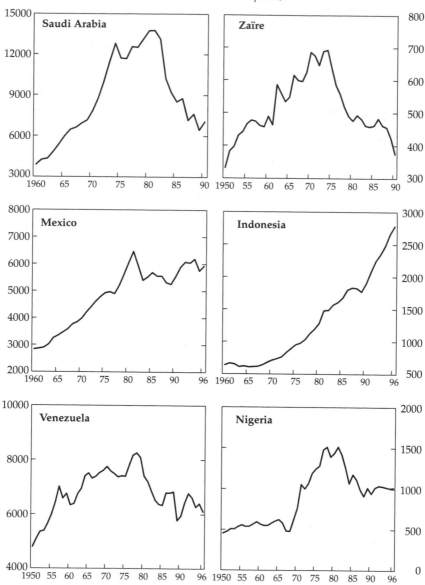

Sources: World Penn tables; and authors' calculations.

work to find a rationale. Is it a consequence of the Dutch disease? Is it caused by the volatility that characterizes resource-based commodity prices? Is it due to political economy forces unleashed by the presence of rents? And what are the policy implications of this problem? Is there such a thing as having too much oil for the country's own good? Should oil income be saved in net terms? Or is the question mainly that of dealing with the volatility in the flows? Are other policies called for?

In this paper we will propose an alternative rationale for the resource curse and discuss some of its policy implications. The approach is based on the interaction between two building blocks: specialization of the domestic economy in the production of nontradables and financial market imperfections. We show that as an oil economy becomes more specialized in the production of nontradables, the real exchange rate becomes more volatile because shocks to the demand for nontradables—associated for example with the fiscal expenditure of shocks to resource income—will not be accommodated by movements in the allocation of capital and labor across sectors but instead by expenditure switching. This requires much larger relative price movements.

Financial frictions such as risk aversion or costly bankruptcy on corporate debt imply that the interest rate will be a function of the volatility in the economy. In fact, the volatility of profits in the nonresource tradable sector can be shown to be larger than in the nontradable sector. As volatility increases, sector-specific interest rates rise causing a decline in the output that is larger for the nonresource tradable sector. A multiplier process is set in motion, where an initial rise in interest rates causes the tradable sector to contract, further raising volatility and interest rates until the sector disappears. At that point, the economy will face an even higher interest rate and a lower level of capital and output in the nontradable sector. An increase in resource income that leads to specialization causes a large decline in welfare: thus the idea of the curse. This form of specialization is inefficient and is characterized by high volatility and interest rates, weak real exchange rates, and low wages and investment. Inefficient specialization is determined by the level and the volatility of resource income and by the international interest rate. The paper discusses the role of fiscal saving of oil revenues as well as stabilization of expenditures. In addition, independent policies that reduce country risk and that improve the functioning of financial markets are seen as being particularly important in this context. More interventionist policies to subsidize investment in the nonresource tradable sector may also have a role to play.

II. Previous Approaches to the Resource Curse

There have been several approaches in the literature to account for the resource curse. The first is associated with the notion of the Dutch disease. The second has to do with the rent-seeking activities generated around the presence of the associated tax revenue. The third approach has to do with the damaging effects of volatility. In this section we will discuss each of these theories and their limitations.

The Dutch Disease Approach

Increases in resource-based revenues, such as oil, generate a greater capacity to import tradables, but typically prompt a greater demand for all goods including nontradables, which cannot be imported but must be produced locally. This requires the economy to move resources out of the nonresource tradable sector—call it manufacturing—in order to expand the production of nontradables such as construction and services. An oil boom would lead to a contraction in manufacturing. A real appreciation is the mechanism that gets the job done (Corden, 1982; Corden and Neary, 1982). This is the Dutch disease.

This logic is compelling, but by itself it does not imply any inefficiency or welfare loss. It only states that booms in resource income would be associated with contractions in manufacturing, not in overall growth. It cannot explain why a country would grow more slowly, just because it has oil.

To get some mileage, one has to assume that nonresource tradables play a special role in the growth process. This is the tradition started by Matsuyama (1992) where he assumed that there are increasing returns to scale in manufacturing, but not in the resource sector. Hence, an abundance of the natural resource makes the economy specialize in the less dynamic sector,[4] which may explain the curse.

One problem with this explanation is that one should expect that over the long run oil-exporting countries would be doing poorly when oil is doing well and that they would be improving when oil becomes less dynamic. However, over the 60-year period between the early 1920s and the early 1980s, Venezuela was the country with the highest growth in per capita income out of the 40 countries for which Maddi-

---

[4]Alternatively, it may want to diversify into resource-intensive industrialization, which has failed in many countries (Auty, 1990).

Table 2.1. *Average Annual Growth in Per Capita GDP*
at Purchasing Power Parity

Country Group	1960–1998	1960–1980	1980–1998	Number of Countries
All developing countries	1.7	3.0	0.2	115
Oil exporters	1.1	5.2	–2.1	15
Others	1.8	2.7	0.5	100

Sources: World Penn Tables; and authors' calculations.

son (1995) has data. During the following 20 years, Venezuela is among the worst performers in the world, a period that coincides with the decline of its oil income (Hausmann, 2001). This is not just a coincidence. The same pattern can be observed if we look at the growth rate of a wider group of countries over a shorter period. As Table 2.1 shows, oil-exporting countries grew faster in the period of rising oil prices and volumes between 1960 and 1980 relative to other developing countries and collapsed when oil revenues declined after 1980. If the Dutch disease story was right, the post-1980 story should have been one of greater growth. Hence, the story as such does not fit the facts.

Moreover, it is not obvious that learning by doing or technological development is slower in resource-based industries relative to others. As de Ferranti and others (2001) have shown in a recent report, several industrial countries such as Australia, Canada, and Finland became rich by developing the technology and capital goods industries associated with their resource sectors. Moreover, whatever bad effects specializing in natural resources might generate, they have to be compared with the benefits of owning large natural resources.

For example, natural resource income may raise national savings and hence facilitate capital accumulation and growth. This is not a minor aspect as oil-exporting economies have averaged twice the savings rate of non-oil exporters (Table 2.2). Moreover, they were able to save more and grow more in the period when oil was growing fast (1960–1980) relative to the more recent episode (1980–1998).

The Rent-Seeking Story

An alternative story is that resource wealth such as oil somehow makes societies less entrepreneurial. There is so much wealth floating around the government that entrepreneurial persons find it much more

Table 2.2. *Average Domestic Savings Rate*

Country Group	1960–1998	1960–1980	1980–1998	Number of Countries
All developing countries	17.1	18.4	16.2	111
Oil exporters	33.2	37.9	30.1	15
Others	14.6	15.3	14.0	96

Sources: World Penn Tables; and authors' calculations.

profitable to engage in unproductive rent-seeking activities to appropriate that wealth rather than in creating more wealth. The presence of common-pool problems or uncertainty over property rights over the resource income may generate low growth by inefficiently focusing economies in fighting over existing resources.

The common-pool problem—caused by situations where costs are shared between many agents but benefits are private (e.g., as in fiscal policy)—may lead to overspending on average and to a distorted allocation of spending over time. Overspending is associated with the idea that different constituencies do not internalize the full cost of their spending requests, as they only pay a small fraction of the additional tax burden (Johnsen, Shepsle, and Weingast, 1981; von Hagen and Harden, 1997). This problem is not specific to resource-rich economies, but instead is present in all countries. However, in resource-rich economies, where nonresource taxes are typically low and resource rents are large, it could be argued that this force could in theory be more powerful.

In a dynamic setting this logic may lead to overborrowing and to a voracity effect (Hausmann, Powell, and Rigobon, 1993; Tornell and Velasco, 1995; and Lane and Tornell, 1999b). Assume that it is best to save a temporary boom until some future time when lower resource income is expected. An individual would choose to smooth consumption. However, when there is a common-pool problem each constituency will ask for a larger share of the pie in good times, fearing that if it does not, other constituencies might take it away.

This story again does not explain why oil economies did so well when incomes were rising and why they have underperformed so strongly in the last two decades.

In yet a different setting, others have argued (Karl, 1997) that oil economies, by not developing the political compact that allows the state to tax its citizens, are poorly equipped to deal with collapses in oil revenues without leading to macroeconomic crises.

This logic may be present, but other factors may well overwhelm it. We already mentioned the fact that resource revenue may allow for higher savings. It may also allow the country to reduce taxation over more mobile factors and hence achieve a less distortionary overall taxation scheme, thus generating a more propitious economic environment for growth. Moreover, the political skills required to allocate rents among different groups may be useful in achieving the necessary reallocations when income declines.

The Volatility Story

An alternative explanation to the curse puts the emphasis on volatility. Volatility has been shown to be bad for growth, for investment, for income distribution, for poverty, and for educational attainment.[5] Natural resource rents tend to be very volatile because the supply of natural resources exhibits low price elasticities of supply (at least in the short term). For example, the standard deviation of oil price changes has been about 30 to 35 percent per year. For a country where oil represents about 20 percent of GDP, a one-standard deviation shock to the price of oil represents an income shock equivalent to 6 percent of GDP. This is huge relative to total GDP volatilities in industrial countries (about 2 percent) or even developing countries (between 3 percent and 4 percent).

But how does volatility in the terms of trade damage the economy? Assume that resource revenues are distributed to the population as a whole, say through government transfers. This means that the fact that the revenue is volatile makes it less valuable to risk-averse consumers. Let us take a relatively severe example. Assume that in a given economy oil is 30 percent of national income and that it has a standard deviation of about 30 percent per year. Assume that utility can be described with a constant relative risk aversion (CRRA) utility function with a relatively high coefficient of risk aversion of 3. This implies that consumers would be willing to sacrifice 4.05 percent of national income in order to make oil revenues perfectly certain. They would be willing to spend that much money in hedging their resource risk: certainly more than a simple nuisance, but nothing that could reasonably be

---

[5]See Inter-American Development Bank (1995), Ramey and Ramey (1995), Gavin and Hausmann (1996), Aizenman and Marion (1999), Caballero (2000). Duryea (1998) and Flug and others (1998) discuss the impact of volatility on educational attainment.

called a curse, when compared with the revenue it generates. This could reasonably justify organizing a seminar to discuss how governments should manage this risk, but is not an adequate explanation for the massive collapse in growth exhibited in Figure 2.1.

So the welfare losses associated with the consumption risk of the flow itself are not particularly large. To get bigger effects, the rest of the economy must somehow be disrupted by the volatility in oil. Interestingly, in a neoclassical setting, it is quite hard to make volatility matter. Imagine first a competitive economy in which capital is perfectly mobile internationally and labor is nationally fixed, but is perfectly mobile domestically across sectors. Assume that there are three sectors: a resource sector—which we will call oil, a tradable sector, and a nontradable sector. Oil is produced without either capital or labor: it is like manna from heaven. One can also think of it as aid. The two other sectors use capital and labor and exhibit constant returns to scale. In this case, *so long as all goods are produced domestically*, the volatility of the oil sector will not affect the value of non-oil output or any non-oil relative price. The income of workers and the rate of return to capital in the non-oil economy will be unaffected by oil volatility. Hence, the only problem will be the dislike for oil volatility itself and this we have already found not to be too serious.

To understand this surprising result it is important to remember that there are five prices in this economy. First, the price of oil is determined abroad. Second, the rate of return to capital will be set by the world interest rate, given perfect capital mobility. Third, the price of tradables will be set internationally through the law of one price. Fourth, the internationally determined price of tradables and cost of capital together with the zero-profit condition required by perfect competition will set the wage that the tradable sector can pay, which will determine, through the free movement of workers between sectors, the wage rate for the whole economy. Fifth, this will determine nontradable prices since wages and the cost of capital are already set and profits must be zero. Shocks to the demand for nontradables (induced possibly by oil shocks) will be adjusted through movements of labor between sectors and movements of capital in and out of the economy. The production possibility frontier will be completely flat. Therefore, an increase in demand driven, for example, by a positive oil income shock would result in an increase in production of nontradables (the shift from Y_{NA} to Y_{NB} in Figure 2.2), to be accommodated by a decrease in the domestic production of tradables, from Y_{TA} to Y_{TB}, without changes in relative prices. At the same time, the upward shift in the budget constraint due

Figure 2.2. *The Benchmark Model: The Diversified Economy*

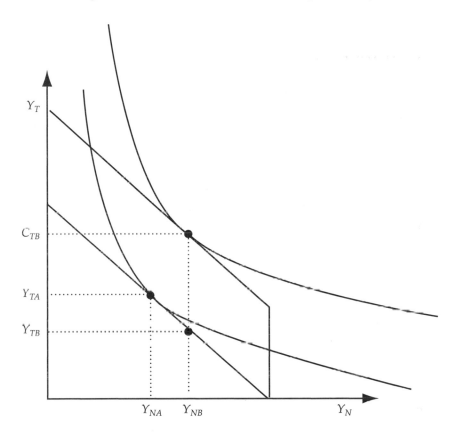

to higher income will result in higher consumption of both nontradables and tradables (the point C_{TB} in Figure 2.2).

This is a very important benchmark not because it is an adequate description of the world, but because it provides a point of departure to think of the possible characteristics of the world—not included in the benchmark—that may explain why oil and its volatility may become really problematic.

With full employment, and set wages and returns to capital, non-oil income will be stable. The only source of volatility will be the direct impact of oil revenues on household income. As we mentioned above, the welfare losses associated with oil revenue uncertainty are not huge—a nuisance more than a curse. To explain the curse, the non-oil economy must be more seriously disturbed by oil volatility.

What features of the world does the benchmark model not take into account? First, capital takes *time to build* and once invested is usually *irreversible*. It cannot move instantaneously between sectors. This is certainly a problem. It means that the production function will be convex and that the volatility in spending of oil income will cause shifts in relative prices. However, the consequences of this are not as serious as one might think. In a standard model, profits are a convex function of relative prices (Caballero, 1991). This means that the greater the volatility in relative prices the larger the expected profits and average investment will be![6] Moreover, if we assume full employment, the welfare of workers may actually go up and not down with volatility, since they would be working on average with more capital. Hence, irreversibility of investment cannot be the basis for a serious curse.

Second, consider the presence of *price and wage rigidities* that prevent the labor market from clearing. In this case, and assuming that capital is predetermined and irreversible,[7] volatility in oil income and government spending will translate into changes in unemployment and output in the nontradable sector. Notice, however, that the tradable sector will remain unaffected: it will face constant prices, wages, and stock of capital. Therefore employment and output in the tradable sector will be constant. The nontradable sector will have constant capital and wages but volatile output. There will also be more capital invested in the nontradable sector than in the benchmark model, given the convexity of the profit function. Welfare losses caused by oil volatility are likely to be larger, because volatility is larger, but the expected average levels of output and consumption should not be much affected.

A New Approach

So where can the curse come from? We will argue that it will arise from an interaction between specialization and financial market imperfections. In the benchmark model we assumed that the economy was producing all goods. What happens if the non-oil economy stops

---

[6]Whether volatility on a variable causes the expected value of some other variable to increase or decrease depends on the concavity or convexity of the relationship between the two. Concavity lowers the expected value while convexity increases it. Hence, if the profit function is convex, then volatility is good for expected profits and leads to more investment.

[7]It makes sense to assume that if prices cannot be readjusted, capital should be even harder to adjust.

Figure 2.3. *The Benchmark Model: The Specialized Economy*

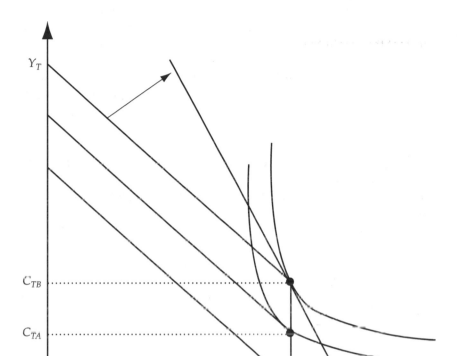

producing non-oil tradables and becomes *completely specialized in nontradables*? Central to the results of the benchmark model is the requirement that there be a positive level of production of tradables: the non-oil economy must not be fully specialized in nontradables. This allows labor movements between sectors to absorb the shocks to nontradable demand. If the economy were fully specialized in non-tradables, this result would disappear (Figure 2.3). Labor would now be fixed and fully employed in nontradables. The only way to expand supply would be by increasing the amount of capital per worker in the sector. But capital is required to get the international rate of return. However, with labor fixed, the productivity of each additional unit of capital would be falling. To avoid a fall in returns to capital, the price of nontradables must go up. Hence, the supply of nontradables will now be upward sloping. But the demand for nontradables must be downward sloping. An increase in the price of nontradables will cause expenditure-switching effects as consumers will substitute away from the now more expensive nontradables and into tradables. The relative price between these two goods—that is, the real exchange rate—will have to move in order to clear the market for nontradables. In the end, the economy will remain "stuck" in the corner solution shown in Figure 2.3, where no tradables are produced, and shifts in demand driven by income changes only affect consumption levels of tradables.

So, in the benchmark model, a specialized economy with volatile re-source revenue will see a volatile real exchange rate, while a diversified economy will have a constant real exchange rate. In this setting, irre-versibility in capital will make relative prices even more volatile, as now the supply of nontradables would be completely predetermined, given that both labor and capital will be fixed. Only expenditure-switching forces will be at play. This will make the real exchange rate even more volatile.

It will be shown below that this still is not enough to generate a real curse. In addition, it is necessary to assume some form of financial fric-tion, either risk aversion or costly bankruptcy. This will make interest rates go up as the volatility of the real exchange rate increases, creating a vicious circle between greater volatility of the real exchange rate and higher interest rates on the one hand and lower investment in tradables (more specialization) on the other, which induces greater real exchange rate volatility. The interest rate faced by the tradable sector increases until the sector disappears and the economy fully specializes ineffi-ciently in nontradables. The inefficiently specialized economy will ex-hibit higher interest rates on nontradables, lower capital and wages, and a more depreciated exchange rate.

III. Modeling the Curse

In this section we offer a formal model of inefficient specialization. The ingredients of the model are the following: assume there are three sectors in the economy—tradables, nontradables, and oil. Oil is as-sumed to consume no inputs and generates a stochastic stream of rev-enues denominated in tradables. We assume it is exogenous and denoted by $\bar{g}L$. For simplicity, we have assumed that government ex-penditure is defined in per capita terms.

The tradable and nontradable sectors comprise a finite number of firms, each using capital and labor.

We assume that capital is owned by foreigners. This simplifies the analysis as it allows us to disregard the effect of changes in capital income. Nevertheless, the results are unaffected (qualitatively speaking) by assuming that domestic agents own some capital. We will assume that capital is irreversible and that it has to be decided one period before production and oil revenues are realized.

We assume that oil belongs to the government, which consumes it entirely in nontradable goods. If the government decides to save its oil revenue, it will do so in foreign assets. We will assume that households derive no utility out of government consumption.[8] This means that the volatile government consumption will not enter directly into the utility of risk-averse households who might want to smooth it. This eliminates the standard justification for stabilization.[9] As discussed above, this cannot possibly be the source of the curse if there is one. We assume that there are no taxes.

Finally, we assume that capital is fully depreciated in one period and that consumers cannot save. Thus, in this regard, the model is equivalent to a single-period model.

Production

We assume that firms are small (price takers). We assume there are N_N firms in the nontradable sector. Each firm requires an investment of one unit of capital to operate, and each production function is given by

$$y_N = l_N^{1-\alpha} \text{ and} \tag{1}$$

$$y_T = l_T^{1-\alpha}, \tag{2}$$

where y refers to the output per firm, l refers to the labor input per firm, and the subscripts N and T refer to the nontradable and tradable sectors, respectively.

Optimal labor decisions conditional on the capital invested in the nontradable sector solves

---

[8]Whether government spending involves directly hiring workers or buying services from the nontradable sector is immaterial for the analysis. Workers are fully employed and indifferent as to the sector of employment.

[9]Volatile government spending will affect welfare through its general equilibrium effects.

$$\max P_N l_N^{1-\alpha} - w l_N, \tag{3}$$

where P_N and w are the price of nontradable goods and wages in domestic currency, respectively. The solution implies that labor demand is

$$l_N = \left[(1 - \alpha) \frac{P_N}{w} \right]^{\frac{1}{\alpha}}; \tag{4}$$

production is

$$y_N = \left[(1 - \alpha) \frac{P_N}{w} \right]^{\frac{1-\alpha}{\alpha}}; \tag{5}$$

and profits in the sector in domestic currency are

$$\pi_N = \frac{\alpha}{1 - \alpha} w \left[(1 - \alpha) \frac{P_N}{w} \right]^{\frac{1}{\alpha}}. \tag{6}$$

The tradable sector is similar. There are N_T firms, where, again, each firm requires one unit of capital. We have assumed that the capital share is the same in both sectors. Hence,

$$l_T = \left[(1 - \alpha) \frac{e}{w} \right]^{\frac{1}{\alpha}}, \tag{7}$$

where e is the exchange rate. Production is

$$y_T = \left[(1 - \alpha) \frac{e}{w} \right]^{\frac{1-\alpha}{\alpha}}, \tag{8}$$

and profits in the sector in domestic currency are

$$\pi_T = \frac{\alpha}{1 - \alpha} w \left[(1 - \alpha) \frac{e}{w} \right]^{\frac{1}{\alpha}}. \tag{9}$$

Government

We assume that oil exports are in foreign currency. Hence, the total government consumption of nontradable goods is

$$\frac{e}{P_N} \tilde{g} L. \tag{10}$$

In this simple setup we are assuming that the government does not face any financial frictions. In other words, the cost of financing is the same as the benefits of saving.

Demand

Households consume tradable and nontradable goods, but not oil. As mentioned above, there are no taxes. We assume that consumers' utility can be represented by the standard Cobb-Douglas utility function. Furthermore, to simplify the number of parameters under study, we assume equal weights on tradable and nontradable goods. Assume the consumers solve

$$\max C_T^{1-\beta} C_N^{\beta}$$
$$s.t.\ eC_T + P_N C_N \le W, \tag{11}$$

where C_T, C_N, and W are the consumption of tradables, consumption of nontradables, and wealth of consumers, respectively; β is the share of nontradables. The first-order conditions (FOC) of the maximization problem implies the standard solution. Given our assumption that the capital is owned by foreigners, then consumers' income is given by total labor income:

$$C_N = \beta L \frac{w}{P_N}, \tag{12}$$

where L is total labor employed in both tradable and nontradable sectors.

Equilibrium

Conditional on the amount of capital in the nontradable sector, we compute the labor market equilibrium:

$$L_T + L_N = L,$$
$$L_T = N_T l_T, \text{ and} \tag{13}$$
$$L_N = N_N l_N,$$

and the nontradable goods market equilibrium in our benchmark model:

$$C_N + \frac{e}{P_N} \tilde{g} L = Y_N, \tag{14}$$

where Y_N is the total nontradable output.

Substituting, the two equations solving for equilibrium are

$$N_N \left[(1-\alpha)\frac{P_N}{w}\right]^{\frac{1}{\alpha}} + N_T\left[(1-\alpha)\frac{e}{w}\right]^{\frac{1}{\alpha}} = L \text{ and} \tag{15}$$

$$\beta L \frac{w}{P_N} + \frac{e}{P_N}\,\tilde{g}L = N_N\left[(1-\alpha)\frac{P_N}{w}\right]^{\frac{1-\alpha}{\alpha}}. \tag{16}$$

Define,

$$q = \frac{P_N}{w} \text{ and} \tag{17}$$

$$Q = \frac{e}{P_N},$$

where q is the relative price of nontradables in terms of wages and Q is the real exchange rate.

This implies that the two equations collapse to

$$N_N + N_T Q^{\frac{1}{\alpha}} = L\left[(1-\alpha)q\right]^{-\frac{1}{\alpha}} \text{ and} \tag{18}$$

$$\frac{N_N}{N_N + N_T Q^{\frac{1}{\alpha}}} = (1-\alpha)\beta + (1-\alpha)qQ\tilde{g}. \tag{19}$$

Note that the total number of firms must be greater than zero. Note also that it is impossible to find a set of parameters in which the number of nontradable firms is zero. However, there exists a set of coefficients where the number of tradable firms indeed is zero. For those circumstances, the set of equations determining the equilibrium in the labor market and the nontradable goods market is identical to the previous ones but with N_T equal to zero.

After some algebra these two equations collapse to the following relationship:

$$[1 - (1-\alpha)\beta - \Psi]\left(\frac{N_T}{L}\right)^{\alpha} = \Psi^{\alpha}\tilde{g}$$

$$\Psi = \frac{N_N}{N_N + N_T Q^{\frac{1}{\alpha}}}. \tag{20}$$

Figure 2.4. *Inefficient Specialization*

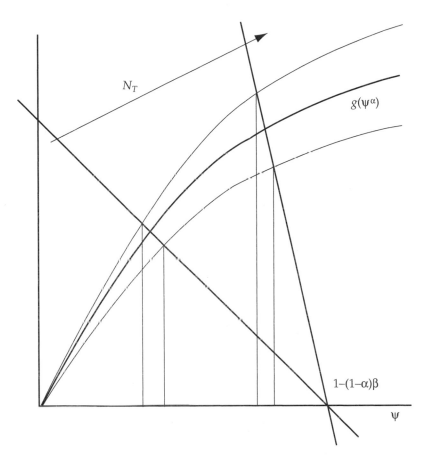

Assume the number of firms in the nontradable sector is given.[10] Then this equation uniquely defines the number of tradable firms in equilibrium. The equilibrium is studied in Figure 2.4.

The downward sloping line corresponds to the left-hand side (LHS) of equation (20), and the increasing concave schedule is the right-hand side (RHS). Notice that all the uncertainty of government oil expenditures appears on the RHS. Hence, we have depicted three schedules reflecting the (supposedly) maximum, median, and minimum of the shocks to oil income.

---

[10] We will relax this assumption in the next section.

As can be seen, the line and the schedule determine (uniquely) the real exchange rate at which both equilibrium conditions are satisfied. Note that for each realization of oil income there is a corresponding real exchange rate (RER).

In the figure, we have depicted an increase in the number of tradable firms. This makes the LHS line steeper. For a given level of uncertainty, this implies an increase in the expected value of Ψ, and a reduction in its variance. Since Ψ is an inverse function of the RER, we conclude that *a larger tradable sector requires a more depreciated exchange rate, but delivers a more stable RER for the same degree of oil-related uncertainty.*

This is an important characteristic of the model and it is useful to understand what drives it. When the number of tradable firms is large (small), reductions in the demand for nontradables can be accommodated through an expansion in the output of tradables with a relatively small (large) decline in the real wage, since the high (low) stock of capital per potential worker invested in tradable production implies that the marginal product of labor declines little (a lot) for every additional worker. In the limit, if there is no capital invested in the tradable sector, there will be no employment in the sector and the adjustment will take place exclusively through the expenditure-switching implications of real exchange rate movements. This fact will become important below when we endogenize the number of firms.

Irreversible Capital and Financial Frictions

The final ingredients of the model relate to the investment decision, which in this setup is equivalent to the number of firms in each sector, as each firm has a single unit of capital. As was mentioned before, all capital is foreign-owned. Irreversibility implies that investors have to decide the number of firms that will operate in each sector before the oil-related uncertainty—in this case, the government expenditure—is realized. If investors are risk neutral, the entry condition for the non-tradable sector is

$$E\left\{\frac{\alpha}{\theta}\left[(1-\alpha)q\right]^{\frac{1-\alpha}{\alpha}}\right\} \geq \rho, \tag{21}$$

and for the tradable sector is

$$E\left\{\alpha\left[(1-\alpha)q\theta\right]^{\frac{1-\alpha}{\alpha}}\right\} \geq \rho, \tag{22}$$

where E is the expectation operator. Substituting equations (18) and (19) we see that the stochastic profits in each of the sectors are

$$\tilde{\pi}_N = \alpha L^{1-\alpha} \frac{N_N}{N_T^\alpha} \frac{\Psi}{(1 - \Psi)^\alpha} - \rho \text{ and} \tag{23}$$

$$\tilde{\pi}_T = \alpha L^{1-\alpha} \frac{1}{N_T^{1-\alpha}} (1 - \Psi)^{1-\alpha} - \rho. \tag{24}$$

Now, we introduce financial frictions in the model by appealing to risk aversion. However, the results presented in the paper would be the same if instead of risk aversion we had assumed costly bankruptcy.

Firms require a rate of return that must compensate them for the volatility of profits. The rate of return will be proportional to their degree of risk aversion σ. Assume that the entry condition is given by

$$\Pi_i = \frac{\tilde{\pi}_i^{1-\sigma}}{1 - \sigma}, \tag{25}$$

where i stands for sectors N or T.

Risk aversion in this setup implies that the expected return has to exceed the risk-free rate by σ times the variance of profits. Notice that the profits of the tradable sector inherit the stochastic properties of Ψ. Indeed, the variance is proportional to the variance of Ψ. When the number of tradable firms increases, the value of Ψ increases (diminishing the expected profit) but reducing its variance. Notice that this effect is different in the nontradable sector. An increase in the number of tradable firms increases the expected value of Ψ, increasing the expected value of the profits, and reducing the volatility of Ψ, reducing further the risk premium. Hence, in the nontradable sector the effect on expected profits and its variance go in the same direction, while they go in opposite directions in the tradable sector.

Simulation

In this section we simulate numerically the model in order to understand the implications of changes in the size of the oil revenues, their volatility, and degree of risk aversion on the economy. In particular, we will study their effect on the number of firms in each sector, the utility of households, and the volatility of the real exchange rate. The parameters chosen for the simulation are as follows. The economy has a size of $L = 1$. We assume that the risk-neutral rate of return required is equal to 5 percent. We set α equal to 0.25 and not the more common 0.3–0.4 because in this model, capital is composed of tradable goods. In real life, capital also has nontradable components. However, assuming a demand for nontradables for investment purposes would have complicated the model unnecessarily.

We let the mean level of oil income move from 0.1 to 0.8. We assume that it is uniformly distributed with a coefficient of variation of zero, 0.25, 0.75, and 0.875. We present our results for two cases: a risk-neutral case (σ = 0, which we interpret as no financial frictions) and an alternative case with a relatively large degree of risk aversion (σ = 15).

In Figures 2.5 and 2.6, the x-axis indicates the mean level of the oil income. Each figure has four panels: the top panel is the number of nontradable firms in equilibrium, the second one is the number of tradable firms, the third is the utility households derive from consumption, and the final panel is the volatility of the real exchange rate. In each panel we represent four curves representing the four degrees of volatility mentioned above, where the thicker lines represent greater volatilities.

The risk-neutral case is studied first (Figure 2.5). As the mean level of oil income increases, the number of firms in the nontradable sector rises and the number in the tradable sector declines. The economy monotonically tends to specialize away from tradables, as would be predicted from the standard Dutch disease literature. Notice that utility is little affected by the level of oil income. Recall that we assume that the government spends the oil revenue in nontradable goods that households do not value and that capital is foreign owned. Hence, the utility of households is determined by the real wage and this does not change with oil income.

Volatility in this setup has surprising effects: it *increases* the number of firms in the tradable sector, *lowers* the number of firms in the nontradable sector, and *increases* utility! This contradicts the conventional wisdom that suggests that the increase in uncertainty should be bad for investment, especially if it is irreversible. This intuition does not hold in this model, a feature amply discussed in the neoclassical literature (see Hartman, 1972; Caballero, 1991; Caballero and Pindyck, 1996). The main reason for this effect is the fact that the profits of tradable firms are a convex function of Ψ. This means that greater volatility increases expected profits and investment in tradables. On the other hand, the profits in the nontradable sector can be concave or convex in Ψ, and hence the volatility may have less salutary effects. For the parameters in this model the function is concave and the num-

Figure 2.5. *Simulation: The Risk-Neutral Case*

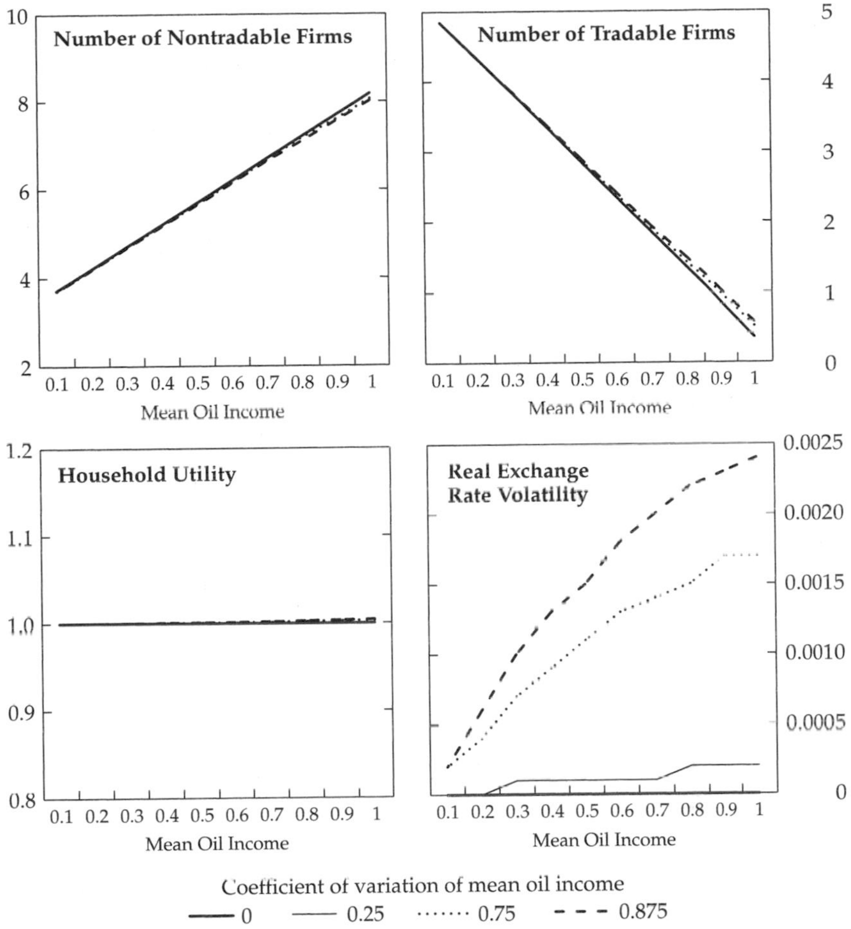

Coefficient of variation of mean oil income
—— 0   —— 0.25   ······ 0.75   – – – 0.875

Source: Authors' calculations.

ber of nontradable firms falls with volatility.[11] Utility increases because wages are also convex in Ψ. Interestingly, specialization in this model is not associated with volatility but, instead, solely with the average level of oil income. Hence, policies geared at stabilization are not welfare improving.

_____

[11]In fact, for most reasonable sets of parameters the schedule is concave. The relationship becomes convex when the number of nontradable firms approaches zero.

Figure 2.6. *Simulation: The Risk-Averse Case*

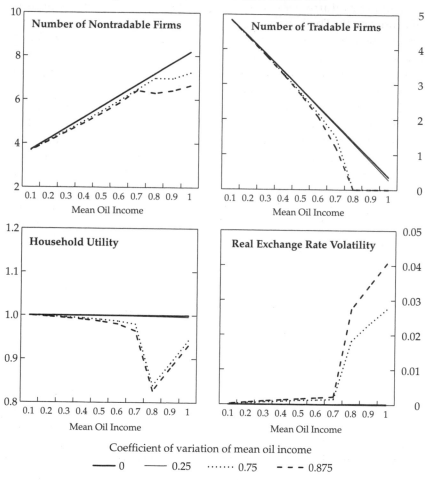

Source: Authors' calculations.

We now turn to the case with risk aversion (Figure 2.6). We assume a level of risk aversion of 15, which is high by conventional standards but significantly less than the coefficient of 40 required to explain the equity premium in developed countries. Remember that we take risk aversion to be a proxy for financial frictions in the economy.

Here we observe a similar initial impact of increases in the mean level of oil income on the number of firms in both sectors. However, notice that now volatility lowers the number of firms in both sectors, as investors demand a higher return to compensate for the greater variance in their returns, overwhelming the otherwise convex relationship of profits on Ψ. There is a point at which the tradable sector completely shuts down. We refer to this phenomenon as *inefficient specialization*. At that point, the number of firms in the nontradable sector also declines (and then rises very gradually), the volatility of the real exchange rate increases by a factor of more than 10, and utility collapses.

The mechanism that brings this about is a vicious circle between specialization and volatility. Remember that the volatility of the real exchange rate and Ψ are inversely proportional to the number of firms in tradables. As the number declines profits become more volatile, but risk aversion now requires a higher risk premium, which lowers investment in tradables further and further increases volatility. The sector disappears because the cost of capital makes expected firm profits negative. This happens only in the tradable sector because its price is exogenously set. In the nontradable sector, the increase in risk premiums lowers investment, but this increases the price of nontradables, preserving profitability.

The decline in utility is related to the magnitude of the inefficiency of the specialization. A measure of this inefficiency is the difference between the number of tradable firms in the zero-volatility curve and the actual number of firms. Notice that as the average level of oil income increases, the economy would naturally specialize, and the gap between the efficient number of firms and the actual number declines. Hence, utility recovers, but does not reach the no-volatility level because the absence of the tradable sector makes the real exchange rate more volatile and lowers the investment in nontradables, where the number of firms also falls relative to the optimal level.

This result might help explain why countries that were very specialized in oil production such as Saudi Arabia, Nigeria, and Venezuela fared so poorly when oil income declined, while countries such as Indonesia, Mexico, and Norway were much less affected. The first group was specialized in oil and when oil income declined that specialization became much more inefficient, while the lack of a tradable sector created a level of volatility and risk premiums that did not allow for investment. Diversified countries could adjust with much smaller costs.

In conclusion, (i) specialization in the production of nontradables creates an economy with more volatile relative prices; (ii) financial frictions interact with this volatility, further specializing the economy as the stock of capital will respond to the greater macroeconomic volatility; (iii) this specialization may lead to the complete and inefficient disappearance of tradable production; and (iv) this specialization reduces the investment in nontradables—which will face a larger cost of capital—and lowers welfare.

Clearly, in this context, a higher level of oil revenues can become a curse if it leads the economy to inefficiently specialize. Moreover, stabilization policies can have large welfare implications.

IV. Policy Implications

The curse of natural resources has so far been explained as being caused by either rent seeking or diversification away from sectors enjoying increasing returns. Separately, expenditure stabilization policies have been advocated based on the welfare benefits of consumption smoothing. This paper has proposed an alternative mechanism for the curse that integrates it with the discussion of stabilization.

An economy that is diversified, in terms of having a significant non-oil tradable sector, will be much less affected by volatility in government domestic spending than an economy that is already fully specialized in nontradables. This is so because in a diversified economy shocks to nontradable demand can be accommodated through changes in the structure of production, while specialized economies have to rely on expenditure switching. We note that countries with more resource rents will naturally produce fewer tradables and hence are more likely to be naturally specialized.

However, the presence of quite standard financial frictions, such as costly bankruptcy, will make relative price volatility affect the cost of capital through risk premiums. This has three major consequences: first, it causes the economy to specialize further by making it harder and in some cases impossible for the tradable sector to access capital; second, it causes higher interest rates and less capital in the nontradable sector under specialization; third, it greatly increases the welfare losses caused by volatility.

The policy implications of this model are relatively straightforward. They have to do with avoiding inefficient specialization and reducing the costs of volatility. We separate our discussion into two parts. First we deal with first-best policies, which are based on reducing the distortions in the economy. Then we move to second-best policies, where we assume that the distortions are hard to remove and look at interventions that can improve welfare, given that the distortions make the market outcome inefficient. This is in general the spirit of the policies we are discussing below.

Fiscal Policy

To discuss fiscal policy it is important to distinguish three types of countries:
- those that are naturally specialized, i.e., those that would special-ize even in the absence of volatility;
- those that are inefficiently specialized; and
- those that are not specialized and would like to stay that way.

Naturally specialized countries

These countries have so much natural resource wealth that it does not make sense for them to engage in the production of other tradables, even in a first-best world. Some Gulf states might be in this category. However, in these countries, specialization makes relative prices very sensitive to the volatility in government spending. These countries would benefit from policies that stabilize government expenditures in order not to transmit volatility to the domestic market.

Inefficiently specialized countries

These countries are suffering from major welfare losses associated with the inability to develop the tradable sector, which makes the cost of capital high, even for the nontradable sector. Countries such as Venezuela and Nigeria may be in this category. Inefficient specializa-tion is the product of a combination of factors: the level of government spending, the volatility of that spending, the "commercial-risk-free" in-terest rate to which firms in the economy have access, and the magni-tude of financial inefficiencies.

These countries need to make a big effort to change the structure of the economy sufficiently to get it over the specialization frontier. Incre-mental changes may not be enough to improve matters significantly. There are three *fiscal* margins in which these economies could work: the average level of government spending, its volatility, and the "commer-cial-risk-free" interest rate.

With respect to the first point, it is useful to be precise in what we call "government spending" in the context of our model. We assumed that there was no domestic taxation. In a world with taxes, the relevant policy variable is the non-oil domestic primary deficit, i.e., the primary deficit excluding oil revenues and external spending by the government. This variable must be *credibly* lowered and stabilized in order to cross the specialization frontier. There is some trade-off between lowering the average value of this deficit and lowering its volatility. The more credible the reduction in volatility, the less important the required reduction in average spending will be. However, our simulations suggest that, for the parameters we studied, feasible cuts in average spending seem quantitatively more effective than feasible reductions in volatility, although the latter brings greater improvements in welfare. Hence, an ideal policy would rely on both: stabilization and cuts in the non-oil domestic primary deficit.

Furthermore, fiscal policy and debt management policies have an important role to play in affecting the interest rate. In our model we assumed a riskless international interest rate to which we added the commercial risks faced by each sector. In real life, on top of this commercial risk, there may be country risk associated with fears about the sustainability of public debt and of the government's fiscal position. Factors that increase country risk will have the effect of moving the specialization frontier inward, causing the economy to specialize at lower average levels of spending and at lower volatilities.

Country risk often arises because of concerns about willingness to pay, or because the budget institutions are perceived as not capable of imposing an effective intertemporal budget constraint. Also, poor debt management can inefficiently expose a country to rollover or other financial risks and thus increase country risk. These problems should be avoided by any country. However, resource-rich countries are at risk of suffering heavily because the higher interest rate these problems cause may inefficiently keep them specialized in a low income–high volatility environment.

It is important to stress that countries in this category do not become specialized because wages in dollars are too high. In fact, if they were able to move to a diversified equilibrium, capital intensity would rise and wages would increase. Moving to a diversified economy is welfare enhancing; it does not imply real wage cuts.

Diversified economies

Economies in this category are characterized by having large nonresource tradable sectors. Examples in this category are countries such as

Ecuador, Mexico, and Indonesia. In these countries, volatility in oil revenues will have smaller effects on relative prices, provided that they have relatively flexible domestic markets.[12] Hence, the benefits of stabilization, other things being equal, are likely to be smaller than in the other two cases. However, these economies run the risk of becoming specialized if they increase the average non-oil primary deficit, its volatility, or have high country risk. For example, Indonesia has seen a big increase in country risk, while Ecuador is undergoing a big expansion in oil production in the context of very high country risk. Here the role of fiscal policy is to keep the economy diversified. It is mainly a preventive strategy that is called for.

First-Best Financial Policies

In our framework, the inefficient disappearance of the non-oil tradable sector is a consequence of financial frictions. Policies that minimize these frictions will allow the financial market to better manage the risks faced by the tradable sector and hence to displace the specialization frontier and to offer financing at lower cost, when the sector exists. We shall start with a list of first best policies. Later, we will discuss some more interventionist policies.

Policies that complete financial markets by expanding the space for credible contracts will have particularly powerful effects on countries that are inefficiently specialized. These include
- policies that make contract enforcement less costly, through effective judicial enforcement and extrajudicial conflict resolution;
- policies that contain willingness-to-pay problems in financial markets such as facilitating the use and effectiveness of collateral; and
- policies that efficiently reduce the cost of bankruptcy.

In addition, the high volatility that characterizes resource-rich economies is bound to make equity particularly valuable, as it allows better risk sharing between firms and investors. This agenda calls for
- policies that facilitate direct investment, especially in the nonresource sector; and
- policies to improve corporate governance so as to make equity claims more credible.

---

[12]After all, in our model we assumed sufficient labor mobility to clear the labor market.

Second-Best Policies

While first-best policies are good for all countries, they are particularly valuable for inefficiently specialized economies. However, this inefficiency might also be addressed through second-best policies, that is, policies that assume that it is hard to credibly avoid fiscal spending volatility or financial frictions. What policies could improve welfare in such a context?

The central problem with the inefficiency described here is that the tradable sector is starved out of capital because it faces too high a real exchange rate volatility for debt markets to manage. Second-best policies involve in one way or the other the need to stabilize the profits of the tradable sector. Two main forms of intervention are discussed: trade policies and financial policies.

Trade policies

If the tradable sector disappears because of unstable expected profits, what role could trade policy play? Let us consider state-contingent protection composed of export subsidies and import tariffs that would go up in times of real appreciation and would be lowered in periods of real depreciation. The idea is that with a more stable expected profit, the sector could attract more capital. In "good times" when oil is high and the real exchange rate is appreciated, export subsidies and import tariffs would kick in and keep profits from collapsing. In "bad times" when the real exchange rate weakens, this extra support could be taken away. The policy is not unrelated to the "price bands" that protects sensitive agricultural products in many countries.

This logic has a strong partial equilibrium flavor. Does it survive the general equilibrium logic? After all, changes in relative prices in this model are equilibrium movements. In the logic of our model, these are the required prices needed to clear both the market for nontradables and the labor market. Interfering with these relative price changes would likely cause even larger changes in underlying prices in order to achieve the requisite reallocation.

However, the policy may survive the general equilibrium counterforces provided it can assure investors that ex post returns will be sufficiently stable. The existence of more capital in the tradable sector does not prevent the sector from shedding labor in "good times" while it is there to absorb it in "bad times." So, labor can still move between sectors, and since it will be working with more capital, it will therefore be more productive. Moreover, if the tradable sector is substantial, its ability to absorb and shed labor will lower the volatility of the economy, reduce interest rates, and support even more capital in the economy.

Furthermore, while in our model movements in relative prices are caused by fundamental forces, in real life they may reflect other shocks and distortions that are less stabilizing. Protecting the tradable sector from their consequences may also be welfare enhancing.

Thus, we find some rationale for state-contingent protection. Obviously, one important drawback is that political economy forces may prevent the government from lowering tariffs and export subsidies when the real exchange rate is weak or may lead to excessive protectionism. However, it is not obvious that trade policy is the most efficient instrument. Further analysis is surely called for.

Financial support for tradables

Trade policy operates by changing the relative prices for goods faced by the whole economy. An alternative approach would be to offer some form of financial assistance to the tradable sector, without getting involved directly in the price-setting process in the goods market. A financial intervention that increases the stock of capital in the tradable sector can help push the economy out of specialization. One instrument to consider is some form of financial guarantee. This guarantee can be made contingent not on the idiosyncratic risks of a project but instead on the real exchange rate, so as to limit moral hazard. Through this mechanism, the probability of having to incur costly bankruptcies would be reduced, thus calling for lower interest rates. If this helps increase the size of the tradable sector, overall volatility might be reduced. However, as these guarantees might be exercised with significant frequency, at least in the transition to a more diversified economy, the potential fiscal liabilities must be considered. It is important to remember that, at least in the typical case, the real exchange rate appreciates in good times, when oil revenues are high and the government spends too much. Having this financial guarantee in place might constitute a mechanism that "punishes the government" for overspending booms and thus might have the right incentive properties from a political economy perspective: it gives the tradable sector a contingent claim on future oil booms that might otherwise lead to their demise.

Having said this, it is important to remember that in practice, money is fungible and that the tradable sector is not precisely defined in real life. Hence, narrowing the definition to include only exportables may be valuable for this and other reasons. After all, exportables are subject to international competition and have a much larger market into which they can potentially expand. However, these policies may collide with current multilateral trade agreements that prohibit export subsidies. Moreover, any initiative involving public monies will be subject to political economy distortions. Assuring that rent seeking does not distort these interventions is critical to their effectiveness.

Bibliography

Aizenman, Joshua, and Nancy Marion, 1999, "Volatility and Investment: Interpreting Evidence from Developing Countries," *Economica*, Vol. 66, pp. 157–79.

Auty, Richard M., 1990, *Resource-Based Industrialization: Sowing the Oil in Eight Developing Countries* (Oxford: Clarendon Press).

Caballero, Ricardo J., 1991, "On the Sign of the Investment-Uncertainty Relationship," *American Economic Review*, Vol. 81, No. 1 (March), pp. 279–88.

———, 2000, "Macroeconomic Volatility in Latin America: A View and Three Case Studies," NBER Working Paper No. 7782 (Cambridge, Massachusetts: National Bureau of Economic Research).

———, and Robert S. Pyndick, 1996, "Uncertainty, Investment, and Industry Evolution," *International Economic Review*, Vol. 37 (August), pp. 641–62.

Corden, W.M., 1982, "Exchange Rate Policy and the Resources Boom," *Economic Record* (Australia), Vol. 58, No. 160 (March), pp. 18–31.

———, and J.P. Neary, 1982, "Booming Sector and Deindustrialization in a Small Open Economy," *Economic Journal*, Vol. 92, pp. 825–48; reprinted in W.M. Corden, 1985, *Protection, Growth and Trade: Essays in International Economics* (Oxford: Basil Blackwell); and in W.M. Corden, 1992, *International Trade Theory and Policy: Selected Essays of W. Max Corden* (Aldershot: Edward Elgar).

de Ferranti, David, Guillermo E. Perry, Daniel Lederman, and William F. Maloney, 2001, *From Natural Resources to the Knowledge Economy—Trade and Job Quality* (Washington: World Bank).

Duryea, Suzanne, 1998, "Children's Advancement Through School in Brazil: The Role of Transitory Shocks to Household Income," IADB Working Paper No. 376 (Washington: Inter-American Development Bank).

Flug, Karnit, Antonio Spilimbergo, and Erik Wachtenheim, 1998, "Investment in Education: Do Economic Volatility and Credit Constraints Matter?" *Journal of Development Economics* (Netherlands), Vol. 55, No. 2 (April), pp. 465–81.

Gavin, Michael, and Ricardo Hausmann, 1996, "Securing Stability and Growth in a Shock Prone Region: The Policy Challenge for Latin America," IADB Working Paper No. 315 (Washington: Inter-American Development Bank).

———, 1998, "Nature, Development, and Distribution in Latin America: Evidence on the Role of Geography, Climate, and Natural Resources," IADB Working Paper No. 378 (Washington: Inter-American Development Bank).

Hartman, R., 1972, "The Effects of Price and Cost Uncertainty on Investment," *Journal of Economic Theory*, pp. 5258–66.

Hausmann, Ricardo, 2001, "Venezuela's Growth Implosion: A Neo-Classical Story?," Kennedy School of Government Working Paper (August) (Cambridge, Massachusetts: Harvard University).

———, Andrew Powell, and Roberto Rigobon, 1993, "An Optimal Spending Rule Facing Oil Income Uncertainty (Venezuela)," in *External Shocks and Stabilization Mechanisms*, ed. by E. Engel and P. Meller (Washington. Inter-American Development Bank and Johns Hopkins University Press), pp. 113–71.

Higgins, M., and J.G. Williamson, 1999, "Explaining Inequality the World Round: Cohort Size, Kuznets Curves, and Openness," NBER Working Paper No. 7224 (Cambridge, Massachusetts: National Bureau of Economic Research).

Inter-American Development Bank, 1995, *Economic and Social Progress in Latin America, 1995 Report* (Washington).

Johnsen, Christopher, Kenneth A. Shepsle, and Barry R. Weingast, 1981, "The Political Economy of Benefits and Costs: A Neoclassical Approach to Distributive Politics," *Journal of Political Economy*, Vol. 89, No. 4.

Karl, Terry Lynn, 1997, *The Paradox of Plenty: Oil Booms and Petro-States* (Berkeley: University of California Press).

Lane, Philip R., and Aaron Tornell, 1999a, "Voracity and Growth in Discrete Time," *Economics Letters*, Vol. 62, No. 1 (January), pp. 139–45.

———, 1999b, "The Voracity Effect," *American Economic Review*, Vol. 89 (March), pp. 22–46.

Maddison, Angus, 1995, "Monitoring the World Economy: 1820–1992," in *Development Centre Studies* (Paris and Washington: Organization for Economic Cooperation and Development).

Manzano, Osmel, and Roberto Rigobon, 2001, "Resource Curse or Debt Overhang?," NBER Working Paper No. 8390 (Cambridge, Massachusetts: National Bureau of Economic Research).

Matsuyama, Kiminori, 1992, "Agricultural Productivity, Comparative Advantage and Economic Growth," *Journal of Economic Theory*, Vol. 58 (December).

Ramey, Garey, and Valerie A. Ramey, 1995, "Cross-Country Evidence on the Link Between Volatility and Growth," *American Economic Review*, Vol. 85, No. 5, pp. 1138–51.

Sachs, Jeffrey, and Andrew Warner, 1995a, "Economic Reform and the Process of Global Integration," *Brookings Papers on Economic Activity: 1,* Brookings Institution, pp. 1–118.

———, 1995b, "Natural Resource Abundance and Economic Growth", Harvard Institute of Economic Research Discussion Paper, No. 517 (Cambridge, Massachusetts: Harvard Institute for International Development).

Tornell, Aaron, and Andrés Velasco, 1995, "Fiscal Discipline and the Choice of the Exchange Rate Regime," *European Economic Review* (Nethelands), Vol. 39, No. 3/4, pp. 759–70.

von Hagen, Jürgen, and Ian J. Harden, 1997, "National Budget Processes and Fiscal Performance," *European Economy, Reports and Studies: Towards Greater Fiscal Discipline,* No. 3 (Brussels: European Commission, Directorate-General for Economic and Financial Affairs), pp. 311–408.

3

Operational Aspects of Fiscal Policy in Oil-Producing Countries

STEVEN BARNETT AND ROLANDO OSSOWSKI[1]

I. Introduction

Oil-producing countries face challenges arising from the fact that oil revenue is exhaustible, volatile, and uncertain and largely originates from abroad. The exhaustibility of oil raises complex issues of sustainability and intergenerational resource allocation. The uncertainty and volatility of oil revenue complicates macroeconomic management and fiscal planning—with the challenge being to avoid transmitting the oil price volatility, which is outside the control of policymakers, into the macroeconomy. Finally, since oil revenue often represents transfers from abroad, changes in oil revenue drive movements in the overall fiscal balance that do not directly affect domestic demand. The fiscal use of these resources, however, has significant consequences for the domestic economy.

Reflecting these challenges, the paper aims at deriving some general principles that are important for formulating and assessing fiscal policy in oil-producing countries. Oil-producing countries are themselves, however, not a homogenous group. There is wide variation in areas such as the relative importance of oil to the economy, the size of oil reserves, maturity of the oil industry, ownership and taxation structure in the oil sector, stage of development of the non-oil economy, and government financial position—all of which would affect fiscal policy

[1]The authors are grateful for helpful comments to Ulrich Bartsch, Nigel Chalk, James A. Daniel, Jeffrey Davis, and George Mackenzie. Alvaro Vivanco provided invaluable research assistance.

decisions. Thus what follows is necessarily general, and certain principles may apply more to some countries than others.

II. Assessing the Fiscal Stance in the Long Run

An assessment of whether a fiscal policy is sustainable, let alone optimal, is especially challenging in an oil-dependent economy.[2] The dependence of revenue on oil proceeds, which are volatile, unpredictable, and exhaustible, significantly complicates fiscal management in the short and long run. This section aims to characterize the fiscal policy consistent with long-run considerations, accepting that fiscal policy may need to deviate from this in the short run (as discussed in the next section).

Several studies have empirically examined the sustainability of fiscal policy in selected oil-producing countries. Tersman (1991), Liuksila, García, and Bassett (1994), and Chalk (1998) employed a framework focused on government wealth, inclusive of oil in the ground—similar to the analytical framework adopted below. The underlying question addressed below, however, goes beyond sustainability, and focuses on the more normative question of how the government should allocate resources over time.

The rest of this section first discusses government wealth and permanent income concepts, and highlights the importance of the non-oil primary fiscal balance for assessments of fiscal sustainability. It then considers the effects of introducing sovereign premiums, precautionary motives, and capital expenditure in the analysis and assesses the sensitivity of wealth estimates to oil prices.

Government Wealth and Permanent Income

The analysis follows what might be considered the standard theoretical approach to the problem.[3] The oil variable of primary interest is oil wealth, defined as the present discounted value of future oil revenue.

---

[2]Chalk and Hemming (2000) provide a survey of fiscal sustainability in general, and include a section addressing countries dependent on nonrenewable resource earnings.

[3]In addition to the above papers, other examples include Alier and Kaufman (1999); Engel and Valdés (2000); Bjerkholt (2002); and Hausmann, Powell, and Rigobon (1993)—although some of these studies go on to develop alternative models.

Fiscal proceeds from oil are then viewed not as income, but rather as financing; specifically, a portfolio transaction that converts oil assets into financial assets. The long-run challenge for fiscal policy is to decide how to allocate government wealth (including the oil wealth) across generations. This challenge, reflecting a concern for intergenerational equity, should be met by targeting a fiscal policy that preserves government wealth—appropriately defined, inter alia, to include oil. Finally, and analogous to the standard permanent income arguments put forth by Friedman, the preservation of wealth would require that consumption in each period be limited to permanent income or, in this case, the implicit return on government wealth.

More formally, the optimal fiscal policy is defined as the path of non-oil revenue and primary government spending that maximizes the government's social welfare function. Appendix I develops and discusses the setup in greater detail. Nonetheless, a few observations are warranted. First, given the focus on intertemporal considerations, the analysis and exposition can be simplified by focusing on a measure of the deficit—which is ultimately what governs the transfer of resources between periods—rather than the specific mixture of taxes and spending. Second, the pertinent deficit measure to substitute into the social welfare function is the (primary) non-oil deficit, which makes explicit that revenue excludes oil income on the grounds that it is more like financing.[4]

This highly stylized and simplified framework is capable of illustrating some of the main points of the analysis. A simulation of the evolution of fiscal policy in such a framework helps develop the intuition. Figure 3.1 (top panel) shows the time path of fiscal revenue—assuming constant non-oil revenue—in an oil-producing economy, which highlights the substantial drop in revenue that will occur when oil is exhausted or becomes obsolete (see Appendix I). However, since there is no uncertainty, the government knows what its wealth is, and can easily determine the optimal non-oil deficit—which is set equal to the return on its wealth. All the fiscal variables are now fully specified, and the evolution of the different balance measures and government debt can be simulated. The simplicity of the framework allows for a clearer

---

[4]For the central or general government, the non-oil balance would normally be defined to exclude all oil-related revenues and expenditures, with the exception of excises and other taxes on refined products sold domestically. For the public sector, it would normally be defined as the overall balance, excluding oil revenues from abroad and oil-related expenditures.

Figure 3.1. *Simulation of Revenue, Expenditure, and Assets*
(In percent of non-oil GDP)

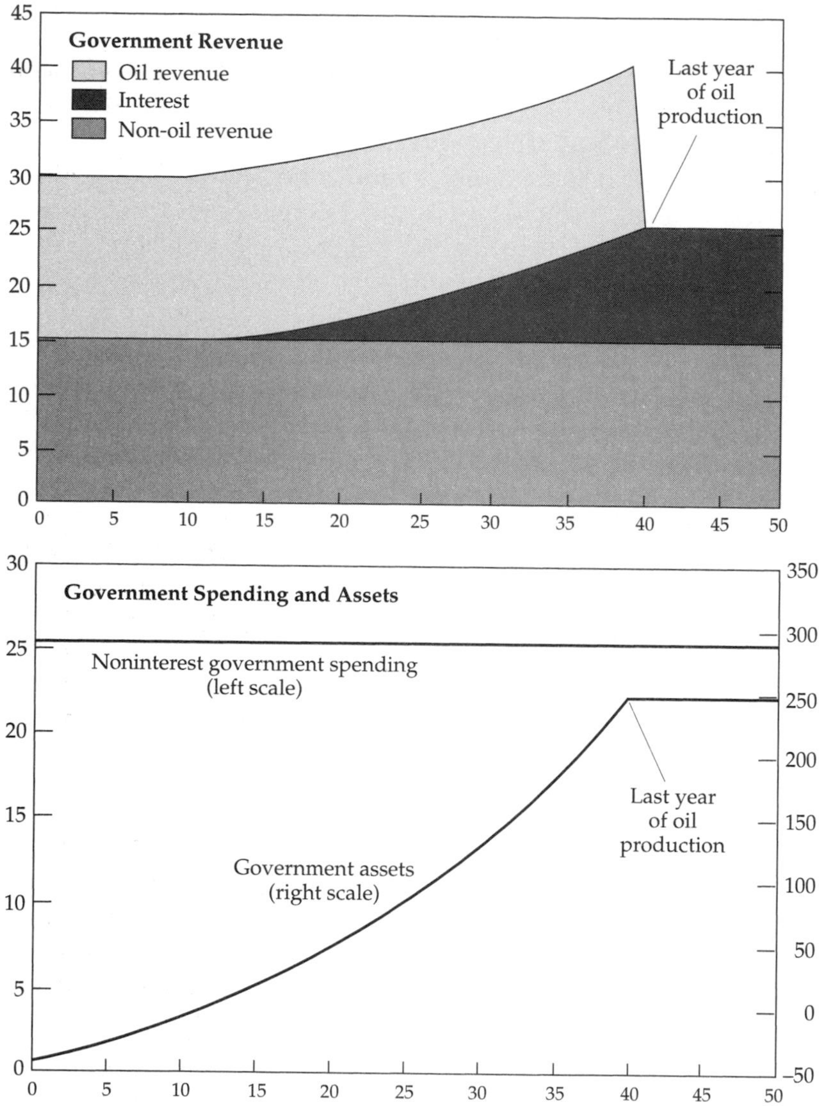

Source: Authors' calculations.

understanding of the driving forces; nonetheless, the results and the underlying intuition should be quite robust to the addition of complicating features, some of which will be discussed later.

First, the primary non-oil balance provides the most useful indicator for measuring the direction and sustainability of fiscal policy. Fiscal policy, in this framework, is essentially constant as both non-oil tax revenue and (primary) government spending are held constant (as a share of non-oil GDP). However, as shown in Figure 3.2 (top panel), of the various fiscal balance measures only the primary non-oil balance is constant throughout. Even though fiscal policy is not changing, the other balance measures are moving due to other factors. The non-oil balance, for example, steadily increases over time as the existing debt stock is paid off and income-generating assets are accumulated.[5] The primary balance and the overall balance are affected by oil revenue, and thus move dramatically when oil revenue is exhausted. In a more general sense, this figure suggests that the government's objective boils down to choosing a primary non-oil deficit consistent with fiscal sustainability.

The importance of focusing on the primary non-oil balance is highlighted when oil price volatility is incorporated. Figure 3.2 (bottom panel) is a repeat of Figure 3.2 (top panel); however, instead of using a constant oil price, the actual series of oil prices over the last 20 years is used.[6] The overall and primary overall balance now swing wildly with the movements in oil prices, again even though fiscal policy is unchanged. Focusing on an overall balance measure would thus give a misleading impression as to developments in fiscal policy. For example, despite substantial increases in the primary surplus in some periods, it would not be appropriate to claim that there was fiscal consolidation—a term that implies a deliberate effort to adjust the fiscal position. All that has happened is oil prices have increased. Changes in the primary non-oil balance should be used as the basis for determining whether there has been a fiscal consolidation. The importance of other fiscal balance indicators will be discussed in Section IV.

---

[5] The return on assets is treated as interest income and, therefore, is not included in the primary non-oil balance.

[6] In keeping with the spirit of the simplified framework, it is necessary to assume that all of the oil price movements were known with certainty. To generate a 40-year simulation, the last 20 years of prices were repeated. Also, the oil price series is normalized such that the present discounted value of wealth, and thus the primary non-oil deficit, is the same as in the top panel of Figure 3.2.

Figure 3.2. *Simulation of Fiscal Balances*
(In percent of non-oil GDP)

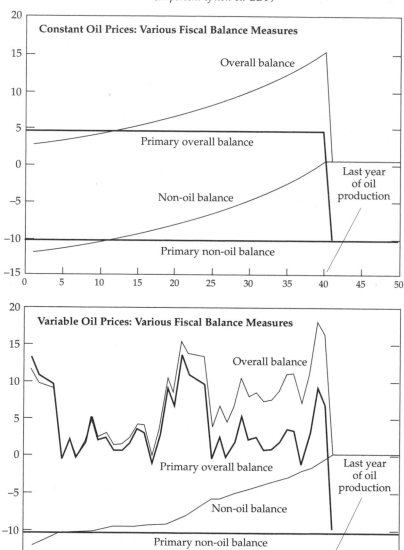

Second, in order to sustain the non-oil deficit when oil has been exhausted, the government should accumulate assets. Specifically, there should be enough accumulated assets for the *return* on those assets to finance the non-oil deficit once the oil revenue has dried up (see the bottom panel of Figure 3.1). In contrast, a strategy of targeting a non-oil deficit that would be financed by drawing down accumulated assets once oil production ceases would not be sustainable. Such a strategy would eventually deplete all of the assets, leading subsequently to steady government borrowing and explosive debt dynamics. The general conclusion is that fiscal policy should be targeted at accumulating substantial net assets during the period of oil production to sustain the non-oil deficit in the post-oil period. Therefore, strategies aimed at stabilizing the (positive) net debt to GDP ratio or even just eliminating all debt would not generally be consistent with fiscal sustainability. Such strategies would result in either the need for substantial fiscal adjustment or explosive debt dynamics in the post-oil period.

Third, government wealth (including the present discounted value of oil revenues), rather than the flow of oil revenue, determines the sustainable non-oil deficit. In this framework, the government would choose a constant primary non-oil deficit (Figure 3.2)—since there is no uncertainty about either oil or non-oil revenue. Intuitively, and as pointed out by Hausmann, Powell, and Rigobon (1993), the government behaves as if it sold all of its oil immediately, thus effectively transforming the flow of oil revenue into a stock of financial assets. While the constant primary non-oil deficit follows from the simplifying assumptions, the underlying intuition that the non-oil balance should be related to government wealth would generally apply.

The above policy guidelines are of significant practical importance as, by and large, many oil-producing countries would seem to fall short of achieving them. For example, few oil-producing countries highlight the (primary) non-oil balance in their budgets. Within the IMF, however, there has been an increasing trend toward presenting the non-oil deficit in country documents. As to the accumulation of financial assets, many oil-producing countries have sizable sovereign net financial liabilities. In mature producers, such liabilities send a potentially troubling signal about the sustainability of fiscal policy and are a source of fiscal vulnerability, especially when oil prices fall. At the same time, while not highlighted above, having oil wealth does afford the luxury of being able to sustain, if properly managed, a potentially sizable primary non-oil deficit.

Sovereign Premiums, Precautionary Motives, and Capital Spending

Sovereign premiums

Many oil-producing countries pay a sovereign premium, suggesting that this is an important consideration for assessing fiscal policy. For present purposes, the reasons underlying the sovereign premium are not as important as its existence. Moreover, these premiums can be quite substantial (Box 3.1). The presence of a sovereign premium alters the problem because the government would now face two interest rates, a higher one for borrowing and a lower one for its gross savings. This functions much like a soft form of liquidity constraints—soft in the sense that the government can borrow, but only at a premium, and thus is not technically liquidity constrained.

A government that pays an interest rate premium on its sovereign debt should pursue a more conservative fiscal policy. Specifically, the government should strive to rapidly pay off its expensive debt. Once the sovereign premium is eliminated, then it would behave as the government in the above framework. The intuition is that the premium paid on debt increases the return to savings (while debt is positive) and thus would induce the government to save more in order to exploit the temporarily high interest rates. Compared to the above framework, the primary non-oil deficit would be smaller while the government has positive debt, with the primary non-oil deficit gradually increasing as the debt is reduced. From a policy perspective, the implication is that governments that pay a sovereign premium should pursue even more conservative policies than they otherwise would—they should spend less than the return on their wealth until the sovereign premium is eliminated.

Precautionary motives

The government of an oil country is confronted with significant uncertainty, including in regard to oil wealth. The volatility of oil revenue due to swings in oil prices is problematic, especially for short-run macro-fiscal management, but it is the uncertainty regarding oil wealth itself that is most important for long-run considerations. Therefore, more than the volatility of prices, it is the uncertainty about the future path of prices—including the statistical properties of oil prices (see below)—that leads to enormous uncertainty about oil wealth. Addi-

Box 3.1. *Selected Countries:*
Ratings and Spreads on Sovereign Debt

	Spread (Basis points)[1]		Rating[2]	
	Nov. 15, 2000	Nov. 15, 2001	Nov. 15, 2000	Nov. 15, 2001
Ecuador	1,332	1,333	B–	CCC+
Mexico	354	348	BB+	BB+
Nigeria	2,001	1,657	...	...
Russia	1,070	809	SD	B
Venezuela	887	1,073	B	B
Memorandum items:				
EMBI+	775	1,025		
Oil price (US$/barrel, monthly average)	32.34	18.66		

Source: Bloomberg.
[1] Based on debt included in the J.P. Morgan EMBI+.
[2] Standard and Poor rating of sovereign long-term foreign currency debt.

tional complicating factors include uncertainty about oil reserves and the cost of extracting them. The following discussion looks at how the presence of these uncertainties would affect the optimal size of the non-oil deficit.[7]

In the standard consumption problem, an increase in uncertainty generally leads to more conservative consumption decisions. For example, adding income uncertainty to a perfect foresight consumption model would generally lead to an equilibrium with higher savings. This is referred to as precautionary savings—see Deaton (1992) for a general discussion. Key for this result is that economic agents are risk averse. Given risk aversion, the intuition is that agents are concerned about the possibility of negative shocks, which would lead them to build up more assets than under conditions of certainty. The larger assets would effectively serve as an insurance policy should there be a bad realization of income.

Analogously, uncertainty about oil wealth would lead a government, for precautionary reasons, to incur a smaller primary non-oil deficit.

---

[7]The potential role of precautionary motives has been cited by others, for example Tersman (1991) and Bjerkholt (2002), but, with the exception of Engel and Valdés (2000), has not featured prominently in the literature.

Since projections of oil wealth are surrounded by considerable uncertainty, the precautionary motive could be quite strong. Uncertainty would depend, inter alia, on estimates of the size of oil reserves and the path of future production. A country with fewer years of production left would face less wealth uncertainty, with, at the limit (end of oil extraction), all oil-related uncertainty fully resolved.

The fact that uncertainty about oil wealth is gradually reduced over time adds a unique dimension to the problem for oil-producing countries. As reserves decline, the precautionary motives would abate. Moreover, a large stock of financial assets should also have been accumulated as the end of production nears, so the uncertainty about the value of remaining oil reserves—especially in relation to the stock of assets—would be small. The reduction in uncertainty would cause a concomitant fall in the importance of the precautionary motive for determining the size of the non-oil deficit. This has consequences for the discussion below about the sensitivity of government spending to price changes.

Bird-in-hand consumption

Bjerkholt (2002) has argued the merits of a rule that targets a non-oil deficit equal to the anticipated return on existing financial assets. He describes this as the bird-in-hand rule, since spending decisions are predicated only on the assets already in hand. In contrast, the above permanent income type framework implies that the size of the primary non-oil balance should be determined by looking also at the expectations of government wealth.

The bird-in-hand rule implies a very conservative approach that could be viewed as an extreme form of precautionary saving, in that it is tantamount to assuming that there would be no future oil revenues. However, prior to the exhaustion of oil reserves or their obsolescence, oil wealth would be greater than accumulated financial wealth, and the rule would thus lead to very restrictive primary non-oil deficits.[8] In this regard, it serves as a lower bound to the solution of the framework that includes precautionary motives. This suggests that the optimal size for the primary non-oil deficit lies above that implied by the bird-in-hand rule but below that of the certainty equivalent framework above.

---

[8]The rule is more applicable to countries with positive net financial assets. In countries with negative net financial assets, the rule would entail running primary non-oil surpluses.

Obsolescence

The bird-in-hand rule highlights the potential for a shock to reduce the value of remaining oil reserves to zero. Technological advances, for example, could lead to alternative fuel sources that are more efficient and cost-effective. Oil would not actually have to become obsolete, but rather its price would just have to fall to such a level that it is no longer cost-effective (at least for most producers) to extract.

The possibility of obsolescence, even remote, creates an additional incentive for precautionary saving. Intuitively, the government would be very concerned about even the remote possibility that oil would become obsolete, an event that would entail the need to reduce significantly the non-oil deficit because of the sharp reduction in wealth associated with the loss of future oil earnings. This concern is manifested in higher savings, as the government attempts to insure itself against such an eventuality by accumulating financial assets.

Capital expenditure

Fiscal sustainability analyses often do not distinguish between capital and current expenditure. If, however, government investment is assumed to be productive in the sense that it boosts output, then investment decisions would be based on the return that the government can get, and the problem would boil down to a portfolio decision between financial and physical assets. Alternatively, government investment could be viewed as if it were a consumer durable, in the sense that the stock of government capital generates social welfare rather than a financial return. As discussed below, these two approaches have significantly different implications.

Productive spending

Government investment in public infrastructure should arguably have a positive impact on growth. In a review of the literature, however, Gramlich (1994) highlights that estimates of the productivity of public infrastructure vary widely, ranging from zero to higher than the return to private capital. For present purposes, the actual productivity of such public infrastructure is less important than the possibility that public infrastructure could be productive. The government is then faced with a portfolio choice regarding the composition of financial versus physical assets. The following conclusions should be taken into account.

First, the return to government investment would have to be quite high for the government to undertake it without a change in fiscal sustainability. Unlike the private sector, the government's financial return is largely limited to what it can recover through higher tax revenue. For a project to be worthwhile—in the sense that it will pay for itself via future returns—output would have to increase substantially (Fischer and Easterly, 1990). For example, with a tax rate of 20 percent, the marginal product of capital would have to be five times the interest rate.

Second, the analysis is not directly affected by the presence of oil wealth. An oil-dependent economy would, in this respect, behave no differently than any other economy: it should borrow to undertake any capital spending that would pay for itself via higher future tax revenues. The productivity of government capital (a supply consideration) and the cost of capital determine the desired stock of government capital. Wealth, oil or otherwise, should not directly impact this decision. There may, however, be an indirect effect to the extent that the presence of (or changes in) oil wealth may lower the cost of capital—although, as noted earlier, many oil producers pay a sovereign premium. Conceptually, there is no reason to believe that the surprise discovery of oil, for example, would change domestic supply conditions so as to increase the productivity of (non-oil) government capital.[9]

The rationale for higher government investment often applied to new oil producers is that there are substantial development needs and an insufficient stock of government capital. However, the discovery of oil would not make such investments (in the non-oil sector) more worthwhile, although, as noted above, the discovery of oil could lower the cost of financing for the government. Ultimately, the decisions confronting such countries are the same as those faced by any other country, and boil down to determining whether the financial return from the investment justifies its expense—a calculation that is independent of oil wealth.

Durable consumption

In contrast, modeling government capital spending as being more akin to durable consumption yields different results. In this interpretation, the government undertakes capital spending not because the capital is productive, but rather because it yields a flow of social benefits.

---

[9]Rodríguez and Sachs (1999) show that over-investment could explain the sluggish growth performance of resource-dependent economies.

That is, once built, government capital provides benefits for many years. The government thus has two types of consumption, durable goods (capital spending) and nondurable goods (current spending).

Viewing capital spending this way would provide a rationale for larger non-oil deficits following an increase in expected government wealth. This has intuitive appeal for many oil-producing countries, especially the new producers. With the discovery of oil, such countries are wealthier and thus justified in wanting to boost consumption (increase the non-oil deficit). The stock of government capital goods—here seen as durable public goods—could in this case be too low, even assuming it had been at the right level just before the discovery of oil. In other words, the desired stock of public capital goods would be higher for a wealthier country, provided government capital is a normal good.

The durable consumption view of government capital would provide a rationale for a tilted pattern of deficits. Specifically, larger primary non-oil deficits would be incurred until the government capital stock reached its new and higher equilibrium level. Even in this case, however, precautionary motives and liquidity constraints as discussed above would maintain their relevance. Indeed, under the assumption that government capital is less liquid than financial assets, the precautionary motives would likely be heightened.

Oil price sensitivity

An issue that was touched upon, but not explicitly addressed above, relates to how sensitive the primary non-oil balance should be to movements in oil prices. As discussed in the next section, in many oil-producing countries government spending has been positively related to oil prices. At the same time, the above analysis emphasized that the primary non-oil balance should respond to changes in oil wealth. The extent that oil price changes translate into changes in oil wealth is thus of fundamental importance for determining how sensitive government spending should be to oil price changes. This question, in turn, depends on the statistical properties of oil prices.

There is evidence that, although oil prices are periodically subject to permanent shocks, most oil price changes have a significant transitory component.[10] This would imply that expectations about long-run

---

[10]See, for example, Engel and Valdés (2000), and Barnett and Vivanco, Chapter 5 in this volume.

wealth would not change that much with a given oil price change. Therefore, based on sustainability considerations, government spending should not be that sensitive to changes in oil prices.[11] However, this needs to be interpreted carefully, because wealth itself is not known with certainty. Indeed, there are numerous factors that lead to great uncertainty about wealth, including parameter uncertainty, uncertainty about future shocks (which have a minimal effect), the possibility of a structural break in oil prices (including obsolescence), and uncertainty about the amount, quality, and ease of extraction of oil reserves. The substantial uncertainty about wealth would imply that precautionary motives would be particularly strong.

Alternatively, assuming oil prices have a unit root leads to somewhat different conclusions. Technically, more than just having a unit root, oil price shocks would have to have a large permanent component. But if this holds, then changes in oil wealth would be strongly correlated with changes in oil prices—since the change in price is effectively permanent. This would provide a stronger rationale for the observed correlation—on fiscal sustainability grounds—between government spending and oil earnings (but see the next section). Perhaps less obvious, but equally important, is that the presence of a unit root would also imply that there is markedly more uncertainty about oil wealth. The variance of expected future oil prices, especially for the distant future, would be substantially higher than the case of oil price changes having a significant transitory component. The higher variance of prices translates into even higher uncertainty about wealth, and thus even stronger precautionary motives.

III. The Short-Run Fiscal Stance and Operational Issues

The long-run factors discussed in the previous section help determine broad fiscal parameters. Within these parameters, however, fiscal policy is ultimately pinned down by short-run considerations.

As in any economy, fiscal policy in oil-producing countries should be consistent with achieving macroeconomic objectives such as macroeconomic stability and an efficient allocation of resources. Given its crucial role in injecting part of the oil rent into the economy, fiscal policy is a

---

[11]An exception would be cases where, for one reason or other, an oil price shock is expected to be permanent.

key tool of short-run macroeconomic management in these countries. Thus, in addition to delivering government savings consistent with optimal consumption out of permanent income, fiscal policy has a key role to play in managing short-term fluctuations in the external and macroeconomic environment.

The rest of this section first discusses the costs of macroeconomic and fiscal volatility and considers some aspects of the short-run macroeconomic impact of fiscal policy. It then examines how the feasibility of various fiscal policy responses to oil revenue volatility depends on the government's financial position.

Macroeconomic and Fiscal Volatility and the Short-Run Impact of Fiscal Policy

Reliance on oil revenue, particularly when it makes up a large share of total revenue, renders short-run fiscal management, budgetary planning, and the efficient use of public resources difficult. The challenges largely stem from the volatility and unpredictability of oil prices.

There is ample evidence that oil prices exhibit volatility in the short run and large fluctuations over the medium term. According to a recent study, one-third of the time the oil market will be faced with the prospect of a monthly price change greater than 8 percent. Therefore, at the average oil price in 2002, in any month there was a one-in-six chance that the spot oil price might drop by some US$2 a barrel (Cashin, Liang, and McDermott, 2000). And the experience of the last few years has shown that large annual price movements can take place in either direction. Annual average oil prices surged by nearly 30 percent in 1995–96, declined by 36 percent in 1997–98, and then more than doubled in 1999–2000. Moreover, these fluctuations are often difficult, or even impossible, to predict.

The volatility of oil prices leads to corresponding volatility in the fiscal cash flow.[12] The dependence of fiscal revenue on the oil sector renders public finances vulnerable to a volatile external variable that is, for the most part, largely beyond the control of policymakers. For example, in Venezuela, mainly reflecting the oil price developments mentioned above, oil revenues accruing to the public sector fell from 27 percent of GDP in 1996 to 12½ percent of GDP in 1998, before rising

---

[12]A distinction should be made between risks posed by oil price uncertainty and volatility to government net worth (as discussed in Section II) and to the fiscal cash flow.

again to 22½ percent of GDP in 2000. And a change in the oil price of US$1 a barrel on an annual basis is associated with a variation of close to 1 percentage point of GDP in Venezuela's public sector revenue.

Thus, dependence on oil as a major source of export earnings and government revenue confronts policymakers in oil-producing countries with the short-run issues of how to address sharp and unpredictable variations in oil prices and revenues, and how to use oil revenues. The analysis of the short-run fiscal stance in oil-producing countries should take into account the macroeconomic and fiscal costs of a volatile fiscal pattern, and the impact of fiscal policy on short-run macroeconomic dynamics.

Macroeconomic costs of fiscal volatility

There is a strong macroeconomic case for smoothing fiscal expenditures. As elaborated below, abrupt changes in government spending—or more generally the non-oil deficit—contribute to macroeconomic volatility, which, in turn, leads to worse economic outcomes. Thus, in the short run, efforts should be made to minimize the correlation between government spending and volatile oil prices.

A number of studies have highlighted the costs of a volatile macroeconomic environment for investment and growth.[13] The disappointing growth and weak economic performance of oil producers has also been the focus of research. Even controlling for other factors, oil-exporting countries have tended to grow slower than resource-poor countries. While several channels have been suggested to account for this stylized fact,[14] a key policy factor contributing to the disappointing

---

[13]For example, Gavin (1997) reports a negative relationship between volatility and economic growth, while Aizenman and Marion (1993) show that investment and growth are adversely affected by volatility in measures of monetary and fiscal policy. Gavin and Hausmann (1996) find that large external shocks—including terms of trade shocks—are one explanation of Latin America's high degree of macroeconomic instability. However, they also argue that the volatility of the domestic policy environment, as reflected in the magnitude of short-run uncertainty about fiscal deficits and monetary growth, has been quantitatively more important.

[14]They include: the postponement—facilitated by the availability of oil resources—of politically painful but ultimately growth-enhancing reforms (Auty, 2001); Dutch disease (Gelb and Associates, 1988; Sachs and Warner, 1995); inefficient specialization in non-tradables (Hausmann and Rigobon, Chapter 2 in this volume); the deleterious effects of competition for natural resource rents accruing to the public sector between fiscal pressure groups (Tornell and Lane, 1998; Leite and Weidmann, 1999); and institutional quality issues in countries that are rich in natural resources (Dalmazzo and de Blasio, 2001).

economic performance of many oil-producing countries has been the procyclicality of government expenditures, evidenced in expansionary and contractionary fiscal impulses associated with fluctuations in oil revenues (Gelb and Associates, 1988; Auty and Gelb, 2001; Bjerkholt, 2002). Indeed, Gelb and Associates has argued that the most important recommendation to emerge from his study of oil windfalls is that spending levels should have been adjusted to sharp rises in oil income far more cautiously than they actually were.

Large and unpredictable changes in expenditure, and the non-oil fiscal deficit, can entail macroeconomic costs. They include the reallocation of resources to accommodate changes in demand and relative prices, real exchange rate volatility, and increased risks faced by investors in the non-oil sector. Sharp fluctuations in government spending make it difficult for the private sector to make long-term investment plans and decisions, with attendant adverse effects on private investment and the growth of the non-oil economy (Hausmann, Powell, and Rigobon, 1993).

International experience suggests that fiscal volatility can be destabilizing for the real effective exchange rate and real output. In the case of oil-producing countries, oil shocks can affect the level and volatility of the real effective exchange rate through several channels. While disposable income and wealth effects are prominent factors, a key transmission channel of external volatility to the real exchange rate is procyclical government spending on nontradables. In this case, the variability of oil receipts can carry over to the real effective exchange rate. The volatility of the latter, in turn, has been shown to be damaging to the non-oil sector and capital formation. World Bank studies suggest that the degree of variability of the real exchange rate is as important as its level for the development of a diversified nontraditional tradable sector (World Bank, 1993; and Servén and Solimano, 1993).

Thus, on macroeconomic grounds there would be merit in smoothing fiscal expenditures. By reducing the volatility of public spending, the government would contribute to a more stable evolution of aggregate demand and the macroeconomic environment.

Fiscal costs of volatile expenditure

There are also strong fiscal arguments for smoothing expenditures. In particular, short-term fluctuations in government expenditure can entail potentially substantial fiscal costs, including a reduction in the quality and efficiency of spending. This provides a further rationale for insulating government expenditure from short-run oil volatility.

The level of spending should be determined taking into account its likely quality and the capacity of the administration to execute it efficiently. In this connection, the sudden creation or enlargement of expenditure programs associated with oil windfalls carries risks. A hasty undertaking of large-scale public spending programs may exceed the government's planning, implementation, and management capacity, with the result that it may be difficult to prevent wasteful spending.[15] For instance, the criteria for the selection of capital projects may become lax, leading to suboptimal decisions. The costs of new projects may also increase due to bottlenecks in the supply of some inputs (Engel and Valdés, 2000). Large-scale capital expenditure programs can also be a fertile ground for governance problems. Expenditures should not rise faster than transparent and careful procurement practices will allow.

Moreover, typically government expenditure proves difficult to contain or streamline following expansions, as spending programs become entrenched and take a life of their own. Booms tend to lock in powerful hysteresis effects that prolong high spending levels and can set the stage for serious macroeconomic imbalances marked by inflation, abrupt demand cuts, and sharp falls in output and growth (Auty and Gelb, 2001). On the other hand, drastic expenditure reductions in the face of negative external shocks (which may involve cuts in social spending and the government payroll, besides capital spending) may lead to social instability, discouraging investment and reducing future growth. Such reductions could involve, in particular, the abandonment of viable capital projects, where the return on some additional expenditure might be high.

Special care needs to be exercised when public expenditure has increased rapidly in recent years. In these cases, the marginal value of additional expenditure is likely to be in question—particularly if, due to institutional constraints, the quality of expenditure is suspect. In any event, the point will be reached where an oil-producing country would benefit more from keeping resources in the form of financial assets or lower gross public debt levels.

---

[15]For examples, see Amuzegar (1999).

Fiscal policy and short-run macroeconomic dynamics

The discussion above suggests that a generally volatile expenditure pattern may entail macroeconomic and fiscal costs, and therefore provides arguments for smoothing the path of spending in the face of oil price fluctuations. In addition, in coming to a view as to the appropriateness of the short-run fiscal stance, macroeconomic issues such as the direct effects of fiscal policy on aggregate demand, inflation, and the balance of payments, and the availability of other policy stabilization instruments must be considered.

The short-run effect of an increase in the non-oil deficit of an oil-producing country financed through higher oil revenues from abroad would be similar to a foreign-financed increase in the fiscal deficit in other countries. A rising non-oil deficit will signal either a relaxation of domestic revenue collection or an increase in expenditure, both of which would tend to put pressure on domestic demand with consequences for activity, inflation, and the external non-oil current account. The relative significance of these effects will depend in part on the initial macroeconomic position, the composition of the increase in spending in terms of imported and domestic goods and services, and the capacity of the economy to absorb increases in government expenditure.

The effects of a fiscal expansion financed with higher oil revenues are likely to include pressure toward the real appreciation of the currency—an adverse shift in relative prices against the production of tradables. For example, large increases in capital spending are likely to have a significant nontradable component. Unless there is substantial initial slack in the economy and supply is responsive, such increases will inevitably put pressure on domestic resources and inflation. Thus, the evaluation of the non-oil fiscal policy stance must include consideration of trends in competitiveness and the potential for Dutch disease effects.

Instead of being spent, an increase in oil revenues could be saved by repaying net public debt. An automatic sterilization of additional oil revenues would be achieved by parallel reductions in net external public debt. Higher revenues could also be used to build up deposits with the domestic banking system or repay domestic debt. In these cases, however, if there is less-than-perfect capital mobility, there may be effects on domestic liquidity and interest rates. This form of asset management response to higher oil revenues could be expansionary, including through the associated reduction in interest rates, and might imply the need for offsetting monetary policy measures.

A variation in oil prices may have effects on activity and the real exchange rate even if the government decides to finance externally (sterilize) the resulting change in oil revenues. First, oil sector activities tend to be correlated (perhaps with some lags) to oil prices. For example, oil booms may lead to an expansion of private oil sector investment, with knock-on effects on demand and activity in the non-oil sector. Second, they may affect private consumption and savings indirectly through wealth effects. Thus, surges in private sector demand associated with higher oil export receipts (which, moreover, may be accompanied by capital inflows or reduced capital outflows) may put upward pressure on the currency and raise inflation concerns.

Policy instruments available to deal with these effects include sterilization, nominal exchange rate appreciation, and fiscal policy. Under a managed or fixed exchange rate system, however, it may not be possible for the central bank to sterilize the foreign exchange inflows,[16] and the use of exchange rate appreciation may be constrained by competitive considerations.[17] In these circumstances, fiscal policy may need to be tightened to contain inflation and prevent an excessive appreciation of the currency, particularly if the foreign exchange inflow is large relative to the absorption capacity of the economy.

In certain macroeconomic settings, therefore, the stabilization function of fiscal policy, the need to address short-term macroeconomic disequilibria, and constraints limiting the use of other policy instruments would provide justification for a countercyclical non-oil fiscal stance that, depending on the circumstances, might need to be more restrained than required by fiscal sustainability. Similar considerations would apply in the case of a rapidly expanding oil sector, where there could be an overshooting of the real effective exchange rate because of large investment projects and broader wealth effects.

---

[16]The ability of the central bank to sterilize the effects of the foreign exchange inflow on the monetary base could be restricted by the lack of suitable instruments and the state of development of the financial markets. Such operations could also be constrained by potentially significant quasi-fiscal costs of sterilization arising from the differences between the interest earned on the central bank's foreign exchange reserves and the borrowing costs incurred to finance its sterilization operations. Moreover, the resulting higher interest rates, by attracting capital inflows, could make such strategies self-defeating.

[17]In the case of a flexible exchange rate system, there would be pressure for the appreciation of the nominal exchange rate.

Fiscal Policy, Stabilization, and the Government's Financial Position

The ability to absorb unanticipated cash flow shocks depends on the robustness of the government's financial position. A government that is liquidity constrained or not able to access credit at reasonable interest rates would likely be forced to undertake potentially costly adjustments even in the case of moderate or temporary downturns in oil revenue. Moreover, the perceived sustainability of the fiscal stance and the credibility of the policy framework would themselves influence a government's creditworthiness and the cost of financing.

A strong fiscal and financial position provides the government of an oil-producing country with room to maneuver during oil price downturns. In particular, the government can accommodate cash flow fluctuations through a mix of adjustment and financing. By doing so, the government can afford to pursue short-run fiscal strategies that avoid fiscal instability and help insulate the domestic economy from oil revenue volatility. Moreover, when the government can smooth expenditures and the non-oil balance in the face of cash flow volatility, the use of oil revenue can be successfully decoupled from current earnings, enhancing the stabilization role of fiscal policy (Bjerkholt, 2002).

In some oil-producing countries, a history of prudent fiscal policies and the existence of large official financial assets and/or low levels of public debt has facilitated an orderly mix of adjustment and financing during temporary oil price downturns. For example, in Norway the solid financial position of the government reflects to a large extent the more fundamental long-run policy objectives of spreading the benefits of oil over time—notably through high government savings rates and the buildup of foreign assets, resisting potential damage to the non-oil tradable sector from Dutch disease, and being able to withstand negative oil market developments. These strategic choices seem to have helped Norway maintain macro stability and reasonable growth rates even in the context of unfavorable oil market environments.

Thus, there are important advantages in pursuing a cautious expenditure policy during oil booms to reduce the country's exposure to adverse oil and other financing shocks (both external and domestic). Such a policy, based on *precautionary motives* in the face of uncertainty, would leave margins to allow for short-run oil revenue risks and provide some insurance against oil revenue fluctuations.

In contrast, in a number of oil-producing countries procyclical fiscal policies and persistent fiscal deficits have led to less favorable financial positions and recurrent fiscal sustainability concerns related to the volatile and excessive use of oil revenues. A regular feature of fiscal policy in many oil-producing countries has been the inability to rein in public expenditure at times of rising oil prices.[18] Expenditures have subsequently proven difficult to reduce during oil price downturns. There may also have been the belief that the oil price decline would be short-lived, prompting the temptation to ride out the downturn.

The resulting fiscal deficits have been financed with external and/or domestic borrowing. However, the former has rendered many borrowers vulnerable to increases in the interest rate on foreign loans, as well as to the drying up of new loans as sustainability concerns set in, while the latter has often been inflationary or has crowded out private sector access to credit. Eventually, mounting external and fiscal imbalances, lack of external financing, and in some cases monetary disequilibria and inflation associated with the domestic financing of deficits force the adoption of belated, costly, and disorderly expenditure cuts (often involving the suspension or abandonment of investment projects), sometimes accompanied by currency depreciations.

Thus, when governments are unable to generate fiscal surpluses during periods of rising oil prices that would permit the budget to withstand adverse oil shocks without falling into deficits that lead to sustainability concerns, fiscal policy tends to transmit oil volatility to the rest of the economy. Lack of financing during oil price downturns, in turn, eventually forces governments to undertake sharp and disruptive fiscal contractions, at a time when the economy can least afford them.[19] Countries where external financing is limited, and available domestic financing fluctuates with shifts in sentiment toward the domestic currency, are particularly vulnerable.

Therefore, in countries that are unable to accommodate oil revenue fluctuations due to financing constraints related to sustainability and other policy concerns, a key policy objective should be to pursue fiscal strategies aimed at breaking the procyclical response of expenditure to volatile oil prices. This would imply eliminating expansionary fiscal policy biases during oil booms, and, critically, targeting prudent non-oil fiscal balances and reducing the non-oil fiscal deficit over time. Such

---

[18]For a discussion of procyclical fiscal policies in Nigeria and Venezuela, for example, see Hausmann, Powell, and Rigobon (1993); World Bank (1994); and García and others (1997).

[19]Gavin (1997) provides a similar discussion of fiscal policy and macroeconomic instability in Latin America.

a strategy would create fiscal room that could become available if needed when a transitory oil boom ends, and restore or enhance creditworthiness to improve access to credit markets. This would place the government in a better position to deal with oil market volatility, and increase the likelihood that it can weather temporary oil shocks without drastic short-run fiscal adjustments.

A strong financial position is also essential to allow for an orderly adjustment to catastrophic oil shocks that turn out to be long-lasting, such as the oil market collapse in 1986. As argued in Section II, there is evidence that oil prices are subject to periodic long-lasting changes or regime shifts. A collapse in oil prices that appears to be permanent may prompt major solvency reassessments, and would require adjustment to restore sustainability. A country with a strong financial position can afford to adjust the non-oil deficit in a gradual and orderly fashion. In contrast, a country that is liquidity constrained would be forced to undertake a sudden and large adjustment with all of the concomitant macroeconomic and fiscal costs.

Medium-term budgeting, fiscal rules, and hedging

To aid the implementation of fiscal policy, some countries have resorted to institutional mechanisms such as medium-term expenditure frameworks and fiscal rules, or have had recourse to contingent financial instruments.[20]

Medium-term expenditure frameworks

The formulation of an overall fiscal policy may be aided by a medium-term expenditure framework, which can help limit the extent of short-run spending responses to rapidly changing oil revenues. Multiyear expenditure planning can also allow a better appreciation of the future spending implications of present policy decisions, including the recurrent costs of capital spending.[21]

Fiscal rules

Many oil-producing countries have faced political difficulties in maintaining stable expenditures. Governments come under recurrent

---

[20]Some countries have created oil stabilization funds to help in the implementation of fiscal policy. For a discussion of oil funds, see Davis and others, Chapter 11 in this volume.

[21]See Potter and Diamond (1999).

political pressures to spend the higher revenues arising from rising oil prices. In countries that face financing constraints, moreover, expenditure increases are typically followed by costly fiscal adjustments during oil downturns. Some oil-producing countries are therefore giving consideration to the establishment of more formal constraints on fiscal policy in the form of fiscal rules, to help insulate fiscal policy from political pressures.[22]

The discussion above makes it clear that, in oil-producing countries, fiscal rules applied in other countries that target a certain overall or primary fiscal balance, or particular public debt levels relative to GDP, would not be consistent with the objective of avoiding procyclical fiscal policies. Such rules would in fact transmit oil price fluctuations to expenditure and the non-oil deficit.[23]

Appropriate fiscal rules should instead seek to decouple expenditure policy and the non-oil deficit from the short-run vagaries of oil prices. This suggests that, from a stabilization perspective, the focus of fiscal rules would be better placed on the ratio of the non-oil primary deficit to non-oil GDP, which could be adjusted for the non-oil economic cycle. This general approach would be consistent with the fiscal sustainability analysis discussed in Section II.

The size of the permissible non-oil primary deficit under the fiscal rule would need to take into account the possibility of financing constraints. In addition, because of the volatility of oil prices, some built-in cushion should be incorporated in the rules to deal with potential oil revenue declines. Significant and protracted oil revenue falls that lead to overall solvency reassessments, however, would entail the need to review the fiscal rules.

Contingent financial instruments

Medium-term expenditure frameworks and fiscal rules take the uncertainty and volatility of oil revenue facing the government as given.

---

[22]Fiscal rules may constrain expenditure or the deficit, or they may restrict the ability to borrow. As discussed in Kopits and Symansky (1998), fiscal rules can have both advantages and disadvantages. For an application to oil-producing countries, see Bjerkholt (2002).

[23]Under an overall balance rule, when oil revenues are buoyant, expenditure can be increased, which may result in a high non-oil fiscal deficit at a time when the private sector may be buoyant. Regarding a debt rule, other things being equal, the ratio of public debt to GDP would fall automatically when oil prices increase (which would raise nominal GDP)—but this may be temporary. A subsequent decline in oil prices could entail the need for fiscal adjustment to comply with the debt rule.

The latter, however, could be reduced through the use of contingent financial instruments such as futures, options, and swaps, which transfer risks to international financial markets (Daniel, Chapter 14 in this volume). Recourse to contingent markets might permit price ranges for oil deliveries in future periods to be "locked in." As a result, budgeting could become more realistic and certain. Hedging could also provide some protection against substantial oil price declines. In practice, however, there are limitations to the extent to which future oil revenue might be hedged, particularly in the case of large oil producers and countries with limited access to credit.

IV. Indicators of Fiscal Stance in Oil-Producing Countries

The special characteristics of oil revenue and their implications for short- and long-run fiscal policy in oil-producing countries require that attention be given to several fiscal balances to interpret the impact of fiscal policy appropriately.

The discussion of long-run fiscal issues in Section II and the short-run analysis of fiscal policy in Section III have highlighted the importance of the *non-oil fiscal balance* as a fiscal indicator in oil-producing countries. From a short-run perspective, the non-oil balance is a key indicator of government demand on the economy. Indeed, in countries such as Norway, budget documents and fiscal policy discussions focus prominently on the non-oil balance and its impact on the domestic economy.

If the government decides to spend an oil export revenue windfall, expenditures can rise without either a deterioration in the overall balance or the imposition of additional tax burdens. However, higher government spending would add to demand pressures, including on imports. This effect would be seen in a higher non-oil fiscal deficit, but would not be picked up by the overall balance, which could improve with rising international oil prices despite the loosening of fiscal policy implied by spending some of the additional oil revenues, and mask an expansionary or unsustainable fiscal policy stance.[24] Conversely, a de-

---

[24]To identify more accurately the direct expansionary impact of government on the domestic economy, the domestic balance could be used. This balance includes only those components of the overall balance that arise from transactions with the domestic economy, and omits those transactions directly affecting the balance of payments. For operational purposes, however, the non-oil deficit will often be a reasonable proxy for the domestic balance.

terioration in the overall balance because of lower oil revenues may mask significant fiscal adjustment efforts (see Appendix II).

The non-oil fiscal balance also provides a clearer picture of the underlying policy stance and is a more reliable measure of discretionary fiscal policy than the overall balance, since it is a fiscal variable largely under the control of the authorities. It also provides a measure of fiscal vulnerability. If expenditures have been increased during a period of rising oil prices, the resulting non-oil deficit may be difficult to finance, or become unsustainable in the absence of compensating fiscal adjustment at lower oil prices.

There are advantages in highlighting the non-oil balance in budget documents that form the basis for legislative and public discussion. This would help make the use of oil revenue more transparent, and delineate policy choices more clearly.

The *overall fiscal balance*, on the other hand, is the relevant indicator for assessing the government's financing requirement and fiscal vulnerability. The evaluation of a particular overall balance will require assessment of the fiscal and macroeconomic impact of alternative methods of financing it. For example, the domestic financing of an overall deficit may be inflationary or may crowd out private sector investment, while external financing may be too costly or unavailable.

Unlike the non-oil balance, however, the overall fiscal balance in an oil-producing country may not be a good pointer for the impact of fiscal policy on domestic demand and the government's adjustment effort. Changes in the overall balance arising from fluctuations in oil revenue that are externally financed should be expected to have limited direct effects on domestic demand.

International lending to developing primary commodity producers with large volatile resource revenues tends to be procyclical. This has particularly important implications for countries facing financing constraints. When assessing the financeability of a given fiscal position under alternative oil price scenarios, it should be borne in mind that these countries may find it difficult to ensure financing when oil prices fall sharply, at a time when foreign resources may be most needed.

It will often be important to gauge the sensitivity of overall fiscal outcomes (and their implications for financing) to variations in key macroeconomic variables (including, prominently, oil prices) and other sources of economic risk.[25] For example, increases in expenditure or

---

[25]Hemming and Petrie (2000) provide a general framework for assessing fiscal vulnerability.

reductions in taxes at a time of rising oil prices may not raise immediate financing concerns, but could increase the budget's exposure to turnarounds in oil prices. Projections of the overall balance under current policies should therefore be made several years into the future under alternative oil scenarios, to examine the trajectory of net government financial assets and possible medium-term financing vulnerabilities.

In the case of oil producers where the financial position of the government is particularly weak, the volatile and uncertain nature of oil revenues would also require undertaking sensitivity analyses of alternative oil price scenarios for the *gross borrowing requirement*. This would be particularly important where market concerns about fiscal sustainability and short-run liquidity raise questions about the availability of credit to finance the overall balance and amortization needs.

V. Conclusions and Policy Recommendations

The main findings from the previous analysis can be broken down into three key guidelines.

First, the non-oil balance should feature prominently in the formulation of fiscal policy. Decomposing the overall balance into an oil and non-oil balance is critical for understanding fiscal policy developments, evaluating sustainability, and determining the macroeconomic impact of fiscal policy. Indeed, highlighting the non-oil balance in the budget would itself be an important step toward improving fiscal policy.

Second, the non-oil balance, especially expenditure, should generally be adjusted gradually. Large swings in fiscal policy—as measured by the non-oil balance—are destabilizing to aggregate demand, exacerbate uncertainty, and induce macroeconomic volatility. Moreover, from a purely fiscal perspective, large swings in expenditure are difficult to manage and reduce its quality and efficiency.

Third, the government should strive to accumulate substantial financial assets over the period of oil production. Oil extraction should be viewed as a portfolio transaction whereby oil wealth is transformed into financial wealth—implying oil revenue is conceptually more like financing than income. Asset accumulation over the years of production needs to be sufficiently large to sustain fiscal policy in the post-oil period.

The above guidelines are theoretically straightforward; nonetheless, they are often not followed in practice. For example, few oil-producing countries publish or include an analysis of the non-oil balance in the budget. At the same time, an excessive focus on the overall balance often leads to fiscal policy (as measured by the non-oil balance) moving in tandem with oil revenue, resulting in a volatile non-oil fiscal deficit with the concomitant adverse macroeconomic and fiscal consequences. And, despite years of oil production, many oil-producing countries have not accumulated financial wealth and have substantial net financial liabilities, raising questions about their fiscal sustainability.

Given the heterogeneity of oil-producing countries and the broad scope of this paper, it is not practical to draw quantitative conclusions as to the desirable non-oil deficit. Such determinations ultimately depend on country-specific factors, including the country's macroeconomic objectives. Nonetheless, the following considerations should help determine appropriate ranges for the non-oil deficit.

First, many oil-producing countries can, indeed, afford to run potentially sizable non-oil deficits. Analogous to a permanent income consumer, decisions on the non-oil deficit should be based on assessments of government wealth (including oil wealth), rather than on current oil income. There are strong precautionary motives, however, that would justify fiscal prudence, including enormous uncertainty regarding oil wealth.

Second, as in any economy, fiscal policy in oil-producing countries needs to support the broader macroeconomic objectives. These include macroeconomic stability, growth, and an efficient allocation of resources.

Third, as a result of procyclical fiscal policies and recurrent fiscal deficits, many oil-producing countries face interest rate premiums on sovereign debt and liquidity constraints related to sustainability and other policy concerns that restrict their ability to accommodate oil revenue fluctuations. These countries should pursue fiscal strategies aimed at breaking procyclical fiscal responses to volatile oil prices, targeting prudent non-oil fiscal balances, and reducing the non-oil fiscal deficit over time.

Appendix I. Intertemporal Allocation of Fiscal Resources (*A Formal Model*)

This appendix sketches the formal model underlying the analysis in Section II of the paper. At the core of the analysis is that the government chooses a tax and spending policy to maximize a social welfare function subject to an intertemporal budget constraint and a transversality or no-Ponzi game condition. These latter two equations are, respectively,

$$B_t = RB_{t-1} + G_t - T_t - Z_t \text{ and} \tag{1}$$

$$\lim_{s \to \infty} B_{t+s} = 0, \tag{2}$$

where B_t is government debt at the end of the period, R is the interest rate (assumed to be constant), G_t is primary government expenditure, T_t is non-oil revenue, and Z_t is oil revenue. It is assumed that there is no uncertainty, that oil revenue Z_t is constant and lasts for exactly N periods, and that non-oil GDP (denoted by Y_t) is also constant.

The setup of the problem allows for the social welfare function to be expressed in several equivalent ways. The above assumptions imply that fiscal policy variables (revenue and expenditure) do not affect the other macroeconomic variables, which are assumed to be constant and exogenous. In this respect, examining equation (1) suggests that it is only the difference between revenue and (primary) expenditure, or equivalently the primary balance, that matters for the evolution of government debt—the levels of revenue and expenditure themselves are not important. It is equivalent, therefore, to express the social welfare function in terms of just the primary balance (as implicitly done in the text), or in terms of revenue for a given level of expenditure (a tax-smoothing approach), or government spending for a given level of revenue. The latter approach, with the assumption that revenue is constant, is adopted in what follows because it simplifies the exposition by accentuating the parallels with the permanent income consumption problem. Formally, the problem then is to maximize the social welfare function,

$$\underset{\{G_t\}_{t=1}^{\infty}}{\text{Max}} \sum_{t=1}^{\infty} \beta^{t-1} U(G_t), \tag{3}$$

where β is the discount factor (and $\beta R=1$ is assumed to hold), $U(G_t)$ is the felicity or utility function, and the maximization is subject to equations (1) and (2).

This problem yields a closed-form analytical solution that is independent of $U(G_t)$. The first-order condition, or Euler equation, is given by,

$$U'(G_t) = \beta R U'(G_{t+1}), \tag{4}$$

where $U'(G_t)$ denotes the derivative. Since $\beta R = 1$, regardless of $U'(G_t)$, the result emerges that $G_{t+1} = G_t \equiv \bar{G}$ or, simply put, government spending is constant. Moreover, spending is just equal to permanent income or the return on the present discounted value of wealth. Formally,

$$\bar{G} = T + \frac{r}{R} \sum_{i=0}^{N} R^{-i} Z - r B_{t-1}, \qquad (5)$$

where the middle term is the return on the present discounted value of oil revenue—that is, oil wealth. To simulate the model, quantitative values of the parameters are set as follows: non-oil GDP is 100 ($Y = 100$); revenue is 15 percent of non-oil GDP, or $\tau = 0.15$ such that $T = \tau Y = 15$; oil revenue is 15 percent of non-oil GDP ($Z = 15$); oil reserves are sufficient to last 40 years ($N = 40$); the discount factor is 0.96 ($\beta = 0.96$), implying that the interest rate is around 4 percent; and the initial debt is 40 ($B_0 = 40$).

The introduction of non-oil GDP and population growth complicates the algebra but does not affect the qualitative results. Following Tersman (1991), the government utility function could be expressed in terms of non-oil GDP, where $g_t = \frac{G_t}{Y_t}$ and $U(g_t)$ is used in the social welfare function (equation (3)) in place of $U(G_t)$.[26] To keep the problem well behaved and simple, the following additional assumptions are also made (where lowercase letters are shares of non-oil GDP): the growth rate of non-oil GDP is constant and equal to η, such that $Y_{t+1} = (1+\eta)Y_t$; the discount factor is adjusted such that; $\beta \frac{1+r}{1+\eta} = 1$; and z_t is constant, which implies that oil revenue is growing at the same rate as non-oil GDP. With these assumptions, the solution is analogous to equation (5), except the government expenditure to GDP ratio is constant, and the interest rate terms are adjusted by η. To keep govern-

---

[26]Scaling in terms of non-oil GDP has advantages over obvious alternatives such as using real spending, real per capita spending, or some rule such as just sharing oil wealth equally. As to the first two options, they would imply that government spending as a share of non-oil GDP is tending toward zero over time (provided non-oil GDP growth is greater than population growth). This does not seem plausible, as in the long run it would seem more realistic to assume that the government expenditure to (non-oil) GDP ratio converges to some steady state value. As Tersman (1991) points out, however, this specification ". . . means that one has to accept the idea that future generations are better off simply because they come later." As to defining the welfare function in terms of sharing the oil wealth equally, Solow (1986) notes "The current generation does not especially owe to its successors a share of this or that particular resource. If it owes anything, it owes...access to a certain standard of living or level of consumption."

ment wealth as a share of GDP from falling in the post-oil period entails a smaller primary non-oil deficit than in the model without
growth (for any given level of assets), as some of the asset returns—an
amount equivalent to the growth in non-oil GDP—have to be rein-
vested. In other words, the non-oil deficit would have to be lower than
the return on government wealth, and instead be the difference between the return and the non-oil GDP growth rate. The following examples, however, are based on the simpler case with zero growth in
non-oil GDP.

Obsolescence can be modeled as a specific form of uncertainty, in
which the future price of oil falls to zero, and stays there forever. Let π
denote the probability (assumed to be constant) of oil becoming obsolete in a given period, then equation (4) would become,

$$U'(G_t) = \beta R[(1-\pi)U'(G_{t+1}^P) + \pi U'(G_{t+1}^0)] , \qquad (6)$$

where G_{t+1}^P is the government spending if oil prices remain positive in
$t+1$, and G_{t+1}^0 is the spending that would occur if prices go to zero. For
the case of oil becoming obsolete, there would be no uncertainty left
and government spending (G_{t+1}^0) would simply be set to permanent income. Permanent income, however, in which oil wealth is zero. In contrast, G_{t+1}^P is based on permanent income in the event that oil prices are
still positive; thus, it is clear that $G_{t+1}^P > G_{t+1}^0$, and G_{t+1}^0 is likely substantially smaller provided that the present discounted value of oil reserves
is relatively large. From equation (6), the obsolescence effect would be
larger the higher the probability of obsolescence (the larger is π), the
larger the value of remaining oil reserves (expanding the gap between
G_{t+1}^P and G_{t+1}^0), and the more risk averse the government is (governed
by $U'(G_t)$).

The impact of sovereign risk premiums are easiest to see by looking
at some of the first-order conditions. In particular, if there is positive
debt (technically at the end of the period) then the following first-order
condition applies,

$$U'(G_t) = \beta \tilde{R} U'(G_{t+1}) , \qquad (7)$$

where $\tilde{R} = 1 + r + \rho$, and ρ is the sovereign premium (such that $\rho > 0$).
Since $\tilde{R} > R$, then it must be the case that $\beta \tilde{R} > 1$ and therefore $G_{t+1} > G_t$.
This indicates that government spending, at least while debt is posi-
tive, is steadily increasing. Once there are positive assets, then the solution is identical to that of equation (5) and government spending is
constant. Given that initially there is debt, the path of government

spending implies a gradually increasing non-oil deficit (until the debt is retired) and, for this to be sustainable, the initial non-oil deficit must be smaller than it would have been in the absence of the premium.

The models that incorporate capital spending can be motivated intuitively. In the case of capital spending boosting non-oil GDP, non-oil GDP becomes a function of government capital (K_t), where $Y(K_t)$ has the usual properties $Y'(K_t) > 0$ and $Y''(K_t) <$ (which rules out increasing or even constant returns to scale). The intuition is the most straightforward if convex adjustment costs and depreciation are abstracted from, in which case government investment is undertaken to the point where,

$$r = \tau Y'(K_{t+1}),$$ (8)

that is, the point where the marginal return to the government, $\tau Y'(K_{t+1})$, is equal to the interest rate (or the marginal cost of investment). What may not be immediately obvious, however, is that $Y(K_t)$ is independent of oil wealth—so, for example, an increase in oil wealth does not affect the productivity of government investment in non-oil GDP. Finally, in the case of modeling capital expenditure as a durable consumption good, the mathematics are somewhat less intuitive. However, the intuition is that provided there are convex adjustment costs—giving an incentive to adjust the capital stock slowly—an increase in oil wealth would lead to an increase in desired government durables. The convex adjustment costs would make the adjustment process gradual, implying a period of larger than normal conventionally measured fiscal deficits.

Appendix II. Fiscal Balances and Measurement Issues

Fiscal analysis and projections in oil-producing countries should take into account the fact that oil prices and the exchange rate are key fiscal variables that can have significant direct effects on the public finances. Moreover, they can also have major effects on the ratios of fiscal variables to GDP because the oil and non-oil GDP deflators can deviate markedly.

Movements in total GDP related to oil sector developments, usually prices, can cause the GDP ratios of non-oil fiscal variables to vary substantially. This could lead to an erroneous conclusion that there has been a modification in the underlying fiscal policy, even though all that has happened is oil prices have changed. For example, assuming unchanged non-oil revenue and expenditure, an increase in oil prices would lead to higher nominal GDP, and thus directly cause the ratios of non-oil deficit to total GDP to fall. Declining ratios of the non-oil deficit to total GDP could mask an expansionary fiscal policy undertaken in the context of rising oil prices.

Changes in the exchange rate may cause similar measurement problems by raising or lowering the share of oil GDP in total GDP. As in the case of changes in oil prices, this has a bearing on the ratios of fiscal variables to GDP. For example, a depreciation of the currency may result in a lower non-oil deficit as a share of GDP as the latter is boosted by the increase in oil GDP. Great care should therefore be exercised when evaluating the ratio of the non-oil deficit or expenditure to GDP in years with large exchange rate fluctuations.[27]

When the terms of trade or the exchange rate display significant fluctuations, it is vital to consider other fiscal indicators besides ratios to total GDP. In particular, important information may be conveyed by percentage changes in the relevant variables—in nominal terms as well as deflated by a broad domestic price index such as the consumer price index or the non-oil GDP deflator—and by ratios to non-oil GDP.[28]

An Illustrative Example

Some of the measurement issues discussed above are illustrated in Table 3.1, which shows fiscal variables and GDP for a hypothetical oil-producing country. The example suggests that care should be exercised in interpreting the fiscal aggregates when the oil price moves from year to year.

In the numerical example in the table, while nominal non-oil GDP is unchanged throughout, oil prices rise sharply in year 2 before falling back in year 3, leading to parallel movements in oil GDP, total GDP, and fiscal oil revenue. In year 2 expenditures are increased, leading to a higher non-oil deficit (in nominal terms and as a share of non-oil

---

[27]A real appreciation of the currency, by reducing the domestic purchasing power of foreign exchange and therefore of oil fiscal revenue, will typically weaken the overall fiscal balance of countries heavily dependent on oil for their fiscal revenues.

[28]For example, the ratio of non-oil revenue to total GDP may provide little information and be hard to interpret. The link between non-oil revenue and oil GDP is likely to be tenuous, and terms of trade and real exchange rate effects of oil GDP on total GDP will affect the share of non-oil revenue to GDP. Therefore it is important to analyze non-oil revenue developments in terms of ratios to non-oil GDP.

Table 3.1. *Fiscal Variables and GDP in a Hypothetical Oil-Producing Country*

	Year 1	Year 2	Year 3
	(In national currency)		
Nominal GDP	1,200	1,350	1,150
Oil GDP	300	450	250
Non-oil GDP	900	900	900
Government finances			
Revenue	230	305	205
Oil revenue	150	225	125
Non-oil revenue	80	80	80
Expenditure	250	265	250
Non-oil balance	–170	–185	–170
Overall balance	–20	40	–45
	(In percent of GDP)		
Government finances			
Revenue	19.2	22.6	17.8
Oil revenue	12.5	16.7	10.9
Non-oil revenue	6.7	5.9	7.0
Expenditure	20.8	19.6	21.7
Non-oil balance	–14.2	–13.7	–14.8
Overall balance	–1.7	3.0	–3.9
	(In percent of non-oil GDP)		
Government finances			
Revenue	25.6	33.9	22.8
Oil revenue	16.7	25.0	13.9
Non-oil revenue	8.9	8.9	8.9
Expenditure	27.8	29.4	27.8
Non-oil balance	–18.9	–20.6	–18.9
Overall balance	–2.2	4.4	–5.0
Memorandum item:			
Oil price (US$/barrel)	15.0	22.5	12.5

Source: Authors' calculations.

GDP), but the non-oil deficit as a share of GDP declines. The deterioration in the non-oil deficit is masked by the improvement in the overall balance, and would become clear if the oil price returned to its initial level. In year 3, although there is an adjustment effort as evidenced in the reduction in expenditures, the non-oil deficit as a percent of GDP deteriorates. Non-oil revenue as a share of non-oil GDP is constant throughout, but its ratio to GDP is volatile and hard to interpret.

Bibliography

Aizenman, Joshua, and Nancy P. Marion, 1993, "Policy Uncertainty, Persistence, and Growth," *Review of International Economics*, Vol. 1 (June), pp. 145–63.

Alier, Max, and Martin Kaufman, 1999, "Nonrenewable Resources: A Case for Persistent Fiscal Surpluses," IMF Working Paper 99/44 (Washington: International Monetary Fund).

Amuzegar, Jahangir, 1999, *Managing the Oil Wealth: OPEC's Windfalls and Pitfalls* (London; New York: I.B. Tauris & Co. Ltd.).

Auty, Richard M., ed., 2001, *Resource Abundance and Economic Development: Improving the Performance of Resource-Rich Countries* (Oxford: Oxford University Press).

Auty, Richard M., and Alan Gelb, 2001, "Political Economy of Resource-Abundant States," in *Resource Abundance and Economic Development*, ed. by R.M. Auty (Oxford: Oxford University Press).

Bjerkholt, Olav, 2002, "Fiscal Rules for Economies With Non-Renewable Resources," paper prepared for the conference "Rules-Based Fiscal Policy in Emerging Market Economies," Oaxaca, Mexico, February.

Cashin, Paul, Hong Liang, and C. John McDermott, 2000, "How Persistent Are Shocks to World Commodity Prices?" *IMF Staff Papers*, Vol. 47, No. 2, pp. 177–217.

Chalk, Nigel, 1998, "Fiscal Sustainability with Non-Renewable Resources," IMF Working Paper 98/26 (Washington: International Monetary Fund).

———, and Richard Hemming, 2000, "Assessing Fiscal Sustainability in Theory and Practice," IMF Working Paper 00/81 (Washington: International Monetary Fund).

Dalmazzo, Alberto, and Guido de Blasio, 2001, "Resources and Incentives to Reform: A Model and Some Evidence on Sub-Saharan African Countries," IMF Working Paper 01/86 (Washington: International Monetary Fund).

Deaton, Angus, 1992, *Understanding Consumption* (Oxford: Clarendon Press).

Engel, Eduardo, and Rodrigo Valdés, 2000, "Optimal Fiscal Strategy for Oil Exporting Countries," IMF Working Paper 00/118 (Washington: International Monetary Fund).

Fischer, Stanley, and William Easterly, 1990, "The Economics of the Government Budget Constraint," *World Bank Research Observer*, Vol. 5, No. 2, pp. 127–42.

García Osío, Gustavo, and others, 1997, "La Sostenibilidad de la Política Fiscal en Venezuela," *Revista del Banco Central de Venezuela*, Vol. 11, No. 2, pp. 11–104.

Gavin, Michael, 1997, "A Decade of Reform in Latin America: Has It Delivered Lower Volatility?" IADB Working Paper Green Series, No. 349 (Washington: Inter-American Development Bank).

————, and Ricardo Hausmann, 1996, "The Roots of Banking Crises: The Macroeconomic Context," in *Banking Crises in Latin America*, ed. by Ricardo Hausmann and Liliana Rojas-Suárez (Washington: Inter-American Development Bank).

Gelb, Alan, and Associates, 1988, *Oil Windfalls: Blessing or Curse?* (New York: Oxford University Press for the World Bank).

Gramlich, Edward M., 1994, "Infrastructure Investment: A Review Essay," *Journal of Economic Liturature*, Vol. 32 (September), pp. 1176–96.

Hausmann, Ricardo, Andrew Powell, and Roberto Rigobon, 1993, "An Optimal Spending Rule Facing Oil Income Uncertainty (Venezuela)," in *External Shocks and Stabilization Mechanisms*, ed. by Eduardo Engel and Patricio Meller (Washington: Inter-American Development Bank and Johns Hopkins University Press), pp. 113–71.

Hemming, Richard, and Murray Petrie, 2000, "A Framework for Assessing Fiscal Vulnerability," IMF Working Paper 00/52 (Washington: International Monetary Fund).

Kopits, George, and Steven Symansky, 1998, *Fiscal Policy Rules*, IMF Occasional Paper No. 162 (Washington: International Monetary Fund).

Leite, Carlos, and Jens Weidmann, 1999, "Does Mother Nature Corrupt? Natural Resources, Corruption, and Economic Growth," IMF Working Paper 99/85 (Washington: International Monetary Fund).

Liuksila, Claire, Alejandro García, and Sheila Bassett, 1994, "Fiscal Policy Sustainability in Oil-Producing Countries," IMF Working Paper 94/137 (Washington: International Monetary Fund).

Potter, Barry H., and Jack Diamond, 1999, *Guidelines for Public Expenditure Management* (Washington: International Monetary Fund).

Rodríguez, Francisco, and Jeffrey D. Sachs, 1999, "Why Do Resource-Abundant Economies Grow More Slowly?" *Journal of Economic Growth*, Vol. 4, (September), pp. 277–303.

Sachs, Jeffrey, and Andrew Warner, 1995, "Natural Resource Abundance and Economic Growth," Harvard Institute of Economic Research Discussion Paper No. 517 (Cambridge, Massachusetts: Harvard Institute for International Development).

Servén, Luis, and Andrés Solimano, eds., 1993, *Striving for Growth after Adjustment: The Role of Capital Formation* (Washington: World Bank).

Solow, Robert M., 1986, "On the Intergenerational Allocation of Natural Resources," *Scandinavian Journal of Economics*, Vol. 88 (June), pp. 141–49.

Tersman, Gunnar, 1991, "Oil, National Wealth, and Current and Future Consumption Possibilities," IMF Working Paper 91/60 (Washington: International Monetary Fund).

Tornell, Aaron, and Philip R. Lane, 1998, "Voracity and Growth," NBER Working Paper No. 6498 (Cambridge, Massachusetts: National Bureau of Economic Research).

World Bank, 1993, "Venezuela—Oil and Exchange Rates: Historical Experience and Policy Options," World Bank Report No. 10481-VE (Washington).

———, 1994, "Nigeria—Macroeconomic Risk Management: Issues and Options," World Bank Report No. 11983–UNI (Washington).

4

The Political Economy of Fiscal Policy and Economic Management in Oil-Exporting Countries

BENN EIFERT, ALAN GELB, AND NILS BORJE TALLROTH[1]

I. Introduction

M ost mineral exporters, and in particular the oil exporters, have done far less well than resource-poor countries over the past few decades, particularly when considering the massive revenue gains to the oil-exporting countries since 1973. Many studies support the "paradox of plenty" (recent examples include Auty, 2001; Gylfason, 2000 and 2001; Hausmann and Rigobon, Chapter 2 in this volume), even though there are certainly exceptions to this pattern. Some of the high-income OECD countries are resource-abundant, Botswana stands out as a successful mineral exporter, and Malaysia has grown and diversified away from resource-based production, including oil. But why has the overall record of oil-exporting countries been so disappointing?

This paper considers the political economy of fiscal policy and economic management across oil-exporting countries with widely differing political systems. Politics affects economics—how oil rents are collected, allocated, and used, including often to sustain a poor policy regime (Auty, 2001). But oil affects politics also—a large, concentrated

[1]The authors would like to thank Ms. Xiao Ye and other colleagues who have provided material for this paper. Responsibility for errors is that of the authors alone. The views expressed in this paper are those of the authors and should not be attributed to the World Bank or to its Executive Directors or the countries that they represent.

rent source in national income can mold the social and political institutions of a producing country into what some have termed the "rentier state" (Karl, 1999).[2] Technical approaches to managing rents
therefore need to be seen in a political context, and implemented in
parallel with approaches to strengthen the constituencies needed to
support them.

In comparing the performance of oil-exporting countries, this paper
attempts to identify factors that have helped them to manage rents
well. Some caveats are in order. Political categories are not robust
enough to provide a clear political-economy linkage. Political regimes
also change, sometimes sharply, but at the same time existing institutions may reflect the impact of years of previous political regimes, in
addition to the impact of the current one. While there is a large literature on the management of oil resources, comparative analysis of the
underlying political determinants of policy is more sparse. The paper
is therefore more suggestive than definitive. It also focuses on spending, rather than revenue policies, not because the latter are uninterest-
ing but because most of the problems of economic management relate
to the use of revenues rather than to their collection.

The following section sets out some general principles for managing
oil rents well, based on the experience of oil exporters over the last
three decades. Section III presents an extended version of Lal's (1995)
topology of political states, which is used in Section IV to discuss selected oil producers. Section V concludes with suggestions for ways to
encourage good practice in managing oil rents.

II. Managing Oil Revenues

Most of the essentials for managing oil revenues well are the same as
those for good budget management in general, but some issues are
more important for oil exporters. These include how much to save for
future generations, how to deal with uncertain revenues and avoid
"boom-bust" cycles, and how to ensure that spending is of high quality, whether in the form of large investment projects, public consumption, or subsidies.

---

[2]Another strain of research considers the role of natural rent in encouraging civil conflict in countries such as Angola, the Democratic Republic of Congo, Liberia, and Sierra
Leone. See, for example, Tallroth (1998); and Collier and Hoeffler (2002).

Saving

Whether countries should save or borrow against anticipated future oil income to fund current consumption and investment (as Algeria and Mexico did in the 1970s) depends on the projected profiles of oil output, extraction costs, prices, discount rates, and returns on alternative investments to keeping oil in the ground. These are slippery numbers. Proven reserves are far larger today than three decades ago. New technology has widened the range of oil substitutes, including tar sands and coal gasification that are now economical at oil prices of US$15–US$20 per barrel. New liberal pricing regimes have stimulated production (Mommer, 1999), as has the opening of the former Soviet Union. On the other hand, the share of natural rent in the price of oil will probably fall as low-cost fields are depleted, and in some countries rent will fall further relative to development needs due to high population growth. Optimal savings rates are very sensitive to such assumptions.

Stabilizing

Oil prices have been highly variable: twice as variable as those of other commodities, even when changes are measured as deviation from recent trends (Dehn, 2001). Changes have also been very poorly predicted, and it has been difficult to separate out temporary fluctuations from trends.[3] If past experience is a guide, shocks will continue to be poorly foreseen, and producing countries will be vulnerable to boom-bust cycles. Instability is very costly, as economies and budgets adjust asymmetrically. On the upside, growth increases little; on the downside, output contracts (Dehn, 2001). Over a series of cycles, countries move toward stagflation. Rapid growth in public spending, which often follows oil price increases, reduces spending quality and introduces entitlements, including recurrent cost commitments, which are often not sustainable in the long run. Efficiency often suffers from a

---

[3]The 1974 and 1979 price increases were not foreseen by consensus forecasts. By the early 1980s, high prices were widely blamed on scarcity, with projections of US$50 per barrel or even higher. Instead, the spike of the early 1980s was followed by the oil slump and a sharp price decline. Prices reached an unexpected nadir in 1998 with the shock of the Asia crisis; projections envisaged a slow rebound toward US$20 per barrel but failed to pick up the spike of 2000 to levels 50 percent higher.

high proportion of unfinished projects as well as from capital invest-ments that cannot be effectively used because of shortages of recurrent resources. These observations point to the need for cautious expendi-ture plans also in times of rapidly increasing government oil revenues.

Simulations using a computable general equilibrium model with a 20-year horizon suggests that optimal savings during revenue booms like those of the 1970s ought to be 60–70 percent of the gains (Gelb and Associates, 1988), far higher than the levels achieved by exporters. They also show that the costs of policies formulated on the basis of overoptimistic projections of prices and revenues during a windfall pe-riod can amount to several times the potential benefit of the windfall it-self (Gelb and Associates, 1988).[4] It is easy to turn potential gains into losses. There is therefore a strong case for making cautious revenue projections, for holding larger than normal reserves, for minimizing outstanding public debt, and for using hedging techniques in order to cushion shocks and gain an additional margin of fiscal flexibility.

Using Rents Well

In almost all producers, oil rents are seen as the property of the na-tion.[5] The problem is how to articulate this concept in an effective and widely agreed way through the political process. Lack of clarity in property rights encourages rent-seeking behavior; mechanisms to dis-tribute rent should thus be clear, and be part of a transparent budget process able to link fiscal choices to current and (conservatively) pro-jected revenues. For any given level of use of oil rents, the mix of chan-nels to distribute them to citizens, whether through public investment or recurrent spending, subsidies and transfers, or lower non-oil taxes, should reflect the marginal value of public resources relative to those in private hands.

Within these general areas, two potential pitfalls tend to be particu-larly important for oil exporters. First, the concentration of fiscal re-sources tends to encourage excessive and imprudent investment: the state implements large projects without sufficient participation of pri-

---

[4]This conclusion agrees with the conclusion of a recent study of countries exposed to large shocks, which shows that the losses are typically far larger than the gains (Collier, 2002).

[5]The United States is one of the very few countries where subsurface rent conveys with ownership of the surface land rights.

vate coinvestors to provide a screen against excessive risk (Gelb and Associates, 1988; and Auty, 2001).[6] Second, some ways of distributing rent, whether through sustained protection of favored activities or firms, or a combination of non-oil taxes and subsidies and public spending, have high deadweight costs and encourage corruption. In some cases, very low non-oil tax rates might be useful as part of a rent-distribution strategy, though this approach should be combined with measures to strengthen tax administration and increase non-oil revenues to diversify potential revenue sources to create a buffer against oil revenue fluctuations. Cheap domestic energy could be one element of such a strategy (particularly in times of high world energy prices), but needs to be viewed in the wider context of non-oil taxation and the long-term risks for inefficiencies in resource allocation.

These prescriptions are well enough in theory. But they often confront the reality of opaque, highly politicized fiscal systems that lack the checks and balances needed to ensure that resources are well employed and to provide the fiscal flexibility needed to adjust spending in line with changes in resources. In extreme cases, when the legitimacy of the government comes to rest on the transfer of oil rent, no fiscal adjustment will be possible unless forced by a crisis. Rents weaken agencies of restraint. For any given group, they divert incentives away from ensuring efficient use of resources across the economy (including by other groups) in favor of appropriating rents unencumbered by the reciprocal scrutiny of the other groups. How this plays out in any given country will depend on whether the political process is able to support a consensus around a sound longer-run social and economic trajectory. If so, rents can provide exports, taxes, and savings to open up additional degrees of freedom for economic policy. If not, they are likely to fuel a destructive process of struggle for the rents that is mirrored in economic crisis and decline.

III. The Political Economy of Rentier States: Toward a Typology

Just as political traditions shape the use of oil rents, rents shape the political economy of petroleum-exporting nations. Revenue streams from

---

[6]Small minority private participation provides little screening as partners expect to gain far more from supplying cost overruns than from profitable projects.

"black gold" can finance productive physical and social investment, or fuel unsustainable consumption booms and eventual fiscal crises; they can improve public welfare through transparent distributional mechanisms, create elite arenas of competition, or underpin kleptocratic governments. Karl (1999) argues that when petroleum exploitation coincides with state-building, it gives rise to a self-reinforcing "legacy of overly-centralized political power, strong networks of complicity between public and private sector actors, [and] highly uneven mineral-based development subsidized by oil rents." Karl's conclusions may be overly deterministic, but her observations ring true for many oil-exporting states. In this section we construct a comparative analytical framework that offers insights into the political economy of oil windfall management in varying political and institutional contexts.

Political scientists have offered insights into the state that have implications for rentier economies. Olson (1986, 2000) emphasizes the importance of horizon constraints in shaping the behavior of governments. Bates (2001) stresses the way in which the relaxation of government budget constraints creates disincentives for economically rational behavior and reform. Work on the theory of rent-seeking behavior illustrates how rent reorients economic incentives toward competing for access to oil revenues, and away from productive activities, especially in nontransparent environments characterized by political discretion and unclear property rights. These studies and others offer insights that can help build an analytical framework for the better understanding of, and improvement in, the fiscal and economic management policies in oil-exporting countries. Still, systems of state classification developed by political scientists remain difficult to operationalize. Some scholars question the utility of classification schemes on the grounds that individual country outcomes are highly context-specific, and arise out of complex sociological interactions combined with leadership and other random factors.[7] Others, including a number of economists, argue that observable variations in political and institutional context have considerable predictive power and are useful.[8] We side with the latter, while recognizing the limitations of any analysis.

Oil-exporting countries may be classified as belonging to one of five main groups: mature democracies; "factional" democracies; paternalis-

---

[7]For example, see Haggard (1990).

[8]For examples of state classification frameworks, see political scientists Andrain (1988), Bratton and van de Walle (1994), and Leftwich (1995), and economists Findlay (1990) and Lal (1995).

tic autocracies; reformist autocracies; and predatory autocracies. These groups reflect qualitative distinctions in (i) the stability of the political framework and of party systems; (ii) the degree of social consensus; (iii) the legitimization of authority and the means through which governments (or aspiring governments) obtain and maintain support; and (iv) the role of state institutions in underpinning markets and the distribution of rents. These political and institutional features foster differences in the length of political horizons, levels of transparency, policy stability and quality, the political power of the sectors producing non-oil tradables, and the power of interests directly attached to state spending (Table 4.1).

The classifications in Table 4.1 are not exhaustive, and some countries have a blend of features from different categories. For example, fiscal federalism is one factor cutting across the categories given in Table 4.1. Therefore, this paper does not aim at creating a *sui generis* classification of oil countries. At the same time, such classification does provide insights into the policy options available to governments. They are also mirrored in comparative ratings such as those of Freedom House and Transparency International (see Table 4.2).

On Transparency International's ratings, mature democracies score high, factional democracies are in the lower half of the sample, and the oil autocracies that are rated score at the bottom. On Freedom House's ratings of political rights and civil liberties, mature democracies score the highest rating, factional democracies quite high, and the autocracies near the lowest ratings. The ratings suggest that democracy may have advanced further in the factional democracies than transparency, a potentially important asymmetry when considering the use of natural rent.

Mature Democracies

Countries and subnational units classified as mature democracies are characterized by relatively stable policies, underpinned by a broad social consensus. Politics is dominated by a few parties. Such political stability encourages long-horizon behavior, as party reputation effects and economic performance become central to competition for political power. The resulting policy regimes are generally based on transparent information; property rights are clear and a swing in government rarely leads to sweeping realignment of policy priorities. Bureaucracies are competent and relatively insulated; professional judicial systems foster depersonalized functioning of markets and reasonable stability

Table 4.1. *Political Economy Classification of Oil Exporters*

Political Features	Institutional Implications	Economic Implications
Mature Democracy: Stable party system. Range of social consensus. Strong, competent, insulated bureaucracy. Competent, professional judicial system. Highly educated electorate.	Long policy horizon. Policy stability, transparency. High competitiveness, low transactions costs. Strong private/traded sector, pro-stabilization interests vis-à-vis pro-spending interests.	Savings likely. Expenditure smoothing, stabilization. Rents partially transferred to public through government-provided social services and insurance or direct transfers.
Factional Democracy: Government and parties often unstable relative to interest groups. Political support gained through clientelistic ties and provision of patronage. Wide social disparities, lack of consensus. Politicized bureaucracy and judicial system.	Short policy horizon. Policy instability, nontransparency. Strong state role in production, high transactions costs. Strong interests attached directly to state expenditures; politically weak private non-oil sector and pro-stabilization interests.	Savings very difficult. Procyclical expenditure; instability. Rents transferred to different interests and to public through subsidies, policy distortions, and public employment.
Paternalistic Autocracy: Stable government; legitimacy originally from traditional role, maintained through rent distribution. Strong cultural elements of consensus, clientelistic and nationalistic patterns. Bureaucracy provides both services and public employment.	Long policy horizon. Policy stability, nontransparency. Low competitiveness, high transactions costs. Strong state role in production. Strong interests attached directly to state expenditures; weak private sector.	Procyclical expenditure, mixed success with stabilization. Risk of unsustainable long-term spending trajectory leading to political crisis. Little economic diversification.
Reformist Autocracy: Stable government, legitimized by development. Social range of consensus toward development. Constituency in non-oil traded sectors. Insulated technocracy.	Long policy horizon. Policy stability, nontransparency. Drive for competitiveness, low transactions costs. Strong constituency for stabilization and fiscal restraint.	Expenditure smoothing, stabilization. State investment complementary to competitive private sector. Active exchange rate management to limit Dutch disease.
Predatory Autocracy: Unstable government, legitimized by military force of arms. Lack of consensus-building mechanisms. Bureaucracy exists as mechanism of rent capture and distribution; corrupt judicial system. Little or no civic counterweight.	Short policy horizon. Policy instability, nontransparency. Low competitiveness, high transactions costs. Strong spending interests vis-à-vis private sector or pro-stabilization interests.	No savings. Highly procyclical expenditure. Very high government consumption, rent absorption by corruption elites through petty and patronage, capital flight.

Source: Authors.

Table 4.2. *Comparative Ratings*

	Transparency and Corruption[1]	Political and Civil Rights[1]
Mature democracies	8.4 (0.7)	1 (0)
Factional democracies	3.6 (1.1)	2.8 (0.9)
Autocracies	1.5 (0.6)	5.7 (0.7)

Sources: www.freedomhouse.org and www.transparency.org; and authors' calculations.

[1]Mean and (standard deviation) of Transparency International ratings for transparency with scores ranging from 1 (lowest) to 10 (highest) for 2001 and Freedom House political and civil rights ratings using scores ranging from 7 (lowest) to 1 (highest).

in rules. State investment tends to complement, rather than substitute for, private investment. These features would facilitate the efficient use of resources, including oil rents, and help to contain rent-seeking behavior. They also give citizens the opportunity to provide a critical counterbalance against the influence of interests attached to government spending. Norway, the state of Alaska, and the province of Alberta can be seen as prototype representatives of this category of states. Botswana shares many of the features of the mature democracies, despite its lower level of development.[9]

Factional Democracies

Countries classified as factional democracies have several features that distinguish them from mature democracies. Income distribution is unequal and social consensus is elusive. Political parties are often weak, and formed around charismatic leaders; military intervention in politics is not uncommon. Governments are often unstable; where they are stable, single-party dominance underlies nominally democratic institutions. In either form, political support derives from systems of patronage. The short-horizon politics of competition for power and state-allocated resources gives rise to unstable policy regimes and nontransparent mechanisms of rent distribution, encouraging the development of clientelistic networks and rent-seeking behavior throughout state and society. Earmarking is pervasive in these systems, as politically powerful interests attached directly to state spending, such as bureaucratic and political elites (including local governments), public sector unions, and the military, tend to capture the state. These preda-

---

[9]Botswana enjoys political rights and civil liberties, has a stable party system, and is rated close to the developed countries in Transparency International's ratings.

tory interest groups can be stronger and more continuous than political parties or governments, and try to lock in their claims on rents. Without a countervailing force, oil rents injected into the political game tend to produce Terry Karl's "petromania": an explosion of inefficient government spending, followed by fiscal and economic crisis. Ecuador, Venezuela, and Colombia can be seen as representatives of this category of countries.

Paternalistic Autocracies

Paternalistic autocracies include Saudi Arabia, Kuwait, and some of the smaller Gulf states. Governments initially derive their legitimacy from traditional and religious authority, but in the process of oil-driven modernization their legitimacy also becomes attached to the mobilization of oil wealth to ensure the material well-being of their citizens (Auty and Gelb, 2001). Such governments can be stable for extended periods; they seek consensus and have a much longer horizon than many democratic governments. Even though conventional politics provides no immediate countervailing force for fiscal restraint, their concern with the longer run means that they may also be able to save when revenue is plentiful. However, the evolving role of state spending toward sustaining political support generates rising and downwardly inflexible expenditure commitments, including subsidies, high levels of public employment in low-capacity, overstaffed bureaucracies, and protected, inefficient enterprises, which in the long run will constrain the scope for productive investment, and consequently, also for long-term growth. Such commitments can eventually push such states toward fiscal crisis.

Reformist Autocracies

Reformist autocracies tend to have autonomous, competent, and politically insulated technocratic elites. Their legitimacy rests on their success in attacking poverty through productive investment and economic growth, ensuring a long horizon in policymaking. Constrained by their political mandate to make real improvements in the welfare of the poor, such states may deploy natural resource rents efficiently to promote economic diversification and growth, despite the lack of transparency inherent in autocratic rule. The political economy equilibrium has to balance out the opportunities for rent-seeking against the importance of sustaining growth in important non-oil sectors, including the need to boost investment and raise employment and incomes in labor-intensive, non-oil traded sectors. Indonesia in the earlier Suharto period is one such case; Taiwan, Singapore, Korea, and to an extent China, offer non-oil examples.[10]

Predatory Autocracies

Predatory autocracies are often less stable than either of the other two types of autocratic regimes. Regimes tend to act as "roving bandits," [11] state power faces few constraints and the exploitation of public and private resources for the gain of elite interests is embedded in institutionalized practices with greater continuity than individual leaders. Such regimes are nontransparent and corrupt; the civil service runs entirely on patronage, as public office brings with it a host of rent-seeking opportunities. Little financial and human capital flows into productive occupations, whose returns are depressed by a dysfunctional environment. Capital flight is likely to be widespread, given the lack of rule of law and the lack of protection of property rights. Government itself is a fundamental obstacle to fiscal restraint and reform; oil revenue fuels the status quo, perpetuating the oppression and poverty of the people. Nigeria under a succession of military rulers offers an example; and while democracy was restored in 1999, its institutions have been shaped by a longer history.

IV. Managing Oil Rents: Some Country Cases

Mature Democracies: The Case of Norway

The orderly quest for rent

Relative to other oil-exporting countries, Norway has been successful in using its highly consensus-oriented and parliamentary institu-

---

[10]Reformist autocracies are similar to the strong developmental state described by Leftwich (1995).

[11]"Stationary bandit" regimes have the strength to control territory for an extended period and thus develop an interest in the productivity of their domain. "Roving bandit" regimes, such as a succession of short-lived military dictatorships, do not develop such an interest. For further discussion of this topic, see Olson (2000).

tions as well as the involvement of interest groups representing business and labor to reconcile competing claims over oil rents with long-term objectives and stabilization goals. This accomplishment is even more remarkable, taking into account that Norway has had several changes in government, and periods of weak minority government, since becoming an oil exporter. However, as a small, trade-dependent nation, Norway also has a strong pro-stabilization constituency in the form of employees, trade union and business leaders, and voters dependent on the non-oil tradables sectors for their well-being, and with a good understanding of the need for restraint in public spending and the avoidance of a volatile expenditure pattern (see also Skancke, Chapter 12 in this volume). Compared to most other countries, political differences are very small, and values are egalitarian. The high level of transparency in political and bureaucratic processes reinforces the general trust in the integrity of politicians as well as in the professional skills of the civil service—few Norwegians would question the government's ability to manage Norway's oil rents in an honest and efficient way. Perhaps for this reason, Norway has not moved to distribute oil dividends directly to citizens as was done in more individualistic Alaska, with the expressed aim of "getting rents out of the hands of the politicians."[12]

Reflecting these features, policies are very stable in Norway, despite changes in government, and policy formulation has a long-term horizon.[13] However, more recently, the move from deficits to structural budget surpluses and the rapid accumulation of assets in the Government Petroleum Fund has led to mounting political pressures for increased government spending of oil export incomes and made restraint more difficult. This, together with growing expenditure commitments in coming decades, in particular for future pensions as the population continues to age, concomitantly with the projected tapering-off of oil revenues, has led to concerns over Norway's ability to sustain its past success in managing its oil wealth.

---

[12]Annual dividends from Alaska's Permanent Fund have recently been close to US$2,000 per state resident. Alaska also increased the private share of oil rents by abolishing state tax. These measures indicate a strong populist tendency underpinned by a tradition of individualism.

[13]In addition, the high educational levels of the general population together with a reality-oriented culture reinforce understanding of, and receptivity to, rather complex analyses of policy choices.

First phase—priority to maintaining competitiveness

As Norway became a significant oil producer in the 1970s, policies focused on the overarching goal of ensuring the long-term competitiveness of "Mainland Norway's" non-oil tradables sectors to maintain full employment. The strength of the constituency for cautious spending of government oil revenues to avoid Dutch disease and loss of job security should be seen against the background of the large number of employees in these sectors. Non-oil traded sectors have also traditionally led wage-bargaining rounds, rather than the urban and public sector unions that have followed. The concern for competitiveness is also closely linked to the geography of the country and the very strong interest in maintaining the economic viability of small, dispersed communities separated by mountains and fiords, where small and fragmented labor markets make it difficult for workers who become unemployed to find another job. Rural interests have traditionally exerted a strong influence on politics in Norway and have ensured control over a main part of Norway's oil rents through large allocations for regional policy, support for agriculture, heavy investments in roads, etc. The experiences of the mid-1970s—Norway saw wages increase by 51 percent in the 1974–76 period, with consequent erosion in international competitiveness—added to these concerns (Norway, Ministry of Finance, 1978, 1981).

Subsequent developments proved these concerns well founded. Strong economic growth, spearheaded by the petroleum sector and compounded by expansionary fiscal and monetary policies in the first half of the 1980s, resulted in an overheated economy with surging inflation and further loss of competitiveness in the non-oil tradables sectors, reflected in a sharp drop in manufacturing employment. In response, the government devalued the krone several times and increased subsidies to domestic industries, including shipbuilding, farming, and fisheries. By the mid-1980s, Norway's industrial subsidies were among the highest in the OECD area (Norway, Ministry of Finance, 1985, 1989). However, these developments cannot be attributed solely to exuberance caused by the inflow of oil rents. Indeed, despite a jump in net cash revenues from the petroleum sector by over 6 percentage points of GDP (from a zero base) during 1970–1985, Norway was able to restrain the increase in government expenditures to a relatively modest 5–7 percentage points of GDP. In contrast, very strong pressures for expanded government services and transfers in Sweden and Denmark resulted in government outlays jumping by about 20 percentage points of GDP—to nearly two-thirds of GDP in the case of Sweden, and Denmark close behind, during the same period. Against this background, Norway can be deemed reasonably successful in managing its oil wealth. In recent years, Norway has sustained public spending at lower levels of GDP than Sweden or Denmark even though public revenues have comprised a higher share of GDP (see Table 4.3).

The sharp drop in oil prices in early 1986, hitting an economy already affected by macroeconomic imbalances, severely impacted the Norwegian economy, causing an economic downturn that lasted for several years. The government set up a commission with representatives of all political parties, labor, business groups, economic experts, and public officials, to formulate new policy guidelines. They called for fiscal policy to be used for countercyclical purposes with monetary policy targeted on maintaining a stable exchange rate, while labor and business leaders committed themselves to wage moderation. There is wide consensus that this new approach played a key role in the strong turnaround of the economy in the early 1990s. Thus, while Norway has seen periods of excessive spending and growth in aggregate demand like other oil exporters, imbalances have been brief and excesses relatively modest. More importantly, Norwegian stakeholders have demonstrated their ability to learn from mistakes and to reach consensus to prevent the recurrence of bad management.

A new policy focus—savings for the future

Long-term demographic projections point to a rapid aging of the Norwegian population over the coming decades, resulting in escalating pension payments and health care expenditures for the elderly that coincide with a projected tapering off of Norway's oil export income as its reserves are exhausted. Using projected pension liabilities over 30 years to put the oil rents in perspective, the government succeeded in creating support for the goal of sustained budget surpluses in order to accumulate savings to fund future expenditure commitments. A Government Petroleum Fund was set up in 1990 to manage accumulated savings (Box 4.1). While maintaining the competitiveness of Mainland Norway remains a key priority, Norway's fiscal and economic management policies are now increasingly shaped by issues related to the appropriate level of saving current oil revenues for the future. From another perspective, while in the past Norway's oil rents were to a large extent captured by rural areas in the form of subsidies for agriculture,

Table 4.3. *Selected General Government Indicators*
(In percent of GDP)

	1970	1975	1980	1985	1988	1988	1990	1995	1996	1997	1998	1999	2000	2001
Norway														
Total outlays	41.0	46.2	48.3	45.6	52.5	49.5	49.7	47.6	45.4	43.8	46.3	45.8	40.8	42.8
Current tax and nontax receipts	43.5	48.7	53.2	55.1	54.1	52.1	52.3	51.1	52.0	51.7	49.8	51.6	55.5	58.8
Fiscal balance	2.5	2.5	4.9	9.5	1.6	2.6	2.6	3.5	6.6	7.9	3.5	5.8	14.7	16.0
Denmark														
Total outlays	40.2	48.2	56.2	59.3	60.2	54.2	53.6	56.6	56.3	54.4	53.4	51.8	49.9	49.4
Current tax and nontax receipts	41.7	46.1	52.2	56.5	59.5	55.7	52.5	54.3	55.3	54.8	54.5	54.9	52.7	51.4
Fiscal balance	1.5	-2.1	-4.0	-2.8	-0.7	1.5	-1.1	-2.3	-1.0	0.4	1.1	3.1	2.8	2.0
Sweden														
Total outlays	43.3	48.9	61.6	64.7	59.6	55.2	55.9	61.9	59.9	58.0	55.5	55.1	52.7	52.9
Current tax and nontax receipts	46.6	50.5	56.3	59.5	61.9	58.1	59.7	54.2	56.8	56.4	57.6	56.8	56.7	56.7
Fiscal balance	3.3	1.6	-5.3	-5.2	2.3	2.9	3.8	-7.7	-3.1	-1.6	2.1	1.7	4.0	3.8

Sources: OECD, *Economic Outlook*, various editions.
Note: The break in 1988 reflects definitional changes.

Box 4.1. *The Use of Petroleum Funds in Mature Democracies—Some Selected Examples*

Norway's Government Petroleum Fund, established in 1990, has two main purposes: (i) act as a buffer to smooth fluctuations in oil revenues and mitigate exchange rate pressures to avoid Dutch disease and preserve a diversified industrial structure; and (ii) save part of current oil rents to help address future needs related to the aging population and the eventual decline in oil revenues. At the end of 2001, the size of the Fund corresponded to about 41 percent of GDP.

The income of the Fund consists of government net cash flow from petroleum activities plus the return on capital. Its expenditures are transfers to the government's budget. Thus, the Fund is an integrated part of the budget: higher government spending or lower taxes from mainland activities result in smaller allocations to the Fund. The annual allocation of oil revenues between the budget and the Fund is flexible, depending on stabilization considerations.

While the detailed guidelines for the Fund's operations are decided by the government, the latter always consults the Parliament before making substantial changes to these guidelines. Transfers to and from the Fund need parliamentary approval, and government informs the Parliament on the Fund's status three times a year. Comprehensive information about the Fund's operations are available in quarterly and annual reports, and the Auditor General has the overriding responsibility for auditing its operations. The transparent rules for the Fund's operations encourage citizens to feel confident to postpone consumption of their entitlements until reaching retirement decades later. To protect the integrity of the budget process, the Fund's assets must be invested abroad rather than become a supplementary source of financing public expenditures.

The new guidelines for the Heritage Savings Trust Fund in the Province of Alberta, Canada, which used to invest much of its assets within the Province as part of the policy to develop the local economy, also mandate that its savings be invested outside of the Province (Hoffman, 1996).

Since its inception, the Alaska Permanent Fund invests its savings out-of-state. The latter fund, however, differs from the Norwegian fund in that it returns part of the earnings as dividends to the residents of Alaska as direct cash payments, amounting to nearly US$2,000 per person in year 2000. The design of the Alaska dividend system reflects the strong individualistic character of Alaskans and their sense of knowing better than their politicians how to use their money.

Sources: Davis and others, in Chapter 11 of this volume; and Norway Ministry of Finance (2002b).

and so on, retirees and pensions will increasingly receive them as the population ages and the growing number of retirees becomes a dominant force in the political landscape. While the goal of maintaining the competitiveness and job security for employees in the non-oil tradables sectors has constituted a strong pro-stabilization force, the future constituency of retirees enjoying indexed pensions may not have the same interest in restraint.

Saving versus spending and tax relief: Toward a balance?

In the 1997 election campaign, the governing Social Democratic Party advocated continued cautious public sector spending to avoid repeating the mistakes of the 1980s, while several smaller opposition parties called for increased spending on various social programs. Failing to garner wide support, a successor minority coalition government proposed increased spending on pensions and family allowances. In 1998, the collapse of global oil prices led to a sharp decline in the budget surplus, but as oil markets bounced back in 2000 and the Petroleum Fund grew, political pressures to boost public spending resumed, especially by local governments, which are responsible for the bulk of spending on health and education. These pressures proved difficult to resist, with the visible accumulation of wealth in the Petroleum Fund blunting the concern for Norway's large, longer-term public pension liabilities. A broad national consensus for a policy change gathered steam in the run-up to the parliamentary elections in the fall of 2001. The governing Social Democratic Party ran on a platform favoring an expansion of expenditures only, but the elections paved the way for a new government, formed by parties favoring both an expansion of the welfare state and a redirection of policy toward reducing Norway's high tax burden. The 2002 budget incorporates a new fiscal plan that accelerates the use of oil revenues over the next ten years and stipulates that the structural deficit in the central government's non-oil budget should be within the 4 percent expected real return on the Government Petroleum Fund assets. Compared to earlier guidelines, this program raises the annual budget deficit by an additional 0.4 percentage points of mainland GDP per year, to 5 percent in 2010. While Norway's record of managing its oil wealth has generally been highly successful in building the foundation for an equitable sharing of its oil wealth with future generations, this recent turn has created some concerns over the long-term sustainability of Norway's fiscal policies, despite large current budget surpluses.

Factional Democracy: Oil Rents in Latin America

Relative to other countries, factional democracies rank quite high in terms of political participation but rather low in terms of transparency and corruption (see Table 4.2). Despite important differences, Colombia, Ecuador, and Venezuela share a tradition of nationalist populism and patronage that has strengthened the political voice of interest groups directly attached to state expenditures. Elites have little incentive for fiscal restraint; leaders who make honest attempts to rationalize spending and stimulate private sector development face general strikes and widespread rioting and, in the case of President Febres Cordero of Ecuador, kidnap by military paratroopers. Interest groups in Colombia, Ecuador, and Venezuela have been more stable than the weak and personalized political parties. These countries also rank low in terms of policy stability,[14] and have performed quite poorly in terms of fiscal discipline and oil revenue management.

Interest groups, instability, and earmarking

Political developments in Ecuador and Colombia have shown striking similarities in recent years. Traditional parties have lost their hegemony and politics have become more personal. The discovery of oil has caused intra-party rivalries to flare as the state becomes increasingly important as a purveyor of resources (Martz, 1997). Lacking a consensus on transparent budget allocation, groups have turned to earmarking to assert their interests, further weakening overall budget management (Box 4.2). In Ecuador, numerous governments have launched attempts at fiscal restraint and structural reform, but none has held up to social pressure long enough to significantly alter its political economy. Urban population growth accelerated during the first boom period in Ecuador, driven by incentives in the form of rising consumer subsidies, the expansion of public sector wages and employment, and a decline in non-oil taxes equivalent to 2 percentage points of GDP (World Bank, 1991). Attempts to introduce fiscal discipline and structural adjustment in the mid-1980s under President Febres Cordero brought mild improvements in a number of macroeconomic indicators; however, in January 1985 Congress called an emergency session to in-

---

[14]In the World Bank's "Business Environment Survey," 2001, Colombia, Ecuador, and Venezuela were rated in the lowest 14 out of 81 countries.

Box 4.2. *Earmarking in Ecuador*

Despite weak non-oil tax administration and the resulting volatility in revenues, in 1999 about 65 percent of total tax revenues (including all oil revenues) were earmarked for specific programs or for transfers to subnational governments. The earmarking system illustrates the strength of Ecuador's network of entrenched interests vis-à-vis the unstable central government. Its complexity and nontransparency has produced unforeseen and irrational distributions of oil revenues, major beneficiaries of which have historically included the inefficient and overstaffed bureaucracy of PETROECUADOR, the military, and the civil service (World Bank, 1991). In 1989, 14.5 percent of all oil revenues were earmarked directly to the military; and 67.6 percent were allocated to finance the public wage bill and other programs, notably the rural roads program, a politically important source of patronage. Earmarking reduces the fiscal flexibility of the central government, locking in spending increases during oil windfalls and forcing drastic cuts in operating and discretionary expenditures during downswings.

---

validate his wage restraint measures and the trade union federation called a general strike. The collapse of oil prices in 1986, followed by disastrous earthquakes in 1987, forced the government to enact emergency measures to address large fiscal deficits, including fuel price increases of up to 80 percent and 25 percent increases in bus fares (Corkill and Cubit, 1988). These measures to adjust to lower oil rents provoked widespread rioting, another general strike, assaults on members of parliament, bombardment of government buildings with Molotov cocktails, and in January 1987, the abduction of the President by air force paratroopers (Espinel and others, 1994). Shamed and devoid of support, Febres Cordero reversed the process of reform and initiated enormous construction projects to benefit his coastal constituency.

President Borja inherited an inflation-riddled economy with a public sector deficit of 16 percent of GDP. His first package of economic reforms included moderate measures of fiscal austerity,[15] but it too was met with a national strike, which was particularly damaging to oil exports. The powerful bus and truck drivers' union shut down transport across the country in June 1989 (Economist Intelligence Unit, *Quarterly Economic Report*, No. 3, 1989), and the President's support quickly

---

[15]However, 17 percent of the 1988 budget had no identified sources of finance and 38 percent was financed through foreign loans.

eroded as continuing austerity measures reduced subsidies and restrained wages. As the Gulf conflict of 1990–91 escalated, the trade
union federation, the military, and the business community descended
on the state, demanding a share of increased oil revenues. Despite the
expected temporary nature of high prices, Borja gave in and the entire
oil windfall was used to finance increases in consumption (World
Bank, 1991). Ecuador fared little better in the 1990s: in eight years out
of the last decade, fiscal impulses exacerbated the oil cycle.

The discovery of significant oil reserves in Colombia in 1993 occurred in the wake of a process of political and fiscal decentralization
initiated by the 1991 constitution. The confluence of these two events
led to an explosion of subnational spending and borrowing as the rules
of the game of competition for rents became "spend more to get more"
(Box 4.3). Politically driven government bailouts of local and regional
entities and state enterprises exacerbated moral hazard problems and
contributed to the doubling of state consumption expenditure in only
six years. A stabilization package initiated in 1999 has moved to check
the more egregious flaws in the decentralization process, but Colombia's weak central government faces enormous arrears in pension payments and spending commitments.

The failure of "sowing the oil"

Oil revenues have shaped Venezuelan politics for decades, creating a
rentier state legitimized by patronage and entrenched constituencies
whose continued loyalty is attached directly to state expenditures
funded by oil rents. Economic performance has been influenced by oil
revenue volatility and "stop-go" policies, resulting in boom and bust
cycles. Transitory oil price increases have led to increased spending,
often maintained even after oil revenues had fallen again. Despite
Venezuela's estimated US$600 billion in oil exports since the early
1970s, real per capita income fell by 15 percent between 1973 and 1985;
since then, the decline in economic conditions has accelerated with
GDP per capita falling on average by 2.2 percent a year during the
1985–2000 period.

Following the sudden large oil windfalls after 1973, Venezuela embarked on a policy of extensive expansion of the state's involvement in
the economy. The oil industry was nationalized and large-scale state investments in capital-intensive projects in steel, aluminum, iron ore, and
energy were made as part of the drive to diversify the economy and reduce import dependency. However, these state enterprises were ineffi-

---

Box 4.3. *Fiscal Decentralization in Colombia*

By the mid-1990s, nearly 40 percent of central government revenue (including all petroleum revenue, regardless of international prices) had been earmarked for transfer to local and regional governments. As with earmarking in Ecuador (Box 4.2), the transfer system tied central government revenue to subnational entities through complex rules, creating a national arena for competition over rents. Under political pressure, based in part on widespread expectations about future oil revenues, central government ignored standards for transfers, making them to departments without adequate capacity while the transfer of responsibilities to subnational governments lagged far behind the transfer of revenues. With weak supervisory practices and regulatory forbearance, moral hazard led local and regional entities to overspend and accumulate excessive debt. The government bailed out several major territorial entities and their creditors in the mid-1990s; the implicit state guarantee further reinforced the borrowing spree. Bailout costs contributed to the rapid acceleration of state consumption expenditure, which skyrocketed from 10 percent of GDP in 1993 (prior to the inflow of oil receipts to the fiscal coffers) to 23 percent of GDP in 1999. Reforms include subjecting subnational governments to credit ratings; it is too early to tell whether recourse to independent evaluation will restore discipline to the consolidated fiscal system.

---

ciently managed by political appointees without professional expertise, and expected world demand for products of the new industries did not materialize (Nissen and Welsch, 1994). Large-scale increases in employment based on patronage and hefty wage increases aimed at enlarging the urban constituency further eroded the financial viability of these enterprises. Despite massive overspending, the government and state enterprises were able to obtain foreign credits without difficulty. Foreign borrowing also supported rapid increases in imports. The rents received during the 1979–82 oil boom were largely used up by budgetary subsidies to prop up these enterprises in the face of huge losses. Despite modest reforms, the country's fiscal position became increasingly fragile and, faced with the oil price downturn of 1982–83, the government was unable to meet its debt obligations. Massive capital flight forced the Black Friday devaluation of February 1983 and sparked a deep recession. Following a series of strikes by the trade unions, most reforms were abandoned. In 1982, the appropriation by the government, without opposition from the Congress, of the US$5 billion saved in the investment fund of the national petroleum company PDVSA widened the gulf between the technocrats of the company and the political establishment and sent a clear message that it was futile to try to sterilize windfalls by (openly) saving abroad (Mommer, 1998).

Entering office in 1984, President Lusinchi introduced fiscal restraints and a multitier preferential exchange rate system to contain the crisis. However, continued strong pressure from organized labor and business soon resulted in another policy reversal with increased minimum wages and subsidies, stimulating economic activity but incurring large deficits and tripling inflation to over 30 percent by 1988. The agency managing the exchange rate system, riddled with corruption, effectively transferred billions of dollars into the hands of political elites (Nissen and Welsch, 1994).[16] Despite the fall in oil revenues following the 1986 price crash, Lusinchi continued to expand fiscal policy, and he left office with the highest recorded popularity of any retiring Venezuelan president.

The new government that took office in February 1989 faced a situation where Venezuelan consumers had to cope with severe shortages even of basic goods and the state was on the brink of bankruptcy. A doubling of petrol prices from their traditionally very low levels in the face of budget deficits running at close to 10 percent of GDP triggered massive riots in urban areas, in which over a thousand people were killed. The trade unions and much of the business sector united in opposition to liberalization of the economy, despite a lack of a coherent alternative, and a general strike was called. The president finally resigned, having failed to find a constituency to support a reform program, and after having barely weathered two bloody coup attempts.

A survey by the Presidential Commission for State Reform in 1989 found that 80 percent of the population was dissatisfied with the democratic administration and that 88 percent believed that politicians did nothing but talk and were holding back the public's rightful wealth (Nissen and Welsch, 1994). Such attitudes, elicited in the midst of reforms, contrast with the popularity of President Lusinchi at the end of an enormous spending binge, and indicate the disillusion that led to the election of President Chávez, backed by the working and lower-middle classes and the military, which had not traditionally partici-

---

[16]Large employers obtained the right to repay their debt at the predevaluation rate of 4.3 bolivars per dollar, a scheme that Minister Matos Azócar called "the most outstanding public subsidy ever paid to the private sector." The rate was 8.1 by 1986 and over 400 by 1996.

pated as members of the political elite. Pressures to take on board even more government workers to create jobs for the unemployed have strengthened as foreign investors have increasingly fled Venezuela. The overall budget balance has continued to fluctuate widely along-side the price of oil—from a surplus of about 7 percent of GDP in 1996 to a deficit of 7 percent in 1998, back to a surplus of 2 percent in 2000 and a 6 percent deficit in 2001. Despite Chávez's inability to bring tangible economic benefits to his supporters, he sustained the passionate support of Venezuela's poorest, as evidenced by the reaction to his temporary ouster in April 2002. PDVSA, faced with a decline in the ratio of operational revenue to expenses, is finding it increasingly difficult to transfer the necessary proportion of funds to the central government, slowly drying up Venezuela's rentier economy, while at the same time the power of the rent-seeking interests that the oil rents have created has not subsided. As of mid-2002, it was not evident where Venezuela would find a constituency for liberal reform and the necessary divorce from oil-dependent statism.

Oil rents and incentives in factional democracies

Especially in patronage-based political systems without the tradition of strong national institutions and the transparency required to establish a clear national consensus, oil revenues encourage rent-seeking behavior as populist competition for resources expands unchecked. In Ecuador, central government authority is weak and unstable, as electoral rules all but ensure the lack of a stable congressional majority; between 15 and 18 parties, largely ad hoc institutions assembled to back the candidacy of charismatic individuals, were represented in congress during the 1980s. Short, intense political cycles give rise to unstable policies and a very short policy horizon. Ecuadorian politics have a strong tradition of direct interference by dominant economic interests with the formal democratic process and weak delegation of representation by organized groups to political parties and congress. As a result, "interest groups are highly divided and parochial in their demands, pursuing predatory ends with little cooperation in the quest for net social gains [. . .] in a rent society, corporate interests are better prepared for defensive action than creative participation in the policy process" (Espinel and others, 1994, p. 19). The ability of Congress to resolve interest group pressures is severely limited; tensions between the executive and the legislature are extraordinary, as the one-house legislature is empowered to act rapidly and unilaterally to impeach technocrats, raise minimum wages without consideration of productivity or inflation, and earmark revenues directly to various interests. Thus, while oil rents did not create Ecuador's political institutions, they do exacerbate their weaknesses, which, at the same time, reduces the ability to use rents well.

Colombia's central government is similarly weak vis-à-vis subnational governments and social interest groups. The Constitutional Court, formed under the 1991 constitution, has established a dominant position in wage and expenditure policy, under the auspices of protecting fundamental individual rights. One recent ruling overturned a public sector wage freeze, requiring that wages be adjusted upwards every year by at least the level of inflation.[17] The judicial branch therefore holds veto power over reforms and fiscal restraint measures.

Political cycles have also become very extreme in Venezuela, with the labor movement, large, state-subsidized firms, and small employers, as well as, more recently, the military, competing for oil rent (Nissen and Welsch, 1994). Even the formally independent central bank has no ability to check politically motivated spending, as presidents can remove the governor of the central bank at will.

Traditional Autocracies: Saudi Arabia and the Gulf Countries

The Gulf states depend heavily on rents from the exploitation of state-owned petroleum reserves to fund their development efforts and generous welfare policies. Over the past 25 years they have gone through a far-reaching social and economic transformation while maintaining social stability. Despite ample reserves, new development challenges over coming decades will test their ability to reconcile traditional institutions with the requirements of a modern economy in an increasingly competitive global environment.

The years of plenty

In the years following the first oil boom, the Gulf governments embarked on massive investment programs, with priority given to basic

---

[17]Another judgment mandated increased expenditures on prisons, basing this on "prisoners' rights" (Colombia Constitutional Court Judgments T-296/98 and T-153/98).

infrastructure, aiming to transfer part of the windfall to the population at large as well as to future generations. Substantial investments were also made in the social sectors. The population at large benefited from generous welfare schemes in the form of access to housing grants, as well as basic foodstuffs, fuels, water, and electricity at highly subsidized rates. Expansion of the government sector served the dual purpose of providing public services for the population and job opportunities for Gulf nationals. Most of the Gulf states also initiated programs to build up domestic industrial capacity, boosted by very generous subsidies. These programs envisioned using abundant hydrocarbon resources as feedstock, and aimed to diversify economies away from extreme reliance on oil rents. After 1973, limited absorptive capacity to formulate and implement development programs—coupled with a small, if rapidly growing, population and the sheer magnitude of the increase in revenues—initially led to a huge accumulation of official foreign reserves. Soon, however, local businesses began to amass fortunes on lucrative government contracts. Since the development programs designed by benevolent governments ensured that everybody gained from the newly acquired fortunes, the programs received broad popular support.

In many ways, the programs initiated during the oil boom years have met with considerable success in raising living standards, including a massive expansion in education. However, the Gulf states generally have not been able to translate the huge investments in infrastructure and human development into vigorous, self-sustained private sector growth. Instead, the efficiency of investment has been steadily declining, reflecting poor screening of the economic viability of projects (Auty, 2001). At the same time, the socioeconomic implication of the "welfare-state" strategies followed by the Gulf states—with focus on the distribution of oil wealth through public programs rather than on developing new sources of wealth—also created severe unintended structural anomalies in the form of persistent dependence on oil for export earnings and fiscal revenues, overgrown public sectors whose omnipresence in the economy stifles the private sector, distorted incentives to work, and extreme dependence on government to provide jobs for Gulf nationals.

The end of the boom

As oil revenues fell dramatically after the mid-1980s, the Gulf governments resorted to large-scale drawdown of accumulated foreign assets to fund the completion of the infrastructure investments initiated during the boom years. However, long-term expenditure commitments also grew due to the expansion of public services, including education, health, and growing public sector employment. Petroleum revenues remaining broadly flat resulted in growing fiscal strains over the coming years.[18] Faced with persistent fiscal deficits since the early 1980s, the Saudi government initiated domestic borrowing in 1988, and domestic debt now significantly exceeds usable official foreign exchange reserves. As fiscal pressures continued to mount, recurrent expenditures for maintenance and subsidies as well as capital outlays were cut back, while efforts were initiated to raise non-oil revenues. As non-oil sector growth stagnated while the number of new entrants to the labor market escalated throughout the 1990s, the tightening fiscal constraint limited the scope for continuing to use the public sector to absorb job-seeking nationals. In the case of Saudi Arabia, annual non-oil sector growth is estimated to have been a minuscule 1.2 percent during the 1990s, relative to a labor force growth rate of over 4 percent, reflecting high fertility rates during the oil boom years. Only some 40,000 of the 120,000 Saudi nationals who entered the labor market in 1999 were able to find jobs in the non-oil private sector.[19]

Cautious reforms aimed at addressing the underlying structural problems behind these trends were initiated during the 1990s. The collapse of oil prices in early 1998 in the wake of the Asian crisis severely affected the fiscal situation of the Gulf countries and strengthened the political awareness of the need for structural and institutional reform. Local discontent has been growing over unemployment and reductions in per capita incomes while privileged "groups" are seen as basking in conspicuous consumption inconsistent with traditional values, and funded by the capture of an undue share of the remaining subsidies. At the same time, the eternal but elusive hope of recovery in oil revenues together with resistance from groups that see their interests threatened have thus far limited the scope of reform. The strong consensus culture of the Gulf countries—while an asset in

---

[18]The Kuwaiti government—which already employs 93 percent of all nationals in the labor force—saw its payroll cost grow by well over 6 percent per annum in the 1995–2000 period, even as total and recurrent budgetary expenditures remained constant in nominal terms, resulting in crowding out of other expenditures, in particular, capital outlays.

[19]Saudi American Bank, August 2001.

terms of solid support for decisions once made—also retards the pace of reform.

The challenge to overcome: Obstacles toward a new development paradigm

Over the next decade, the Gulf states will face mounting fiscal pressures to expand public services because of population growth—on top of high payroll costs. While remaining oil and natural gas reserves may last for up to 100 years at current levels of production for several of the Gulf countries, the scope for boosting oil revenues beyond current levels is constrained by OPEC agreements and the realities of competition from other suppliers with liberal oil tax regimes. The public sector can no longer be used to absorb the rapidly increasing number of new entrants to the labor market. These trends generate an urgent need to accelerate non-oil private sector growth to create new job opportunities for Gulf nationals. However, to realize this objective, Gulf governments will have to abandon development strategies pursued over the past quarter century and overcome severe political hurdles toward a sustainable strategy.

Despite stable macroeconomic conditions, the dominance of petroleum and the strength of the local currencies continues to frustrate progress on developing the non-oil tradables sectors. The notable exception is the United Arab Emirates—spearheaded by the Dubai Emirate (which anticipates the depletion of its oil reserves over the next decade) that has followed a liberal, business-friendly, and market-oriented strategy aimed at diversifying the economy. However, given the generally high import content in private consumption in the economies of the Gulf states, exchange rate adjustment to promote economic diversification and create non-oil private sector jobs in the long run would meet strong resistance from the general population facing immediate price increases and reductions in real per capita incomes and would create social discontent that could be exploited by powerful groups. At the same time, the prospective gains, in terms of future job opportunities in the non-oil sectors for Gulf nationals, are likely to be too abstract to create a strong constituency. Influential groups with interest in investing abroad to raise returns or avoid real or perceived political risks would also probably oppose an exchange rate adjustment of the required magnitude. Gulf governments would see net gains from an exchange rate adjustment, but their expenditure commitments are now such as to preclude the option of sterilizing part of these gains in the form of assets held abroad to sustain the adjustment—a viable option until some 5–10 years ago.

Opposition to the reform of widespread producer and consumer subsidies will also have to be overcome if a more rational price structure is to support efficient investments in line with comparative advantage. Saudi Arabia has made progress by eliminating budgetary transfers to fund subsidies for agriculture, industry, and housing in recent years—thus limiting subsidized credits to what is available through the repayment of old loans. But the Gulf countries will still have to overcome strong consumer resistance (and worries that some groups might exploit consumer discontent) to rationalizing charges for water and electricity with the aim of enhancing the private sector's interest in investing in these sectors as well as curtailing waste. Entrenched interests are also likely to delay education reform to make curricula more relevant to the needs of a modern economy.

Strong and deeply entrenched interests have also largely frustrated attempts to address the perceived lack of transparency and predictability in legal and regulatory frameworks that continues to constrain private sector takeoff in the Gulf.[20] The judiciary is widely seen as lacking appreciation for the requirements of modern business legislation and the need for a level playing field, while suffering from capacity problems that results in extremely long delays in settling commercial disputes. Red tape, in the form of requirements for permits and licenses, still persists in varying degrees and contributes to a generally poor competitive environment, slowing structural change while creating handsome rents for well-connected business interests. As the world increasingly moves toward an integrated, information- and knowledge-driven economy, the general lack of even basic statistical information and easy access to rules and regulations—making, for example, market analyses and feasibility studies hard—will become an even more severe drawback.

Predatory and Modernizing Autocracies: Nigeria and Indonesia

Like the Gulf States, Nigeria and Indonesia have both had autocratic governments over most of the last three decades, and both rank very

---

[20]A beginning to reform has been made with the recent adoption of new investment laws and other institutional reforms in Kuwait, Oman, and Saudi Arabia.

low in terms of transparency. Yet they offer contrasting experiences in the management of oil rents, with much of the difference traceable to political factors.

From predatory autocracy to factional democracy?

Oil represents an estimated 37 percent of GDP in Nigeria, and 63 percent of consolidated government revenues.[21] Management of this resource has historically been driven by political economy considerations. Oil resources are controlled by the public sector and have traditionally greased the functioning of an extensive machinery of rent seeking and political patronage. Oil has also been used, with some success, to hold together a fragile "political coalition" of diverse ethnic and religious interests. Not surprisingly, public expenditures have always ratcheted out of control during oil booms, creating considerable macroeconomic instability. Forced and painful adjustment has typically followed. Desire for, and ability to, achieve reforms have also been low or nonexistent. During the past 20–30 years, Nigeria's estimated US$300 billion in oil revenues has largely enriched a small group of politically and socially influential elite, while the majority of Nigerians have become impoverished. Growth has been stagnant and per capita income is estimated to have fallen from about US$800 in the early 1980s to about US$300 today.

Under Nigeria's periods of military dictatorship, the federal executive alone determined how the oil cycle was managed. After an initial lag in 1973 and 1974, when large surpluses were accumulated abroad, public capital spending accelerated so strongly that by 1976 it alone accounted for more than the entire increase in oil revenue. Current spending too rose sharply, with a doubling of pay for civil servants, following the review of the Udoji Commission, a decision widely interpreted as an effort to rally support behind the announcement by General Gowon that the country was not ready to return to civilian rule. Even the second oil price rise was not sufficient to bring the budget back into surplus, so that after 1975 the country faced growing fiscal and current account imbalances, and after 1981 a rapid accumulation of external debt, accompanied by capital flight. Increased government spending did not accelerate growth; neither is it easy to find evidence of the massive, if temporary, increase in overall welfare

---

[21]Average of the seven years 1995–2001.

that would have been expected during the period of sharp real appreciation that followed the spending binge. One explanation is that Nigeria's potential gains were absorbed in the sharply growing inefficiency of a corrupt and progressively more wasteful and distorted economy (Gelb and Associates, 1988). Agriculture and manufacturing atrophied, and the country has steadily de-electrified.

In Nigeria's emerging democracy there are more actors and consequently things are more complex. But fiscal policies following the oil price boomlet of 2000–2001 were not much different from those during previous periods. States and local governments now control a larger share of oil revenues, mainly because constitutional provisions on revenue sharing between the three tiers are now being strictly adhered to. Over the course of 2001, state and local government demands—backed by constitutional mandates that shares of *all* oil proceeds be distributed to them to fund their rapidly expanding spending programs—frustrated federal government efforts to institute a savings mechanism for oil windfall revenues that would have sterilized revenues corresponding to 10 percentage points of GDP. Following recent decisions, states receive almost half of all federal income, while the federal government faces massive pension obligations and domestic debt service. At the federal level, the legislature, absent for 18 years, is again a player with a strong belief it has constitutional powers to change the executive's budget to reflect its own (or multiple members') agenda for spending. The 2000 and the 2001 appropriations bills have both been much larger than the executive's proposals. Finally, there is increased tension between demands for "derivation of revenues to the oil-producing states" and "redistribution across all states." Oil-producing states have been successful in getting 13 percent of oil revenues to be paid to them as derivation since 2000.

No effective agents of restraint have emerged from this larger number of actors. The federal executive's efforts in this regard were neither credible nor successful. Between 1999 and 2001, as Nigeria's oil receipts rose from US$7.8 billion to US$15.3 billion, consolidated government spending increased from US$12.2 billion to US$21.7 billion. The fundamental drivers of the process—the politics of patronage, support of a large bureaucracy (in May 2000 public sector wages were more than doubled), and keeping a diverse and often fractious polity together—remain the same. Over the years, this has created a dynamic that has not only led to huge levels of government spending but to a widely shared belief in Nigeria that large public programs and spending are normal and desirable. The most recent factor—the need to deliver "democracy dividends"—is unfortunately seen as a call for larger public sector spending and thus perversely continues the same approach. Overall, it is estimated that the general government may itself absorb some 70 percent of Nigeria's oil income; the poor quality of the counterpart expenditures has done little to improve the living standards of the impoverished population. Efforts to contain spending through "value for money" audits and compliance with due process in spending appear to have little impact on its effectiveness.

Outcomes in the management of Nigeria's oil cycle in the new democracy are thus far not much different from the past pattern, illustrating the fact that political institutions are shaped by a longer history than the current political regime. The key feature remains excessive and unsustainable increases in public spending on the upswing, with considerable macroeconomic instability, and little to show in growth and economic development. This was a central factor in the recent agreement between Nigeria and the IMF not to pursue a monitoring program. Faced with mounting resource shortfalls, Nigeria's 2002 budget proposed to significantly raise non-oil revenues to 19 percent of GDP or 45 percent of total revenue, despite the likely adverse effect on an already costly and unattractive investment environment and the ineffectiveness of state spending (Box 4.4).

From reformist autocracy to—what?

Like Nigeria, Indonesia was a poor, largely rural economy, and its initial response to the oil windfall of 1973–74 was to rapidly increase development spending. Half of the rent earned during the first oil boom was devoted to a wide variety of programs especially in agriculture and economic infrastructure, largely in rural areas. Assessments of these programs suggest that, despite some problems, they laid the foundation for agricultural growth at rates well exceeding the average for developing countries, let alone oil exporters. Instruksi Presiden (INPRES), the labor-intensive public works programs, also appear to have been successful, creating 1.5 million person-years of work in 1982. Among other achievements, primary school construction helped boost enrollment from 77 percent in 1970 to 100 percent by 1978. Fertilizer subsidies averaged 11 percent of development spending, and Indonesia's abundant gas reserves were harnessed to provide a supply of low-cost agricultural inputs to complement the introduction of high-yielding rice varieties.

Box 4.4. *Should Nigeria Cut Non-Oil Taxes?*

Viewed in the context of other countries, Nigeria's proposed non-oil tax ratio of 19 percent of GDP seems not unreasonable. Yet it may be excessive in a context where the marginal value of public resources is surely lower than that of income circulating in the private economy, and where the fiscal problems have been mainly on the spending, rather than the revenue, side. Some have proposed a drastic cut in tariff and tax rates as a mechanism to reduce the state's role, to decrease corruption, and to transfer income to private agents. Others have suggested investing heavily in electrification so that cheap power can help the reindustrialization of the country. Political realities suggest that efforts to radically scale back the weight of the state in Nigeria are unlikely to be successful. Yet the economic record also suggests that fiscal deficits may not constitute a sound longer-run argument to increase non-oil tax rates.

Concern over real appreciation of the rupiah led to a devaluation in November 1978, but this came just before the second oil price spike. A less cautious government might have encouraged greater foreign borrowing by public firms or increased its own borrowing: it might at least have maintained its balanced budget rule that had been applied by the Suharto government since 1967, albeit somewhat flexibly.[22] But although the budget was balanced in a formal sense, spending controls were applied to create a substantial de facto surplus that was not widely known, including to the parliament. Claims of the banking system on the government fell sharply, and reserves doubled to US$5 billion.[23] As oil prices fell after 1981, Indonesia also moved aggressively with a drastic rephasing of its development plan, canceling investments and cutting subsidies and spending, as well as stabilizing its real exchange rate through progressive devaluations. Growth, high during the boom years, was sustained far better than in other oil exporters, and non-oil exports, notably manufacturing and, after 1979, liquefied natural gas (LNG), continued to grow.

---

[22]In implementing the rule, development assistance was considered as "above the line" and therefore a revenue item rather than financing.

[23]In interviews with government officials, one of the authors asked why the extent of the surplus was not widely apparent to parliamentary representatives, despite being clear from the monetary accounts. The response was that few members understood the accounts, and those few that did also understood the reason for saving and for doing so quietly, to avoid accusations that "the people's money" was not being spent on them.

The shaping of political economies

Why did Indonesia manage so much better than Nigeria during this period, both in terms of fiscal and macroeconomic control and in terms of the effectiveness of public spending? A large part of the answer lies in their different political economies. Since independence, political power and economic strategies in Nigeria have tended to be defined in regional and ethnic, rather than in occupational or class, terms. This has led to a continuous search for a constitutional formula to hold together the Nigerian Federation and to an ongoing battle over the regional allocation of public revenues. In none of the dominating parties prior to military rule were farming interests well represented; neither was there active commitment to increasing equity. Pressures from poor farmers were blunted by ethnic cleavages (Bates, 1981, and Bienen, 1986) and the widespread desire to leave the agricultural sector, while pressures from the urban elite—with interests increasingly tied to spending decisions funded by oil revenues—grew sharper.

History shaped Indonesia's politics differently. The condition of its economy when the Suharto regime came to power in 1967 could hardly have been worse. The increasingly chaotic "Guided Democracy" of the Sukarno government had been more destructive, in economic terms, than many conflicts. Inflation had reached 600 percent; shortages of food, especially rice, contributed to political instability and to a huge drop in GDP, the magnitude of which will never be known because of the demise of the statistical system. Economic stabilization and reconstruction, especially in rural areas, was crucial for the survival of the new regime. A team of economic advisers was constituted, which proved to have both exceptional influence and continuity.[24] Food security was the prime objective of the new development policy (Tracee Baru), together with exports, macroeconomic stabilization, and financial sector reform, and an impressive turnaround bolstered the credibility of the new government. The remarkable Pertamina crisis—the failure of the economic fiefdom constructed around the national oil company to service its debts in 1975—both strengthened the hand of the technocrats and reinforced the cautious elements in government.

Good economic management was further encouraged by two features. First, the power base of the government—in addition to the army—was Golongan Karya Party (GOLKAR), a coalition of diverse

---

[24]Three of the five core members were recent graduates of the University of California and became known as the "Berkeley Mafia."

functional groups with a strong representation of farmers, women, workers, and youths, rather than a narrowly based political party. This provided a vehicle for developing consensus, and reduced rivalries over how oil revenues were to be spent. Second, Indonesia's economy was overwhelmingly rural—in 1970 only 17 percent of the population lived in urban areas, most with strong rural ties—and stabilization of the rural population, especially in land-scarce Java, was a critical policy priority. Even in an autocratic setting, the non-oil tradables sector, agriculture, and, increasingly, labor-intensive industry therefore constituted a major political interest group with a direct concern for the quality of public spending as well as for avoiding extreme appreciation of the real exchange rate.[25] Unlike Nigeria, Indonesia therefore had the benefit of effective agents of restraint through the first oil windfall. Its political challenge would only emerge later.

V. Conclusions

This study has reviewed the political economy of fiscal and economic management in a number of oil exporters with widely differing political systems, emphasizing the issues of long-term savings, short- to medium-term stabilization, and the effective use of rent income. While these are different objectives, they are all part of good economic and fiscal management, and countries that have been able to do well in one area have typically been able to do well in others. Not all objectives are reasonable for all countries; in particular, it may not be realistic to expect poor exporters still dependent on official development assistance to save for extended periods.

Oil rents widen the set of policy choices: in principle, countries can do better than they would have done without rents. However, as has been demonstrated in numerous studies, oil exporters' economic performance has, with few exceptions, been poor. Since the first oil booms, evidence has accumulated on better technical approaches toward managing resource rents, especially rents from geographically concentrated oil and hard-mineral resources, as well as on the high cost of "stop-go" and failure to use rents well to support a broader process of development. Looking forward, the main factors determining the success of

---

[25]Non-oil traded sectors were also important constituencies for stable economic management in Malaysia, in particular tin, rubber, and increasingly assembly operations.

mineral exporters are less likely to be technical and more likely to relate to the political economy of managing rents.

More and less successful cases offer some suggestions. Mature democracies clearly have some advantages because of their ability to reach consensus, their educated and informed electorates, and a level of transparency that facilitates clear decisions on how to use rents over a long horizon. Yet even in these systems (with institutions that were shaped well before oil rents became large), conservative management is a continuing struggle. Reformist or traditional autocracies can also sustain long decision horizons and implement developmental policies. But their resistance to transparency and the danger that oil-led spending becomes the major legitimizing force behind the state raises problems of "locking in" mounting corruption and political transition. Little positive can be expected from predatory autocracies, which sometimes have shorter horizons and the characteristics of "roving bandit" regimes.

Factional democracies present particular challenges, because they lack a sufficiently effective political system to create a consensus among strong competing interests. Special attention will be needed to increase transparency and raise public awareness. There may be a threshold of democratic maturity, below which political competition will not help in managing oil incomes well. And oil income makes it more difficult to sustain a constituency in favor of sound, longer-run economic management, because it weakens incentives for agents to support checks and balances that impinge on their individual plans to appropriate the rents.

Constituencies in favor of cautious management can include a well-informed civic society ("keep it out of the hands of the politicians," as in Alaska); parliament (effective consensus building underpinning a transparent budgetary process as in Norway); and those dependent on the non-oil traded sectors (agriculture and fisheries, which lead wage-bargaining in Norway, rice in Indonesia, and tin and rubber in Malaysia). These constituencies will benefit from public information and education programs.

Similarly, attempts must be made to get the political debate to span longer horizons. Oil euphoria can be dampened by comparing rents to long-run obligations, such as the present value of pension obligations or to debt service: paying off Pertamina's debt while oil prices were high was a great stabilizer for Indonesia.

Norway's experience also suggests a case for integrating the treatment of special funds into the budget—technical rules will not prevail against lack of political will, and this also can provide a check against manipulation. Surpluses should be invested abroad, to reduce the risk of politicization. Integration of oil funds with the regular budget avoids the risk of competing decisions on spending and facilitates accountability and oversight.

Hedging has been little used by exporters but can help buffer export price risk. However, it will be more politically salable if integrated into budget formulation, and recast as buying a slice of government spending forward, or buying debt service forward, rather than selling oil forward. There may be a role for international agencies in guaranteeing hedging contracts to neutralize part of the risk.[26]

External agents of restraint may also have a role in strengthening management. For large-scale industrial projects, private investors can only be agents of restraint and risk sharing if their shares are large enough to make their profits depend on performance of the investment rather than supplying inputs. Credit ratings for subnational governments offer possible indicators of management effectiveness. If there is a lack of trust between federal and state governments, possibly international agencies could help by offering certified savings facilities for states wishing to retain control of their own surpluses. In extreme cases, such as Chad (Box 4.5), the government can commit to be restrained by the rules set by external agents. Such cases are likely to be very rare, but may suggest approaches to exporters that are still aid-dependent.

Transfers can be a mechanism for both distributing oil rents and economic stabilization. Only a few countries can implement a transparent "Alaska-style" system of direct rent check transfers to individuals, but there may be potential for using rents to make transparent transfers to communities or schools as in Uganda (Reinikka and Svensson, 1999).

Particularly in countries with poor tax administration and low-quality public spending, the combination of high non-oil taxes and oversized government suggests the existence of large deadweight

---

[26]In 1990–91 Mexico bought put options, sold oil futures, and used oil swaps to hedge price risk, as well as establishing a special contingency fund against oil price declines. The objective of the strategy was to ensure that it received at least US$17 per barrel, the basis for its 1991 budget. Mexico's experience shows that such strategies can be successful, but they are rarely used by oil-exporting governments. One reason is asymmetric political risk: governments will be blamed for losses of potential revenue if oil prices rise but will receive little credit for hedging if prices fall. This suggests that any hedging strategy should be integrally built into the budget and clearly presented with the budget, more as a forward purchase of revenues than as a forward sale of oil. For a further discussion of the use of hedging, see Daniel, Chapter 14 in this volume.

Box 4.5. *Chad's Management of Oil Revenues*

Chad will become an oil exporter in 2003 under unique arrangements, designed in consultation with the principal private investor in the project and international donors, and aimed at addressing the risk of fiscal and economic mismanagement when a poor and institutionally very weak country suddenly sees a large inflow of oil income. The key elements of the law that will govern the management of Chad's oil revenues are:

1. Net incomes (dividends and royalties) shall be deposited in an offshore escrow account.

2. Direct net incomes shall be allocated as follows:

   a. Ten percent in a savings account (Future Generations Fund) to be opened in an international financial institution;

   b. Out of the remaining 90 percent of direct net incomes,

- Eighty percent to be used for expenditures in priority sectors (public health and social affairs, education, infrastructure, rural development, environment, and water resources);
- Five percent of royalties to be used for the development of the producing region (Doba);
- Fifteen percent to be allocated for government operating and investment expenses.

3. An Oil Revenues Control and Monitoring Board is charged with the responsibility to ensure that commitments from the accounts meet the requirements of the Finance Act, and to authorize and monitor disbursements. The Board comprises nine members, four of whom are representatives from the civil society (one NGO, one trade union representative, one religious leader, and one representative for the human rights associations) and one is a parliamentarian from the opposition in the parliament.

The main purpose of the offshore accounts is to ensure proper accounting, including annually published audits, of the revenues. Donors will undertake annual public expenditure reviews to monitor the use of oil revenues. While oil will represent a very large boost to Chad's development options, adding 50 percent to annual budgetary revenues, the country will still need to attract other private investment and foreign aid. The level of future donor assistance will depend on the government's compliance with the above agreements.

---

losses. There can also be strong arguments for a combination of initially very low non-oil tax rates to ensure compliance and create a culture of paying taxes in the longer term, in parallel with measures focused on improving tax administration to provide greater fiscal flexibility and macroeconomic stabilization.

In the end, no single mechanism is likely to provide a silver bullet: oil-exporting governments will need to use a combination of approaches. They should hedge more; hold larger reserves; adopt more conservative, transparent, and flexible budgeting; and transfer part of the rents to individual citizens during boom periods to reduce pressure for explosive spending followed by lock-in and fiscal - crisis during the downturn. Some countries are well-placed to learn from experience; others, unfortunately, appear to have a long way to go.

Bibliography

Andrain, C. F. 1988, *Political Change in the Third World* (Boston, Massachusetts: Allen & Unwin).

Auty, Richard M., 2001, "The Political State and the Management of Mineral Rents in Capital-Surplus Economies. Botswana and Saudi Arabia," *Resources Policy*, Vol. 27, No. 2, pp. 77–86.

———, and Alan Gelb, 2001, "Political Economy of Resource-Abundant States," in *Resource Abundance and Economic Development*, ed. by R.M. Auty (Oxford: Oxford University Press).

Bates, Robert, 1981, *Markets and States in Tropical Africa: The Political Basis of Agricultural Policies* (Berkeley: University of California Press).

———, 2001, *Prosperity and Violence: The Political Economy of Development* (New York: W.W. Norton & Co.).

Bienen, Henry, 1986, *Political Conflict and Economic Change in Nigeria* (London: Frank Cass & Co. Publishers).

Bratton, Michael, and Nicolas van de Walle, 1994, "Neopatrimonial Regimes and Political Transitions in Africa," *World Politics* (U.S.), Vol. 46 (July), pp. 453–89.

British Petroleum, 2001, *Statistical Review of World Energy* (June).

"Chavez's Muddled New World," 1999, *Economist*, Vol. 353, No. 8146, pp. 37–39.

Collier, Paul, 2002, "Primary Commodity Dependence and Africa's Future," paper prepared for the World Bank Annual Conference on Development Economics.

———, and Anke Hoeffler, 2002, "Greed and Grievance in Civil War," CSAE Working Paper No. 2002–01 (London: Center for the Study of African Economies). Also published in 2000 as World Bank Policy Research Paper No. 2355 (Washington: World Bank).

Corkill, David, and David Cubitt, 1988, *Ecuador: Fragile Democracy* (London: Latin American Bureau).

Dehn, Jan, 2001, "The Effects on Growth of Commodity Price Uncertainty and Shocks," World Bank Policy Research Working Paper No. 2455 (Washington: World Bank Development Research Group).

de la Torre, Carlos, 1997, "Populism and Democracy: Political Discourses and Cultures in Contemporary Ecuador," *Latin American Perspectives*, Vol. 24, No. 3, pp. 12–24.

Dillinger, William, and Stephen Webb, 1999, *Decentralization and Fiscal Management in Colombia*, Latin America and Caribbean Region, Poverty Reduction and Economic Management Sector Unit (Washington: World Bank).

Echeverry-Garzón, Juan Carlos, and Verónica Navas-Ospina, 1999, Colombian National Planning Department, "Confronting Fiscal Imbalances via Intertemporal Economics, Politics, and Justice: The Case of Colombia," in *Sustainable Public Sector Finance in Latin America*, conference of Latin America Research Group, November 1–2, Federal Reserve Bank of Atlanta Press.

Economist Intelligence Unit, *Quarterly Economic Reports*, various issues.

Espinel, Ramón, Alison Graham, Alain de Janvry, Elisabeth Sadoulet, and Walter Spurrier, 1994, "Ecuador" in *The Political Feasibility of Adjustment in Ecuador and Venezuela*, ed. by Alain de Janvry and Christian Morrisson (Paris: OECD Development Center).

Fasano, Ugo, 2000, "Review of the Experience with Oil Stabilization and Savings Funds in Selected Countries," IMF Working Paper 00/112 (Washington: International Monetary Fund).

———, and Qing Wang, 2001, "Fiscal Expenditure Policy and Non-Oil Economic Growth: Evidence from GCC Countries," IMF Working Paper 01/195 (Washington: International Monetary Fund).

Findlay, Ronald, 1990, "The New Political Economy: Its Explanatory Power for LDCs," *Economics and Politics*, Vol. 2, pp. 193–221.

Forero, Juan, 2002, "Venezuela Wipes Away Marks of Its Fallen President," *New York Times*, April 14.

Gavin, Michael, 1996, "The Mexican Oil Boom 1977–1985," IADB-OCE Working Paper No. 314 (Washington: Inter-American Development Bank).

Gelb, Alan, and Associates, 1988, *Oil Windfalls: Blessing or Curse?* (New York: Oxford University Press for the World Bank).

Gelb, Alan, Arye Hillman, and Heinrich Ursprung, 1998, "Rents as Distractions: Why the Exit from Transition Is Prolonged," in *Economic Interdependence and Cooperation in Europe*, ed. by N. Baltas, G. Demopoulos, and J. Hassid (Heidelberg: Springer-Verlag Berlin).

Giusti, Luis E., 1999, "La Apertura: The Opening of Venezuela's Oil Industry," in *Journal of International Affairs* (U.S.), Vol. 53, No. 1, pp. 117–28.

Gylfason, Thorvaldur, 2000, "Resources, Agriculture, and Economic Growth in Economies in Transition," CESifo Working Paper Series No. 313 (Munich: Center for Economic Studies & Ifo Institute for Economic Research).

————, 2001, "Nature, Power and Growth," CESifo Working Paper Series No. 413 (Munich: Center for Economic Studies & Ifo Institute for Economic Research).

Haggard, Stephan, 1990, *Pathways from the Periphery: The Politics of Growth in the Newly Industrializing Countries* (Ithaca, New York: Cornell University Press).

Harrison, P., 1994, *The Impact of Oil on Trinidad and Tobago, 1966–1990*, Institute of Social Studies Working Paper Series No. 171 (Hoveniersberg: University of Ghent, Institute of Social Studies).

Hoffman, Michael D., 1996, "The Economic Impact of the Alberta Heritage Savings Trust Fund on the Consumption-Savings Decision of Albertans," Western Centre for Economic Research Information Bulletin No. 36 (Edmonton: University of Alberta).

Karl, Terry Lynn, 1997, *The Paradox of Plenty: Oil Booms and Petro-States* (Berkeley: University of California Press).

————, 1999, "The Perils of the Petro-State: Reflections on the Paradox of Plenty," *Journal of International Affairs* (U.S.), Vol. 53, No. 1, pp. 31–48.

Lal, Deepak, 1995, "Why Growth Rates Differ: The Political Economy of Social Capability in 21 Developing Countries," in *Social Capability and Long-Run Economic Growth*, ed. by B.H. Koo and D.H. Perkins (Basingstoke: Macmillan), pp. 288–309.

Leftwich, Adrian, 1995, "Bringing Politics Back In: Towards a Model of the Developmental State," *Journal of Development Studies*, Vol. 31, No. 3, pp. 400–27.

Martz, John D., 1997, *The Politics of Clientelism: Democracy and the State in Colombia* (New Brunswick: Transaction Publishers).

Mommer, Bernard, 1998, "The New Governance of Venezuelan Oil," Oxford Institute for Energy Studies Working Paper No. 23 (Oxford: Oxford Institute for Energy Studies).

————, 1999, "Oil Prices and Fiscal Regimes," Oxford Institute for Energy Studies Working Paper No. 24 (Oxford: Oxford Institute for Energy Studies).

Nissen, Hans-Peter, and Friedrich Welsch, 1994, "Venezuela," in *The Political Feasibility of Adjustment in Ecuador and Venezuela*, ed. by Alain de Janvry and Christian Morrisson (Paris: OECD Development Center).

Norway Ministry of Finance, 1978, "The Long-Term Programme, 1978–1981" (April).

————, 1981, "The Long-Term Programme, 1982–1985" (April).

————, 1985, "The Long-Term Programme, 1986–1989" (March).

————, 1989, "The Long-Term Programme, 1990–1993" (March).

————, 1997, "The Long-Term Programme, 1998–2001" (March).

————, 2001, "The National Budget, 2002, A Summary" (October).

————, 2002a, "The Long-Term Programme, 2002–2005" (April).

————, 2002b, "The Norwegian Government Petroleum Fund."

Olson, Mancur, 1986, "Toward a More General Theory of Governmental Structure," *American Economic Review, Papers and Proceedings*, Vol. 76, No. 2, pp. 120–25.

————, 2000, *Power and Prosperity: Outgrowing Communist and Capitalist Dictatorships* (New York: Basic Books).

Organization for Economic Cooperation and Development, *Economic Outlook* (Paris: various issues) and *Economic Survey* (Paris: various issues).

"Recortes al gasto público, anticipa Ernesto Zedillo," 2000, *El Financiero*, January 6, p. 8.

Reinikka, Ritva, and Jakob Svensson, 1999, "Confronting Competition: Investment Response and Constraints in Uganda," World Bank Policy Research Working Paper No. 2242 (Washington: World Bank Development Research Group).

Satyanarayan, Sudhakar, and Eduardo Somensatto, 1997, "Trade-offs from Hedging Oil Price Risk in Ecuador," World Bank Policy Research Working Paper No. 1792 (Washington: World Bank).

Saudi American Bank, quarterly reports, various issues.

Saudi Arabia, *National Development Plans*, various issues.

Tallroth, Nils Borje, 1998, "The Political Economy of Modern Era Wars in Africa" (unpublished; Washington: World Bank).

United States General Accounting Office, 1999, "Budget Surpluses: Experiences of Other Nations and Implications for the United States," Report to the Chairman and Banking Minority Member, Committee on the Budget, U.S. Senate, Washington, November.

Usui, Norio, 1997, "Dutch Disease and Policy Adjustments to the Oil Boom: A Comparative Study of Indonesia and Mexico," *Resources Policy*, Vol. 23, No. 4, pp. 151–62.

van der Meulen Rodgers, Yana, 1998, "Empirical Investigation of one OPEC Country's Successful Non-Oil Export Performance," *Journal of Development Economics*, Vol. 55, pp. 399–420.

Varangis, Panos, Takamasa Akiyama, and Donald Mitchell, 1995, *Managing Commodity Booms—and Busts* (Washington: World Bank).

World Bank, 1991, "Ecuador: Public Sector Reforms for Growth in the Era of Declining Oil Output," Country Study (Washington).

————, 2001, "World Business Environment Survey," pp. 161–203. Available via the Internet: http://info.worldbank.org/governance/wbes/index1.html.

5

Statistical Properties of Oil Prices: Implications for Calculating Government Wealth

STEVEN BARNETT AND ALVARO VIVANCO[1]

I. Introduction

U nderstanding the statistical properties of oil prices is important for fiscal policy formulation in oil-producing countries. Specifically, the extent to which oil price changes are believed to be persistent or temporary is likely to have substantial implications for the optimal fiscal policy. Barnett and Ossowski (see Chapter 3 in this volume) argue that government oil wealth—defined as the present discounted value of government oil revenue—is a key input for assessing the sustainability of fiscal policy. Therefore, and looking only at sustainability considerations, the optimal fiscal response to an oil price shock depends on how much the shock changes government wealth.[2] This, in turn, hinges on the extent to which the shock is permanent or transitory.

The reasoning is identical to the standard permanent income consumption argument (Friedman, 1957). Specifically, consumption should respond to permanent income shocks but not to transitory ones that

[1]The authors are grateful to Paul Cashin, Nigel Chalk, James Daniel, Jeffery Davis, Lucien Foldes, and Rolando Ossowski for helpful comments. The views expressed in the paper, as well as any errors, are the sole responsibility of the authors and do not necessarily represent the opinions of the Executive Board of the IMF or other members of the IMF staff.

[2]Barnett and Ossowski, however, highlight that there are a variety of macroeconomic and fiscal factors that need to be considered in assessing the appropriate fiscal response to an oil shock.

leave wealth largely unchanged. Davis and others (see Chapter 11 in this volume) find strong empirical evidence that in a number of oil-producing countries government spending is indeed positively related to oil export earnings. Whether such responsiveness is warranted—based on sustainability considerations—depends on the extent to which changes in current oil revenue translate into changes in oil wealth.

Empirically, therefore, the objective of this paper is to assess the extent to which oil price shocks are transitory or permanent. Conventional tests for unit roots (nonstationarity) are informative in this regard, but at the same time are not decisive. At the simplest level, empirical evidence of nonstationarity (that is, a unit root) in oil prices would suggest that wealth could be quite sensitive to price shocks, and, by extension, government spending as well. However, evidence of a unit root needs to be interpreted carefully on several grounds. First, as argued by Rudebusch (1993), tests for unit roots have low power against near alternatives. Or, more plainly, it is nearly impossible with the available sample sizes to distinguish between a true unit root and a stationary process with slow mean reversion. Second, even if there is a unit root or permanent component to price changes, the process could be dominated by transitory shocks. In this case, most of a given shock is transitory; thus, even though a price shock contains a small permanent component, the value of oil wealth may not change much. Finally, the possibility of structural breaks in the oil price process further complicates matters. The presence of a structural break in a series—for example a one-time shift in the mean—would generally bias results in favor of a unit root, and the erroneous conclusion that all shocks are permanent (when in fact most shocks could actually be transitory).

II. Review of the Literature

There is a diverse literature that examines the statistical properties of oil prices, and many studies do find evidence of mean reversion. The findings from the literature can be roughly grouped as follows. In the very long run, that is, periods of more than 100 years, there is evidence of mean reversion in real oil prices. Studies looking at just the post–World War II period, however, usually find that oil prices are not mean reverting. Nonetheless, when the sample is further divided, many studies find evidence of mean reversion during the more recent periods (since the mid-1970s or mid-1980s).

Pindyck (1999) finds strong evidence of mean reversion in real oil prices looking at an extremely long sample; the sample includes 127 years, 1870–1996, of data on real oil prices. In the longest samples, 1875–1996 and 1900–1996, the null hypothesis of a unit root is rejected using the augmented Dickey-Fuller test.[3] Variance ratio tests also indicate that the transitory component of shocks is quite large, further supporting the finding of mean reversion. The paper also develops a model with richer dynamics, allowing for both a stochastic mean and trend, but still finds substantial reversion in price shocks. Moreover, despite the richer dynamics, the long-run out-of-sample forecasts appear to converge to a relatively narrow range (whether the forecast begins in 1970, 1980, 1981, or 1996), and outperform a simpler AR(1) process. The richer dynamics stem from consideration of a model that strives to capture the supply and demand considerations that govern the evolution of prices.

Videgaray (1998) also finds strong evidence of mean reversion using a similar dataset. He estimates a two-state Markov switching model, with the parameters suggesting mean reversion in each state. In particular, he finds that most of the time—around 80 percent—oil prices are in a low mean, low volatility, and high persistence state (slower mean reversion), and the remainder of the time are in a high mean, high volatility, and low persistence state. The possibility of switching states introduces another form of uncertainty, that all else being equal would be expected to increase the variance of long-run price forecasts (and therefore oil wealth).

Focusing on the post–World War II period, Cashin, Liang, and McDermott (2000) find evidence of strong persistence in oil price shocks. They use monthly data on oil prices in real terms from 1957 to 1998 and a median-unbiased estimator to help mitigate the problems associated with regressions on series that may have a unit root. They find strong evidence that oil price shocks are persistent, with the estimate that the half-life of a shock is infinite (that is, no mean reversion). The 90 percent confidence interval for the half-life of a shock ranges from a minimum of more than seven years up to infinity.

---

[3]In only one of the six tests reported (longest sample with four lags), the null hypothesis could not be rejected at the 10 percent level. In the shorter samples (1925–1996 and shorter), however, the unit root hypothesis is not rejected, although the author cautions that the sample size is insufficient to reject the unit root hypothesis given the slow mean reversion, and that failure to reject is not the same as accepting. These points are also pertinent for what follows.

Engel and Valdés (2000) use quarterly real oil price data from first quarter (QI) 1957 to second quarter (QII) 1999 and come up with somewhat mixed results. Similar to the findings of this paper, they find that the unit root hypothesis cannot be rejected for the entire sample, but that it can be rejected in smaller samples. In particular, in the 1974QI–1999QII and 1986QI–1999QI samples the unit root hypothesis is rejected. They find that the variance ratio tests support evidence of shocks having both a transitory and a permanent component; however, the small samples (especially the sample 1974QI–1998QIV) make it difficult to draw firm conclusions from this test. They also run 15 different models or forecasting techniques and conclude that none performed significantly better than the random walk over a two-year horizon. However, it is not clear whether these results would generalize to longer forecast horizons— which is relevant for calculating wealth—or different forecasting periods.

Akarca and Andrianacos (1995, 1997, and 1998) have a series of papers that find results similar to, and supportive of, the findings in this paper. Their studies focus on the natural log of monthly real oil prices from January 1974 to October 1994. In their 1995 paper, they find evidence of a structural break in oil prices following January 1986 using regression techniques, corroborated by the examination of the variance ratios in the different periods. Building on this, Akarca and Andrianacos (1997) find that oil prices in the earlier period (January 1986 and earlier) are nonstationary, but that in the latter period oil prices are stationary. In their 1998 paper, they refine this argument, and argue that with the exception of two shocks, oil price shocks have all been transitory. In particular, they find that there was a permanent upward shift in the mean oil price in March 1979 and a permanent decline in January 1986, but that all other shocks have been transitory. This supports one of the main conclusions of their paper, namely that most oil shocks should be viewed as being transitory.

Bessembinder and others (1995) find strong evidence, based on the term structure of futures prices, that markets expect oil prices to be mean reverting. Based on daily futures prices from March 1983–December 1991, they find that 44 percent of an oil price shock is expected to be reversed in eight months. They also argue that among the possible causes of mean reversion in oil futures prices, the main factor is an expected mean reversion in actual prices. That is, market participants expect that there is a large temporary component to oil price shocks. Moreover, the authors highlight that one possible explanation for the mean reversion is that oil supply is more elastic in the long run than in the short run.

Cashin, McDermott, and Scott (2002) take an alternative approach to studying oil prices, characterizing a cycle in oil price movements. Similar to the techniques used to date business cycles, they date the cycles in oil prices. They examine numerous commodity prices, including oil, from January 1957 to August 1999. For oil, while they find that there is a good deal of variability in the duration of booms and slumps, on average an oil boom lasts 22 months with prices rising nearly 50 percent, and a slump lasts 51 months with prices also falling nearly 50 percent. Loosely speaking, therefore, oil prices are characterized by relatively fast rises in prices followed by more prolonged declines.

Oil prices are the outcome of a market process—a fact that is easily overlooked in the quest to model prices as if they were random drawings from a statistical process. It is supply and demand considerations that ultimately drive oil prices (see, for example, Wickham, 1996, or Pindyck, 1999, for a discussion). Market forces, moreover, could point to some mean reversion in oil prices. For example, whereas oil supply may not be able to respond immediately to an uptick in prices, over time production may increase, causing prices to fall back over the medium term. Likewise, higher oil prices may cause demand to fall over time as alternatives to oil are exploited. Focusing just on oil prices, as is done below, abstracts from these structural demand and supply considerations that underlie the observed movements in oil prices.

III. Futures Market Evidence

In the last two decades financial derivatives for oil have been developed and reached significant levels of liquidity. Oil futures embody market expectations about future prices and, therefore, provide clues as to the degree that markets regard oil shocks as permanent or transitory. An analysis of the futures market data strongly suggests that there is—or market participants believe that there is—a substantial amount of mean reversion in oil prices. This is demonstrated using more informal evidence, based in part on Daniel (see Chapter 14 in this volume), and some econometric evidence along the lines of Bessembinder and others (1995).

Informal Evidence

Futures market data support the hypothesis that there is a large transitory component to most oil price shocks—or, to be more precise, that markets expect that there is.[4] We demonstrate this by comparing the properties of spot and futures prices and examining the term structure of oil prices.

Futures oil prices exhibit substantially less variation than spot prices, suggesting that there is an important transitory component to oil price shocks. Figure 5.1 compares a proxy for the spot price with the 12-month- and 18-month-ahead futures prices.[5] The futures prices fluctuate much less than the spot price proxy, as seen by the fact that the futures have smaller-size peaks and higher-size troughs. Indeed, the standard deviation of the spot proxy is US$4.98 compared to only US$2.97 and US$2.44 for, respectively, the 12- and 18-months-ahead futures prices. Moreover, the ratio of the standard deviation for a given futures price to the spot proxy is monotonically declining with the time to maturity of the contract.[6] It falls from 96 percent for the 2-month-ahead futures price (which matures 1 month after the spot proxy), to 60 percent for the 12-month-ahead and 49 percent for the 18-month-ahead.

The standard deviations of the futures prices also provide clues as to the expected persistence of shocks. The ratio of the standard deviation of the futures price to the spot proxy can be used to derive a measure of persistence. Specifically, if we assume that the term structure is equal to the expected price (but see below) and that the expected price can be modeled as an AR(1) process, then the ratio of the standard deviation can be used to calculate the implied coefficient on the lagged price. For example, the coefficient in an AR(1) equation consistent with the 18-month standard deviation being 49 percent of the spot proxy is 0.96. Looking at each of the ratios from 2 to 18 months, the implied coefficient varies little, ranging from 0.95–0.96. This has implications for the regressions and unit root tests performed in the next section, as it suggests that the coefficient estimate on the lagged oil price (in the

---

[4]The data are monthly averages of futures contracts for sweet oil as traded on the New York Mercantile Exchange between March 1983 and November 2001.

[5]The nearby futures price—that is the futures price that expires next—is used as a proxy for the spot price in this section (see Bessembinder and others, 1995, regarding the advantages of proceeding this way).

[6]This holds for contracts with up to 18 months' maturity (for which there are no missing observations during the sample period); for longer-dated contracts there are significant missing observations, which makes the comparisons less straightforward.

Figure 5.1. *Oil Futures Prices*
(In U.S. dollars per barrel)

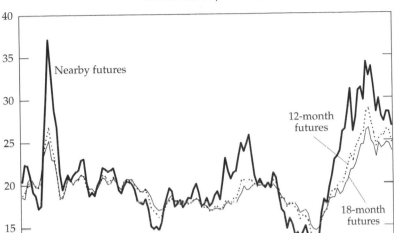

Source: NYMEX.

monthly regressions) could be around 0.95—or, if more than one lag is included, that the sum would be close to 0.95.[7]

The term structure of oil futures provides further evidence that oil prices are expected to be mean reverting. Figure 5.2 shows an average of the futures price curves grouped by the level of the spot price. The mean reversion of futures prices is demonstrated by the fact that, regardless of the spot price, the futures tend to converge to prices close to US$20 per barrel.

Looking at the term structure from selected days further highlights the underlying mean reversion in futures prices. Figure 5.3 shows the term structure going out to nearly six years on three different days.[8]

---

[7]The regressions and unit root tests below use the log of oil prices; however, repeating the above calculations expressing the futures prices in logs yields very similar results—the range, with rounding, is still 0.95–0.96.

[8]Only contracts that had volume reported for that day are included in the graph. Since we are interested in the longer-dated futures, days (each in January to facilitate comparison) with the most activity in the longer-dated futures were selected. The December futures contracts often have activity six years in advance.

Figure 5.2. *Average Crude Oil Futures Prices Grouped by Spot Price, 1983–2001*
(In U.S. dollars per barrel)

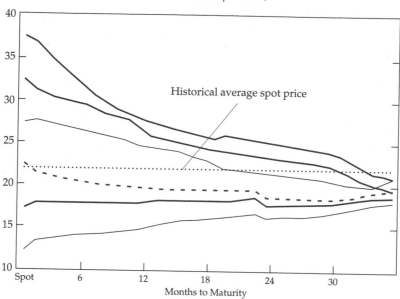

Sources: NYMEX data; and authors' calculations.

Despite substantial variation in the nearby futures price, the six-year-ahead (technically 71-month) futures do not change that much. The January 22, 1998 term structure, coinciding with low spot prices, actually corresponds to higher-priced long-dated futures than the January 18, 2000 term structure (when the spot price was substantially higher). This suggests that while there is most likely mean reversion, the mean that is reverted to may not be constant over time or even necessarily correlated with the spot price.

The finding of mean reversion in the term structure needs to be interpreted carefully. First, the futures prices may not coincide exactly with the actual price expectations. For example, the futures price could also depend on factors such as the interest rate and risk premium, both of which may vary over time, causing the futures price to deviate from the expected price (see Bessembinder and others, 1995). Kumar (1992), however, finds that futures prices for the most part provide unbiased forecasts, although his longest-dated contract is nine months ahead (the sample period also terminates in 1990). Second, the finding of mean reversion, as highlighted above, does not imply that the mean is

Figure 5.3. *Oil Futures Term Structure, Selected Days*
(In U.S. dollars per barrel)

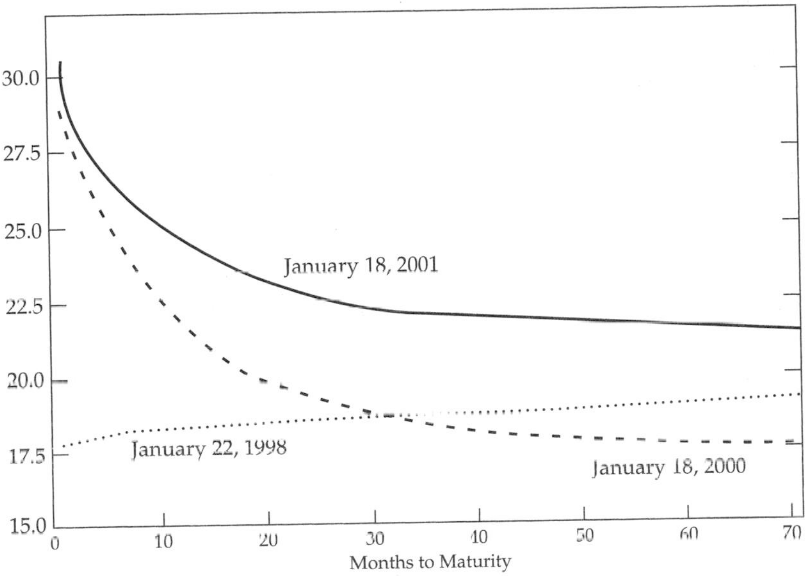

Source: NYMEX data from Bloomberg.

constant over time. Schwartz (1997) finds strong evidence of mean re-version in oil futures prices, but also finds that a simple model with a constant mean is outperformed by models that allow for time-varying factors.

Regressions

Futures prices can be used to estimate the expected persistence of oil price shocks, along the lines of Bessembinder and others (1995). In particular, the elasticity of the change in the longer-dated futures prices relative to a change in the spot (or nearby futures) price provides a measure of expected persistence. The following regressions repeat those presented in Bessembinder and others (1995), but using different data. The key differences are that monthly averages instead of daily data are used, the data cover a longer sample period, and longer-dated futures are examined. The sample period is January 1990–August 2001, for which there is continuous data on all contracts out to 18 months. For longer-dated contracts there are missing observations for some months (which, due to the differencing, results in two lost observations).

The results are consistent with those in Bessembinder and others (1995) and suggest that the markets expect price shocks to be largely transitory (Table 5.1). Both the qualitative and quantitative results are strikingly similar. The eight-month future, for example, has a coefficient estimate of 0.535 compared to 0.564 in Bessembinder and others (1995), which implies that 46 percent of a shock is expected to be reversed in eight months. After one year, nearly 60 percent of the shock is expected to be reversed and after 1½ years more than 70 percent is expected to be reversed. The results beyond this are based on smaller samples and thus may not be comparable, but, with this caveat, would seem to imply that after two years more than 80 percent of the price shock is expected to be reversed.

The futures market data, both the informal evidence and the econometric results, suggest that markets believe that there is a large transitory component to oil price shocks. However, this does not shed light on whether oil prices are stationary or not. Oil price shocks could have both a permanent and a transitory component, and thus could technically follow a random walk even with the substantial evidence for mean reversion presented above. Nonetheless, the mean reversion is quantitatively significant, which already suggests that the transitory component of price shocks needs to be considered when projecting future revenue from oil production.

IV. Oil Price Regressions

Annual and monthly Brent oil price data for the period 1957 to 2001 are used in the following empirical exercises.[9] There are certain advantages to working with annual average price data. From a fiscal policy perspective, the average annual price corresponds to the variable of interest for most budgets. Moreover, the lag structure is likely to be simpler, relative to higher-frequency data, thereby avoiding some of the specification selection problems. There are also drawbacks, including the significant loss of observations and intrayear variation. The use of monthly data avoids these problems, but makes the lag structure more

---

[9]Data are from IMF's *International Financial Statistics* unless noted otherwise. Prices in real terms are constructed using the U.S. manufacturing unit value (MUV) index as the deflator.

Table 5.1. Elasticities of Futures Price Changes[1]

Future	Elasticity	Standard Error	P-value	Observations	R-squared	Bessembinder and others (1995) Elasticity	Standard Error
2	0.899	0.020	45.399	140	0.937	0.808	0.016
3	0.808	0.020	40.021	140	0.920	0.742	0.020
4	0.738	0.022	34.131	140	0.893	0.701	0.022
5	0.679	0.023	30.177	140	0.867	0.669	0.023
6	0.623	0.024	26.335	140	0.833	0.632	0.025
7	0.577	0.024	24.054	140	0.806	0.617	0.024
8	0.535	0.024	22.363	140	0.782	0.564	0.028
9	0.493	0.025	20.008	140	0.742	…	…
10	0.482	0.024	19.877	140	0.739	…	…
11	0.454	0.024	18.634	140	0.713	…	…
12	0.409	0.025	16.554	140	0.663	…	…
13	0.386	0.025	15.503	140	0.633	…	…
14	0.365	0.027	13.522	140	0.567	…	…
15	0.353	0.027	13.045	140	0.549	…	…
16	0.344	0.027	12.548	140	0.530	…	…
17	0.322	0.030	10.801	140	0.455	…	…
18	0.284	0.028	10.006	140	0.417	…	…
19	0.263	0.042	6.334	71	0.354	…	…
20	0.240	0.046	5.225	68	0.275	…	…
21	0.276	0.051	5.421	64	0.314	…	…
22	0.173	0.052	3.326	55	0.236	…	…
23	0.203	0.050	4.088	50	0.209	…	…
24	0.185	0.051	3.619	50	0.182	…	…

Source: Authors' calculations; and Bessembinder and others (1995).
[1]The dependent variable is the change in the log of the futures price as indicated in the first column, and the independent variable is the change in the log of the nearby future (no constant is included).

complicated. From a technical point of view, however, the larger number of observations is advantageous.

The nominal and the real oil price display qualitatively similar characteristics, although there is more variation in real prices (Figure 5.4). From 1957 to 1970 the price is essentially constant, then in the run-up to the 1974 shocks there is a modest increase in prices before the big spike in 1974, and then another spike in 1979. The 1979 spike, while substantially larger in absolute value, is actually smaller in percentage terms. Prices plunged in 1986 and then went through a period of relative tranquillity until the late 1990s, when, after a dip in 1998, there was a pronounced increase through 2000 that only unwound late in 2001. Comparing the annual and monthly data highlights the extent that the monthly volatility is masked by the annual averages.

Unit Root Tests

There is strong evidence of a unit root in the full (1957–2001) sample of data for both the annual and monthly series. Unit root tests were performed on both real and nominal prices and using a variety of specifications.[10] In particular, for the annual data, 12 tests were performed for each price series involving the permutations of (i) zero, one, or two lags; (ii) constant or constant and time trend; and (iii) Augmented Dickey-Fuller or Phillips-Perron test. The results show that the hypothesis of a unit root cannot be rejected in any of the 12 tests on either series. For the monthly series the number of lags was extended to 12 and the same combinations of tests were performed, for a total of 52 tests. The results are similar to those based on annual data as the unit root hypothesis is not rejected in any of the tests. In the post-1973 sample, however, there is strong evidence in favor of rejecting the unit root hypothesis for the annual data using the nominal price. The real oil price series, in contrast, yields somewhat more mixed results. The unit root hypothesis cannot be rejected in the tests that assume no trend in the data. But in the tests that allow for a trend, the unit root is rejected at the 10 percent level in four of the six tests.

The bottom line from this battery of unit root tests is that the answer regarding the presence of a unit root depends on the sample period and

---

[10]All the empirical exercises, unless otherwise noted, use the natural logarithm of the given price. A description of the unit root tests and results is available upon request from the authors.

Figure 5.4. *Nominal and Real Oil Prices*
(In U.S. dollars per barrel)

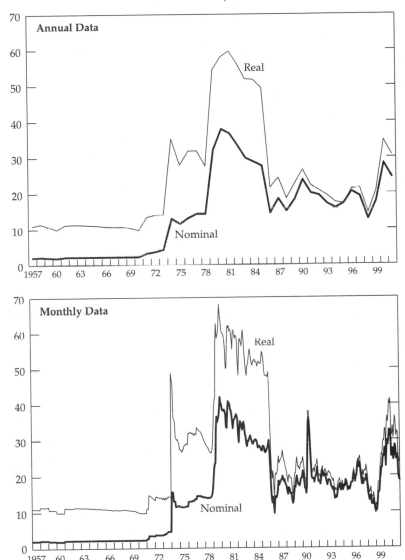

Source: IMF, *International Financial Statistics.*

whether nominal or real prices are used. The results regarding the sample period are consistent with those in the literature noted above. Specifically, in the longer samples (1957–2001) there is evidence of a unit root, but in shorter samples (1974–2001) oil prices appear to be stationary. This result holds for both annual and monthly data and is strongest for nominal prices, as there is some ambiguity regarding the results for real prices depending on whether a trend is included or not.

Empirical considerations suggest that the nominal oil price is the more appropriate variable to use for the purposes of this study. Testing for a unit root using the log of real oil prices is tantamount to testing for whether the deflator and nominal oil price are cointegrated. Indeed, it imposes that they are cointegrated with a specific vector. This, however, could be problematic on several fronts. First, focusing on the 1974–2001 sample, using both annual and monthly data, the evidence suggests that the unit root hypothesis cannot be rejected for the MUV. Thus, the nonstationarity in the MUV could be behind the seeming nonstationarity of the real oil price—the sum of a stationary (nominal oil prices) and nonstationary variable (MUV) is by construction nonstationary. Second, the failure to find a unit root in the nominal price series for 1974–2001 means that the series cannot be cointegrated, which would require that both series have a unit root. Finally, even in the longer sample (1957–2001), where both the nominal oil price and MUV seem to have a unit root and thus cointegration tests are valid, there is little evidence that the series are actually cointegrated.[11]

Regression Results

Consistent with the unit root tests, the regression results depend on the sample used. The following discussion focuses on nominal oil prices. For the 1957–2001 annual sample, the coefficient on lagged oil is estimated to be 0.96, quite close to one and lending credence to the failure to reject the unit root hypothesis (Table 5.2). In contrast, the 1974–2001 sample yields an estimate on lagged oil of around 0.5 for the annual data, clearly less than one and suggestive of why the unit root hypothesis is rejected for this sample. Also, the coefficient of around 0.5 on lagged oil would suggest that shocks are not that persistent.

---

[11]Specifically, cointegration tests were performed allowing for either zero or one lag in the data. In none of the five common permutations (that is no trend, linear trend, or quadratic trend in the data combined with various combinations of a trend or constant in the cointegrating relationship) was there evidence of any cointegrating relationship.

Table 5.2. *Regressions of Log of Brent Oil Prices (Annual Average Series)*[1]

| Coefficient | 1974–2001 | | 1957–2001 | | | |
	Nominal	Real	Nominal	Real	Nominal	Nominal
Constant	1.49*	1.07**	0.15	0.36***	0.26**	0.41*
	(0.33)	(0.44)	(0.09)	(0.21)	(0.12)	(0.10)
Brent (t–1)	0.51*	0.69*	0.96*	0.89*	0.73*	0.56*
	(0.11)	(0.13)	(0.04)	(0.07)	(0.12)	(0.09)
Dum74–01	...	...	...	...	0.54***	0.94*
					(0.28)	(0.21)
Dum74	...	...	...	...	0.68**	...
					(0.30)	
Time Trend	...	...	...	...	0.001	...
					(0.005)	...
D Brent (t–1)	...	...	...	...	–0.01	
					(0.13)	
R-squared	0.45	0.52	0.94	0.80	0.96	0.96
Standard error	0.26	0.30	0.28	0.26	0.23	0.23
Number of observations	28	28	44	44	43	44

Sources: WEO database; and authors' calculations.

Note: * significant at the 1 percent level; ** at the 5 percent level; and *** at the 10 percent level.

[1]The dependent variable is the log of Brent oil prices. Dum74-01 is a dummy variable that equals one in 1974–2001, and zero otherwise; Dum74 equals one in 1974 and zero in all other periods.

Using the longer 1957–2001 sample, but allowing for a shift in the mean beginning in 1974, yields results similar to the 1974–2001 sample. The persistence of shocks is about the same and the implied unconditional mean for the post-1974 period is US$21.65, only slightly different than that from the US$21.35 for the 1974–2001 sample.

However, even if we allow for a structural break in 1974, formal tests are still unable to reject the unit root hypothesis for the full 1957–2001 sample. Perron (1989) suggests a testing procedure and critical values applicable to such situations, and neither the residual-based tests nor the one based on regressions reject the null hypothesis of a unit root.

The failure to formally reject the unit root hypothesis, even with a structural break, is not surprising. As it is well known, unit root tests have low power against local alternatives, especially in the relatively small sample sizes used here. Moreover, the failure to reject the unit root does not mean that there is indeed a unit root. Thus, we are left in the position of having to rely on more subjective assessments as to whether there is a unit root or not, and whether to rely on the longer 1957–2001 sample or the shorter 1974–2001 sample. The subsequent exercises rely on the shorter 1974–2001 sample. There is clearly evidence of a structural break in 1974, as a regime of essentially constant oil prices was coming to an end and a new regime with much more volatile—and higher—oil prices was beginning.

Mean Oil Prices

The regressions have implications regarding the mean oil price, a notion that needs to be interpreted carefully. While an unconditional mean oil price may be readily calculated from the above regressions, it is really better viewed as a conditional mean, that is, a mean conditional on there being no further structural breaks in oil prices. Indeed, by basing the assessment on the presumption that there was a structural break in 1974, the analysis actually admits that there are, at least occasionally, permanent shocks to the oil price series. By definition, therefore, the oil price series is not stationary. The following, therefore, is not only conditional, but explicitly assumes that there would be no further structural breaks or permanent shocks to oil prices.

The assumption that there would be no further structural breaks warrants further discussion. It is justified on the grounds that such shocks are infrequent and little is known about their likely distribution or arrival rate. By ignoring the possibility of such shocks, the analysis effectively says that policymakers can quantitatively do no better than to assume that the present regime will exist into the future. By ignoring the possibility of there being a future permanent shock, the following exercise underestimates the true degree of uncertainty.

The reasoning, more heuristically, is that most shocks to oil prices seem to be temporary and not permanent. That is not to say that there are not permanent shocks as well, but rather that most shocks are not, and that from a policy point of view it is better to assume that a given shock is transitory. This leaves open perhaps the most difficult question, which is to identify in real time when a permanent shock has occurred. That is a question beyond the realm of this study, although clearly one that policymakers have to confront.

With the caveats above, it is relatively straightforward to derive the mean oil price from the above regressions.[12] Ultimately, however, it is

---

[12]The annual regressions use the results from an AR(1) regression, while the monthly regressions are based on AR(2) in line with the results for the Schwarz criterion and consistent with Akarca and Andrianacos (1998).

not just the mean but also the variance (and perhaps higher moments) of oil prices—and therefore oil wealth—that need to be considered. The imprecision in the underlying parameter estimates translates directly into uncertainty about the mean oil price, and a few dollars plus or minus could have significant implications for oil wealth.

Parameter Uncertainty

Parameter uncertainty introduces a good degree of variation into the estimated mean. While the unconditional mean oil price for the 1974–2001 sample, using annual data, is estimated to be US$21.35, the standard deviation is US$2.29. If we take ±2 standard deviations—corresponding roughly to the 95 percent confidence interval—then the range for the estimated mean price goes from US$16.77 to US$25.92 (Table 5.3). This is a relatively large range that, in turn, translates into a fair amount of uncertainty about oil wealth.

Using the monthly data for the 1974–2001 sample, we find a lower unconditional mean and standard deviation, US$20.83 and US$1.78, respectively (Table 5.4). This translates into a shorter range for the 95 percent confidence interval from US$17.27 to US$24.39. This result is expected given the number of observations used for each specification.

Rolling regressions are performed to examine the robustness of the above results. The 1974–2001 sample is broken up into nine subperiods of 20 observations (Table 5.3). The results are broadly consistent with those for the whole 1974–2001 sample, but would point to relatively more uncertainty as to the unconditional mean. The estimates of the unconditional mean range from a low of US$19.53 for the 1980–1999 sample to a high of US$22.40 for the 1977–1996 sample. Moreover, the standard deviation is also higher in all of the subsamples, peaking at US$4.39 for the 1975–1994 subsample—implying a 2 standard deviation range from US$12.39 to US$29.96. Given the smaller sample and higher estimates on the coefficient of lagged oil, the unit root hypothesis could not be rejected for most of these subsamples. Only in two cases is it rejected, although the estimate on lagged oil never exceeds 0.72.

The same time periods are used to run rolling regressions on the monthly data, each with 240 observations (Table 5.4). The estimates of the unconditional mean range from a low point of US$19.57 for the 1982–2001 period to a peak of US$22.19 for the period between 1977–1996, again showing slightly less volatility than the annual series.

Table 5.3. Regressions of Log of Brent Oil Prices (Nominal, Annual Average Series)

Coefficient	1974–2001	1974–93	1975–94	1976–95	1977–96	1978–97	1979–98	1980–99	1981–2000	1982–2002
Constant	1.49*	1.47*	0.86***	1.00**	1.10**	1.17**	1.17***	0.84***	1.17**	1.39**
	(0.33)	(0.37)	(0.47)	(0.47)	(0.50)	(0.53)	(0.60)	(0.47)	(0.51)	(0.52)
Brent (t–1)	0.51*	0.52*	0.72*	0.67*	0.65*	0.62*	0.62*	0.72*	0.61*	0.53*
	(0.11)	(0.12)	(0.15)	(0.15)	(0.16)	(0.17)	(0.19)	(0.15)	(0.17)	(0.17)
R-squared	0.45	0.5	0.55	0.52	0.46	0.42	0.36	0.55	0.43	0.35
Standard error	0.26	0.28	0.26	0.25	0.25	0.25	0.27	0.22	0.23	0.31
Number of observations	28	20	20	20	20	20	20	20	20	20
Unit root test	1	1	NR	NR	NR	NR	NR	NR	NR	10
Unconditional mean										
(US$/barrel)	21.35	22.04	21.17	21.92	22.40	22.36	21.50	19.53	20.29	19.87
Standard deviation										
(US$/barrel)	2.29	3.00	4.39	3.84	3.62	3.37	3.42	3.59	2.71	2.15
–2 Standard deviations	16.77	16.04	12.39	14.24	15.16	15.62	14.66	12.34	14.86	12.57
+2 Standard deviations	25.92	28.04	29.96	29.60	29.64	29.10	28.35	26.72	25.72	24.18

Sources: WEO database; and authors' calculations.
Note: * significant at the 1 percent level; ** at the 5 percent level; and *** at the 10 percent level; NR means that the unit root hypothesis is not rejected.

Table 5.4. *Regressions of Log of Brent Oil Prices (Nominal, Monthly Average Series)*

Coefficient	1974:1–2001:12	1974:1–1993:12	1975:1–1994:12	1976:1–1995:12	1977:1–1996:12	1978:1–1997:12	1979:1–1998:12	1980:1–1999:12	1981:1–2000:12	1982:1–2001:12
Constant	0.20*	0.20*	0.09*	0.11*	0.12*	0.13*	0.10*	0.13*	0.16*	0.18*
	(.04)	(.05)	(.03)	(.04)	(.04)	(.04)	(.05)	(.04)	(.05)	(.05)
Brent (t–1)	1.10*	1.12*	1.35*	1.34*	1.33*	1.32*	1.32*	1.28*	1.23*	1.20*
	(0.05)	(0.06)	(0.06)	(0.05)	(0.05)	(0.04)	(0.06)	(0.06)	(0.06)	(0.06)
Brent (t–2)	–0.16*	–0.19*	–0.38*	–0.37*	–0.37*	–0.36*	–0.35*	–0.32*	–0.28*	–0.27*
	(0.05)	(0.06)	(0.06)	(0.05)	(0.05)	(0.06)	(0.06)	(0.06)	(0.06)	(0.06)
R-squared	0.92	0.93	0.96	0.96	0.95	0.95	0.95	0.95	0.93	0.92
Standard error	0.10	0.11	0.07	0.07	0.07	0.03	0.08	0.08	0.08	0.08
Number of observations	336	240	240	240	240	240	240	240	240	240
Unit root test	1	1	NR	NR	NR	NR	NR	10	5	5
Unconditional mean (US$/barrel)	20.83	21.32	20.92	21.61	22.29	21.86	20.55	20.38	20.01	19.57
Standard deviation (US$/barrel)	1.78	2.23	3.18	2.85	2.78	2.59	3.17	2.35	2.01	1.72
–2 Standard deviations	17.27	16.87	14.56	15.90	16.64	16.67	14.21	15.69	15.98	16.14
+2 Standard deviations	24.39	25.77	27.28	27.31	27.75	27.05	26.89	25.07	24.03	23.01

Sources: WEO database; and authors' calculations.

Note: * significant at the 1 percent level; ** at the 5 percent level; and *** at the 10 percent level; NR means that the unit root hypothesis is not rejected.

The standard deviation is also higher for most of the subsamples, but it is contained within a smaller range, going from a low point of US$1.72 for the 1982–2001 sample to US$3.18 for 1975–1994. The hypothesis of the unit root is rejected for the first subperiod (1974–1993), and for all the samples starting after 1980. The rolling regressions are also performed on the monthly data for the post-1987 sample to allow for the possibility of a break in 1986 as found by Akarca and Andrianacos (1995, 1997, and 1998). These results (not presented) suggest a lower mean price (US$18.71) relative to the 1974–2001 sample and a lower standard deviation.

The above regressions provide strong evidence of mean reversion, but also highlight that there is uncertainty as to the true underlying parameters. The implied unconditional mean of oil prices varies depending on the sample period, as does the standard deviation. This could reflect normal sample fluctuation, or the fact that despite strong evidence in favor of mean reversion, the underlying mean that is being reverted to fluctuates modestly over time.

V. Oil Wealth

One of the objectives of this paper is to understand how movements in oil prices affect estimates of government oil wealth. As noted above, oil wealth is a key determinant of the size of the sustainable non-oil fiscal deficit, and thus an important variable for fiscal policy formulation. For example, if oil price shocks have a large impact on estimates of government oil wealth, then, at least on sustainability grounds, there would be a basis for adjusting the non-oil balance in line with oil price movements.[13] At the same time, the variance of the oil wealth estimates also matters. The larger the uncertainty about the estimate of wealth, the stronger the precautionary savings motives would be.

Translating oil price movements into changes in fiscal oil wealth, however, is complicated and requires making numerous assumptions. The first set of complications relates to the calculation of the present discounted value of total oil revenue. In addition to the path of prices, such a calculation depends on the interest (discount) rate, the amount

---

[13]Barnett and Ossowski (see Chapter 3 in this volume) elaborate on this, and also discuss why, in general, the non-oil balance should often be adjusted cautiously to increases in prices, even if a greater increase might be warranted based solely on sustainability considerations.

of oil reserves, the number of years that it will take to exhaust the reserves, and the amount of extraction that will take place in any given period. Moreover, these factors may themselves depend on oil prices. For example, price movements could affect decisions on how much oil to extract in a given period, or might induce more exploration that may result in finding additional reserves.

The second set of complications relates to translating the flow of gross oil revenue into government oil revenue. This would depend on the profits in the oil sector, which are likely to be a nonlinear function of oil prices. In particular, if extraction costs contain a large fixed component (as they probably do), then a given percentage change in prices would translate into an even larger change in profitability. For example, if the cost of extraction per barrel is US$10, a 20 percent increase in the price from, say, US$20 to US$24 results in a 40 percent increase in profitability, from US$10 to US$14 per barrel. Another consideration is the financial relationship between the government and the oil sector, including whether most fiscal oil revenue comes from ownership in the oil company, royalties, or taxation—a fiscal regime, moreover, which could be nonlinear in profitability. These considerations suggest that some caution is warranted in translating oil price movements into changes in fiscal revenue.

In light of the above considerations, the following examples should be seen as illustrative. In any event, country-specific estimates could be calculated by making the corresponding adjustments to the assumptions. To keep matters simple, it is assumed that extraction lasts for a fixed number of years, a constant amount of oil is extracted in each period, and the discount rate is constant. The per-period extraction is also normalized to one—the results, therefore, could be equivalently viewed as the expected return for producing a barrel of oil each year for the given number of years. Finally, the cost of extraction is assumed to be a fixed amount per barrel.

The specific values of these parameters are varied in the calculations below to assess the sensitivity of the results. In all cases, however, the interest rate is fixed at 3 percent. This is somewhat low for a nominal interest rate—given that nominal prices are being projected—but it could also be interpreted as a proxy for the real interest rate under the assumption that in the very long run oil prices grow in line with inflation. The period during which extraction is projected to take place is set at either 25 years, 50 years, or infinite. The extraction costs are either set at zero—implying that gross oil revenue is actually being calculated—or US$10 per barrel, to proxy for a relatively high-cost producer.

Mean of Wealth

Variations in the current price do not have a very strong impact on estimates of oil wealth. Intuitively, this follows from the finding that oil shocks are not that persistent, as embodied in the relatively fast mean reversion. Thus, whether oil prices at a particular point in time are high or low only affects the near-term price forecasts. The medium- to long-horizon forecasts are unchanged, so the impact on oil wealth would be limited to the impact of a few years of higher or lower prices. The sensitivity, therefore, would also depend on the remaining years of production, with short-term price changes more important for producers with fewer years of production remaining.

To illustrate this, oil wealth is simulated using a continuum of oil prices. Figure 5.5 shows the deviation of wealth from a reference value as a function of the current price, where the reference value of wealth is calculated by setting the price to its long-run average. The parameters from the regressions on annual data (1975–2001) are used, which, as an AR(1), has the advantage that the current price is all that is needed to determine the future path of prices and therefore wealth. Focusing on the top panel, which assumes that extraction costs are zero, the sensitivity to changes in price is greater (as seen by the higher slope) the fewer years of production remaining. The magnitude of the changes, however, are not that large even for the producer with only 25 years of production remaining; for example, an increase in the price from US$10 to US$30 would only increase wealth by around 12 percent. The bottom panel of Figure 5.5 repeats the exercise with extraction costs set to US$10 per barrel. The sensitivity, as expected, increases; for example, an increase from US$10 to US$30 for the high-extraction-cost producer with 25 years of oil remaining results in a 24 percent increase in wealth.

It follows, therefore, that the changes in oil wealth induced by the yearly fluctuations in oil prices are generally not too large (see Table 5.5).[14] For example, when oil prices increased by 60 percent in 2000, a "no extraction cost" producer would have experienced an increase in oil wealth ranging from 5½ percent to around 3 percent depending on the years of production remaining. As highlighted above, a high-cost

---

[14]The change in oil wealth is approximated by comparing oil wealth for a given type of producer (no cost or high cost, and number of years of production remaining) in a given year with the previous year. For example, the oil wealth of a producer with 25 years of production remaining in 2000 is compared to a producer with 25 years of production remaining in 1999.

Figure 5.5. *Oil Wealth Simulations*
(In percent of reference value of wealth)[1]

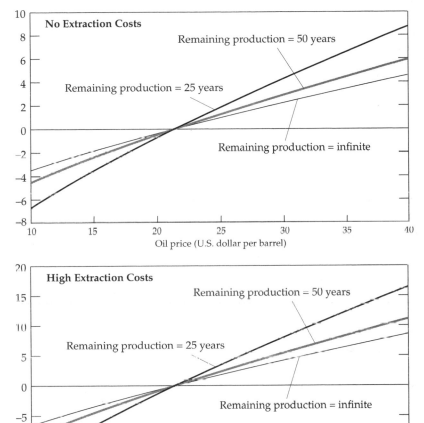

Source: Authors' calculations.
[1]Reference value of wealth is calculated by setting the oil price to its long-run average.

producer would experience a larger change in wealth, but the amounts still are not that large. Again looking at 2000, oil revenue would have increased by nearly 140 percent for the high-cost producer, yet wealth would have grown by only 10 percent or so (for a producer with 25

Table 5.5. *Annual Change in Oil Wealth and Revenue*
(*In percent*)

| | Brent Price | | No Extraction Cost | | | High Extraction Cost | | |
| | | | Wealth (production years) | | | | Wealth (production years) | |
Year	US$/barrel	Revenue	25	50	Infinite	Revenue	25	50	Infinite
1975	11.50	...	–1.0	–0.6	–0.5	...	–1.9	–1.2	–0.9
1976	13.14	14.3	1.1	0.7	0.6	109.3	2.2	1.4	1.1
1977	14.31	8.9	0.7	0.5	0.4	37.2	1.5	1.0	0.7
1978	14.26	–0.3	0.0	0.0	0.0	–1.1	–0.1	0.0	0.0
1979	32.11	125.2	9.6	6.4	4.9	419.1	18.7	12.3	9.4
1980	37.89	18.0	2.5	1.7	1.3	26.1	4.5	3.1	2.4
1981	36.68	–3.2	–0.5	–0.3	–0.3	–4.4	–0.9	–0.6	–0.5
1982	33.42	–8.9	–1.4	–0.9	–0.7	–12.2	–2.4	–1.7	–1.3
1983	29.78	–10.9	–1.6	–1.1	–0.9	–15.5	–2.9	–2.0	–1.6
1984	28.74	–3.5	–0.5	–0.3	–0.3	–5.3	–0.9	–0.6	–0.5
1985	27.61	–3.9	–0.5	–0.4	–0.3	–6.0	–1.0	–0.7	–0.5
1986	14.43	–47.7	–6.8	–4.6	–3.6	–74.8	–12.4	–8.5	–6.7
1987	18.44	27.7	2.4	1.6	1.2	90.3	4.6	3.1	2.3
1988	14.98	–18.8	–2.0	–1.3	–1.0	–41.0	–3.8	–2.6	–2.0
1989	18.25	21.9	1.9	1.3	1.0	65.8	3.8	2.5	1.9
1990	23.71	29.9	2.9	2.0	1.5	66.2	5.6	3.7	2.9
1991	19.98	–15.7	–1.9	–1.3	–1.0	–27.2	–3.6	–2.4	–1.9
1992	19.41	–2.8	–0.3	–0.2	–0.2	–5.7	–0.6	–0.4	–0.3
1993	17.00	–12.4	–1.3	–0.9	–0.7	–25.7	–2.6	–1.7	–1.3
1994	15.83	–6.9	–0.7	–0.5	–0.4	–16.7	–1.3	–0.9	–0.7
1995	17.05	7.8	0.7	0.5	0.4	21.1	1.4	0.9	0.7
1996	20.45	19.9	1.9	1.3	1.0	48.2	3.6	2.4	1.9
1997	19.12	–6.5	–0.7	–0.5	–0.4	–12.8	–1.4	–0.9	–0.7
1998	12.72	–33.5	–3.8	–2.5	–1.9	–70.2	–7.1	–4.8	–3.7
1999	17.70	39.2	3.1	2.1	1.6	183.2	6.1	4.0	3.0
2000	28.31	59.9	5.5	3.7	2.9	137.8	10.6	7.1	5.4
2001	24.41	–13.8	–1.8	–1.3	–1.0	–21.3	–3.4	–2.3	–1.8

Sources: IMF, *International Financial Statistics;* and authors' calculations.
Note: The wealth estimates assume that the log of oil prices follows an AR(1) with a constant of 1.487 and AR(1) coefficient of 0.514.

years of production remaining) and less for a producer with more years of production remaining. On the rough assumption that the sustainable non-oil deficit moves in line with oil wealth, the implied elasticity (which depends on the price) of the sustainable non-oil deficit with changes in oil prices is generally well below 10 percent.[15]

---

[15]For example, suppose that a non-oil deficit equivalent to 5 percent of GDP is deemed sustainable and oil revenue is 6 percent of GDP (implying some wealth accumulation). An elasticity of 10 percent would imply that if oil revenue doubled to 12 percent of GDP (an increase of 6 percentage points of GDP), the sustainable non-oil deficit would rise by only ½ percentage point of GDP. Moreover, most of the implied elasticities in Table 5.5 are well below 10 percent.

Videgaray (1998) finds qualitatively similar but generally larger effects of oil price changes on wealth. His calculations are roughly comparable to the no-extraction-cost infinite producer in Table 5.5. Whereas he estimates a decrease in wealth of 26 percent in 1986 (the largest decline in his table), Table 5.5 implies a decrease in wealth of only 3.6 percent. Nonetheless, he reports a change in wealth greater than 5 percent in only 7 of the 17 years of data (1980–1996). The main reason for the higher sensitivity is that there is more persistence of the shocks in his model and thus slower mean reversion.

Variance of Wealth

The impact of oil price changes on wealth needs to be viewed in the context of the more general uncertainty surrounding wealth expectations. As highlighted above, the parameters of the oil price equation are themselves unknown. This implies that the variance (or standard deviation) of wealth expectations could be calculated by factoring in the parameter uncertainty. The parameter uncertainty affects both the long-run average price and the persistence of price shocks—both of which would have an impact on the variance of wealth expectations. In particular, the sensitivity of wealth to changes in the oil price depends on the persistence of shocks. If the persistence is underestimated, for example, then the sensitivity of wealth to price changes—as analyzed above—is also underestimated. While this effect is potentially quite important, the uncertainty about the long-run prices is algebraically easier to examine and sufficient to demonstrate that there is a good degree of uncertainty surrounding wealth expectations.

Uncertainty about the parameters to use in estimating oil wealth translates into a high variance in wealth expectations. As noted above, the standard deviation for the long-run oil price in the 1974–2001 annual regression (Table 5.5) is around 10 percent of the price. This implies that for the no-extraction-cost producer (with infinite production years remaining) the standard deviation of wealth is also 10 percent. Or, viewed alternatively, the 95 percent confidence interval spans roughly from 80–120 percent of expected wealth. In contrast, an oil price variation from US$10 to US$30 translates into movements equivalent to 96–102 percent of expected wealth (see Figure 5.5). In light of the variance of wealth expectations, such a change in expected wealth would not be statistically significant. For the high-extraction-cost producer, the uncertainty about wealth is substantially greater as the appropriate standard deviation to use would be in excess of 20 percent.

VI. Summary and Conclusions

The empirical investigation of the statistical properties of oil prices suggests that most oil price movements are transitory. In particular, accepting that there are periodic permanent oil shocks (such as in 1973), the evidence suggests that oil prices are mean reverting. Mean reversion is supported both by conventional unit root tests and an analysis of price expectations as embodied in the term structure of futures prices. The futures price data imply that around 60 percent of a given price shock is expected to be reversed after one year. Conventional unit root analysis on nominal oil prices generally rejects the unit root hypothesis using both monthly and annual data—with the important caveat that the sample must begin after 1973.

The presence and the pace of mean reversion in oil prices suggest that the year-to-year fluctuations have only a minor impact on oil wealth. This implies that for the most part (and looking only at sustainability considerations) a government should not adjust the non-oil balance that much in response to oil price changes. Moreover, the change in expected oil wealth from changes in prices is likely to be quantitatively insignificant relative to the uncertainty surrounding projections of oil wealth. This reinforces the view that a given change in oil prices does not convey too much new information about government wealth nor the sustainability of fiscal policy.

Bibliography

Akarca, Ali T., and Dimitri Andrianacos, 1995, "Is the Oil Still Persistent?," *The Journal of Economics*, Vol. 21, No. 2, pp. 17–21.

———, 1997, "Detecting Break in Oil Price Series Using the Box-Tiao Method," *International Advances in Economic Research*, Vol. 3, No. 2 (May), pp. 217–224.

———, 1998, "Identifying Crucial Oil-Price Shocks," *The Journal of Economics*, Vol. 24, No. 1, pp. 115–124.

Bessembinder, Hendrik, Jay F. Coughenour, Paul J. Seguin, and Margaret Monroe Smoller, 1995, "Mean Reversion in Equilibrium Asset Prices: Evidence from the Futures Term Structure," *Journal of Finance*, Vol. 50, No.1, pp. 361–375.

Cashin, Paul, Hong Liang, and C. John McDermott, 2000, "How Persistent Are Shocks to World Commodity Prices?," *IMF Staff Papers*, Vol. 47, No. 2, pp. 177–217.

Cashin, Paul, C. John McDermott, and Alasdair Scott, 2002, "Booms and Slumps in World Commodity Prices," *Journal of Development Economics*, Vol. 69 (October), pp. 277–96.

Engel, Eduardo, and Rodrigo Valdés, 2000, "Optimal Fiscal Strategy for Oil Exporting Countries," IMF Working Paper 00/118 (Washington: International Monetary Fund).

Friedman, Milton, 1957, *A Theory of the Consumption Function* (Princeton, New Jersey: Princeton University Press).

Kumar, Manmohan S., 1992, "Forecasting Accuracy of Crude Oil Futures Prices," *Staff Papers*, International Monetary Fund, Vol. 39 (June), pp. 432–61.

Perron, Pierre, 1989, "The Great Crash, the Oil Price Shock, and the Unit Root Hypothesis," *Econometrica*, Vol. 57, No. 6 (November), pp. 1361–401.

Pindyck R., 1999, "The Long-Run Evolution of Energy Prices," *Energy Journal*, Vol. 20, No. 2, pp. 1–27.

Rudebusch, Glenn D., 1993, "The Uncertain Unit Root in Real GNP," *The American Economic Review*, Vol. 83, No. 1 (March), pp. 264–72.

Schwartz, Eduardo S., 1997, "The Stochastic Behavior of Commodity Prices: Implication for Valuation and Hedging," *Journal of Finance*, Vol. 52, No. 3, pp. 923–73.

Videgaray, Luis, 1998, "The Fiscal Response to Oil Shocks," Ph.D. dissertation (Cambridge, Massachusetts: Massachusetts Institute of Technology).

Wickham, Peter, 1996, "Volatility of Oil Prices," IMF Working Paper 96/82 (Washington: International Monetary Fund).

Part II.
Dealing with Oil Revenue

6

Revenue from the Oil and Gas Sector: Issues and Country Experience

EMIL M. SUNLEY, THOMAS BAUNSGAARD,
AND DOMINIQUE SIMARD[1]

I. Introduction

Oil and gas extraction plays a dominant role as a source of export earnings and, to a lesser extent, employment in many developing countries. But the most important benefit for a country from development of the oil and gas sector is likely to be its fiscal role in generating tax and other revenue for the government. To ensure that the state as resource owner receives an appropriate share of the economic rent generated from extraction of oil and gas, the fiscal regime must be appropriately designed.

The government, as resource owner, has a valuable asset in the ground. This asset—a crude oil or natural gas deposit—can only be exploited once. In order to convert this asset into financial resources, the government must attract capital on terms that ensure it gets the greatest possible value for its resources—under uncertainty about what the value of the resources will turn out to be.

There is a fundamental conflict between oil and gas companies and the government over the division of risk and reward from a petroleum

---

[1]Comments from Phillip Daniel and John Bartlett are gratefully acknowledged. This paper draws on previous work undertaken in the Fiscal Affairs Department of the International Monetary Fund, including Sunley and Baunsgaard (2001) and Baunsgaard (2001).

project. Both want to maximize rewards and shift as much risk as possible to the other party. Nevertheless, the right choice of fiscal regime can improve the trade-off between each party's interests—a small sacrifice from one side may be a big gain for the other. Oil and gas agreements and the associated fiscal rules establish the "price" of the resource in terms of the bonuses, royalties, taxes, or other payments the investor will make to the government over the life of the project. Designing fiscal arrangements that encourage a stable fiscal environment and efficient resource development maximizes the magnitude of the revenues to be divided.

In designing fiscal (tax and nontax) instruments, the government will need to weigh its desire to maximize short-term revenue against any deterrent effects this may have on investment. This will require a balanced sharing of risk and reward between the investor and the government. The aim should be for fair and rising government share of the resource rent as profitability increases, without scaring off potential investors.

This paper reviews the various fiscal instruments available to policymakers to design a fiscal regime for the oil and gas sector that will attract investment as well as secure a reasonable share of economic rent for the government. It is organized as follows. Section II discusses types of tax and nontax instruments used to generate revenue from the oil and gas sector. Section III provides an overview of current practices in a variety of countries and discusses the evolution of the fiscal regimes in selected countries. Section IV summarizes the policy implications.

II. Revenue Issues

The government can collect revenue from the oil and gas sector through a variety of tax and nontax instruments. Most countries collect the government share of economic rent primarily through production-based or profit-based instruments. In some countries, the government participates more directly in oil and gas projects by taking an equity interest. Policymakers will also have to decide on the treatment of indirect taxes such as value-added tax (VAT) and customs duties applicable to oil and gas.

Multiple fiscal instruments may be needed to create an identity of interests between the government and the oil and gas companies over the life of the agreement. Production-based instruments, such as royalties, can ensure that the government receives at least a minimum payment for its mineral resources. Profit-based instruments allow the government to share in the upside of highly profitable projects, but they also increase the government's share in the project's risk inasmuch as the government may receive no revenue if the project turns out to be unprofitable.

In addition to product-based and profit-based instruments, there may be bonuses and rental payments of various types. Bonuses can ensure some up-front revenue for the government and may encourage companies to explore and develop contract areas more rapidly. They are usually suitable only in highly prospective areas where there is strong competition among investors for petroleum rights. Annual rental payments typically are not a significant source of revenue but can be designed to encourage companies to explore and develop contract areas or to relinquish their rights.

In many countries with petroleum resources, revenues from different instruments accrue to different parties; for example, royalty payments may be made to local units of government, landowners, or the petroleum ministry.

Tax/Royalty Regimes

A common way of taxing the oil and gas sector involves a combination of tax and royalty payments. A tax/royalty regime may involve three levies: (i) a royalty to secure a minimum payment, (ii) the regular income tax that is applicable to all companies, and (iii) a resource rent tax to capture a larger share of the profits of the most profitable projects.

Royalties

Royalties are attractive to the government, as the revenue is received as soon as production commences and they are easier to administer than many other fiscal instruments, at least in the case of simple royalty regimes. Furthermore, they ensure that companies make a minimum payment for the minerals they extract. Royalties are typically either specific levies (based on the *volume* of oil and gas extracted) or ad valorem levies (based on the *value* of oil and gas extracted). Some countries have introduced a profit element in royalties by having the royalty rate depend on the level of production (e.g., Chile, Ecuador,

Norway, and Thailand) or on a measure of nominal return such as the R factor (e.g., Peru, and Kazakhstan).[2]

As royalties raise the marginal cost of extracting oil, they can deter investors if imposed at too high a level. They may also discourage development of any marginal reserves that have been discovered and lead to early abandonment of productive oil and gas wells. Investors are resistant to the use of royalties, even on potentially rich deposits, partly on the grounds that royalty payments are only a deductible expense in determining taxable income in the home country and are not allowed as a foreign tax credit against the home country's income tax.

A key issue for policymakers is to determine an appropriate method for the valuation of the extracted oil and gas used as a base for royalties and other taxes. Ad valorem royalties are generally levied on the sales price or the f.o.b. export price, at times after netting back certain costs.[3] An overriding concern should be the use of an observable price. When using a generally quoted market price (e.g., North Sea oil), it should be adjusted to reflect differences in gas and crude oil quality and the wellhead value should be established by netting back transportation and other costs.[4]

Income tax

The income tax should be levied on oil and gas companies, as on all other companies. It is not unusual for the profit tax rate for oil companies to be higher than the general rate for other companies. This is one way to capture a share of the resource rents from the project.

Many countries provide an incentive for exploration and project development by allowing exploration costs to be recovered immediately and allowing accelerated recovery of development costs, for example,

---

[2]The R factor equals cumulative revenues, net of royalties, divided by cumulative costs.

[3]Some countries (e.g., OPEC countries until 1974 and Nigeria until 1986) have historically used government-set prices, which were often independent from market prices. This practice is disappearing. In contrast, Norway introduced in 1974 a government-set price for oil defined as the market price of the same type of crude over a given period.

[4]Governments can exercise a considerable amount of discretion in determining price adjustments. For instance, in order to establish gross revenue at the wellhead, the U.K. inland revenue allowed as deductions from the landed price not only transport costs from North Sea fields but also around 70 percent of production platform costs. This practice was abandoned by the end of the 1970s (Kemp, 1987).

over five years. Accelerated cost recovery brings forward payback for the investor and, possibly, retirement of debt. It can therefore reduce both investor risk and tax-deductible interest costs; it also facilitates project financing. Some countries offer special incentives to encourage exploration in particular regions.

To protect the tax base, countries may place limits on the use of debt financing to limit "earning stripping" through the payment of interest abroad.[5] To limit abusive transfer pricing between related companies, the tax authority should have the power to adjust income and expenses where under- or overpricing between related companies has resulted in a lowering of taxable profit (Box 6.1).

A related issue for the taxpayer is the treatment of tax credits. Many multinational companies expect to be subject to an income tax in the producing country, as this tax will be creditable against the income tax levied in the home country. Absent an income tax in the producing country, the multinational may be subject to higher tax payments in the home country. Whether or not a tax is creditable depends on the particular tax law in the home country and on any tax treaties in place.[6] However, a tax paid in the producing country that in nature resembles a home country tax is most likely to qualify for a tax credit. Some specialized mineral taxes, such as a resource rent tax, may be deemed to differ in nature from a standard corporate tax and, therefore, could face difficulties in qualifying for a tax credit.

It is important to determine the extent of "ring-fencing" of tax accounts. Ring-fencing means a limitation on consolidation of income and deductions for tax purposes across different activities, or different projects, undertaken by the same taxpayer. Some countries ring-fence oil and gas activities, others ring-fence individual contract areas or projects. This can become complex if a project incorporates extraction, processing, and transportation activities. If the oil and gas tax regime is more onerous than the standard tax regime, the taxpayer could seek to have certain project-related activities treated as downstream activities outside the ring-fence. If they are treated as a separate activity, the taxpayer through transfer pricing may attempt to shift profits to the lightly taxed downstream activities.

---

[5]For instance, in Norway, liberal rules (the current limit on external financing is 80 percent) for the deduction of financial costs from both the corporate income tax and the Special Tax have been identified as one of the basic problems of the Norwegian petroleum taxation (Noreng, 2002).

[6]Unless foreign-sourced income is exempt in the home country.

Box 6.1. *Transfer Pricing*

Through transfer pricing, a taxpayer seeks to minimize income and maximize deductible expenditures in high-tax jurisdictions and vice versa in low-tax jurisdictions. A transfer pricing mechanism that could affect revenue in the oil and gas sector is, for example, the creative use by firms of price hedging mechanisms perhaps involving transactions between related parties, causing great difficulty in assessing whether hedging instruments are used for transfer pricing purposes rather than to reduce risk.

More common measures to maximize expenditure deductions include the following:
- The provision by related parties of highly leveraged debt finance at above-market interest rates.
- Claiming excessive management fees, deductions for headquarters costs, or consultancy charges paid to related parties.
- The provision of capital goods and machinery in leasing arrangements at above-market costs charged by a related-party lessor.
- If the petroleum tax rate is above the standard tax rate, there may be an incentive to establish a domestic shell firm that will on-lend financing capital from related parties to the oil company giving rise to an interest deduction at a higher tax rate than is charged on the interest earnings in the shell company.

Abusive transfer pricing can be very difficult to detect and prevent. Properly designing the tax code, though, is an important first step. At a minimum, the tax legislation should include safeguards requiring that transactions between related parties be assessed on an arm's-length basis, or perhaps that certain deductions be capped as a share of total costs. Some countries also impose a limit on the allowable (for tax purposes) debt leverage of a project. It is also advisable to seek close cooperation with the tax authorities in the home countries of the more important investors.

Ring-fencing rules matter for two main reasons:
- Absence of ring-fencing can postpone government tax revenue because a company that undertakes a series of projects will be able to deduct exploration or development expenditures from each new project against the income of projects that are already generating taxable income.
- As an oil and gas area matures, absence of ring-fencing may discriminate against new entrants that have no income against which to deduct exploration or development expenditures.

Despite these points, a very restrictive ring-fence is not necessarily in the government's interest.[7] More exploration and development activities may occur if taxpayers can obtain a deduction against current income, generating more government revenue over time by increasing the taxable base. The right choice is again a matter of balance within the fiscal regime, the degree of the government's preference for (modest) early revenues over (larger) revenues later on, and the extent of the government's bargaining power with oil and gas companies.

Resource rent tax

An innovative attempt both to provide the government with an appropriate share of economic rent *and* to make the tax system less distortive to investors is the resource rent tax (RRT). The RRT (as applied in Australia and Papua New Guinea, for example) is imposed only if the accumulated cash flow from the project is positive. The net negative cash flow (in the early years of a project) is accumulated at an interest rate that, in theory, is equal to the company's opportunity cost of capital (adjusted for risk).[8]

The RRT takes a share of returns once the company has earned this hurdle rate of return. If the only tax imposed is the RRT, the government's revenue stream becomes back-loaded, and for less profitable projects, the government may not receive any revenue at all. Therefore, a resource rent tax is usually combined with royalties and a standard profit tax to provide some early revenue.[9] Only for very profitable projects will the resource rent tax then apply.

Conceptually, an RRT has strong economic features. When properly designed, an RRT captures a share of the natural resource rent, which is the return over and above the company's opportunity cost of capital. Proponents argue that the RRT can enhance contract stability because it automatically increases the government share in highly profitable

---

[7]Oil and gas companies see this provision as a major disincentive. For instance, they proposed repeatedly that the Indonesian government relax its restriction on transferring expenses from one contract area to another. However, the government maintained its ring-fencing provision (Gao, 1994). Indonesia's relatively tough fiscal arrangements (Barrows, 1988) are compensated by its attractive oil and gas potential.

[8]The "opportunity cost of capital," which is equal to the discount rate, means the expected return on the best alternative use of available funds.

[9]Palmer (1980) recommends that the resource rent tax be combined with a traditional company profits tax.

projects. For the RRT to be efficient, each contract area needs to be ring-fenced. That is, costs incurred in one contract area cannot be used to offset the revenues in another contract area. One exception to this rule may be to allow unrecovered costs from an abandoned contract area to carry over to a contract area that remains active. This helps to prevent an RRT from discriminating against exploration.

While the resource rent tax has much theoretical appeal, it has not been a significant revenue raiser in practice. There may be many reasons for this. It could reflect the difficulty of designing the tax, particularly the choice of the discount (or hurdle) rate and tax rate. If the hurdle rate is set too high, chances are that the resource rent tax will never apply; if it is set too low, the tax may become a major deterrent to investment.[10] If either the hurdle rate of return is too low or the tax rate too high, the RRT will also increase the incentives for oil companies to engage in tax avoidance, which in countries with a weak tax administration may be very difficult to detect and control.[11]

Production Sharing

An alternative to a tax/royalty regime is production sharing. Under a production-sharing arrangement the ownership of the resource remains with the state, and the oil and gas company is contracted to extract and develop the resource in return for a share of the production. The government retains the right to petroleum reserves in the ground but appoints the investor as "contractor" to assist the government in developing the resources. Instead of paying the contractor a fee for this service, while the government bears the risk, cost, and expense, the parties agree that the contractor will meet the exploration and development costs in return for a share of any production that may result. The contractor will have no right to be paid in the event that discovery and development does not occur. In principle, the government retains and disposes of its own share of petroleum extracted, though joint-marketing arrangements may be made with the contractor.

---

[10]A weakness of a tax based on rates of return is that it does not take geological risks into account (Van Meurs, 1988, p. 72).

[11]In this respect, it should be noted that a properly designed RRT is probably less distortionary than the regular corporate income tax. The latter postpones the achievement of a desired rate of return (particularly if slow depreciation rates are specified) and therefore encourages other behavior likely to increase current deductions.

The mechanics of production sharing are in principle quite straight-forward. The production-sharing contract (PSC) will usually specify a portion of total production, which can be retained by the contractor to recover costs ("cost oil"). The remaining oil (including any surplus of cost oil over the amount needed for cost recovery) is termed "profit oil" and is divided between the government and the contractor according to some formula set out in the PSC.

Royalties can also be introduced into the production-sharing regime. In some PSCs there is an explicit royalty payment that is paid to the government before the remaining production is split between cost and profit oil. An alternative to a royalty is to have a limit on cost oil (e.g., 60 percent of production), which ensures there is profit oil, as soon as production commences. Where a cap is imposed on the deduction of costs and costs are at this limit, the cap will have a similar economic impact as a royalty, with the government receiving revenue—its share of profit oil—as soon as production commences.

Unrecovered costs in any year are carried forward to subsequent years, but some PSCs allow these costs to be uplifted by an interest factor to compensate for the delay in cost recovery. Interest expense is generally not a recoverable cost. If interest expense is allowed to be recovered, then there should be no uplift for unrecovered costs as this would involve a double counting to the extent unrecovered costs are debt financed.

The split of profit oil is often fixed—60 percent for the government and 40 percent for the investor, for example. It may vary according to the level of production, the price of crude oil, or the internal rate of return earned on the project. Contractors often pay income tax on their share of production. This tax could be paid out of the government's share, but then the government's share should be increased, all other things being equal.[12] A significant advantage of this approach is that the contractors would have fiscal stability—any future changes in the tax rules would affect only the allocation of the government's share between tax and nontax oil. The assurance of fiscal stability is an important investment incentive, carrying the cost of reduced flexibility for the government to increase tax on a given project in the future (see Box 6.2 on explicit fiscal stability clauses).

A versatile production-sharing framework can be attractive to both the contractor and the government since it can be adjusted to suit par-

---

[12]As an example, see the Indonesian case, as detailed in the Appendix.

Box 6.2. *Fiscal Stability Clauses*

Given the nature of investment in oil and gas extraction—long-term, large-scale, and up-front—a particular concern for investors is to guard themselves against unforeseen changes to the financial premises of the project. One safeguard mechanism that is often sought by investors is the inclusion of a fiscal stability clause in the project agreement. While the government may view this as an attractive and, in the short run, inexpensive way of minimizing investor risk, a final stability clause does limit the government's flexibility to set tax policy, potentially resulting in a revenue loss and increased administrative costs.

Fiscal stability clauses come in different forms. One approach is to "freeze" the tax system at the time of the project agreement. If the tax system is later changed, this will imply a special treatment of a particular taxpayer, adding to the administrative burden, especially if several projects are operating under different tax systems. Another approach is to guarantee the total investor take. If one tax is increased, this will be offset by a reduction in another tax (or in principle by paying a compensatory subsidy), which perhaps better preserves the integrity of the tax system. Still, it may be quite difficult in practice to agree on compensatory measures that can satisfy both government and investor. There are also some stability clauses that are asymmetric: protecting the investor from adverse changes to the fiscal terms but passing on benefits of economy-wide reductions in tax rates.

Fiscal stability clauses are widespread in the oil and gas sector. Of 109 countries surveyed in 1997, a majority (63 percent) provided fiscal stability clauses for all fiscal terms (Baunsgaard, 2001). A small group (14 percent) had partial fiscal stability clauses excluding income tax. Finally, a minority (23 percent) did not provide any fiscal stability clauses in project agreements (at least up until 1997). However, a fiscal stability clause does of course not prevent an investor from seeking to renegotiate fiscal terms in response to policy changes. Kazakhstan provides a recent example of a country that repealed its tax stability clause for contracts signed from 2002 onwards (Page, 2002). Tax conditions set in contracts may now be adjusted in compliance with amendments to tax laws, by the mutual consent of the government and the contractor.

---

ticular project circumstances without changing the overarching fiscal framework. However, it might include design and administrative complexities causing a PSC to be as complex to administer as profit-based taxes. Difficulties relate particularly to the determination of allowable costs. Moreover, it is possible that the ex ante agreement becomes quite inappropriate as the real profitability of a project becomes known.

Table 6.1. *Comparison Between Royalty and Production-Sharing Regimes*

Risk/Reward Trade-Off for the Government Arising from Various Fiscal Instruments	Tax/Royalty Regime	Production-Sharing Regime
Low risk/low reward	Royalty	There may be an explicit royalty; or there may be a limit on cost oil that functions as an implicit royalty.
Medium risk/medium reward	Income tax that applies to all companies	Income tax that applies to all companies, which may be paid out of the government's share of production.
High risk/high reward	Resource rent tax	The determination of the amount of profit oil can be highly progressive and mimic a resource rent tax.

Source: Authors.

The Choice Between Tax/Royalty and Production-Sharing Regimes

There is no intrinsic reason to prefer a tax/royalty regime to a PSC regime, since the fiscal terms of a tax/royalty regime can be replicated in a PSC regime, and vice versa (Table 6.1). Each can include fiscal instruments for which the risk/reward trade-off for the government is low, medium, or high. For example, the tax/royalty regime may include an explicit royalty—a low risk/low reward trade-off for the government. The PSC regime may have an explicit royalty, or there may be a limit on cost oil that functions as an implicit royalty. Under both regimes the contractor can be subject to the same income tax as other companies—a medium risk/medium reward trade-off for the government. Finally, to capture a larger share of the resource rents of the most profitable projects, there can be resource rent tax or, under the PSC regime, the split of profit can be made highly progressive and even mimic a resource rent tax—a high risk/high reward trade-off for the government.

PSCs permit the conditions governing petroleum exploration and development to be consolidated in one document. They may be particularly helpful to newcomers, not familiar with the operating environment, since the necessary provisions (including those relating to fiscal stabilization) can be consolidated in the PSC, thus clarifying the way in which the law will be applied. The PSC is a straightforward way in which contractual assurances, additional to statutory rights, can be offered to investors.

State Equity

A government may also participate more directly in an oil and gas project by taking equity in the project. State equity can take several forms, including: (i) a full working interest—paid-up equity on commercial terms, which places the government on a par with the private investor; (ii) paid-up equity on concessional terms, where the government acquires its equity share at a below-market price, possibly being able to buy into the project after a commercial discovery has been made; (iii) a carried interest, where the government pays for its equity share out of production proceeds, including an interest charge; (iv) tax swapped for equity, where the government's equity share is offset against a reduced tax liability; (v) equity in exchange for a noncash contribution, for example by the government providing infrastructure facilities; and (vi) so-called "free" equity, which is a bit misleading since even the noncash provision of equity usually results in some, more or less transparent, offsetting reduction in other taxes.[13]

State equity participation is mainly motivated by a desire to share in any upside of a project, but can also reflect noneconomic reasons. These can relate to nationalistic sentiment, to facilitate transfer of technology and know-how, or to provide more direct control over project development. But full equity participation can become a costly option when consideration is given to the resulting cash calls.[14] There are also possible conflicts of interest arising from the government's role as regulator overseeing the environmental or social impact of a project, which may differ from its objectives as a shareholder. In many instances, the government may be better off by focusing on taxing and

---

[13]See Daniel (1995) for a comprehensive discussion. Furthermore, in some transition economies, the government's inability to honor its financial commitments under a joint partnership has led to numerous tax concessions to oil and gas companies due to the government's weakened bargaining position.

[14]Cash advances required to be paid by each joint venture company to meet the net cash requirement of the joint venture.

regulating a project rather than being directly involved as an equity participant.[15]

Cash-rich, resource-rich countries, particularly in the Middle East since the mid-1970s, have tended to assume all the risk of financing their own upstream investments through a national oil company, and, in return, reap all the rewards of a successful exploration and production. In such cases, the involvement of international oil companies is usually limited to the supply of the relevant technology and engineering know-how. In other words, they act as contractors in return for agreed cash payments.[16]

Indirect Taxes

The imposition of indirect taxes, such as customs duties and VAT, though often ignored in discussions of petroleum taxation, plays an important role in the fiscal regime. In principle, oil and gas projects should be treated similarly to other economic activities when it comes to indirect taxation. In practice, however, the oil and gas sector is often treated differently, either due to its special nature or as a fiscal incentive to attract investors.

Import duties

If there were no special treatment for import duties, these would be an attractive way for the government to secure an up-front revenue stream. Given the very substantial import needs, particularly during project development, this revenue is typically even more front-loaded than royalty payments. For the same reason, duty exemptions are highly attractive to investors to improve project economics. Duty exemptions can also be sought as a way to minimize dealings with customs officials, where foreign enterprises with substantial import needs can be an easy target for rent-seeking behavior.

---

[15]It should also be kept in mind that tax instruments can replicate the economic impact of an equity share. For example, a 25 percent carried interest with a 15 percent interest charge is equivalent to a 25 percent resource rent tax with a 15 percent hurdle rate of return. In both cases the government receives payments—with respect to its equity share or taxes—only after the project has earned a 15 percent rate of return. See Nellor and Sunley (1994) for an illustration of this point.

[16]The role of state-owned oil companies as active participants (operators) is discussed by McPherson in Chapter 7 of this volume.

It is quite common for specialized equipment for exploration and development to be exempted from import duties. It is advisable to restrict this exemption by requiring that the equipment is reexported after its use. In some countries, all project-related inputs (perhaps restricted to purchases that are not available locally) receive a blanket exemption. Some countries provide guarantees against discriminatory duties being imposed on oil and gas companies, for example by applying a maximum allowable duty. This can result in reverse discrimination whereby duties on imports for petroleum projects are in effect lower than for other importers.

Value-added tax

The treatment of the oil and gas sector for VAT purposes is often influenced more by administrative realities than by principles of good tax policy. In a developing country, typically a large share, if not all, of the output from a petroleum project will be exported. Combined with the very large investment needs, this can complicate the treatment for VAT purposes. If exports are zero-rated under a destination-based VAT regime, the taxpayer will likely be in a continuous net refund situation reclaiming VAT paid on investment goods or on inputs. While this, in an economic sense, is the correct treatment of an exporter, it may be difficult to pay refunds in a timely fashion if the administrative capacity is weak. This situation is further exacerbated by the magnitude of the VAT refunds, particularly during periods with large investment requirements.

Faced with this refund problem, many countries provide VAT exemptions for imported capital goods and sometimes imported inputs for oil and gas extraction. This treatment may also be sought for domestic suppliers to projects, though this can be particularly problematic since it opens a loophole for domestic firms to evade VAT. That said, if the capacity is not in place to administer a refund-based system, it may be an unavoidable option to introduce a sector-specific exemption for capital goods, perhaps extended to certain specialized inputs used exclusively for oil and gas extraction. It is desirable that the exemption should not apply to inputs that can be easily used by other sectors in the economy, for this would open another loophole for tax evasion.

The standard international practice is to levy VAT on the destination basis, under which imports are taxed and exports are zero-rated. An exception to this practice was the treatment of trade between the new countries (other than the Baltics) formed after the dissolution of the Soviet Union (hereinafter referred to as the "CIS countries"). In part because the former Soviet Union was viewed as a common economic space, the CIS countries adopted the origin basis for CIS trade, under which goods were taxed in the country in which they were produced. Non-CIS trade was taxed under the destination basis.[17] The IMF staff advised the CIS countries to use the destination basis for VAT to avoid production distortions and be consistent with international best practice. The CIS countries have now adopted the destination basis for CIS trade, other than oil and natural gas.[18] As Russia is a large net exporter of oil and natural gas, this special rule involves a transfer of tax revenue to Russia, primarily from Ukraine. This revenue loss for Ukraine and other CIS countries might be partly offset by the revenue gain from the preferential excise rate for Russian gas exports to the CIS countries. The current situation may change as the Russian Ministry of Finance is considering proposals to switch to the destination basis—first for oil and later for natural gas.

Export duties

Most export duties that countries levy are concentrated in a few products. These duties are sometimes justified as a means of taxing away windfall gains, as a substitute for income taxation (on agricultural products), and as a way to improve the terms of trade. Many countries have removed export duties as part of tariff reform programs aimed at establishing outward-oriented trade regimes.

Export duties are generally not levied on oil and gas. However, Russia levies export duties on oil, natural gas, and oil products. The oil tariff is a sliding scale tied to the Ural oil price, and the rate is adjusted every two months. Below US$15 per barrel, there is no export duty. This levy, which has been justified as a revenue measure, primarily burdens producers and distorts the price of exports and domestic oil supplies.

Other Nontax Payments

A number of other nontax instruments are available, though these are often of lesser importance in terms of revenue generation. Many countries require payment of various fees—either fixed or auctioned,

---

[17]See Baer, Summers, and Sunley (1996) for a discussion of the destination VAT for CIS trade.

[18]However, there is one other exception to the switch to destination principle. All trade between Belarus and Russia remains based on the origin principle.

such as license, rental, or lease fees. These are commonly paid to the petroleum department and to some extent act as an incentive for the investor to carry out exploration and development work on the granted license area. It is a common requirement for oil and gas projects in many countries to pay signature, discovery, and production bonuses. Bonus payments are attractive to the government because they are received early in the project cycle;[19] for the same reason, however, they may discourage marginal investments. Collecting bonus payments requires little administrative effort and is a desirable way to ensure some early revenue from an oil and gas project.

Auctions for exploration or development rights could in theory be a very attractive way of securing the state's share of economic rent. However, for countries where political risk is perceived to be large, or with a high level of geological uncertainty, investors will be fewer and very risk averse prior to development. The bids received will therefore be lower than the expected net present value of a mineral deposit in a situation of no uncertainty. This could lead to demands to increase the government take if a project turns out to be more profitable than the original bid would reflect. Despite this bias, an auction can be a desirable way to administer the allocation of exploration rights among oil and gas companies, as it is done in some countries, though it would be unrealistic to rely on this instrument as a major revenue source. Empirical evidence on the effectiveness of auctioning exploration or development rights is mixed across countries.[20] Although auctions have performed very efficiently in the U.S., they were not as successful in the U.K. due to a much lower number of bidders. In Venezuela, the 1997 bidding round was viewed as successful in raising government revenue, though some industry sources suggest that the winning bids were at a substantial premium.

III. Country Experience

Cross-Country Evidence

Reflecting the fact that there is not one optimal model for taxing oil and gas projects, countries make use of a broad range of tax and non-

[19]Signature and discovery bonuses are received prior to project development, whereas production bonuses are paid when production commences or reaches certain prescribed levels.
[20]See Frewer (2000).

tax instruments. To illustrate the range of fiscal regimes, Table 6.2 provides an overview of current practice in a large number of developing countries.[21] While fiscal regimes for oil and gas exploration are strikingly diverse across countries, some general observations can be inferred.[22] The majority of countries in the sample apply royalties in order to secure an up-front revenue stream. Moreover, while almost all countries assess royalties on an ad valorem basis, the actual rates vary from 2 percent to 30 percent; a common range for countries with royalties would be around 5–10 percent.

The choice of tax rate reflects the typically higher economic rent in the petroleum sector. Countries without production-sharing arrangements or a resource rent tax typically apply a higher income tax rate to the oil and gas sector than to other economic activities. Some countries have combined a corporate income tax with a resource rent tax, often rate-of-return based, whereas a few countries apply a higher income tax rate when oil prices exceed a certain trigger level. Some countries have provided for more lenient taxation of natural gas projects, partly reflecting lower resource rents, the typically higher investment requirement, and at times larger risk involved than under an oil project. Key issues in gas development are the identification of a market for the gas and the determination of the most economic means of transporting gas to the market.

As in many other economic sectors, investment incentives are widely available. The most common are full current expensing of exploration and/or development costs, accelerated depreciation allowances, and investment tax credits. Tax holidays or reduced tax rates are less common, but some countries do offer them, particularly for smaller projects or to encourage investments in less explored regions. Many countries provide exemptions from customs duties and VAT on imports, at times only for specialized equipment to be reexported after use. Another common incentive is flexible loss carry-forward provisions, in many countries for an unlimited period of time.

---

[21]Since some countries apply special fiscal terms to individual projects, either through separate legislation or on a contractual basis, the information should only be regarded as indicative of general fiscal terms or standard contracts in the petroleum sector, whereas a particular project may actually be operating under different fiscal terms.

[22]A priori, one would expect that (i) countries with large proven oil reserves and relatively low exploration and development costs will be able to have a tougher fiscal regime; and (ii) high-cost countries with smaller oil reserves will have to offer more lenient fiscal terms to be successful in attracting investment.

Table 6.2. Key Characteristics of Fiscal Petroleum Regimes, Selected Developing Countries

Country	Royalties	Production Sharing[1]	Income Tax Rate	Resource Rent Tax	Dividend Withholding Tax[2]	Investment Incentives[3]	State Equity[4]
Africa							
Angola	...	15–80% (P)	50%	None	...	Yes (E)	25%
Cameroon	Negotiable	None	48.65%	None	25%	Yes (O)	50%
Chad	12.5%	None	50%	None	20%	None	10%
Gabon	10–20%	65–85% (V)	Gov. share	None	...	Yes (E)	15%(C)
Mozambique	8%	10–50%	40%	None	...	Yes (E)	None
Niger	12.5%	None	45%	None	18%	Yes (E)	...
Nigeria	0–20%	20–65%	50–85%	None	10%	Yes (E,Cr)	Variable
Sudan	None	60–80%	None	None	None	...	None
Asia and Pacific							
Bangladesh	None	65–80% (V)	None	None	...	Yes (I)	None
Brunei	8–12.5%	None	55%	None	None	Yes (A)	50%
Cambodia	12.5%	40–65% (V)	20%	None	None	Yes (E)	None
Indonesia	...	75–90% (V)	30%	None	15%	Yes (I,A,Cr)	10%
Malaysia	10%	50–70%	38%	70%	None	Yes (A,E,U)	25%
Papua New Guinea	2%	None	45%	20–25%	None	Yes (I,Cr)	22.5%(C)
Philippines	None	60%	32%	None	15–32%	Yes (E)	None
Thailand	3.5–10.5%	None	50%	None	10%	Yes (E)	None
Vietnam	6–25%	65–80% (V)	Gov. share	Formula	15%	Yes (H)	15%
Middle East							
Algeria	10–20%	60–88% (P)	Gov. share	None	20%	None	30%(C)
Bahrain	None	70%	46%	None	...	None	None
Egypt	10%	70–87% (V)	Gov. share	None	None	Yes (I)	None
Libya	16.67%	5–90%	None	None	...	...	...

Oman	None	77.5–80%	None	None	None	None	None
Qatar	None	35–90%	Gov. share	None	None	None	65%
Tunisia	2–15%	None	50–75%	Yes	None	Yes (E,U,I)	Negotiable
Yemen	3–9%	50–86%	None	None	None	Yes (E,U)	None
Latin America							
Belize	7.5%	5–15% (V)	25%	None	15%	Yes (U)	5%
Bolivia	18%	None	25%	25%	12.5%	Yes (E,U)	None
Chile	28–45%	None	15%	None	35%	Yes (A)	35%
Colombia	5–25%	None	35%	None	7%	None	50%(C)
Ecuador	12.5–18.5%	None	25%	Formula	25%	...	None
Guatemala	5–20%	30–70% (V)	30%	None	None	Yes (E,U,I)	None
Guyana	None	12.5–55% (V)	35%	None	10%	Yes (E)	None
Mexico	None	None	35%	None	7.7%	Yes (E,I)	None
Trinidad & Tobago	12.5%	Variable	50%	0–36%	...	Yes (A,H,I)	51%
Venezuela	30%	None	50%	None	None	Yes (E,Cr)	
Transition Economies							
Azerbaijan	None	50–90% (P)	32%	None	15%	Yes (E,O,U)	7.5–20%
Kazakhstan	Up to 20%	Negotiable	30%	0–30%	15%	...	50%
Kyrgyz Republic	None	60–80% (V)	Gov. share	None	15%	Yes (H)	None
Turkmenistan	3–15%	40–60%	25%	None	15%	...	None
Uzbekistan	5%	75%	25%	None	15%	...	50%(C)

Sources: Barrows (1997); Petrocash (online); Coopers & Lybrand (1998); PricewaterhouseCoopers (1999); and International Bureau of Fiscal Documentation (various).

[1]Production sharing linked to physical volume of production (V), or realized profitability (P).

[2]Nonresidents.

[3]Investment incentives: tax holiday (H), accelerated depreciation (A), tax credit (Cr), current expensing of exploration and/or development cost (E), exemption of imports of equipment and capital goods (I), unlimited loss carry-forward (U), and other (O).

[4]The maximum equity share that the state can select to take, often on a carried basis (C).

Production-sharing arrangements are widespread in the petroleum sector, where about two-thirds of the countries surveyed have this as the main core of their fiscal regime. Quite common is a formula-based system with the share of profit oil linked to the volume of production. It is typical to have at least 50–60 percent of profit oil going to the state, but in some countries a higher share applies. Countries also differ regarding limits for allowable costs the operator can recover as cost oil. In some countries, even if income taxes are nominally due, these are paid out of the state's share of production.

The extent to which countries participate directly in projects as equity holders differs. Countries typically retain the right to take equity in a project. Often this is done on a carried interest basis, whereby the cost of the equity is paid back to the company out of production proceeds. However, many countries do not actually exercise their right to equity participation or at least not fully, in part due to the costly financial obligations that can arise from project participation, particularly when the equity interest requires the country to meet cash calls and to make other cash payments.

Some regional patterns are also apparent. In Africa, about one-half of the surveyed countries rely on production sharing. Of the other half with a tax/royalty regime, some apply a resource rent tax in addition to the corporate income tax. In Asia, production-sharing arrangements are widespread. Only a few countries in the Pacific use resource rent taxes. In the Western Hemisphere, production sharing is quite rare outside of the Caribbean, and very few countries apply resource rent taxes. There are also several Latin American countries that have reduced tax rates noticeably over the last couple of years—particularly Argentina, Chile, and Peru—to attract investment. In the Middle East, the majority of countries rely on some form of production sharing, which is also common among the surveyed transition countries.

Evolution of Selected Fiscal Regimes

The evolution of fiscal regimes for upstream oil and gas activities in four diverse countries (Norway, Indonesia, Kazakhstan, and Angola), summarized in the Appendix, provide some insights into how oil and gas taxation varies over time and across countries.

There are four main features of the dynamic evolution of these fiscal regimes. First, the fiscal terms appear to have been influenced by oil prices, becoming more generous in periods of price decline and vice versa. As declining world oil prices lead to expectations of lower profitability and reduced investment activities, there is some evidence that host country governments have responded to this by offering more attractive fiscal conditions. Whether this observation is generalized to most oil- and gas-producing countries in periods of sustained petroleum price changes remains to be confirmed. If so, it would imply that conservative oil and gas revenue projections should reflect an assumption of relaxed fiscal terms along with projected persistently lower oil and gas prices. Second, fiscal terms have been influenced by tax policies set in the home countries of international petroleum companies. For example, Indonesia modified the terms of its production-sharing contracts in 1978 in response to the U.S. Internal Revenue Service (IRS) that disallowed a tax credit for "income taxes paid" by the Indonesian government on behalf of American companies, and Norway raised the Special Tax rate and restricted capital depreciation provisions in 1979, following the introduction of the U.S. windfall profits tax. Third, bonuses have become streamlined and less important over time as a method of petroleum revenue collection. Fourth, the case studies suggest that as the petroleum fiscal system matures, the revenue regime becomes more progressive. For example, in 1972, Norway moved from a single-rate royalty regime to a multiple-rate one based on the scale of production. In 1995, Kazakhstan introduced the excess profits tax with a range of rates corresponding to different rates of return brackets. In 1988, Indonesia adopted a progressive production-sharing scheme, where the production split between the contractor and the government depended on the nature of the field and on production volumes. In Angola, the 1988 model production-sharing contract provided five different share parameters between the government and the contractor, based on different rate of return brackets.

An important explanation of the wide difference in fiscal patterns observed across countries lies in their difference in bargaining power when negotiating fiscal terms with international oil and gas companies. In turn, a country's bargaining power is derived from its particular circumstances. The strictest fiscal regimes tend to be in countries that offer very attractive geological prospects, combined with political and macroeconomic stability (Indonesia is a good example of such a country until recently). While it can be argued that all countries embody some degree of most forms of risk, from political to commercial, certain risks tend to influence the bargaining position, and hence the fiscal terms, more so in some countries than in others.

In Norway, an important risk issue concerns the competitiveness of its oil and gas in highly contested markets. Although characterized by a stable political regime and reasonably strong geological prospects, Norway must compete with several other North Sea producers (the U.K., The Netherlands, and Denmark) to attract international companies' investments in North Sea exploration and production activities. The main market for North Sea oil and gas is Western Europe, a fairly saturated and competitive market. This market-based risk has likely influenced Norway to further focus on its lenient ring-fencing, interest deductibility, and depreciation rules. These provisions are believed to have undermined the effectiveness of the Special Tax, which underscores the importance of combining a tax on excess rents with strict ring-fencing and thin capitalization rules.

Kazakhstan is an investment location characterized by significant resource commercialization risks. Kazakhstan's landlocked geography makes it dependent on either Russian-owned pipelines or its ability to secure investment for, and build, alternative routes (across other jurisdictions) in order to ship its oil and gas to international markets. Transportation fees to the pipeline companies dissipate some of its petroleum sector rents across jurisdictions, leaving fewer rents to be collected by the Kazakh government. Until recently, this weakened the government's bargaining position and led to more relaxed fiscal terms over time, such as streamlined bonuses and the deductibility of bonuses and royalties from the income tax and the excess profits tax. However, this situation changed dramatically following the opening of the private Caspian Pipeline Consortium (CPC) pipeline in late 2001. Faced with a new competitive situation, the Russian pipeline monopoly offered better terms and greater access to Kazakh exporters. Hence, opening of the CPC pipeline has attracted developers by cutting export costs by more than half. In this environment, the Kazakh authorities—who repealed the fiscal stability clause for new contracts in 2002—have been pressing for revisions to long-established contracts (e.g., the Tengiz field) to capture some of the higher earnings. This intensified fiscal pressure might have backfired somewhat since Chevron (the operator of the Tengiz field) recently announced a suspension of the next phase of its field development, involving some US$3 billion in investment, which would have almost doubled production.

Finally, Angola—a country with strong geological prospects (Barrows, 1989)—is an investment location characterized by relatively high-perceived political risks. The fiscal regime concluded between investors and the Angolan government is specific to each production-sharing contract, which includes a tax stability clause. Other terms of the contracts have become more discretionary over time—for instance, model production-sharing contracts used to specify a maximum cost recovery share, an uplift factor, and a depreciation rate for development expenditures. These provisions became determined on a contract-by-contract basis in 1997. Furthermore, the list of expenditures admissible (at the government's discretion) under cost recovery has been expanded.

V. Conclusions

A broad range of fiscal instruments is available to policymakers to design a fiscal regime for the oil sector that will attract investment as well as secure a reasonable share of economic rent for the government. Some may favor greater reliance on production-based levies to ensure a steady stream of revenue for the government. Others would put greater emphasis on profit-based levies to minimize distortions. Most countries have both profit-based and production-based levies. Fiscal terms accepted by a country reflect the negotiating strength and experience of the country, geological prospects, and the track record of previous projects. During negotiations, potential fiscal revenue may be lowered to compensate for particularly high costs of extracting oil, reflected in market, commercial, or political risk premiums.

There is clearly not one optimal fiscal regime suitable for all petroleum projects in all countries. Countries differ, most importantly in regard to exploration, development, and production costs; the size and quality of petroleum deposits; and investor perception of commercial and political risk. Likewise, projects may differ sufficiently that some flexibility is necessary in deriving an appropriate fiscal regime. At times, this could justify a case-by-case approach to project negotiations, though it is desirable that the chosen fiscal framework be sufficiently flexible to respond to unforeseen developments so as to minimize the need for ad hoc changes. These factors will influence the size of the government's revenue take: a country with large proven reserves and low exploration and development costs will be able to negotiate a higher revenue share than a country that has a short, and perhaps somewhat uneven, track record, particularly if there is uncertainty regarding the size, quality, and extraction costs of its petroleum reserves.

Despite these qualifications, it is possible to outline some desirable features to target when designing a fiscal regime for the petroleum sector. Ideally, this should combine some up-front revenue with sufficient progressivity to provide the government with an adequate share of economic rent under variable conditions of profitability. This result can be achieved through a tax-based system combining a corporate income tax with a rate of return-based resource rent tax (or a progressive income tax), and a royalty at a modest level to secure some up-front revenue. However, it could also be achieved by a production-sharing arrangement with a moderately progressive government take linked to product prices or project rate of return. The latter, however, may be more difficult to negotiate for countries with few successfully developed projects. Under those circumstances, a resource rent–based tax system could prove more flexible while requiring less information ex ante about potential project profitability. Still, the capacity of a particular country to competently administer a complex taxation-based system must be taken into account when designing the fiscal regime. Attempts should be made to keep the administrative burden as low as possible, while maintaining sufficient safeguards to counter tax avoidance, particularly the risk from transfer pricing.

The case studies in this paper provide useful insights into the dynamics of fiscal terms. First, there is some evidence that these react endogenously to world petroleum prices, at least to sustained medium-term changes. Second, fiscal terms set by host countries are influenced by tax policies in the home countries of oil and gas companies. Third, there may be some tendency for revenue collection schemes to become more progressive as a country's petroleum fiscal system matures.

The government's share of economic rent can become excessively low as countries compete to attract investment for oil and gas extraction, particularly if the fiscal regime is used to try to compensate for an otherwise unattractive investment environment or high political, market, or commercial risk. Though the pressure to provide generous fiscal terms to attract investment can be almost irresistible, the overall investment climate is a more important determinant for attracting investment than tax factors.[23] Moreover, there must be a lower bound for the government share from oil and gas extraction below which it

---

[23] Tax incentives may also be insufficient in determining a firm's location decision. In a recent survey of 75 multinational companies, including 12 firms in the energy sector, most of the energy firms identified nontax factors, such as geology or market opportunities, as more important for the location of a foreign subsidiary (Wunder, 2001).

would be better for the country to postpone a project rather than forgo a reasonable share of the economic rent.

From the perspective of the multinational oil companies, the primary concern is how attractive the oil and gas prospects are, how the fiscal terms affect their risk, what the expected reward is if petroleum is found, and how these factors—for any particular regime—compare to investment opportunities elsewhere.

Ultimately, there is a market test for each country's fiscal regime— can the country attract investment in its oil and gas sector? If not, the fiscal regime may be inappropriate for the country, given its exploration, development, and production costs; the size and quality of petroleum deposits; and investor's perception of commercial and political risk.

Appendix. Evolution of Petroleum Tax Systems for Selected Countries

Royalties/Cost Oil Limit

Norway   Royalties changed from 10 percent to a range of 8 to 16 percent (1972).

Lifted for new fields (1987).

Royalty will be phased out so that no royalty will be paid after 2005.

Indonesia   Cost recovery limited to 40 percent of annual production (1960–1975).

Abolished after 1973 (oil price crisis of 1973 and U.S. Internal Revenue Service disallowing tax credits for Indonesian corporate taxes paid by Pertamina (the state company)).

Cost recovery feature based on a double-declining balance depreciation method. Period extended from 7 to 14 years (1976).

Royalty in kind, First Tranche Petroleum, a 20 percent portion of oil and gas production to be split (before any deduction of cost recovery) between Pertamina and the contractor. Split ratios vary with the volume of production (1988).

Kazakhstan Fixed royalty (increase in increments of US$10 million over three years starting from US$20 million and remaining at US$40 million the fourth year) and, after four years, 18 percent royalty (25 percent if the nominal return exceeds 17 percent) (1991).

Contracts negotiated include royalty up to 20 percent (1995). Profit-sharing contracts introduced in 1997. Cost recovery parameter is negotiable.

Angola   Cost recovery determined on a contractual basis, but limited to a maximum of 50 percent per year of annual production (1988–1997).

Maximum unspecified after 1997.

Income Tax

Norway   Corporate income tax reduced from 50.8 percent to 28 percent (1992).

Special Tax of 25 percent on full income net of corporate income tax of 50.8 percent (1974–1975, following quadrupling of oil and gas prices), raised to 35 percent (1979–1980, following sharp increases in oil and gas prices and introduction of U.S. windfall profits tax), reduced to 30 percent (1987, following drop in oil and gas prices), raised to 50 percent (1992).

Indonesia   Production net of cost split 65/35 in favor of the government (1960–1975).

Proportion increases from 65 percent past a base level (1972). Minimum government share increases to 85 percent. Introduction of a tax on foreign companies (1974–1975).

Post-tax split of 85/15 in favor of Pertamina is decomposed as follows: contractor's pretax profit share of 34 percent is subject to 45 percent corporate income tax. Also a 20 percent tax on interest, dividends, and royalties after deducting the corporate tax (1978).

Kazakhstan   Maximum corporate income tax of 30 percent (1991).

Angola   Determined on a contractual basis. Equal to 50 percent of the contractor's share in profit oil, reduced by an amount equivalent in volume to the price cap excess fee valued at the market price.

Deductible Expenses

Norway   Special tax relief provisions in the offshore industry abolished (1972).

10 percent depreciation allowance for 15 years on capital (1974–1975). Lower rate and fewer number of years (1979–1980). No longer available (1987).

5 percent depreciation allowance over 6 years allowed as additional depreciation (uplift) under the Special Tax (1992).

Deductibility of financial costs (applied to oil companies, not to individual prospects) limited to 80 percent of external financing. Deficits incurred after January 1, 2002 can be carried forward increased by interest.

Indonesia	Carry forward of unrecovered costs allowed, but no uplift factor. Interest payment on debt not included in recoverable operating costs (1960–1975).

Interest treated as recoverable costs subject to the following limitations: financing must be with nonaffiliates, loans should be obtained at rates not exceeding prevailing commercial rates, financing plans and amounts must be included in each year's budget of operating costs for the prior approval of Pertamina (1976).

Introduction of investment incentives (1974–1975).

Investment credit of 20 percent of production subject to a guarantee to the government of a 49 percent share of gross revenue over the life of the field (1977).

Investment credit decreases to 17 percent subject to a guarantee to the government of a 25 percent share of gross revenue over the life of the field (1984).

Kazakhstan Royalties and signature bonus become deductible from the income tax (1997).

Angola Uplift factor of 1.4 for development expenditures, with subsequent linear depreciation of 20 percent (1988).

Linear depreciation parameter for development expenditures increased to 25 percent for offshore agreements (1991).

Uplift and depreciation parameters no longer specified after 1997.

Exploration expenditure recoverable from unused balance of cost recovery crude oil from each development area after recovery of development and production expenditures. Each year, exploration expenditures are recoverable first from any cost recovery crude oil balance having the most recent date of commercial discovery and then any balance of total exploration expenditure not already recovered is recoverable in sequence from development areas with the next most recent dates of commercial discovery.

5-year loss carryover for development expenditures, after which the contractor's share of crude oil is increased to allow for cost recovery. Indefinite carry forward with no change in cost recovery parameter for other types of expenditure.

Between 1991 and 1997, list of admissible expenditures under cost recovery widens to: technical, health, safety, and environmental audits items (provided by affiliates of the operator or of SONANGOL), and communications studies.

Range of items falling under costs recoverable only with prior approval of SONANGOL has increased.

Ring-Fencing

Norway   50 percent of losses from other activities in Norway deductible from offshore income. No other ring-fencing provision (1974–1975).

Indonesia   Yes.

Kazakhstan   Introduced in 1995.

Angola   For development expenditures.

Resources Rent Tax/Profit Oil

Norway   Not applicable.

Indonesia   Not applicable.

Kazakhstan   Excess profits tax, which starts with a 20 percent internal rate of return and comprises up to 4 rates applicable to thresholds stipulated in individual contracts (1995).

Deductibility of royalties and the signature bonus (1997).

Angola   Development area profit oil is shared between SONANGOL (state company) and the contractor according to the after-tax nominal rate of return achieved in the preceding quarter. The model PSA agreement has five different rates of return (unspecified) brackets with different share parameters.

Other Nontax Payments

Norway   Not applicable.

Indonesia   Bonus payments vary considerably between individual PSCs. Not included in the operating costs, which are recoverable from production, but can be charged against tax liabilities once profitable operations commence (1960–1975).

Signature bonus ranges from US$1 million and US$5 million. There may be 2 to 5 production bonuses triggered by the volume of production. Total bonus commitments range from US$15 million to US$50 million.

Requirements for bonus payments decline sharply over the years. Total bonus payments reported in the 46 PSCs concluded in 1979–1982, US$306 million, are much higher than the total of US$60 million from the 45 PSCs concluded in 1987–1990.

Kazakhstan   Signing, commercial discovery, and mining bonuses (1992).

Signature bonus becomes deductible from the income tax and the excess profits tax. Other bonuses are repealed (1995).

Signature bonus repealed in 1997.

Angola   Signature bonus, to be determined on a contractual basis.

State Equity

Norway   35 percent on a carried interest basis on all new licenses (1969).

The State Direct Financial Interest (SDFI) was established in 1985. Until recently the SDFI has taken a share in all licenses. The policy has now changed and the SDFI only takes a share in prospects with a large expected net present value.

Indonesia   10 percent is usual under a First Tranche Petroleum (FTP) contract.

Kazakhstan   State companies participate up to 50 percent as full working partners—usually carried through exploration.

Angola   SONANGOL must take a minimum of 51 percent of all contracts unless in water depths greater than 150 meters, where this share is reduced.

Fiscal Stability

Norway   Not applicable.

Indonesia   Not applicable.

Kazakhstan   Introduced in 1996, but repealed in 2002 for all new contracts.

Angola   Government is open to revisions subject to the fact that it does not impact negatively on either party's economic benefit. SONANGOL reimburses the contractor for increases in clearance, stamp duty, and/or the statistical levy applicable to imports.

Government-Set Price for Cost Recovery and/or Tax Calculations

Norway — Price of the same type of crude over a given period determined by independent traders on a free market (1974–1975).

Norm prices used for calculating income for tax purposes are set by an independent Norm Price Board.

Indonesia — Set according to an OPEC-type guide price (1972).

Set on the basis of monthly average spot prices for a basket of five internationally traded crude oils (1988).

Kazakhstan — Not applicable.

Angola — Not applicable.

Bibliography

Baer, Katherine, Victoria P. Summers, and Emil M. Sunley, 1996, "A Destination VAT for CIS Trade," *Moct-Most*, Vol. 6, No. 3, pp. 87–106. Also, IMF Working Paper 96/35 (Washington: International Monetary Fund).

Barrows, Gordon, 1988, "A Survey of Incentives in Recent Petroleum Contracts," in *Petroleum Investment Policies in Developing Countries*, ed. by N. Beredjick and T. Wälde (London: Graham & Trotman).

———, 1997, *World Fiscal Systems for Oil* (Calgary: The Barrows Company Inc.).

———, 2000a, *Angola: 1988 Model Production Sharing Agreement Between SONANGOL and International Companies; 1991 Model Production Sharing Agreement for Deep Water Blocks Between SONANGOL and International Companies; 1992 Model Production Contract; 1997 Model Production Sharing Agreement Between Sociedade Nacionale de Combustiveis de Angola—Unidade Economica Estatal (Sonangol, UUE) and Contractor* (Calgary: The Barrows Company Inc.).

———, 2000b, *Kazakhstan: Tax Decree of the President of Kazakhstan dated 25 April 1995 as amended on 28 February 1997* (Calgary: The Barrows Company Inc.).

Baunsgaard, Thomas, 2001, "A Primer on Mineral Taxation," IMF Working Paper 01/139 (Washington: International Monetary Fund).

Coopers & Lybrand, 1998, *International Tax Summaries* (New York: John Wiley & Sons Inc.).

Daniel, Philip, 1995, "Evaluating State Participation in Mineral Projects: Equity, Infrastructure and Taxation," in *Taxation of Mineral Enterprises*, ed. by J. Otto (London: Graham & Trotman).

Frewer, Geoff, 2000, "Auctions vs. Discretion in the Licensing of Oil and Gas Acreage," in *The International Experience: Markets, Regulations and the Environment*, ed. by G. MacKerron and P. Pearson (London: Imperial College Press).

Gao, Zhiguo, 1994, "International Petroleum Contracts: Current Trends and New Directions," International Energy and Resources Law and Policy Series (London: Graham & Trotman).

International Bureau of Fiscal Documentation, *African Tax Systems* (Amsterdam, various editions).

————, *Taxation and Investment in Asia and the Pacific* (Amsterdam, various editions).

————, *Taxation and Investment in Central and East European Countries* (Amsterdam, various editions).

————, *Taxation and Investment in the Caribbean* (Amsterdam, various editions).

————, *Taxation and Investment in the Middle East* (Amsterdam, various editions).

————, *Taxation in Latin America* (Amsterdam, various editions).

Kemp, A.G., 1987, *Petroleum Rent Collection Around the World* (Halifax: The Institute for Research on Public Policy).

Machmud, T.N., 2000, *The Indonesian Production Sharing Contract* (The Hague: Kluwer Law International).

Nellor, David C.L., and Emil M. Sunley, 1994, "Fiscal Regimes for Natural Resource Producing Developing Countries," IMF Paper on Policy Analysis and Assessment 94/24 (Washington: International Monetary Fund).

Noreng, Øystein, 2002, "The Concept of Economic Resource Rent and Its Application in U.K. and Norwegian Petroleum Taxation," expert testimony for the Centre for Energy Studies, BI Norwegian School of Management, Sandvika, Norway.

Page, Bill, 2002, "Kazakhstan's New Tax Code," *Tax Notes International*, January 21.

Palmer, Keith F., 1980, "Mineral Taxation Policies in Developing Countries: An Application of Resource Rent Tax," *Staff Papers*, International Monetary Fund, Vol. 27, No. 3, pp. 517–42.

PricewaterhouseCoopers, 1999, *Corporate Taxes 1999–2000* (New York: John Wiley and Sons).

Sunley, Emil M., and Thomas Baunsgaard, 2001, *The Tax Treatment of the Mining Sector: An IMF Perspective*, presentation at the World Bank and International Finance Corporation Workshop on Sustainability and the Governance of Mining Revenue Sharing, Washington, April.

Van Meurs, Pedro, 1988, "Financial and Fiscal Arrangements for Petroleum Development—An Economic Analysis," in *Petroleum Investment Policies in Developing Countries*, ed. by N. Beredjick and T. Wälde (London: Graham & Trotman).

Wunder, Haroldene, 2001, "The Effect of International Tax Policy on Business Location Decisions," *Tax Notes International*, Vol. 24 (December 24), pp. 1331–55.

7

National Oil Companies: Evolution, Issues, Outlook

CHARLES MCPHERSON

I. Introduction

Oil is of special importance to developing countries. It accounts for very high percentages of GDP, government revenues, and foreign exchange earnings in many of the countries where it is produced. In importing countries, it typically accounts for a significant share of foreign exchange expenditures, and in all countries in the developing world, taxes on oil consumption contribute importantly to fiscal revenues.

How well the oil sector performs in these countries depends critically on industry structure and patterns of ownership. More often than not, the national oil company (NOC) plays a central role in determining outcomes.

This paper examines the origins and evolution of NOCs, the issues they have raised, and the outlook for their future.

There has been surprisingly little systematic research on NOCs. Literature on NOCs is limited, their importance notwithstanding, and organized, comprehensive data is virtually nonexistent.[1] This paper, then, is an initial essay. Its arguments are based on "armchair empiricism" rather than rigorous analysis, and should be regarded more as testable hypotheses than research findings. Motivated by the relevance

---

[1]Discussion of NOCs, where it does occur, tends to be embedded in books or articles whose main topic is something other than NOCs, at least in the sense they are dealt with in this paper. Mommer (2002), which includes a discussion of the political economy of Mexico's Pemex and Venezuela's Petróleos de Venezuela S.A. (PDVSA), is one recent example.

of NOCs to the economic performance of many of its client countries, and by the limited work done to date, the World Bank now has further research under way.

II. The Origins and Evolution of NOCs

NOCs date back to the 1920s when Yacimientos Petrolíferos Fiscales (YPF) was founded in Argentina. Petróleos Mexicanos (Pemex) came a bit later in the 1930s. The major increase in numbers of NOCs, however, occurred in the 1970s, triggered by a worldwide tide of nationalism and enthusiasm for state intervention and ownership. The Organization of Petroleum Exporting Countries (OPEC) was formed at that time, and its members were stunningly successful in wresting control of international oil markets from the international oil companies, and in dramatically increasing oil prices.

Oil was viewed as a commodity of strategic importance, or, to borrow from Lenin, and a recent book title, as one of the "commanding heights" of the economy (Yergin and Stanislaw, 1998). As such, oil was considered as something the government must control. Legislation and regulation were not thought sufficient for this purpose. Direct participation through ownership was regarded as key in this regard, and NOCs proliferated. NOCs were expected to operate "upstream," that is, in oil exploration and production, as well as "downstream," that is, in crude oil refining, product importing, and marketing. Upstream, the principal motivation for NOCs was the creation (through OPEC action) and capture of a large share of the economic rents associated with oil production. Interest in NOC involvement downstream in oil-producing countries stemmed from a pursuit of the value added to production by refining and marketing activities. In oil-importing countries, the oil shocks of the 1970s and concern for supply security moved oil to center stage and led to the creation of downstream NOCs. In both oil-exporting and oil-importing countries, interest in a downstream role for the NOCs also revolved around gaining control over the pricing of petroleum products to final consumers, an area of great political and social sensitivity.

Today, there are more than 100 NOCs, found in almost all oil-exporting and many oil-importing developing countries. The early years saw NOCs established in a number of OECD countries—the United Kingdom, Canada, Norway, and Denmark—as well as in the developing world.

NOCs in developing countries quickly became the focal point for accomplishing a broad range of national economic, social, and political objectives that went well beyond their original sector-focused objectives. These roles expanded rapidly based on perceptions of almost limitless cash available to the NOCs, their size (often the largest local enterprises by a wide margin), and their near monopoly on local technical and commercial talent.

At the same time, NOCs were expected to emulate the international oil companies (IOCs) in the areas of technical and managerial skills and the ability to generate profits, with the aim of either effectively counterbalancing the local influence of the IOCs, or of replacing the IOCs altogether.

While high real oil prices lasted, both the NOCs and their governments believed it was possible to accomplish both noncommercial and commercial objectives. Politics, however, meant that priority was assigned to the achievement of social, economic, and political goals; and the cracks that began to emerge with respect to attainment of commercial goals were ignored, papered over by massive cash flows.

The oil crisis of 1986, the dramatic revenue drops associated with it, and continued lower real oil prices exposed these cracks and the incompatibility of the dual roles the NOCs were expected to play (Figure 7.1). As a consequence, the late 1980s and the 1990s saw concerns increasingly expressed with respect to the commercial performance of the NOCs, and, at the same time, the wisdom of the noncommercial agendas assigned to the NOCs was increasingly challenged.

This debate has led to a reconsideration of the NOCs' role and a closer look at their organization and management. Some NOCs have disappeared, or have had their roles reduced, as a result of full or partial privatization. Others have gone through wide-ranging commercialization exercises. But so far, most NOCs remain a major presence in their home countries, and, as a group, they continue to have a significant influence on the international oil industry. NOCs control 90 percent of world oil reserves and account for 73 percent of production. And 25 of the world's top 50 oil companies are NOCs.[2] "Getting it right" with respect to NOCs can be expected to have major political, social, and developmental consequences.

---

[2] Petroleum Intelligence Weekly (2000).

Figure 7.1. *Oil Prices*
(Crude oil price in U.S. dollars per barrel)

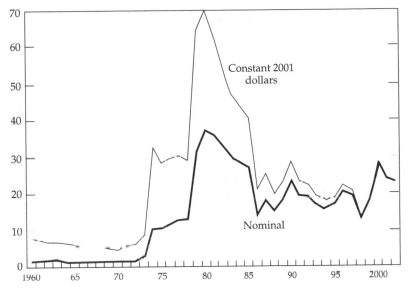

Source: World Bank.

III. Issues

This section looks at the wide range of NOC-related issues that have arisen over their past 30 years of history. Most of these issues are interrelated. They include commercial efficiency, noncommercial objectives, governance, cash requirements, and conflict of interest.

Commercial Efficiency

With few exceptions, the NOCs score poorly in this area. A recent management audit of Pertamina, Indonesia's NOC, exposed losses of over US$2 billion per year,[3] an amount equal to 10 percent of the national budget. A similar audit of the Nigerian National Petroleum Company (NNPC) estimated losses at between US$800 million and US$1 billion annually (World Bank, 2000a). The Pertamina audit calculated

---

[3]PricewaterhouseCoopers (1998).

direct production costs of US$5.50 a barrel for Pertamina's own-oper-
ated production versus an industry average of US$1.20, a significant
gap.[4] A casual comparison of SOCAR, Azerbaijan's NOC, with Mobil,[5]
a major IOC operator in Central Asia, suggests that the NOCs have a
long way to go if they are to catch up with IOCs in efficiency. At the time
of comparison, both SOCAR and Mobil employed about 65,000 people,
but Mobil operated in 100 countries, not one country; produced 1.6 million barrels per day of crude oil compared to SOCAR's 100,000 barrels
per day; and operated 33 refineries compared to SOCAR's two.[6]

Losses due to inefficiencies may be expected in both the upstream
and downstream operations of the NOCs. Upstream operations attract
a lot of attention because of the sheer volume of revenues generated at
that level. However, NOC losses frequently appear to be concentrated
downstream. Daunting technological and financial challenges have
caused most NOCs to opt for joint ventures or other forms of contract
with the IOCs in upstream operations. IOC operatorship of these ventures ensures efficiency standards will be at or close to the IOCs' own,
thus minimizing losses, at least at the project level (overhead inefficiencies at the NOC may be unaffected). Downstream, the story is often
very different. Although the situation has begun to change, NOCs, in
many countries, have held virtual monopoly positions over petroleum
refining, transportation and storage, and imports. A report commis-
sioned by the World Bank in 1993, but whose findings are still considered to be robust, put annual losses attributable to inefficient NOC
operations in sub-Saharan Africa at over US$1.4 billion, an amount that
was equivalent at the time to the World Bank's entire sub-Saharan
lending program in all sectors.[7]

A variety of factors have contributed to the low levels of commercial
efficiency in NOCs. Lack of competition to the NOCs, especially downstream, is surely an important cause. A major 10-year study recently
released by McKinsey,[8] the management consultants, found that lack of
competition was the key factor in explaining enterprise underperfor-
mance in developing countries. Other causes, issues in themselves,

---

[4] Part of this difference may be explained by economies of scale. Pertamina's own-
operated production is small relative to industry averages. Directionally, however, the
finding is expected to be robust.

[5] Now ExxonMobil.

[6] The list could go on. See, for example, the analysis of YPF in Shaikh (1996).

[7] Findings are summarized in Schloss (1993).

[8] McKinsey, Presentation at the World Bank, March 2002.

such as the assignment of noncommercial objectives to NOCs, and governance issues, discussed next, have also been important explanatory factors.

Noncommercial Objectives

As already suggested, noncommercial objectives—whether social, economic, or political—featured importantly on NOC agendas almost from the outset, and have since become far-reaching. A nonexhaustive list might include the following:

- *Job creation.* Oil is a capital-, not labor-intensive, industry. Yet most states have looked to their oil sectors, and their NOCs in particular, to provide employment, presumably on the presumption that the NOCs can afford to do this. Typically higher than industry average employee per barrel or employee per dollar of net income for NOCs bears witness to the governments' success in this area. Many of those employed have very low productivity, either because they are not needed, or because they have not had the necessary training or education.
- *Local capacity.* NOCs are almost invariably expected to develop local technical, commercial, and managerial capacity in the oil sector, the oil services and supply sector, and beyond. They are often not well equipped to take on this role because of their limited operational experience (upstream) or because of their constrained ability to operate commercially (see the discussion on "Governance" below). A common approach to developing the service and supply sector is to incorporate these activities into the NOC either on a 100 percent basis or an affiliated basis, a practice that creates problems of its own (see the discussion on "Conflict of Interest" below).
- *Social infrastructure.* NOCs may be asked to fund and directly support local schools, hospitals, and related community services—activities that can be expensive and that take them well outside their core competencies. Pemex is famous for its support in these areas. In Russia, withdrawal of NOC support of this type was one of the most contentious aspects of the privatization of Russia's several state oil companies.
- *Regional development.* Local roads, bridges, airports, telecommunications, and water would all come under this heading.
- *Income redistribution/transfers.* The most common example of this is a government-imposed, politically popular requirement to sell pe-

troleum products locally at prices that are below—and usually well below—market levels. The costs of such policies, initially to the NOC but ultimately to government, can be enormous. The annual cost of Pertamina's subsidies has been calculated at US$3 billion, or 15 percent of the budget. Similar policies implemented by NIOC in Iran impose costs that are conservatively estimated to equate to 10 percent of the country's GDP.[9]

- *State borrowing.* Using the leverage of their oil, NOCs may be asked to raise finance for government for non-oil activities. This is common practice in many countries. Sonangol's regular approaches to the capital markets on behalf of the government of Angola provide just one example.

These objectives are considered the proper province of government in most countries, but in oil-producing countries NOCs have been enlisted to perform them because of the cash they control, and because of their perceived capacity, a perception that may not be true in absolute terms, but is probably correct in relative terms. Time has shown that the NOCs cannot discharge these obligations and at the same time develop commercially. Noncommercial obligations drain the cash flow needed for reinvestment and distract management attention from its proper business.

Governance

Weak governance has also undermined the performance of NOCs. More often than not, transparency, accountability, commercial oversight, management structures, and commercial "signaling" are all lacking.

Where there is only one shareholder, that is, government, NOCs are subject to little pressure to be transparent in their operations. Indeed, it may often be more convenient to their owners to obscure the uses to which funds are put, many of which uses may have been politically or personally motivated. Few NOCs to date publish accounts that are either consistent with International Accounting Standards, or independently or externally audited.[10] Internal financial controls—accounting

---

[9]See Gupta and others, Chapter 15 in this volume; and Espinasa, Chapter 16 in this volume.

[10]It is noteworthy that net income figures are available for only 6 of the 25 NOCs that rank among the world's top 50 oil companies.

and management information systems and internal audit functions—are often lax for the same reasons.

Reluctance to relinquish political influence over NOCs or surrender discretionary control over the use of NOC funds has led politicians to (i) deliberately avoid clarity concerning the NOC's organizational positioning in the government structure; (ii) put in place politically constituted Boards of Directors, without requisite professionalism or independence; and (iii) obstruct the formation of adequately capitalized or independent enterprises, or business units within enterprises with incentives to act commercially. Budget procedures often require that NOCs return all revenues to the government, forcing the NOCs to rely on uncertain annual allocations to finance ongoing operations or new investments, and severely limiting their ability to plan or even to meet their existing obligations to financiers or joint venture partners in a predictable and timely fashion.

Examples of this type of behavior abound. Government's concern to exercise more direct political control over NNPC in Nigeria resulted in NNPC being without a board of any kind for 10 years. More recently, in Venezuela a highly professional board and management team at PDVSA, very rare in the world of NOCs, was replaced with a hand-picked political team. While NNPC established Strategic Business Units (SBUs) within its organization some time ago, these have never been adequately funded and have been obliged to seek authorization for even relatively minor expenditures. Further, the incentive system in place has neither rewarded good performance nor sanctioned poor performance (for example, most SBUs operate on a cost pass-through basis), making it difficult to hold them accountable. As a result, NNPC has operated more like a government department than a commercial entity. Although this appears about to change, Nigeria also provides an example of the damage annual government budget dependence can do to planning and financing. The same situation exists in Mexico, where draconian taxes effectively confiscate all of Pemex's net income and force Pemex into virtually continuous item-by-item negotiation of its budget with the ministry of finance, often under very nontransparent circumstances.

The intrusion of government into the governance of NOCs has clearly hampered achievement of commercial objectives. It has also led to NOCs being commonly referred to as "states within states." The lack of transparency and accountability in the NOC—the government's "cash cow"—has made it possible for government to adopt the same traits, causing an erosion of governance at the country level, with negative consequences for economic and social development and political stability. This is the "resource curse" that has attracted so much attention in research and policy debate in recent years.[11]

Cash Requirements

NOCs may be attractive to their governments for the cash they generate, but they are also very cash hungry. Oil is a cash- and capital-intensive industry and the budgetary demands of NOCs are often very large relative to the requirements of other sectors, particularly social sectors such as education and health, and even physical infrastructure, such as transport. As a result of the competition for funding, oil sector investments are likely to be delayed or less than optimal, and social needs, frequently urgent, may go unmet. Figure 7.2 illustrates dramatically the dilemma posed by NNPC's financing requirements.

Mexico faces an even more extreme situation. Without massive new investments, oil production in Mexico will begin to decline. Yet over the same time period, the government expects the demand for new social and physical infrastructure to mushroom as the country's very young and rapidly growing population matures. While it may have been possible in the past, with difficulty, to address both needs, it will be impossible in the future to fund both Pemex and the country's non-oil priorities.

The issue is especially worthy of debate because: (i) under appropriate terms and conditions most oil-producing countries will have no problems in attracting private sector investment; and (ii) progress in petroleum tax design has made it possible for governments to efficiently collect a major share of oil rents from the private sector through the tax system without investing themselves (through the NOC) and without investment risk.[12] The risks associated with the oil business, which are by no means confined to the exploration phase, have led many to question whether investment in the sector constitutes an appropriate use of public funds.[13]

---

[11]Karl (1997) contains an excellent discussion of the relationship between NOCs and their governments and the consequences for governance at the country level.

[12]See Sunley, Baunsgaard, and Simard, Chapter 6 in this volume. For an explicit discussion of the trade-off between taxes and NOC participation in the Nigerian context, see World Bank (2000c).

[13]An interesting counterargument is sometimes encountered, namely that investments in the oil sector, at least when these are made in the context of joint ventures with IOCs, are more secure than public investments outside the sector, which are often wasted or abused.

Figure 7.2. *Competing Budgetary Allocations in Nigeria, FY 2002*[1]
(In billions of naira)

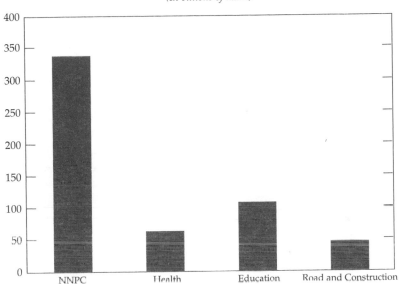

Sources: Central Bank of Nigeria; and IMF staff estimates.
[1]Funding for social programs and infrastructure is for federal spending (current and capital) only. An unknown amount of funding also occurs at the state level.

Conflict of Interest

NOCs in many countries are expected to formulate and implement oil sector policy, and to enforce sector regulations. Even where other government ministries and agencies exist to perform these functions, they more often than not lack the resources, expertise, and political support necessary to carry them out, and the NOC by default becomes more or less involved, giving rise to a range of potential conflict of interest situations.

It is hardly appropriate for a major player in the sector at the same time to be writing sector policy and enforcing the rules of the game. This "poacher turned gamekeeper" type of arrangement will almost certainly tilt the playing field against existing or potential private sector participants, and is highly likely to prove detrimental to protection of the public interest.

The harm arising from this conflict of interest situation will vary widely, depending on the precise nature of the tasks delegated to the

NOC, but may include preferential treatment of the NOC's own operations; preferential allocation of exploration acreage and development approvals; discretionary penalties or waivers related to the enforcement of regulations; and extortion of benefits arising from control over permitting.

One particularly contentious area relates to the promotion of local capacity and content, a role that, as noted earlier, is often assigned to the NOC. Typically, this involves employment policies, and procurement of goods and services for oil operations. The risk is that this role will encourage cronyism in the advancement of employment candidates and unwarranted preference to local enterprises in the supply of goods and services, which are often affiliated, formally or informally, with the NOC and/or its management. In at least two major oil-producing countries, Angola and Indonesia, IOC operators have estimated that this kind of distortion of the procurement process has occasioned delays and increased industry standard costs in the order of 25 percent to 30 percent, while at the same time creating unnecessary tensions between the IOC and NOC. The increased costs represent a diversion of revenues away not only from IOC profits but also from the government's budget to the NOC and/or its affiliates.

Setting the Stage for Reform

Widespread recognition of the foregoing issues and ills has set the stage for oil sector reform and a reconsideration of the role and functions of the NOC in a growing number of countries. The conditions existing in Argentina in the early 1990s, just before the country embarked on a sweeping oil sector reform program, echo the discussion above. The list of concerns at the time included poor YPF performance against standard industry benchmarks; declining reserve additions and production; a wide range of noncore, noncommercial obligations; frequent political interference; urgent competing claims on the budget; and the "poacher-gamekeeper" issue. The same list could be, and indeed has been, drawn up for the oil sector in many other countries.

IV. Outlook

A considerable variety of remedies have been proposed and/or adopted in response to the issues just reviewed, and together they suggest the future outlook for the NOCs. They are discussed below, following the order of topics in the preceding section.

Commercial Efficiency

Remedies to the observed commercial inefficiencies of NOCs cover a broad range and include these items:

- *Benchmarking.* Comparison of key indicators of operating and financial efficiency between the NOC and IOCs. To maximize the impact of this exercise, the comparisons should be made public. Pemex and several other large NOCs conduct benchmarking exercises on a regular basis, but the results are rarely published. Benchmarking is normally done by qualified international consultants.
- *Limited competition.* Limited competition among NOCs, which may be independent of one another, or different subsidiaries of a single NOC holding company. China has adopted this approach by setting up competition among its three government-owned oil companies—CNPC, Sinopec, and CNOOC.
- *Unrestricted competition.* Competition of the NOC with private sector operators. Ideally, a level playing field should apply, but in practice the NOC often enjoys preferential status. Unrestricted competition is most common in the retail phase—petroleum product marketing—but can be observed upstream as well, for example in Brazil, where private sector companies can compete successfully against Petrobras for exploration and production licenses, and in Nigeria where the government has announced a program of licensing for "green field" private sector refinery construction, that is, new refinery competition to existing NOC refinery capacity.
- *Joint ventures.* As noted earlier, unincorporated joint ventures between the NOC and IOCs, or more rarely, the domestic private sector, are commonplace in the upstream sector. Thirty-four out of 49, or 70 percent, of the oil-producing developing countries recently surveyed by the World Bank had adopted joint ventures in one form or another in their upstream sectors (Bacon, 1999). The NOC is seldom the operator, but benefits from the technical, managerial, and commercial skills of its partner(s).
- *Partial privatization.* Sale of part of the NOC to a "strategic investor" or to the public. Sale to a strategic investor on a bid or negotiated

basis is usually, but not always, of a controlling interest and brings many of the same advantages as an unincorporated joint venture covered above. Partial sale to the public does not typically involve the loss of control associated with the sale to a strategic investor, but does bring the discipline of the stock market to bear on the NOC's commercial performance. It also has the broader positive impact of helping to develop local capital markets.

- *Divestiture of nonperforming or noncore assets.* The first of these assets to go should be those outside the oil and gas business, but many ancillary activities in the service and supply areas should be considered for divestiture as well. A common feature of NOC reform programs, divestiture of noncore assets allows management to focus on activities where it has, or should have, a comparative advantage. The divested assets as well as the retained assets can be expected to perform better under new owners prepared to give them more focused attention. Divestiture of Sonatrach's noncore assets is one of the central features of Algeria's ongoing program to improve efficiency at its NOC.

- *Full privatization.* Transfer of the NOC in its entirety to the private sector through sale to a strategic investor, the public, or a combination of the two. Because it means a complete break with state ownership, and the multiple conflicting roles associated with that ownership, full privatization can be expected to be more effective than other remedies in delivering commercial efficiency. However, it can also be expected to be the most difficult remedy to "sell." Opponents of privatization range from those who are ideologically opposed to private ownership, through nationalists, who suspect that privatization will result in at least partial foreign ownership and domination, to those who are directly interested in preserving the status quo, including employees, beneficiaries of the noncommercial services provided by NOCs, and other less defensible stakeholders who have used nontransparency and/or conflicting NOC roles for their own political or personal ends. The mechanism used to privatize has proven to be one of the keys to success. A number of different approaches have been suggested or implemented. Political palatability is critical and depends on, among other things: (i) placing ownership at least in part in the hands of deserving stakeholders, such as employees and their pension funds, local regions, or communities; (ii) a social safety net for those disadvantaged groups adversely affected by privatization (Gupta, Schiller, and Ma, 1999); (iii) transparent and worthwhile use of the proceeds of privatization; and (iv) a transaction structured to produce early improvements in performance. The privatization mechanisms adopted in three Latin American countries and Russia illustrate the options, good and bad (Box 7.1).

Focusing solely on the efficiency issue is unlikely to meet with success absent parallel action on other fronts, for example, noncommercial obligations, governance, and conflict of interest, as discussed next.

Noncommercial Obligations

Most NOC reform "packages" transfer noncommercial social, economic, and political functions to the government, thus leaving the NOC free to get on with commercial activities. Weaning noncommercial activities from their dependency on NOCs can be very difficult, however. Careful attention needs to be paid to the transition period. Best practice usually includes transitional social safety nets for those individuals or institutions—employees, schools, hospitals, and so on—most negatively impacted by the withdrawal of NOC support. Government's concern over the lack of viable alternatives to employment at SOCAR is one of the main obstacles to the launch of an NOC reform program in Azerbaijan. The transfer of noncommercial obligations away from NOCs will not be successful unless the institutions taking over from the NOCs are adequately funded, staffed, and managed.

Governance

Transparency is a critical ingredient to good governance and starts with the NOC's publication of properly prepared and externally audited accounts. Transparency is not only important for its contribution to governance, it is a sine qua non for access to commercial finance based on a balance sheet assessment, rather than oil-backed or sovereign basis. Until the NOCs are in the position to raise finance on this basis, they will not have closed the gap between themselves and the IOCs.

If anything less than full privatization is contemplated, commercialization of the NOC will also be essential to ensuring good governance. Commercialization implies an adequately constituted Board of Directors capable of providing independent and objective oversight and di-

Box 7.1. *NOC Privatization Options*

Argentina (YPF)	Noncore activities sold to employees/private sector investors.
	YPF shares distributed 55 percent, 35 percent, 10 percent to federal and provincial governments and employees, respectively.
	Federal and provincial governments to sell 50 percent of shares on international capital markets in three years.
	Licensing terms enhanced to attract private sector.
	NOC/public "buy-in." Substantial new investment.
Bolivia (YPFB)	YPFB divided into three independent companies.
	50 percent of each transferred to a strategic private sector investor.
	Bids based on investment in the corporation ("capitalization") rather than purchase of assets.
	Government share transferred to Bolivian public through pension fund.
	Politically sensitive privatization of downstream activities deferred to later date.
Brazil (Petrobras)	Partial privatization. Government share reduced from 82 percent to 50 percent. Retention of state ownership politically palatable.
	Shares sold to local and international private sector, individual, and institutional investors.
	Future sales will focus on providing local benefits from sales proceeds.
	Petrobras management reorganized to be more competitive. Question mark persists over state-appointed management.
Russia (State Vertically Integrated Companies)	Controlling interests in state companies mortgaged on noncompetitive basis to private investor groups.
	Government option to reacquire debt lapsed and ownership passed to private sector.
	Nontransparent process deeply resented by the public.

rection. Commercialization also means profit-oriented internal restructuring, creating business units that are adequately capitalized or
funded and independent, yet accountable. Strong internal financial
oversight and corporate planning functions are equally important. Finally, an NOC cannot behave commercially unless it is allowed to retain net cash flow adequate to meet current and near-term obligations
and plan over a reasonable time horizon.[14]

Cash Requirements

Consideration of competing demands on public funds can be a key
determinant in deciding on a move to partial or full NOC privatization.
The privatization transaction itself may bring in considerable cash on a
one-time basis, but equally importantly, privatization reduces or eliminates significant annual demands on the budget.

More commonly than through outright privatization, governments
reduce the oil sector's demands on the budget by relying on NOC contracts with the private sector structured to delay or avoid altogether
NOC equity contributions to operations. So-called "carried interest"
provisions, or production-sharing contracts, are typical. Transferring
part of the financing burden to the private sector in this way is financially equivalent to partial privatization—the nominal equity share of
the state is shifted to the private sector along with full risks and, since
the private sector will require it, an appropriate award.

Finally, shifting financing to the private sector IOCs, which have
much better access to finance than most NOCs or their governments,
has the benefit of reducing the overall cost of operations.[15]

Conflict of Interest

The simple solution to the conflict of interest issue is to transfer policy and regulation roles from the NOC to government, ideally to a min-

---

[14]Sometimes a "catch-22" dilemma gets in the way of satisfying this requirement.
Good governance may depend on the right to retain an adequate share of net cash flow,
while that right may be denied by government or the legislature on the grounds that
governance in the NOC is weak.

[15]Petroleum Finance Company (2002). The highest cost of finance probably occurs
when NOCs, unable to access commercial finance, turn to their IOC partners for loans.

istry and a quasi-independent regulatory agency, respectively, leaving the NOC with a primarily or purely commercial role. This is more easily said than done, given the likely resistance of entrenched interests, and the all too common failure to provide the ministry or agency involved with the capacity, resources, salaries, and skills necessary to perform these roles properly.

Difficult as it may be to put into practice, the triangular configuration of roles recommended here, sometimes referred to as the "Norwegian Trinity Model," is proving effective in a number of countries. In Norway, policy and licensing, and, in collaboration with the Ministry of Finance, petroleum taxation and related fiscal issues, are the responsibility of the Ministry of Petroleum. The Norwegian Petroleum Directorate, reporting to the Ministry of Petroleum, but with considerable independence on matters under its jurisdiction, provides advice to the ministry on technical matters and is responsible for the management of all technical data and the enforcement of technical regulations. The NOC, Statoil, is expected to focus on commercial operations, a role that was recently reinforced through partial privatization. NOCs in countries adopting this model appear to be performing better than those in countries where roles are blurred.

Reform Strategies

Just as reference to one country's prereform circumstances helped summarize the various NOC issues urging reform, reference to one country's reform strategy (again Argentina's, and again not unique to Argentina) helps bring together the range of remedies that may be adopted to address those issues. Reacting to the deteriorating sector conditions described earlier, the Argentine government implemented a strategy in the early 1990s that called for limiting government's role to sector policy, legislation, and regulation; withdrawing government from commercial operations through the privatization of YPF and its oil service and noncore subsidiaries; introducing fiscal and other incentives to enhance private sector participation and competition; and deregulating downstream markets. The strategy was a success, resulting in substantial savings for government, efficiency gains, new entry into the sector, and a significant increase in investment.

Box 7.2 summarizes a number of recent or ongoing NOC reform initiatives, suggesting not only their future but the possible future of other NOCs that have yet to act.

Box 7.2. *Recent and Ongoing NOC Reform Initiatives*
(1990s and Current)

Algeria	Divestiture of policy and regulatory roles from Sonatrach. Commercialization of Sonatrach. Private sector entry to all phases of business. Downstream price deregulation.
Argentina	Privatization of YPF and Gas del Estado. Promotion of private sector participation.
Bolivia	Privatization of YPFB. Promotion of private sector participation.
Brazil	Partial privatization of Petrobras. Commercialization of Petrobras. Promotion of private sector participation.
China	Partial privatization of NOCs through sale of shares. Creation of three competing NOCs
Indonesia	Withdrawal of Pertamina's monopoly. Commercialization of Pertamina. New entry encouraged. End downstream price distortions.
Nigeria	Planned privatization of downstream activities. Commercialization of NNPC.
Russia	Privatization of state-owned companies.

V. Summary and Concluding Remarks

The environment in which the NOCs find themselves has changed enormously since they were first formed in the 1970s.

Firstly, the environment has become much more commercially demanding. It is not enough to control the resources to be profitable. Real oil prices are down sharply, and all firms, including the NOCs, must increasingly rely on technical and managerial skills and agility to survive and operate efficiently.

Secondly, the expectations of civil society with respect to government and state-owned enterprises, and NOCs in particular, given the volume of revenues they control, have changed and go well beyond bottom-line profitability, demanding, in addition to efficiency, transparency and accountability.

Thirdly, perceptions of oil as one of the "commanding heights" are changing. Broad, deep, and competitive global markets for both crude oil and petroleum products have resulted in the commoditization of oil, reducing its strategic value to many market participants. Further, new organizational models have emerged that rely successfully on competition, private sector participation, and light-handed but efficient regulation to protect the public interest, rather than relying on state ownership.

While a significant number of NOCs have yet to take concrete steps to catch up with their changed environment, a growing number have begun a process of profound change. In some countries, the NOC has altogether or effectively disappeared through privatization, for example, in Argentina, Bolivia, Canada, Peru, and the United Kingdom. In others, partial privatization, commercialization of the NOC, and increased direct private sector participation have been the adopted route to reform. This route has been followed or is under active discussion in Brazil, Indonesia, Nigeria, and Pakistan.

NOC reform programs face serious obstacles: ideological opposition, nationalism, entrenched interests, and suspicion. To be successful, these programs will need to have support from the top, and, at the same time, from a wide range of public opinion. Normally, they will have to be part of a broader package of economic, political, and social reform. They will need to be carefully designed to ensure the institutional capacity is there to take on the roles the NOC divests itself of, and, during the transition period, to safeguard deserving stakeholders who may be adversely affected by change in policies.

These are still the "early days," but the evidence available to date suggests that the new directions in the air for the NOCs produce substantial developmental benefits in terms of increased opportunities, increased investment, superior allocation of resources, and reduced losses.

Bibliography

Bacon, Robert, 1999, *Global Energy Sector Reform in Developing Countries: A Scorecard* (Washington: World Bank Energy Sector Management Assistance Program).

Gupta, Sanjeev, Christian Schiller, and Henry Ma, 1999, "Privatization, Social Impact, and Social Safety Nets," IMF Working Paper 99/68 (Washington: International Monetary Fund).

Karl, Terry Lynn, 1997, *The Paradox of Plenty: Oil Booms and Petro-States* (Berkeley: University of California Press).

McKinsey & Company, 2002, *Lessons Learned from Ten Years of Economic Research by the McKinsey Global Institute*, presentation at the World Bank (March).

Mommer, Bernard, 2002, *Global Oil and the Nation State* (Oxford: Oxford University Press).

Petroleum Finance Company, 2002, *Presentation to the National Oil Companies Forum* (Algiers), April.

Petroleum Intelligence Weekly, 2000, *PIW's Top 50: How the Firms Stack Up*, (March).

PricewaterhouseCoopers, 1998, *Pertamina's Restructuring Blueprint: The Roadmap Towards A World-Class Oil And Gas Company* (July).

Schloss, Miguel, 1993, "Does Petroleum Procurement and Trade Matter?" *Finance & Development*, Vol. 30 (March), pp. 44–46.

Shaikh, Hafeez, 1996, *Argentina's Privatization Program — A Review of Five Cases* (Washington: World Bank).

World Bank, 2000a, *Nigerian National Petroleum Company Management Audit*, December (Washington).

———, 2000b, *Nigeria Petroleum Sector Review*, December (Washington).

———, 2000c, *Nigeria Petroleum Taxation and State Participation*, December (Washington).

Yergin, Daniel, and Joseph Stanislaw, 1998, *The Commanding Heights* (New York: Simon and Schuster).

8

The Assignment of Oil Tax Revenue

CHARLES E. McLURE, JR.

This paper provides a conceptual statement of the considerations that might lead one to conclude that revenues from the taxation of oil should be assigned to one level of government or the other in a multilayer system of government and discusses techniques that might be used to implement assignment of revenues to a subnational level of government. The assignment of oil tax revenues is one aspect of the theory of tax assignment, the question of who (which level of government) should tax what, and how.[1] In this case what to tax (oil) is given, and we need only ask who should tax it, and how. Revenues from oil could be assigned to only one level of government or to both central and subnational governments. The paper focuses on whether subnational governments should have the power to tax oil, why, and (if so) how.

The analysis presented here is best applied before oil is discovered. In that context, decisions on revenue assignment can be made behind the "veil of ignorance," not knowing how much revenue will be at stake or which will be the oil-rich jurisdictions. Regional vested interests will not yet have arisen and a nationally oriented view of costs of compliance and administration, of distributional equity, and of allocative efficiency is possible. Once oil has been discovered, the political dynamic is likely to be very different. If reserves are extremely valu-

---

[1]This wording of the question is adapted from the title of Musgrave (1983). Views summarized here are explained in greater detail in, for example, McLure (1994), (1998), (1999), and (2000).

able, and especially if they are highly concentrated geographically, regional interests will come to the fore and a different view of distributional issues—the distribution of revenues between the central and subnational governments and among subnational governments—is likely to dominate all other issues in political discussions. When the stakes are high, such discussions may become especially acrimonious.[2]

The paper concentrates on the division of taxing powers between the central government and the highest subnational tier of government. Though written in the context of federal systems, for the most part and with obvious modifications, the ideas presented here are equally applicable to unitary systems. Also, it is assumed that enough revenue is at stake to make the question important. Finally, as in most other normative literature on fiscal federalism, it is assumed that subnational governments respond to the wishes of their constituents.[3]

I. Forms of Revenue Assignment

Before turning to the question of who should tax oil, it is useful to ask how subnational governments might tax oil and how oil revenues might otherwise be channeled to subnational governments, if there is a desire to do so. The aspects of revenue assignment to be considered, aside from the crucial question of who gets the money and under what conditions, are who defines the tax base(s), who sets the tax rate(s), and who administers the tax(es). Together these determine how much fiscal autonomy subnational governments have in raising revenue from oil.

The following five alternatives are distinguished, ranked in order of subnational control over the power to raise revenues from oil.[4] Except for the first, each of these may merge into the one below, depending on specific details.

Royalties from subnational ownership of resources. If subnational governments own natural resources, revenues from exploiting the re-

---

[2]The high energy prices of the 1970s, which saw consumers in the United States paying higher prices while energy-rich jurisdictions enjoyed large increases in revenues, led to references to a "new war between the states." References in consuming states to "blue-eyed Arabs" were countered in Texas with bumper stickers that said, "Let the bastards freeze in the dark."

[3]Prud'homme (1995) questions the relevance of this basic assumption for many developing countries.

[4]There is, unfortunately, no uniformly accepted terminology in this area. These terms are used below because they clearly and accurately describe most of the alternatives.

sources accrue to them as owners, in the form of royalties. They have no need to use taxation to gain these revenues, although they may also receive oil revenues in one or more of the following four ways. This describes the situation in Canada and to a limited but important extent in Alaska, but, for the most part, not in the rest of the United States.[5] There is no reason, in principle, that national taxation could not reduce the amount subnational governments can realize from the ownership of oil reserves. This case is not discussed at length, but many of the same concerns that are relevant for tax assignment (e.g., vertical fiscal imbalance and horizontal fiscal disparities) are as relevant for assigning ownership of natural resources as for tax assignment.

Subnational legislation and implementation of taxes. Subnational governments may have the legal right to legislate and collect taxes on natural resources. This is the situation in the United States and Canada. Subnational taxing powers may be exclusive or concurrent with national powers, and constitutions or national laws may limit such legal rights. For example, there may be limits on the types of taxes subnational governments can impose on oil, on tax rates, and even on the definition of the tax base. For example, it might be required that key provisions such as depletion allowances follow national law, or the required conformity might be more far-reaching. Conformity facilitates compliance and administration, without seriously compromising subnational fiscal autonomy. Conformity is not required in the United States, where the lack of uniformity across jurisdictions (for example, in corporation income taxation) complicates compliance and administration, as well as creating undesirable gaps and overlaps in state tax bases. Unless severely restricted, this approach provides maximum subnational autonomy in taxation of oil.

Subnational surcharges on national taxes. Conformity may be so comprehensive that subnational governments utilize the same tax base as the national government. This may occur voluntarily, mandatorily, or as a requirement for tax administration by the national government. The result, either de jure or de facto, is a subnational surcharge on the national tax. While fiscal autonomy of subnational governments may be compromised in the last two situations, the most important aspect of autonomy, the power to set subnational tax rates and obtain revenues from oil, is retained in all three situations.

---

[5]In the United States, unlike much of the rest of the world, private ownership of mineral rights is common, except in the case of public lands.

Subnational governments may collect surcharges on the national tax, or the national government may collect surcharges for them. Federal administration of provincial income tax surcharges is available on a voluntary basis to Canadian provinces that choose to adopt the federal income tax base. Other provinces, while administering their own taxes, rely heavily on the federal definition of taxable income.

Subnational surcharges may be imposed on either the national tax base or the national tax liability. Subnational autonomy is greater if the surcharge is levied on the national tax base than if it is levied on the amount of the national tax, as in Canada until recently. In the latter case the structure of subnational taxes depends on the structure of the national tax.

Tax sharing. The term tax sharing is used in this paper to describe the practice of returning revenues from particular taxes to subnational jurisdictions on a derivation basis, that is, to the jurisdictions where the revenues originate (or are deemed to originate). Conceptually this system can be viewed in either of two ways: as a surcharge system in which the subnational government lacks the power to choose the tax rate or, because subnational governments lack all aspects of fiscal autonomy in the raising of revenue, as tantamount to a grant system. Sharing rates can be the same in all jurisdictions, or they can vary across jurisdictions, as in the former Soviet Union. In the latter case tax sharing shades into revenue sharing and the similarity of tax sharing and grants is clear.

Revenue sharing. In revenue sharing, revenues are shared with subnational jurisdictions on the basis of a formula, rather than being channeled to their jurisdictions of origin, as in the techniques considered above. As with tax sharing, revenue sharing allows no subnational fiscal autonomy.[6] Revenue sharing is one way to offset vertical fiscal im-

---

[6]Revenue sharing may also create less incentive than the other techniques for subnational governments to spend public funds in ways that enhance productivity. The techniques that assign revenues to the jurisdictions where they originate create incentives for subnational governments to spend public funds in ways that enhance productivity within their boundaries, as that makes it easier to raise revenues. By comparison, revenue sharing generally creates smaller incentives of this type, as the amount of funds available to subnational governments depends less on efforts to enhance productivity, and may even be negatively affected by them. See Careaga and Weingast (2001). The ease of raising revenue would seem to be a more important consideration in societies where governments do not respond to the will of their constituents than in those where they do. The incentive to spend revenues in ways that increase job opportunities, wages, the return to capital, and the value of land—considerations of prime importance to the electorate—would exist under both revenue sharing and techniques that channel revenues to subnational governments of jurisdictions where they originate.

Table 8.1. *Four Methods of Assigning Oil Tax Revenues*
to Subnational Governments: Functions
(Level of government responsible for functions; subnational jurisdiction receiving revenue)

	Method of Revenue Assignment			
	Separate legislation and administration	Subnational surcharges	Tax sharing	Revenue sharing
Choice of tax base	Subnational	National	National	National
Choice of tax rate	Subnational	Subnational	National	National
Tax administration	Subnational	Either	National	National
Recipient jurisdiction	Origin	Origin	Origin	Formula

Source: Author.

balance. The central government can also share its oil revenues with subnational governments in a way that offsets horizontal fiscal disparities created by the geographical concentration of oil.

Tables 8.1 and 8.2 summarize the key features of the last four methods of assigning revenues to subnational governments. The key points are (i) that only separate legislation and administration and subnational surcharges provide subnational autonomy over tax rates, the key to subnational fiscal autonomy; (ii) that independent legislation and administration may entail an unacceptable level of duplication and cost of compliance and administration and is thus not likely to be appropriate for many countries, especially developing countries; (iii) that, except in the case of revenue sharing, revenues flow to jurisdictions of origin, which may create horizontal fiscal disparities; and (iv) that only

Table 8.2. *Four Methods of Assigning Oil Tax Revenues to Subnational*
Governments: Effects

	Method of Revenue Assignment			
Effects	Separate legislation and administration	Subnational surcharges	Tax sharing	Revenue sharing
Subnational Fiscal Autonomy over				
Tax base	Yes	No	No	No
Tax rates	Yes	Yes	No	No
Administration	Yes	Possibly	No	No
Duplication/Costs of Compliance and Administration	Potentially high	Low	Low	Low
Reduction of Fiscal Disparities	None	None	None	Possible

Source: Author.

revenue sharing (and horizontal equalization) can be used to offset horizontal fiscal disparities.

II. Economic Considerations in Revenue Assignment

Several types of economic considerations are relevant for revenue assignment.

Benefit taxation. Subnational governments should have access to taxes (or fees or other charges) that compensate them for benefits provided to (and other costs imposed by) those who exploit their natural resources. Examples of costs that may be incurred by subnational governments or their citizens include the costs of roads needed to carry heavy machinery, costs of hospitals needed to care for those injured on the job, and costs of health problems caused by damage to the environment. Taxes (and fees and charges) of this type should be levied, to the extent possible, in a way that reflects costs incurred by subnational governments or their residents. This implies that taxes on resource rents or the value of production are not likely to be optimally designed for this purpose; taxes on the volume of production are likely to be much more appropriate. This type of tax is not examined further in what follows.

Subsidiarity. National governments ordinarily have greater capacity to raise revenue than do subnational governments. This, combined with the advantages of decentralized government, suggests that subnational governments should have access to revenues from any tax that is not inappropriate for them, for example, because it interferes with international trade. This principle, commonly called subsidiarity, implies examination of other considerations to see what kinds of taxes are inappropriate for use by subnational governments. The implications of geographic concentration of oil revenues are first ignored and then these implications are considered. Legal and political issues are addressed in the next section.

Considerations That Are Independent of Geographical Concentration

Unstable revenues. Oil revenues are notoriously unstable. National governments are in a better position to offset this instability than are subnational governments, for example, because they have larger budgets (in relation to GDP), more sources of non-oil revenues, greater access to credit markets, and the power to engage in monetary policy. They may also be better equipped, technically as well as politically, to withstand the pressure to increase spending when current revenues are high (and even to borrow against future revenues) than are subnational governments, but this is not inevitable.

Taxation of resource rents. Taxation of resource rents is (aside from benefit taxation) the preferred form of oil taxation, as it minimizes distortion of economic decisions. It is also fairly complicated to implement.[7] Thus national governments are likely to be more able to implement rent taxes than are subnational governments, which are more likely to rely on production taxes—taxes that encourage inefficient "high-grading" (cessation of production once revenues no longer cover costs, including taxes).[8] Finally, rent taxes are likely to be more unstable than other forms of taxation of natural resources. This feature also makes them inappropriate for subnational governments.

Ring-fencing. If a tax on natural resources is to be economically neutral, it is important to allow losses incurred in one period to be carried forward or back to offset income earned in another period. The question of whether to allow taxpayers also to offset expenses incurred in one area against revenues gained in another raises interesting issues that cannot be addressed here. Subnational governments are unlikely to allow a deduction for expenses incurred in another jurisdiction. National governments can either allow it or not, via ring-fencing.

Locational mobility. Subnational taxation of economic activities that are geographically mobile can induce inefficient tax-motivated locational decisions. Subnational taxation of oil has the advantage, compared to many other types of taxes, that oil resources are geographically immobile.

Tax exporting. Taxes are exported when they reduce the real incomes of nonresidents of the taxing jurisdiction (perhaps by reducing the income of companies owned by nonresidents). Tax exporting is unfair, unless the exported taxes compensate for benefits received by (or costs

---

[7]McLure (1994) explains the difficulties of implementing three types of taxes on economic rents. These include standard problems of income taxation, such as the need to deal with transfer pricing on transactions between related parties, timing issues (in the recognition of income and expenses), and perhaps adjustment for inflation. In addition, since economic rents are the excess of returns over all costs, including the imputed cost of equity capital, it is necessary to know the normal return to equity investments.

[8]Even worse, they may rely on property taxes, which encourage early depletion.

due to) those who bear the burden of taxation. Also, if a subnational jurisdiction can export its nonbenefit taxes, it will have an incentive to expand public services beyond the point where marginal social benefits of public services equal marginal social costs of taxation, because only taxes paid by residents will be considered in making decisions on the proper level of taxation and spending.[9] This suggests that subnational governments should not levy taxes that would be exported.[10]

Tax exporting to consumers of oil is probably less pervasive than sometimes thought. The fact that oil is exported does not imply that oil taxes can be exported. That depends on the degree to which the taxing jurisdiction dominates the world market. With few exceptions the requisite market domination is lacking.[11]

Exporting to nonresident owners of oil may occur if oil reserves are privately owned. Exporting to owners of concessions to exploit oil reserves may occur if unanticipated tax increases are not contractually precluded.[12]

Duplication of administration and compliance. Concurrent national and subnational taxation can create duplication of costs of compliance and administration. Compliance and administration can be further complicated if subnational jurisdictions do not utilize the same taxes, define tax bases the same way, or cooperate in tax administration. Tax surcharges, tax sharing, and revenue sharing minimize duplication and complexity.

---

[9]The fact that various jurisdictions may reciprocally export taxes to residents located in other jurisdictions within the same nation does not imply that tax exporting does not have the efficiency effects indicated. Imported taxes have only an income effect, whereas tax exporting also has a substitution effect, by affecting the tax price of public services.

[10]By comparison, few would suggest that national governments should not levy taxes that would be exported, merely because it reduces the local cost of public services. The difference in answers to what is seemingly the same question depends on the difference in the two policy contexts. Both ask what is the best fiscal arrangement from a national point of view.

[11]This statement assumes that the consequences of the actions of a single jurisdiction are being examined. When oil-producing jurisdictions act collusively to raise taxes (for example, under the auspices of OPEC), forward shifting is more likely. Note, however, that if the actions of OPEC lead to higher prices and higher profits of oil companies and a single country raises its taxes to capture some of the profits that result, the tax is not shifted to consumers. It is the actions of OPEC, not the tax, that causes prices to be higher.

[12]The availability of foreign tax credits (FTCs) for source-country income taxes creates a particularly common form of tax exporting, to the treasuries of home countries of multinational oil companies. This is not unique to oil taxes and thus is not considered further.

Vertical fiscal imbalance. If oil revenues were to be assigned entirely to subnational governments, an unusual form of vertical fiscal imbalance might develop, in which subnational governments have adequate revenues, but the national government does not. Under such circumstances it might be appropriate to assign part of revenues to the central government.

Considerations That Depend on Geographical Concentration

Horizontal fiscal disparities. Assignment of oil revenues to the jurisdictions where they originate allows resource-rich jurisdictions to provide a given level of public services with non-oil taxes that are lower than those levied elsewhere or to provide higher levels of public services than elsewhere with a given level of non-oil taxes. This result can be challenged on grounds of both distributional equity and economic efficiency.

Distributional inequity. The implications of horizontal disparities for distributional equity are fairly apparent;[13] it may seem unfair that residents of oil-rich jurisdictions receive more public services or pay lower taxes (or both) than residents of other jurisdictions.

Uneconomic locational decisions. The lower taxes and greater public spending made possible by oil revenues may cause more labor and capital to be attracted to oil-rich jurisdictions than is optimal.[14] Empirical evidence suggests that these distortions may not be a significant problem, except where extraction of oil is highly concentrated in jurisdictions with extremely low population density, such as Alaska.[15]

Wasteful government expenditures. Another implication of horizontal fiscal disparities is that oil revenues may be spent on government programs and projects that have lower social value than if spent elsewhere. A particularly popular form of waste is local investment of oil

---

[13]Actually, the implications for equity may be more apparent than real if factors of production (capital and labor) are mobile. As with many other instances of differential taxation, what appear on the surface to be horizontal inequities (which they are, before adjustments are made to them) may be reduced dramatically or eliminated by adjustments. That is, once capital and labor have adjusted to the differences in wage rates, returns to capital, taxes, and levels of public services, little or no inequity may remain. What remains is likely to be reflected, if at all, in land values.

[14]See Boadway and Flatters (1982) and McLure (1983).

[15]See Mieszkowski and Toder (1983). The fact that Alaska has a relatively inhospitable climate presumably reduces the likelihood that locational decisions will be badly distorted.

revenues, particularly in uneconomic "downstream" processing activities.[16]

Equalization: Responding to Horizontal Fiscal Disparities

Where assignment of oil revenues to subnational jurisdictions creates unacceptable horizontal fiscal disparities, equalization is likely to be advocated. This is where revenue sharing comes into its own. All of the other forms of revenue assignment examined here channel revenues to the jurisdiction where they originate and are thus likely to create horizontal fiscal disparities. By comparison, revenue sharing can be designed to channel revenues to "have-not" jurisdictions and thus reduce horizontal disparities.

III. Legal and Political Considerations

Most of the considerations examined above suggest that revenues from oil (other than those required to offset costs of providing public services and social costs imposed by exploitation of oil resources) should be reserved for national governments. But no matter how the issues examined above are resolved, there may be overriding legal and political issues.

First, a nation's constitution may assign the power to tax oil to subnational governments. This fact may trump all the considerations discussed thus far.

Second, subnational governments may claim that natural resources are the "patrimony" of the subnational jurisdictions where they are found.[17] This raises the interesting philosophical question of whether the patrimony at issue belongs to the residents of the nation or to those of the subnational jurisdiction.

Third, the very continued existence of a federation may depend on whether subnational governments are allowed to tax oil. This issue is

---

[16]This is common even at the national level. See Gelb and Associates (1988). The very different experiences of the state of Alaska, which followed a rational investment model, and of Alberta and the native peoples of Alaska, which followed the "development" model, is instructive; Alaska realized a far higher rate of return. See McLure (1994) and literature cited there.

[17]See Link (1978) and the papers in Smith (1980).

particularly important when it arises in combination with separatist tendencies based on ethnic differences, as in the case of Tatarstan in Russia.[18]

Fourth, subnational governments where oil revenues originate may simply not trust the national government to deliver revenues due to them under systems based on tax surcharges and tax sharing. They may prefer to administer their own taxes, even if the definition of their tax base is severely constrained.

Bibliography

Boadway, Robin W., and Frank R. Flatters, 1982, "Efficiency and Equalization Payments in a Federal System of Government: A Synthesis and Extension of Recent Results," *Canadian Journal of Economics*, Vol. 15, No. 4 (November), pp. 613–33.

Careaga, Maite, and Barry R. Weingast, 2001, "Fiscal Federalism, Good Governance, and Economic Growth in Mexico" in *In Search of Prosperity: Narratives on Economic Growth,* ed. by Dani Rodrik (Princeton: Princeton University Press), pp. 399–435.

Gelb, Alan, and Associates, 1988, *Oil Windfalls: Blessing or Curse* (New York: Oxford University Press for the World Bank).

Link, Arthur A., 1978, "Political Constraint and North Dakota's Coal Severance Tax," *National Tax Journal*, Vol. 31, No. 3 (September), pp. 263–68.

Litvack, Jennie I., 1994, "Regional Demands and Fiscal Federalism," in *Russia and the Challenge of Fiscal Federalism*, ed. by Christine I. Wallich (Washington: World Bank), pp. 218–40.

McLure, Charles E., Jr., 1983, "Fiscal Federalism and the Taxation of Economic Rents," in *State and Local Finance: The Pressure of the 80's,* ed. by George Break (Madison: University of Wisconsin Press), pp. 133–60.

———, 1994, "The Sharing of Taxes on Natural Resources and the Future of the Russian Federation," in *Russia and the Challenge of Fiscal Federalism*, ed. by Christine Wallich (Washington: World Bank), pp. 181–217.

———, 1998, "The Revenue Assignment Problem: Ends, Means, and Constraints," in *Public Budgeting and Financial Management*, Vol. 9, No. 4 (Winter), pp. 652–83.

———, 1999, "Tax Assignment," in *Fiscal Transition in Kazakhstan* (Manila: Asian Development Bank), pp. 273–316.

---

[18]See Litvack (1994) and McLure, Wallich, and Litvack (1995). The ability of Texas and Alaska to retain much of their public lands—and Alaska's ability to choose land known to contain oil reserves—may have influenced their willingness to become states.

————, 2000, "Tax Assignment and Subnational Fiscal Autonomy," *Bulletin for International Fiscal Documentation*, Vol. 54, No. 12 (December), pp. 626–35.

————, Christine I. Wallich, and Jennie I. Litvack, 1995, "Special Issues in Federal Finance," in *Decentralization of the Socialist State: Intergovernmental Finance in Transition Economies*, ed. by Richard M. Bird, Robert D. Ebel, and Christine I. Wallich (Washington: World Bank), pp. 379–404.

Mieszkowski, Peter, and Eric Toder, 1983, "Taxation of Energy Resources," in *Fiscal Federalism and the Taxation of Natural Resources*, ed. by Charles E. McLure, Jr., and Peter Mieszkowski (Lexington, Massachusetts: Lexington Books), pp. 65–91.

Musgrave, Richard A., 1983, "Who Should Tax, Where, and What?" in *Tax Assignment in Federal Countries*, ed. by Charles E. McLure, Jr. (Canberra: Centre for Research on Federal Financial Relations), pp. 2–19.

Prud'homme, Rémy, 1995, "On the Dangers of Decentralization," *World Bank Economic Review*, Vol. 10, No. 2 (August), pp. 201–20.

Smith, Roger S., ed., 1980, *The Alberta Heritage Savings Trust Fund*, a special issue of *Canadian Public Policy*, Vol. 6 (February), pp. 141–8.

9

Oil Revenue Assignments: Country Experiences and Issues

EHTISHAM AHMAD AND ERIC MOTTU[1]

I. Introduction

The assignment of oil revenues in multilevel countries raises a number of issues, including the right of subnational regions to raise revenues on natural resources, the ability of subnational jurisdictions vis-à-vis the central government to stabilize revenues in response to oil price uncertainty and volatility, inter-jurisdictional equity and redistribution, and the financing of a stable level of public services provided by subnational governments, as well as environmental concerns. There is also an overriding emotive or political economy consideration associated with the assignment of natural resource revenues—particularly with oil—reflected in demands for a direct share of the oil revenues from the regions where the oil fields are located. Factors in determining appropriate revenue assignments would also include macroeconomic stabilization, efficiency, and redistributive considerations traditionally addressed in the literature.

The paper describes arrangements to assign oil revenue to different levels of administration in a range of countries—ranging from large federations to relatively small unitary states. Based on country studies, the paper presents a simple typology of existing arrangements, includ-

[1]The authors benefited from comments from Giorgio Brosio, Jeffrey Davis, Gene Handel, Charles E. McLure, Jr., and Rolando Ossowski, as well as from input from M. Alier, A. Bauer, D. Chua, T. Dabán, S. Danninger, A. Espejo, U. Fasano, M. Guin-Siu, H. Hirschhofer, L. Leruth, A. Rambarran, S. Schwartz, A. Vivanco, and D. Zakharova on individual countries. All errors remain ours.

216

ing full centralization, full decentralization, and various revenue-sharing schemes including the definition of various overlapping revenue bases.

While the paper considers a large number of oil-producing countries, the following countries are examined in more detail: Canada, Colombia, Indonesia, Mexico, Nigeria, Russia, United Arab Emirates, United States, and Venezuela—representing differing constitutional and political arrangements touched on above.

Arguments for centralization of oil revenues are based on a number of considerations. A central government can better absorb the uncertainty and volatility of oil prices because it usually has a broader tax base, less correlated with oil prices, than subnational jurisdictions. And if subnational governments do have other assigned taxes, oil-rich regions may have less incentive to use such bases if they are also assigned oil revenues—this can lead to internal beggar-thy-neighbor outcomes within federations, and a misallocation of factors of production. Moreover, a central government can contribute to horizontal equity by redistributing oil revenue between resource-rich and resource-poor regions. As a depletable resource, oil cannot be considered as a buoyant long-term source of revenue for subnational governments.[2]

The main arguments for assigning oil revenues to subnational jurisdictions are mainly political and turn on either constitutional stipulations that delineate the regional or local ownership of the natural resources, or the right to levy taxes on certain bases or sources of income. Another common arrangement—sharing revenues—is often the result of attempts by central governments to appease separatist tendencies in natural resource producing regions. We examine the merits and problems associated with such arguments in the context of possible arrangements for different types of countries.

The case of the small unitary state may appear trivial, as oil revenues are necessarily centralized in these countries. However, a number of considerations are important, and the preconditions for effective macroeconomic stabilization in such countries indicate the necessary conditions in larger unitary states or federations for decentralization of oil revenues to subnational jurisdictions.

The paper assesses the advantages and drawbacks of the various types of arrangements, including their ability to contribute to macro-

---

[2]See Boadway and Shah (1994); Brosio (2000); McLure (1983), (1998), (2000), and (2001); Mieszkowski (1983); Norregaard (1997); and Ter-Minassian (1997a).

economic stabilization and fiscal discipline. It concludes that centralization of oil revenues would be a desirable arrangement, along with
the assignment of other tax bases to subnational governments accompanied by a transfer system to address distributional or equalization
concerns. An alternative solution is to assign more stable oil-tax bases
to oil-producing subnational governments, such as production excises,
and to design the transfer system accordingly to guarantee a minimum
level of resources for all subnational governments to finance a stable
level of public services. The least preferred solution is oil-revenue sharing. By taking away large amounts of revenue from the central government, it precludes and complicates macroeconomic management.
By fully transmitting the volatility of oil revenue to subnational governments, it does not provide stable financing of local public services,
and it usually does not manage to diffuse separatist tendencies, since
oil-producing regions can still be better off by keeping 100 percent of
their oil revenues.

II. Experiences in Oil-Revenue Assignments

Data on oil revenue disaggregated by level of government are scarce.
For both sets of unitary and federal countries, Table 9.1 presents oil revenue collections as well as total revenues over the period 1997–2000. A
major feature that is apparent is that *oil revenues are more volatile than
total revenues*—in all major countries and groupings of countries (small
and large, predominantly oil producing, and so on). Volatility of oil
revenues, defined as the standard deviation relative to the mean, was
roughly similar for unitary and federal countries. However, within
each group there were considerable differences across countries. For
unitary states, for instance, oil revenue volatility was higher for countries such as Iran, Indonesia, and Colombia than for Saudi Arabia or
Kuwait—reflecting a lower ability to use quantity adjustments to compensate for price variations. A similar pattern was apparent for federal
states, with Nigeria, the United States, and Venezuela being subject to
greater oil-revenue volatility than Mexico, Russia, or the United Arab
Emirates.

The data also confirm that the *volatility of total revenues is greater when
the share of oil revenues in total revenues is higher.* This, which is seen
clearly from Figure 9.1, has implications for states that lack non-oil revenue bases, as well as subnational governments that come to rely extensively on oil-revenue shares or assignments.

Table 9.1. Oil-Revenue Volatility in Selected Countries, 1997–2000[1]

	Oil Revenue (In percent of GDP)[1]	Volatility (In percent)[2]	Total Revenue and Grants (In percent of GDP)[1]	Volatility (In percent)[1]	Oil Revenue (In percent of total revenue)[1]	Coverage
Unitary countries[3]						
Algeria	16.6	27.6	32.8	12.6	48.2	Central government
Azerbaijan	21.4	25.9	32.7	13.3	64.4	General government
Bahrain	5.7	29.1	19.6	5.1	28.6	Oil and gas
Colombia	13.0	26.3	24.6	15.1	51.9	Nonfinancial public sector
Ecuador	2.6	38.3	27.7	2.8	9.4	Nonfinancial public sector
Indonesia	7.4	32.1	25.1	15.9	31.3	Oil and gas. General government[4]
Iran	5.6	32.7	17.5	11.5	31.1	Oil and gas. Central government[5]
Kuwait	13.3	42.0	25.5	18.2	49.8	Oil and gas[6]
Libya	38.6	19.2	60.7	13.3	63.0	Consolidated government
Norway	23.0	8.0	39.0	14.7	59.9	General government
Oman	8.9	30.8	52.3	4.0	16.9	General government
Qatar	30.2	15.6	39.5	6.9	76.0	General government[4]
Saudi Arabia	16.7	27.4	23.6	19.5	57.3	General government
Syrian Arab Republic	24.6	27.4	33.6	15.5	72.0	Central government
Yemen	21.6	31.9	33.1	20.4	63.8	Central government
Federal countries[3]						
Canada	12.7[7]	28.2	29.0	9.9	44.7	General government[4]
Mexico	...	25.9	46.2	0.5	...	Public sector. Excludes excises on gasoline
Nigeria	5.3	17.7	21.5	4.4	24.7	General government
Russia	23.8	39.3	31.8	28.6	72.4	Oil and gas. Federal government
United Arab Emirates	3.8	26.4	13.1	14.2	28.8	General government
United States	18.2[8]	22.4	34.6	6.3	52.0	General government[9]
Venezuela	...	31.1	29.9	1.6	...	Public sector (excl. nonrecurrent operations)

Sources: IMF country reports; and authors' estimates.

[1] Average during 1997–2000.
[2] Defined as the standard deviation in percent of the mean over the period 1997–2000.
[3] Unweighted average.
[4] Fiscal year starting on April 1.
[5] Fiscal year starting on March 20.
[6] Fiscal year ending on June 30.
[7] Resource revenue in the provinces of Alberta and Saskatchewan.
[8] Oil revenue in the state of Alaska.
[9] Fiscal year ending on September 30.

Figure 9.1. *Volatility of Total Revenue in Selected Oil-Producing Countries,*
1997–2000[1]

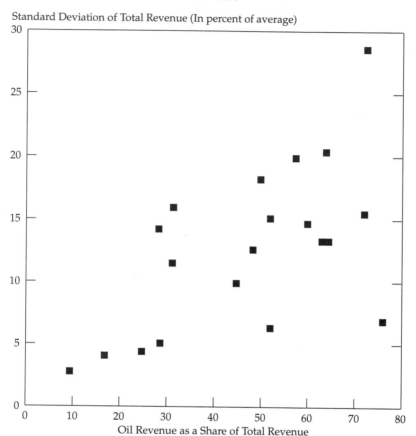

Standard Deviation of Total Revenue (In percent of average)

Oil Revenue as a Share of Total Revenue

Sources: IMF country reports; and authors' estimates.
[1]Based on data found in Table 9.1.

Specific arrangements to assign oil revenues in unitary and federal countries can be broadly classified into four categories: full decentralization, full centralization, assignment of overlapping/shared tax bases, and revenue sharing. Table 9.2 shows a classification of a number of oil-producing countries according to their assignment of oil revenue. The general principles of tax assignment and revenue-sharing arrangements are set out in the Appendix.

Most *small unitary countries* centralize oil revenues, often because local governments in these countries do not have important expendi-

Table 9.2. *Classification of Oil-Revenue Assignments
in Unitary and Federal Countries*

	Full Decentralization	Full Centralization	Shared Revenue Bases	Revenue Sharing
Unitary countries		Algeria Azerbaijan Bahrain Indonesia (until 2000) Iran Iraq Kuwait Libya Norway Oman Qatar Saudi Arabia United Kingdom Yemen		Colombia (D) Ecuador (C) Indonesia (since 2001) (C) Kazakhstan
Federal countries	United Arab Emirates[1]		Canada United States	Mexico (C) Nigeria (D) Russia (D) Venezuela (D)

Source: Authors.
Note: C = Rather centralizing arrangement. D = Rather decentralizing arrangement.
[1]Upward revenue-sharing arrangement.

ture responsibilities or have other revenue sources. The challenge for these countries is to develop non-oil revenue bases and to deal with the stabilization and saving of volatile oil revenue at the national level.

Large unitary states (such as Colombia and Indonesia) tend to be pressed into revenue-sharing arrangements with subnational governments, but these lead to many difficulties, not least in terms of macroeconomic management. Moreover, oil-producing regions are generally dissatisfied with the arrangement, leading to potential political instability.

The same issues arise in *federal countries*, particularly in Nigeria. While expenditure responsibilities of subnational governments remain relatively stable over time, oil revenue transferred through revenue-sharing arrangements is highly volatile, leading to major fiscal management problems that these governments cannot address for lack of alternative revenue bases.

Two federal countries (Canada and the United States) assign oil tax bases to subnational governments (overlapping with the federal government) instead of sharing oil revenue collected centrally. This tax assignment creates more accountability for the governments concerned. The revenue disparities with respect to non-oil-producing regions can be addressed through the national equalization system (Canada). Only one country, the United Arab Emirates, fully decentralizes oil revenue and has an upward revenue-sharing arrangement.

These arrangements are discussed in more detail in the following sections.

III. Unitary States

Most small unitary states reflect a *full centralization model,* where all oil revenues accrue to the central government. Proceeds of taxes on the extraction and production of oil are included in general revenue of the central government. Such countries include those in the Gulf Cooperation Council (GCC) region: Bahrain, Kuwait, Oman, Qatar, Saudi Arabia, and Yemen (the case of the United Arab Emirates is somewhat different and is examined with the federal countries). Most other large unitary oil-producing countries (Algeria, Azerbaijan, Indonesia—until 2000, Iran, Iraq, Libya, Norway, and the United Kingdom) also follow this model.

The *advantages* of full centralization of oil revenues are that (i) the central government fully absorbs oil-revenue fluctuations, which it is able to do because of more diverse tax bases uncorrelated with oil; (ii) interregional disparities can potentially be reduced if the central government is assigned oil revenues, as the latter may be in a better position to establish horizontal equalization mechanisms; and (iii) there may be less scope for a competitive "race to the bottom"[3] for other subnational taxes than if oil revenues were assigned to regions or localities.[4]

Issues in Small Unitary States

A number of policy responses to oil-price volatility and exhaustibility of oil in small oil-producing states are noteworthy. First, most oil-

---

[3]An interjurisdictional competition that would drive tax rates down and result in suboptimal outputs of public services. See Breton (2002).

[4]Mieszkowski and Toder (1983) find that efficiency losses due to the migration of capital and labor to energy-producing states in the United States (which benefit from oil revenues) may range from 2 percent to 9 percent of the revenue raised.

producing states recognize the need to develop a *significant non-oil revenue base* to minimize the variance in total revenues. Such a base is also needed to compensate for a reduction in customs tariffs that have occurred during the past decade, either due to regional initiatives or the impending membership in the WTO of some of the oil-producing states. Countries such as Azerbaijan have made significant progress in the establishment of a value-added tax (VAT).

Second, some countries have attempted to address the issue of oil-price volatility by the *establishment of a stabilization fund,* with a view to smoothing revenues, hence expenditures, over time.[5] Examples include Azerbaijan, Norway, Oman, and Venezuela. One of the main difficulties with such an arrangement is the possibility of establishing a parallel budget mechanism, often with less oversight than the regular budget. This difficulty is particularly pronounced at the subnational level, especially in developing countries. Norway's responses to the potential difficulty are noteworthy: all resources coming into the oil fund are reported to parliament—which must also authorize any transfers from the fund to the budget. All spending is done from the regular budget.[6]

Third, the finite duration of oil extraction is sometimes addressed by setting up *a savings fund,* with a share of annual oil revenue being saved for future generations.[7] An example is the Kuwaiti Reserve Fund for Future Generations (RFFG)—spending from which is expressly curtailed. However, the government was permitted to borrow from the RFFG because of the country's reconstruction at the end of the Iraqi occupation. Neither a stabilization fund nor a savings fund necessarily stabilizes public finances or effectively raises public savings—these depend on the overall stance of fiscal policy. The potential difficulties noted above may far outweigh potential benefits and the introduction of such a fund should be very carefully assessed at the outset.

Trends in Larger Unitary States

At a time when small nation states are seeking to offset problems caused by the variance in oil revenues, there has been considerable

---

[5]For a full discussion of the advantages and problems associated with oil stabilization funds, see Davis and others, Chapter 11 in this volume.

[6]See Skancke, Chapter 12 in this volume.

[7]This is also the case in Alaska.

pressure in the larger unitary states (and federations) to enter into *revenue-sharing arrangements* or *assign oil-revenue bases* to producing regions or localities.

In addition to the problems also faced by the small oil-producing regions, the sharing or assignment of oil revenues to the producing regions or localities also has to address a number of issues: (i) it is difficult to determine the relevant jurisdiction that should receive the "largesse," especially if the relevant unit for revenue sharing is the district or county—typically an oil well in one district may draw on reserves technically under several district jurisdictions; (ii) the assignment of such revenues to producing districts or regions may exacerbate horizontal inequalities across districts or regions; (iii) as stated above, it may lead to distortions in economic development by allowing non-oil taxation to be lowered in a "race to the bottom" in oil-producing districts; and (iv) it makes the stabilization function of the central government more difficult to achieve.

Fiscal discipline may be difficult to enforce if subnational governments receive large amounts of fluctuating oil revenues. In developing countries, governments may not be able to resist the temptation to spend the "oil windfall" during periods of high prices—given the relatively low-income levels and the substantial developmental needs. Moreover, the transparency in expenditure management needed to ensure an effective stabilization fund would be difficult to establish at the central level and more so at the subnational level, where expenditure management procedures and reporting practices are likely to be rudimentary.

If regional governments provide significant amounts of services and infrastructure for the exploitation of natural resources, some charges may be considered a compensation for the associated costs, justifying that some share of the revenues (e.g., a proportion of royalties) could be returned to them under the benefit-tax linkage principle. There could also be production excises or severance taxes.[8] These alternatives to the sharing of oil revenues may also be less volatile than oil revenues per se, and thus more appropriate as revenue sources for subnational governments.

While oil production is not a good source of subnational revenue, political economy realities might dictate that some form of regional taxation of natural resources is inevitable if there is distrust that the

---

[8]Severance taxes are levied on the extraction or removal of natural resources.

center will provide sufficient untied grants for regional expenditures. There are also a number of economic arguments (based on the benefit principle and externalities) that may justify the levy of taxes on such resources. In addition, since oil and gas are subject to income taxation, a piggybacking arrangement with this and other sources may be considered (this might be quite attractive and might not exacerbate regional inequalities if applied across all income sources). There may thus be a number of taxes or charges on oil and gas that could accrue to regional governments.

Three case studies are illustrative of some of the difficulties discussed above—including Indonesia, Colombia, and Nigeria (discussed later in Section IV on federations).

Indonesia

Until 2000, all oil and gas revenue accrued to the central government and was not subject to any revenue-sharing arrangement with provincial and district-level governments. Between 1997 and 2000 oil and gas revenues represented 33 percent of total revenue of the central government (5.6 percent of GDP).

The laws on decentralization, which went into effect in 2001, transferred expenditure responsibilities such as education, health, and local infrastructure to provinces and districts. They also instituted revenue-sharing arrangements for onshore oil and gas revenue, whereby 15 percent of oil revenue and 30 percent of gas revenue were to be transferred to the originating provinces, districts, and adjacent districts, starting in 2001.[9] However, unlike in Canada and the United States, where the provinces own the natural resources and have the right to tax earnings from these resources, in Indonesia the latter are owned by the unitary state.

Given the political economy considerations in Indonesia, it was inevitable that recognition of residents' demands for a share in the resource rents be accommodated in some fashion. However, sharing of oil revenues with producing regions within the country may not in itself satisfy the aspirations of regional separatists—since by definition they would be better off if they kept all the oil revenues.[10] Thus, for the

---

[9]In addition, at least 25 percent of central government revenue (net of revenue sharing) is to be transferred to all lower level governments through a general transfer mechanism, and additional grants may be distributed for specific purposes (IMF, 2002).

center and the producing regions it may be difficult to establish the politically acceptable level of resource sharing, particularly of oil and gas revenues, and there is plenty of scope for building up further resentments. National unity would thus have to rest on other factors, such as the services that the center could provide with greater efficiency, defense, and national identity.

Moreover, the sharing of oil and gas revenue is likely to further increase regional disparities in revenue capacities, as the sources of oil and gas revenue are concentrated in a small number of provinces and districts. It is estimated that districts in five provinces would likely receive over four-fifths of the local share, while those in the remaining 25 provinces would receive zero or near zero oil and gas revenue shares. Thus, there remains a need for "equalization transfers" for non-oil/gas-producing provinces or districts.[11] Finally, revenue from oil and gas production is highly volatile and does not provide a stable source of financing.[12]

In sum, there are considerable risks in sharing oil and gas revenues in Indonesia. This could widen regional disparities; prove difficult to administer, particularly at district level, as volatile oil prices lead to a divergence between budgets and realized revenues; complicate the functioning of a grants system; add to "unsatisfied aspirations"; and significantly increase the central government deficit.

Colombia

Colombia is a unitary republic, but with significant subnational governments. Considerable expenditure responsibilities, as well as some revenue, were devolved to districts and municipalities by the 1991 constitution—the provinces perform deconcentrated functions on behalf

---

[10]The equilibrium may be less than 100 percent, however, because of the costs associated with secession. See Ahmad and Singh (2003) for a discussion. In Indonesia in 2001, Aceh Province accepted the offer of an asymmetric deal based on retention of 55 percent of oil revenue and 40 percent of gas revenue.

[11]Ahmad and Mansoor (2002).

[12]For example, as of mid-December 1998, the price of benchmark Minas crude oil stood at about US$10 per barrel, compared with an assumed price of US$13 for purposes of the central budget, causing monthly average revenue to fall to US$600 million in the third quarter of 1998, compared with US$1 billion per month in the fourth quarter of 1997. The rupiah's strengthening to about Rp 7,500 to the dollar from the Rp 10,600 assumed in the central budget compounded the fall in revenues in domestic currency. The revenues from oil rose dramatically during the rebound of oil prices in 1999–early 2000. The seesaw pattern continued during 2001–02.

of the center (as in Indonesia). As a result, municipalities have taken over several important functions, and their expenditures represent over one-third of total nonfinancial public sector (NFPS) expenditure (35 percent on average during the period 1997–2000). The municipalities are mainly responsible for health and education expenditures,[13] as well as for local capital expenditure.

Until 2001, the constitution specified compulsory intergovernmental transfers to subnational governments, and these were to reach 46.5 percent of the central government's current revenues by 2002. This imposed a considerable constraint on the central government's overall fiscal effort. Since subnational governments have not fully used their powers to collect own taxes, a large share of their revenue (close to one-half) comes from the central government or public enterprises, making them dependent on intergovernmental transfers. A constitutional amendment was approved in 2001, however, delinking transfers to subnational governments from current revenues of the central government.

In this context, oil revenue represents a nonnegligible share of total revenue of the NFPS, on average 8 percent during the period 1997–2000 (about 2½ percent of GDP).[14] This revenue is shared among the various levels of government and public enterprises. Oil revenue comprises the operating surplus of the public oil company (Ecopetrol) and direct transfers from Ecopetrol to an oil savings and stabilization fund (FAEP).[15] Part of the operating surplus is transferred to the central government, another part as royalties for subnational governments, mostly in producing regions, harbors, or regions crossed by pipelines. Resources from the FAEP fund are shared among all subnational governments and Ecopetrol, according to a formula established in the law (the formula takes into account population and tax revenue performance). In sum, a large share of oil revenue accrues to subnational governments, either through direct transfers to the FAEP fund or through royalty payments.

The law on the oil-revenue-sharing system was established to prevent political considerations from influencing use of the revenue. However, these oil-revenue shares (together with guaranteed transfers)

---

[13]As there have been difficulties in the assumption of teachers' salaries by the municipalities, the education function has been only partially decentralized.

[14]This share increased from 5½ percent in 1997 to about 14 percent in 2000.

[15]The fund's objectives are to save part of oil revenues and to stabilize oil-revenue fluctuations.

have had a deleterious effect on macroeconomic stability by inducing some territorial governments to contract debt beyond their repayment capacity. Several subnational governments have been brought to the brink of bankruptcy, and in 2000, seven provinces and two municipalities had to restructure their debt. Moreover, the sharing of oil-related royalties favors relatively small and rich oil-producing subnational governments, exacerbating regional disparities (Ahmad and Baer, 1997).

IV. Federations

Most federal countries use some form of revenue sharing or assignment of tax bases. In the revenue-sharing model, oil revenues are collected by the central government (or by a subnational government in the case of the United Arab Emirates) and redistributed to all or some levels of government according to a specific rule or formula. The alternative assigns specific tax bases to different levels of government— some of these might be overlapping bases.

Revenue-Sharing Arrangements

There are numerous types of revenue-sharing arrangements for oil. Some apply the same rule or formula to share oil revenues as is used for other fiscal transfers, while others have a different rule. Some arrangements favor the derivation principle, whereby each subnational government's share is related to the oil revenue originating in its territory. Others follow criteria such as population, needs, or tax capacity (this makes the resulting revenue share similar to a transfer).[16] Some revenue-sharing arrangements provide relatively large amounts of revenue to subnational jurisdictions (these are rather *decentralizing* arrangements), others provide small amounts (rather *centralizing* arrangements) (see Table 9.2). The first category would include Colombia, Nigeria, Russia, and Venezuela. The second category would include Ecuador, Indonesia, and Mexico.

The main advantage of revenue sharing is that it is a convenient form of transferring fiscal resources to subnational governments, especially

---

[16]See Ahmad and Craig (1997).

if oil is a major source of revenue. While administrative considerations often militate for centralization of tax assignments, including oil revenues, revenue sharing provides a way to redistribute funds to subnational governments. The sharing formula may also be tailored to address various concerns regarding equalization or compensation for special regional needs.

Revenue sharing, however, has major drawbacks with regards to macroeconomic management and overall fiscal discipline (Ter-Minassian, 1997b). Revenue-sharing arrangements reduce the revenue base that the central government can use to stabilize the economy or to adjust the fiscal policy stance—they may distribute revenues that are not commensurate to subnational governments' spending needs—and they leave subnational governments vulnerable to potentially large swings in oil revenues. In addition, these arrangements tend to be politically controversial and unstable.

The alternative to revenue sharing would be assigning specific revenue bases (such as production excises) to the subnational level. Specific excises linked to oil production—instead of prices—may be relatively stable, as well as positively correlated with environmental damages. The United States and Canada represent examples of this variant.

Mexico (limited revenue sharing)

Oil revenue in Mexico represents a significant share of revenue for the public sector, close to one-third during 1997–2000. Over this period, revenues from oil extraction rights, oil excess return levies, and the net income of the state-owned oil company amounted to about 5.3 percent of GDP.

Although most of the oil revenue accrues to the central government, a small part is shared with the subnational governments according to a formula-based system established by the law on fiscal coordination.[17] Specifically, lower level governments receive (i) 20 percent of so-called ordinary oil extraction rights; and (ii) 3.17 percent of the additional oil extraction rights. The former share is incorporated into a general fund, which is distributed to the states based on a fixed formula taking into

---

[17]Subnational governments have considerable expenditure responsibilities, mostly the provision of education (elementary and middle schools), public health care and social services, basic social infrastructure, security, and utilities. Most of their revenues are in the form of conditional transfers and revenue-sharing arrangements with the central government, totaling about 7 percent of GDP.

account their characteristics.[18] The latter share is earmarked for municipalities located in oil-producing regions or where oil is shipped abroad, to compensate for environmental damage caused by the extraction and sale of oil (Amieva-Huerta, 1997).

Revenue sharing from oil has not been a source of political contention in the recent past, mainly because the resources are channeled through a general pool of shared resources and distributed according to a transparent formula. Except for a small part transferred to municipalities involved in oil production and export, there is no direct link between oil-producing subnational governments and oil revenues in the general revenue-sharing arrangement. Moreover, because oil revenue represents a small part of the revenue of the subnational jurisdictions, the oil-revenue sharing has not been a source of fiscal instability.

Nigeria (extensive revenue sharing)

Oil is the main source of revenue in Nigeria, amounting to 82 percent of the total revenue of the general government, or 40 percent of GDP, in 2000.[19] After so-called first charges[20] are withheld, oil revenue is shared among the federal government and state and local governments according to an arrangement whereby the remainder (over 75 percent of gross oil revenue) is divided between the federal government and subnational governments. More specifically, the 1999 constitution assigns the control and collection of oil revenue to the federal government, but attributes at least 13 percent of the net oil revenue to the oil-producing states. In addition, about half of the net proceeds (after deduction of first charges) are redistributed to state and local governments according to a formula decided by parliament every five years. Excess proceeds over the budgeted revenue are also redistributed in the same way, after assigning 13 percent to oil-producing states.

---

[18]In addition, states receive a 20 percent share of the excise tax on gasoline and of the overall VAT revenue. They must redistribute at least 20 percent of their shares to municipalities. Central government transfers are based on revenue estimates included in the annual budget, but are automatically adjusted each month to reflect actual revenues.

[19]Oil revenues consist of (i) crude export earnings of the Nigerian National Petroleum Company (NNPC); (ii) profit taxes and royalties of oil-producing companies (usually joint venture companies with a government majority ownership); and (iii) domestic crude sales and upstream gas sales.

[20]First charges comprise mainly the government share of the production cost of oil ("cash calls") and priority projects of the national oil company, the external debt service, and the 13 percent allocated to oil-producing states.

The formula is clearly defined and based on an oil price assumption used in the budget documents. If the actual price exceeds the budgeted price, the excess proceeds are to be distributed. Excess proceeds need not be spent; they could be saved for spending in the following years. If prices are lower than envisaged, the actual amount is distributed.

State and local governments are highly dependent on revenue-sharing arrangements with the federal government.[21] In 1999, 75 percent of state revenue and 94 percent of local government revenue came from redistributed revenue from the federal government, including for the former, their share of the VAT (85 percent of total proceeds). Most of this revenue was oil related. Federation revenue released to subnational governments rose from 7.4 percent of GDP in 1999 to about 15.3 percent of GDP in 2001.

The two key challenges posed by the Nigerian model of fiscal federalism are the conflicting claims over oil resources and the lack of fiscal discipline of subnational governments (IMF, 2001). As sharing arrangements for oil revenue combine the derivation and distribution principles, they remain highly contentious. Given large disparities in natural resource endowments, oil is concentrated in only a few of the 36 states, which have onshore or offshore oil production. Several oil-producing states claim that they should have total control over their own oil revenues. Others contend that the 13 percent share accruing to oil-producing states should also be applied to oil revenue from offshore production (which represents about 40 percent of oil revenue). Clearly, the sharing agreement has led to severe political problems with oil-producing states demanding an increasing share of oil revenues, and non-oil producers demanding greater redistribution of oil resources.

There is no legal mechanism to impose fiscal discipline on the lower tiers of government. The high oil prices in 2000–2001 led to a large increase in the distribution of financial resources to subnational governments, particularly to oil-producing states, without the corresponding assignment of new expenditure responsibilities. As these transfers were immediately spent, the rapid increase in aggregate demand con-

---

[21]State and local governments are responsible for providing education, health, public works, and local utilities and infrastructure. However, there is little information on subnational governments' budgets, much less on the precise level and composition of their expenditure. In general, it is assumed that subnational expenditures are equal to their revenues, but some subnational governments have accumulated considerable debt vis-à-vis banks.

tributed to a rise in inflation and a sharp depreciation of the currency in the parallel market.

The revenue-sharing arrangement leaves little room to maneuver on the fiscal side. It places the burden of macroeconomic adjustment on the federal government with control over less than half of the federation revenue.

Ideally, financial resources to state and local governments should be insulated from oil price fluctuations, and should be commensurate with the tasks they are assigned to perform and their capacity to effectively spend such resources. This would imply a shift from a transfer system, which relies on the sharing of volatile natural resource revenues, to one that provides for stable financing of the provision of at least a minimum set of essential subnational public services.

Russia

Oil and gas revenues are considerable in Russia. At the federal level, oil revenue is estimated to make up to about 25 percent of total revenue, and 45–50 percent including gas revenues. This includes oil- and gas-related revenue from profit taxes, VAT, excises, export duties, and some resource mineral taxes. Most taxes are collected by the federal government and shared, to a certain extent, with subnational governments according to either negotiated or fixed rate systems.[22] However, natural resource taxes are mainly collected by subnational governments and are important sources of own revenue in oil-producing regions. These taxes include petroleum production royalties, charges for use of mineral deposits, and exploration fees.

Because natural resources, including oil, are highly concentrated in a few regions, decentralization of taxes on these resources creates large disparities in revenue between resource-rich regions and others. In 1997, the five richest regions, accounting for only 5½ percent of the population, collected 53 percent of all subnational government revenues from taxes, fees, and charges on natural resources (Martínez-Vázquez and Boex, 2000).

There have been strong pressures for local control over natural resources. Resource-rich regions with high per capita revenues have demonstrated a strong desire for greater autonomy, and particularly for control over revenue from their own resources. While economic

---

[22]For specific revenue-sharing arrangements, see Martínez-Vázquez and Boex (2000).

arguments would favor centralizing oil rents to minimize large horizontal fiscal disparities, producing regions may resist (McLure, 1994a and 1994b). As in other oil-producing countries (e.g., Nigeria), revenue sharing may not be a fully satisfactory solution, as it would not protect regions from price fluctuations, and they would always be better off keeping a larger share. An alternative may be to assign part of the revenue base (e.g., production excises) and implement an appropriate and reliable fiscal transfer system.

Venezuela

Oil revenue accounts for a large share of central government revenue in Venezuela, on average 47 percent of total revenue during the period 1997–2000 (about 9 percent of GDP). Oil revenues include royalties, income taxes, and dividends, which all accrue to the central government.

Subnational governments play a relatively important fiscal role in Venezuela, with expenditure representing about one-third of central government expenditure. Most of subnational governments' revenues come from revenue-sharing arrangements and transfers, making them dependent on the central government. It is estimated that about half of subnational government revenues are oil related. In addition to receiving 20–25 percent of total central government revenues through various schemes, subnational governments are entitled to 20–30 percent of oil royalties.

Revenue-sharing arrangements are a continuous source of political and fiscal contention. The central government believes that resources assigned to subnational governments are excessive, and that there is little control over the ways these funds are spent. State and local governments, on the other hand, would like to see their share of revenue increased. The issue of oil-revenue sharing will be discussed once again in the context of the draft law on public finance of state and local governments.

United Arab Emirates

The United Arab Emirates is a federation formed in 1971, comprising seven emirates.[23] Each emirate retains a considerable degree of eco-

---

[23]The seven emirates are Abu Dhabi, Ajman, Dubai, Fujairah, Ras Al-Khaimah, Sharjah, and Umm Al-Qaiwan.

nomic and political autonomy, and has full ownership of and control over its oil resources. Oil and gas revenue accounted for about half of total revenue of the consolidated government on average during 1997–2000 (18 percent of GDP).

Oil and gas revenue accrue to emirate governments through royalties, company profit transfers, and income tax receipts. For the largest emirate, Abu Dhabi, 58 percent of revenue came on average from crude oil royalties and taxes during 1997–2000 (about 15 percent of GDP).

The federal government is mostly financed by an upward revenue-sharing arrangement, whereby the oil-producing emirates—mostly Abu Dhabi and, to a lesser extent, Dubai and Sharjah—make cash or in-kind contributions. These contributions and services provided, which represent 60 percent to 106 percent of Abu Dhabi's oil revenue, account for about two-thirds of federal government revenue. As cash contributions are negotiated each year between the federal government and each emirate, there is considerable smoothing between high- and low-price years, providing the federal government with a relatively stable source of revenue despite price fluctuations.

Overlapping Revenue Bases: North America

Assigning specific tax bases—possibly with some overlap between levels of government—represents an attractive alternative to revenue sharing. Canada and the United States are examples of this model, although Canada is close to full decentralization.

United States

The United States assigns resource revenue bases to the states, which are sovereign under the constitution and own the resources (except on federally owned land), but with a sharing of the income tax base—following from its specific political and historical setting (McLure, 1994b). Alaska—where oil revenue represents about four-fifths of own revenue—presents an interesting example of the methods used.

On oil, the state of Alaska levies a property tax (at 2 percent on appraised value); a severance tax ranging from 12¼ percent to 15 percent on oil, subject to a minimum tax per barrel; royalties; a production tax surcharge for hazardous spill; and a corporate income tax. The corporate income tax is based on worldwide corporation net income apportioned to Alaska under a three-factor formula involving (i) the percentage of corporate sales and tariffs from Alaskan operations; (ii) the percentage of production from Alaska; and (iii) the percentage of property represented by Alaska holdings—at a maximum marginal rate of 9.4 percent. All state taxes and royalties are deductible for federal income tax purposes.

The main advantage of this type of system is that the subnational government is fully accountable for the fiscal policy choices related to oil revenues and their possible uses for spending or savings. Alaska has created a fund to save part of the oil revenue for future generations[24] (as has the province of Alberta in Canada).

Canada

In Canada, taxes on natural resources, mostly oil, are also assigned to the provinces, and Canadian provinces levy a range of taxes (including minimum taxes) and royalties on natural resources.[25] However, oil revenues are strongly concentrated in a few provinces, mainly Alberta where these revenues account for about one-quarter of revenue, and Saskatchewan where they represent about one-tenth (Krelove, Stotsky, and Vehorn, 1997). On aggregate, however, oil revenues account for only 3½ percent of the total revenue of subnational governments. While decentralization of oil revenue contributes to the disparities in fiscal capacity among provinces, the federal equalization system takes these into consideration by withholding any equalizing grants from the relatively rich provinces, including oil-producing Alberta.

However, decentralization and the imposition of oil and gas royalties have led to a heavy taxation of these industries (possibly deterring investment) relative to other industries. In addition, the oil-producing provinces have reduced sales and income taxes relative to other non-oil-producing provinces. Some Canadian scholars would prefer to reallocate natural resource taxes from provinces to the center, but rec-

---

[24]The Alaska Permanent Fund was created in 1976 to save part of the large oil revenue derived from the exploitation of the state's oil resources. The fund receives about one-fifth of oil revenue, as well as other discretionary state transfers. It saves part of its revenues and distributes the other part to its residents in the form of an annual dividend. At end-2001, the fund totaled close to US$25 billion in net assets (about 95 percent of state GDP); see Alaska Permanent Fund Corporation (2001).

[25]For a discussion of the role of natural resource rents on the design of the transfer system in Canada, see Boadway and Hobson (1993).

ognize that this is unlikely to happen given the political constraints and the constitutional rights of the provinces.[26]

Canada and the United States have found means to compensate for the drawbacks of assigning oil revenues to subnational governments. First, oil-producing states in these two countries have created oil funds that aim at shielding their budgets from fluctuations in oil revenue and prevent excessive public spending. Second, the federal equalization system in Canada compensates for the large revenue generated by oil-producing provinces by excluding these provinces from the equalization framework. Third, the piggybacking arrangements for personal and corporate income taxes, whereby provinces can set their own tax rates on the federal tax base, contribute to mitigating the volatility of oil revenue by providing a somewhat more stable revenue source.

V. Policy Options

Based on country experiences, this section assesses the various policy options to assign oil revenue to the different levels of government, given the objective of financing a stable level of public services provided by subnational governments.

In an unconstrained world, it would be best to fully centralize oil revenue. This should be accompanied by (i) appropriate revenue assignments that give the subnational administrations control over some major tax rates at the margin (needed for accountability); and (ii) well-designed transfers with appropriate transparency and based on equalization principles—these sources of finance allow a stable level of public services to be provided by the subnational governments and the financing, if necessary, of large infrastructure projects. This would address the issues of oil revenue volatility and uncertainty, disparities in oil revenue among subnational governments, and fiscal discipline and accountability.

However, given the political realities in most countries, some degree of subnational control over natural resource bases or revenues is likely to be needed—this could take the form of revenue sharing or assignment of revenue bases.

Because revenue-sharing arrangements take away large amounts of revenue from the central government, they complicate macroeconomic

---

[26]See Ip and Mintz (1992).

management. Sharing a large revenue source—such as oil taxation—reduces the capacity of the central government to run countercyclical fiscal policies or implement effective fiscal adjustment. The central government may be left with little revenue to exert a significant macroeconomic impact, and subnational governments may not be willing to follow a policy determined at the central level, especially in the case of fiscal adjustment.[27] Further, by fully transmitting the volatility of oil revenue to subnational governments, revenue sharing does not provide stable financing of local public services. Finally, revenue sharing may not always diffuse separatist tendencies, as it may be difficult to agree on the proportion of revenues to be shared—the oil-producing subnational governments can always be better off keeping 100 percent.

For these reasons, *sharing tax bases, with stable elements assigned to subnational governments* (such as specific production excises), may be preferable to revenue sharing. It may also be more desirable, for example, on environmental grounds, since revenue would be correlated with environmental damage. These revenue assignments encourage stronger accountability for the subnational governments concerned, which can determine oil tax rates and the use of oil revenue, and can potentially provide adequate financing. They would need, however, to be assessed against expenditure assignments, and transfer systems designed accordingly. Moreover, subnational governments remain exposed to oil-price volatility, and the oil-revenue base may be at times insufficient.

Hence, several conditions must be met to assign oil revenues to subnational governments:

- Oil should not be assigned solely to subnational governments—that is, there should be some degree of overlap in the oil tax base.
- The amounts of revenue involved should be kept relatively small, if possible.
- If the assignment leads to large or fluctuating revenues, appropriate safeguards and transparency would be needed (such as in Alaska). This is not likely to be possible at the subnational level in most developing countries.

---

[27] Although not related to oil revenue, in Argentina there were several "pacts" between the federal government and the provinces during the 1990s, aiming at sharing the burden of fiscal adjustment. However, these arrangements proved difficult to set up (not all provinces participated) and to enforce (mechanisms to that effect were weak). See Schwartz and Liuksila (1997), and Jiménez and Devoto (2002).

- Subnational governments should be assigned other sources of stable revenues, for example, production excises and piggybacked income taxes supplemented by stable transfers from the center.

If these conditions are met, assigning oil tax bases to subnational governments may provide—for the reasons discussed above—an attractive alternative to oil-revenue sharing.

Appendix. Subnational Taxation, Revenue Assignment, and Revenue-Sharing Arrangements

Subnational Taxation and Revenue Assignment

Arrangements assigning revenue-raising responsibilities to central and subnational governments (SNGs) should seek to promote economic efficiency, distributional equity, macroeconomic stability, and accountability.

First, arrangements should induce the least possible *economic inefficiencies* or *distortions* in the location of economic activities and individuals by limiting wide differences in the tax burden across jurisdictions, and by limiting excessive tax competition. To limit tax-induced movements of businesses, SNGs should be assigned a more *immobile* tax base.

Second, arrangements should favor distributional *equity* by providing all SNGs with a fair share of the national tax base, and by promoting positive incentives with respect to local economic development. Equalization grants may have to correct for an uneven distribution of the tax base or to support jurisdictions facing particularly high costs; but there are limits to the degree of equalization achievable. Thus, the ideal subnational tax base is one that is relatively *evenly distributed* across jurisdictions.

Third, arrangements should provide the central government with *stabilization* instruments, and conversely, shelter the budgets of SNGs from cyclical fluctuations. Thus, subnational taxes should be relatively *insensitive* to movements in GDP and national income. Table 9.3 below summarizes these criteria.

In addition to these criteria, revenue-raising responsibilities should be closely associated with expenditure responsibilities. This links the benefits of public expenditure to their price, namely the taxes levied to finance them. Such a link promotes *fiscal responsibility* and *accountability* of subnational policymakers to their electorate. Instead of relying on

Table 9.3. *Criteria for Assigning Revenue-Raising Responsibilities*

	Central Tax	Subnational Tax
Mobility of tax base	Mobile	Immobile
Distribution of tax base	Uneven	Even across SNGs
Sensitivity to GDP	High	Low

transfers from the central government, SNGs have to adjust the marginal tax rates when they decide to increase expenditure.

According to these criteria, it is generally accepted that corporate income taxes, VAT, taxes on natural resources, and taxes on international trade should be assigned to the central government. Personal income taxes appear more suitable for—at least partial—assignment to the subnational level, since the mobility of individuals and households tends to be less than that of businesses. However, to minimize distortions and tax-induced movements of labor and capital, it is preferable that the definition of the subnational tax base be homogeneous throughout the country and that rate differentials among SNGs be kept relatively small. Single-stage sales and excise taxes can be assigned to SNGs, provided that the rates do not differ excessively among regions. Property taxes, business license taxes, and user fees for local services are also good potential subnational taxes, since their base is relatively immobile.

Tax Assignment and Revenue-Sharing Arrangements

Tax bases can be assigned either exclusively to one level of government (separation of tax bases) or shared among several levels (overlapping tax bases). In the latter case, the same tax base, for example personal income, would be used by both central and subnational governments (SNGs) as the base of their own taxation, which may have different tax rates and schedules.

Once a tax has been assigned to one level or another, there remains the possibility to share the tax receipts among levels of government (*revenue sharing*). This requires a definition of the share of receipts to be allocated to SNGs, and the appropriate formula for distributing this share among the different SNGs. Typically, the formula can be based either on the revenue that has been collected in each jurisdiction (derivation principle), or on other criteria such as population, expenditure needs (needs assessment), and tax capacity (resource base).

Box 9.1. *Revenue Assignments and Fiscal Autonomy of Subnational Governments*

Own taxes	Base and rate under local control.
Overlapping tax bases	Nationwide tax base, but total rates (national and subnational governments) under SNG control.
Nontax revenues	Fees and charges under SNG control, but sometimes with specific provisions set by the central government.
Revenue sharing	Nationwide tax base and rates. A fixed proportion is allocated to SNGs, according to the derivation principle or some needs- or resource-based formula.
General purpose grants (block grants)	Determined by the central government, but SNGs are free to determine how the grant should be spent. The amount received may have an equalization component.
Specific or conditional grants	The central government specifies the expenditure program for which the funds should be spent.

In addition to tax or revenue-sharing arrangements, *grants* from the central government to SNGs are often an important component of intergovernmental financial transfers. Grants can be unconditional transfers usable for general purposes, or can be conditioned by the grantor to specific uses, for example to finance specific programs or projects. Box 9.1 summarizes the various possible arrangements for assigning revenue to SNGs, which result in decreasing degrees of fiscal autonomy (see Norregaard, 1997).

Bibliography

Ahmad, Ehtisham, and Katherine Baer, 1997, "Colombia," in *Fiscal Federalism in Theory and Practice*, ed. by Teresa Ter-Minassian (Washington: International Monetary Fund), pp. 457–503.

Ahmad, Ehtisham, and Jon Craig, 1997, "Intergovernmental Transfers," in *Fiscal Federalism in Theory and Practice*, ed. by Teresa Ter-Minassian (Washington: International Monetary Fund), pp. 73–107.

Ahmad, Ehtisham, and Ali Mansoor, 2002, "Indonesia: Managing Decentralization," IMF Working Paper 02/136 (Washington: International Monetary Fund).

Ahmad, Ehtisham, and Raju J. Singh, 2003, "Political Economy of Oil-Revenue Sharing in a Developing Country: Illustrations from Nigeria," IMF Working Paper 03/16 (Washington: International Monetary Fund).

Ahmad, Ehtisham, and Vito Tanzi, eds., 2002, *Managing Fiscal Decentralization* (London: Routledge).

Alaska Permanent Fund Corporation, 2001, *An Alaskan's Guide to the Permanent Fund* (Juneau, Alaska).

Amieva-Huerta, Juan, 1997, "Mexico," in *Fiscal Federalism in Theory and Practice*, ed. by Teresa Ter-Minassian (Washington: International Monetary Fund), pp. 570–97.

Boadway, Robin, and Paul A.R. Hobson, 1993, "Intergovernmental Fiscal Relations in Canada," Canadian Tax Paper No. 96 (Toronto: Canadian Tax Foundation).

Boadway, Robin, and Anwar Shah, 1994, "Fiscal Federalism in Developing/ Transition Economies: Some Lessons from Industrialized Countries," in *National Tax Association: Proceedings of the 86th Annual Conference on Taxation, 1993* (Columbus, Ohio), pp. 64–71.

Breton, Albert, 2002, "An Introduction to Decentralization Failure," in *Managing Fiscal Decentralization*, ed. by Ehtisham Ahmad and Vito Tanzi (London: Routledge).

Brosio, Giorgio, 2000, "Decentralization in Africa," IMF Conference on Fiscal Decentralization, November 20–21, 2000. Available via the Internet: http://www.imf.org.

International Monetary Fund, 2001, *Nigeria: Selected Issues and Statistical Appendix*, IMF Staff Country Report No. 01/132 (Washington).

———, 2002, *Indonesia: Selected Issues*, IMF Staff Country Report No. 02/154 (Washington).

Ip, Irene K., and Jack M. Mintz, 1992, *Dividing the Spoils: The Federal-Provincial Allocation of Taxing Powers* (Toronto: C.D. Howe Institute).

Jiménez, Juan Pablo, and F. Devoto, 2002, "Argentina: Coordination of Subnational Borrowing," in *Managing Fiscal Decentralization*, ed. by Ehtisham Ahmad and Vito Tanzi (London: Routledge).

Krelove, Russell, Janet G. Stotsky, and Charles L. Vehorn, 1997, "Canada," in *Fiscal Federalism in Theory and Practice*, ed. by Teresa Ter-Minassian (Washington: International Monetary Fund), pp. 201–25.

Martínez-Vázquez, Jorge, and Jameson Boex, 2000, *Russia's Transition to a New Federalism* (Washington: World Bank).

McLure, Jr., Charles E., 1983, "Fiscal Federalism and the Taxation of Economic Rents," in *State and Local Finance: The Pressures of the 1980s*, ed. by George F. Break (Madison, Wisconsin: University of Wisconsin Press), pp. 133–60.

————, 1994a, "The Taxation of Natural Resources and the Future of the Russian Federation," in *National Tax Association: Proceedings of the 86th Annual Conference on Taxation, 1993* (Columbus, Ohio), pp. 87–91.

————, 1994b, "The Sharing of Taxes on Natural Resources and the Future of the Russian Federation," in *Russia and the Challenge of Fiscal Federalism*, ed. by Christine I. Wallich (Washington: World Bank), pp. 181–217.

————, 1998, "The Revenue Assignment Problem: Ends, Means, and Constraints," *Journal of Public Budgeting, Accounting, and Financial Management*, Vol. 9 (Winter), pp. 652–83.

————, 2000, "Tax Assignment and Subnational Fiscal Autonomy," *Bulletin for International Fiscal Documentation*, Vol. 54 (December), pp. 626–35.

————, 2001, "The Tax Assignment Problem: Ruminations on How Theory and Practice Depend on History," *National Tax Journal* (Washington), Vol. 54, No. 2, pp. 339–64.

Mieszkowski, Peter, 1983, "Energy Policy, Taxation of Natural Resources, and Fiscal Federalism," in *Tax Assignment in Federal Countries*, ed. by Charles E. McLure, Jr. (Canberra: Australian National University), pp. 129–45.

————, and Eric Toder, 1983, "Taxation of Energy Resources," in *Fiscal Federalism and the Taxation of Natural Resources*, ed. by Charles E. McLure, Jr. and Peter Mieszkowski (Lexington, Massachusetts: Lexington Books), pp. 65–91.

Norregaard, John, 1997, "Tax Assignment," in *Fiscal Federalism in Theory and Practice*, ed. by Teresa Ter-Minassian (Washington: International Monetary Fund), pp. 49–72.

Schwartz, Gerd, and Claire Liuksila, 1997, "Argentina," in *Fiscal Federalism in Theory and Practice*, ed. by Teresa Ter-Minassian (Washington: International Monetary Fund), pp. 387–422.

Tanzi, Vito, 1996, "Fiscal Federalism and Decentralization: A Review of Some Efficiency and Macroeconomic Aspects," *Annual World Bank Conference on Development Economics, 1995*, ed. by M. Bruno and B. Pleskovic (Washington: World Bank), pp. 295–316.

Ter-Minassian, Teresa, 1997a, "Intergovernmental Fiscal Relations in a Macroeconomic Perspective: An Overview," in *Fiscal Federalism in Theory and Practice*, ed. by Teresa Ter-Minassian (Washington: International Monetary Fund), pp. 3–24.

————, 1997b, "Decentralization and Macroeconomic Management," IMF Working Paper 97/155 (Washington: International Monetary Fund).

10

Oil Revenue and Fiscal Federalism

Giorgio Brosio

Introduction

Although the theory hardly recommends revenues from oil and gas as an ideal source of finance for subnational governments—with the exception of funds to compensate social and environment damages and to finance additional needs for infrastructure in the producing areas—the role these revenues play in subnational budgets is expanding worldwide. Matching the current general trend toward more decentralized governments, national regulation and taxation policies of the oil sector are increasingly recognizing the right of subnational governments to have a greater share of the resources generated by this sector. In fact, a large number of oil- and natural gas-producing countries have recently introduced sharing arrangements among different levels of government (see Table 10.1). A similar trend is taking place in favor of indigenous peoples and their formal, or informal, organizations (see Andrews-Speed and Rogers, 1999; Clark and Clark, 1999; O'Faircheal-laigh, 1998; United Nations ESCAP, 2001). Basically, the allocation of oil rents among levels of governments is following a pattern quite similar to that of other mineral rents.

Decentralization expands the bargaining power of subnational governments by institutionalizing their demands, particularly where centrifugal forces are in action. These demands have been strengthened by frequent disregard of the problems created to local communities by exploration and exploitation activities. In fact, sound theoretical principles and technical arguments stressing the merits of national governance of natural resources are not easily expendable among local politicians when the central government neglects their problems.

Table 10.1. *Systems for Sharing Oil Revenue in Selected Countries*

Country	Onshore Production	Offshore Production	Equalization System for Oil Revenue	Legal Basis or Source
Argentina	Royalties up to a maximum rate of 12.0 percent paid to producing provinces.		Fondo de Regalías Petroleras distributes collections between federal government and provinces.	Ley de federalización de hidrocarburos 24,145.
Australia	States impose royalties and excise tax on onshore projects and coastal waters. Share royalties on coastal waters with Commonwealth.	Commonwealth levies a Petroleum Resource Rent Tax (PRRT) or crude oil excise and royalty on offshore projects. Shares royalty with states. The PRRT on offshore projects is shared 75 percent federal, 25 percent to Western Australia (WA).		See sources.
Bolivia	Oil royalties are attributed to provincial governments and also 25 percent of collections from the special hydrocarbons tax.		Up to 10 percent of taxes on oil are distributed by the Fondo Compensatorio Departamental to provinces with below the national average per capita royalties.	Law 1702 of 1996. (Ley de Participación Popular, 1994 www.congreso.gov.bo/11leyes/leyes/1551.htm.)
Brazil	Share of royalties exceeding 5 percent of value of production is distributed as follows: 52.5 percent to producing states; 15 percent to producing municipalities; 7.5 percent to transporting	Royalties referring to continental shelf are distributed as follows: 22.5 percent to facing producing states; 22.5 percent to facing producing municipalities; 7.5 percent to transporting		Law 9478 of 1997. The proceeds of the first 5 percent share are distributed according to law 7990 of 1989.

	municipalities. Remaining 25 percent goes to federal government. In addition, there is a sharing system by which gross revenue on production (minus investments, costs, taxes, and royalties) is distributed: 40 percent to producing states; 10 percent to producing municipalities; 50 percent to federal ministries.	municipalities; 7.5 percent to Fundo Especial to be distributed to all states and municipalities. Remaining share goes to the federal government.	
Canada	Provinces are free to levy taxes and royalties on natural resources.	The federal government has the right to levy royalties. A sharing system with the province of Labrador and Newfoundland is in operation.	See sources.
Colombia	Royalty rates are determined by central government. A ceiling determined on the basis of production is imposed on royalty earnings. Proceeds are distributed as follows: 47.5 percent to producing departments; 25 percent to producing municipalities; 8 percent to transporting municipalities and harbors; 19.5 percent to Fondo Nacional de Regalías.	Fondo Nacional de Regalías. Distributes proceeds according to development projects presented by departments and municipalities (including the producing ones).	The constitution assigns property rights on land to the states. Offshore projects are governed by the Offshore Constitutional Settlement of 1979. Royalties by Petroleum (Submerged Lands) Act of 1967.

Table 10.1. (*continued*)

Country	Onshore Production	Offshore Production	Equalization System for Oil Revenue	Legal Basis or Source
Indonesia	70 percent of royalties from the sale of oil and natural gas to the provinces of Aceh and Irian Jaya, which have a special autonomous status. Other producing provinces receive 3 percent of royalties on oil and 6 percent on gas. Local governments receive 6 percent and 12 percent.			Mining Royalties Act, 1992.
Italy	Onshore royalties are set at 7 percent of annual net production, or the equivalent value. No royalties have to be paid on annual production up to 20,000 metric tons of liquid oil. Producing regions receive 55 percent of royalties; municipalities where facilities and wells are located receive a share of 15 percent.	Four percent of offshore royalties are paid to the regions. Royalties on production in territorial waters are also attributed to the regions.		Law 141 of 1994.
Malaysia	5 percent of oil royalties are attributed to the states of Sabah, Sarawak, and Terengganu.			Decree no. 625/96.

Nigeria	The constitution mandates 13 percent of total oil revenue to be distributed to the producing states. These states also have access to general transfers.	Constitution.
Papua New Guinea	A royalty of 2 percent on sales revenue is shared between provincial government (80 percent) and landowners (20 percent). In addition, the Special Support Grant—equivalent to a royalty of 1 percent—is paid on a derivation basis to the provincial government (20 percent goes to the producing local government).	See sources.
Peru	20 percent of income taxes collected from mining activities are distributed to regional and 30 percent to local governments.	Law of July 2001.
Philippines	According to the "National Wealth Revenue Sharing," 40 percent of mining revenues are returned to the producing subnational governments.	See sources.

Table 10.1. (*concluded*)

Country	Onshore Production	Offshore Production	Equalization System for Oil Revenue	Legal Basis or Source
Russia	A petroleum royalty with a tax rate of 6–16 percent is shared: 40 percent to federation; 30 percent to producing oblasts, republics; 30 percent to rayon and cities. Excise tax: variable specific rates. Shared: 30 percent to federation; 70 percent to first tier governments.	Royalties are federally determined and shared: 40 percent to federation; 60 percent to producing oblasts, rayons, or cities.		Russian Federation Law on the Subsoil, 1992, and later changes.
United States	The states are free to levy taxes and royalties, but not on federally owned land.			

Sources: Garnaut and Ross (1983); PricewaterhouseCoopers (1998); Otto (2001); Daniel and others (2000). In addition, legal texts shown in the table can be found on the official government websites of the concerned countries. Additional country-specific sources are: for Argentina, San Miguel (1999); for Australia, Government of Australia (2001); for Canada, Government of Canada, The Atlantic Accord (1985), and Rodgers (1998); for Indonesia, Malaysia, and the Philippines, United Nations Economic and Social Commission for Asia and the Pacific (2001); for Papua New Guinea, Daniel and others (2000); for Russia, Gray (1998).

Harmonizing conflicting claims and making efficient use of the revenue generated by oil and natural gas resources are therefore daunting tasks. There are, however, instruments available to governments, along with evidence showing how these conflicts can be softened and related problems can be alleviated. For example, when it is not politically feasible to resist the demands from producing areas for a share of the resource, a revenue-sharing scheme that leaves the taxing decisions to the central government is a better system than devolving oil taxation power to local governments. This is because, as will be shown in Box 10.1 later, taxation of oil is better managed at the central than at the local government level. Equalization mechanisms also have to be used to allow nonproducing regions to share a part of the oil revenue and to alleviate the equity and efficiency problems deriving from assigning oil revenue to the producing regions.

The paper is organized as follows. Section II presents the main features of oil exploitation activities that impact on intergovernmental relations. Section III reviews the pros and cons of assigning oil revenue to subnational governments. While the main argument against revenue sharing is the sizable geographical concentration of these revenues, claims by the producing areas cannot be completely dismissed on efficiency and equity grounds. Systems for sharing oil revenue and their main features—with a stronger emphasis on sharing of tax bases—are examined in Section IV, focusing on the unsuitability of natural resources to form the base of local taxes; evidence showing the increasing access by subnational governments to oil revenue is also presented. Equalization mechanisms are analyzed in Section V, where the focus is on how and to what extent these mechanisms can be adjusted to accommodate large disparities in oil revenue across regions. Section VI concludes.

Although the paper does not focus explicitly on developing countries, the arguments presented are of relevance to them.

Features of Oil Exploitation Impacting on the Assignment of Revenue

A few features concerning oil exploitation are important when discussing its implications for intergovernmental relations.

The first and most important feature is the sizable geographic concentration of oil production—the most common case in large and medium-sized countries. Oil production in Colombia is located in only two provinces; the Siberian oblast of Tyumen produces almost two-thirds of total Russian oil; and in Argentina a single province, Neuquén, produces more than one-third of total oil output. In addition, in a number of countries, oil is discovered and exploited in sparsely populated areas. Russia shows, possibly, the most striking case, with the oblast of Tyumen having only 1 percent of the Russian population. The province of Neuquén in Argentina comes close: its inhabitants are a mere 1.5 percent of the total population.

When oil rents are assigned exclusively to subnational governments, they tend to produce vast horizontal imbalances—that is, extremely large disparities in per capita revenues of subnational units. In Alaska, for example, petroleum revenue peaked in 1981 at US$3.3 billion, equivalent to about US$8,000 per capita. Presently, dividends from Alaska's Permanent Fund, where most oil revenue is accumulated, are close to US$2,000 per capita (see Eifert, Gelb, and Tallroth, Chapter 4 in this volume). Obviously, large imbalances across subnational jurisdictions foster political pressures and provide theoretical ground for national equalization of these resources. At the same time, sparsely populated regions carry little weight in national politics, particularly in weak democracies with limited mechanisms of checks and balances. This factor increases subnational jurisdictions' perceived risks of having to bear the costs of exploitation without reaping the benefits, if oil revenue entitlements are transferred to the national government. In general, when local jurisdictions have little power at the central level, they make increased demands for decentralization of powers and resources.

Secondly, oil and natural gas are rapidly depleting resources, sometimes creating the typical "boomtown" phenomenon. Exploration and production attract individuals and capital, but reserves can be rapidly exhausted. Large-scale projects require vast investments and impact geographically on small areas. Even when local governments do not benefit from oil revenue, the economic impact of oil on local communities is large and difficult to regulate. Inflow of workers[1] and population can be significant, with related substantial risks of social disruption and environmental damage. In addition, oil exploration and, to a lesser extent, its production entail large pecuniary externalities, such as higher land rents and increased local costs of living in the nearby communities. Potentially, those risks could be compensated by

---

[1]For example, in the oil-producing department of Casanare in Colombia, more than 7,000 workers, in a population of fewer than 200,000, were attracted to the area during the construction period.

higher development at the local level (however, pecuniary externalities impacting on the price of inputs and factors can seriously hamper it) and by construction of infrastructure in transport and communications. Local governments' involvement in controlling damages, providing infrastructure, and diversifying growth can hardly be denied, but it requires resources and skills.

Thirdly, oil prices show large and unpredictable fluctuations. According to empirical evidence (Barnett and Vivanco, Chapter 5 in this volume; and Davis and others, Chapter 11 in this volume) prices do not seem to have a well-defined time-invariant average. In other words, there is no notion of a "normal" price toward which actual price reverts to at the end of boom or slump periods. Hence, volatility of oil revenue is much higher than for other sources of fiscal revenue. This compromises fiscal management and the efficiency of spending, particularly in countries whose revenue base is highly dependent on natural resources.

Finally, energy policy is mostly a national responsibility, worldwide. This is particularly the case when the oil sector represents a large share of economic activity and is the dominant source of public revenue.[2] High shares of oil revenue in total revenue also reflect the disincentive effects of oil discovery on tax efforts and on the diversification of the economy. At the same time, high oil revenue shares give rise to an intense struggle for the division of the "pie" among a number of organized and strongly competing parties. These include, in addition to the producing companies, national and subnational governments, local communities, and, in some countries, the army.[3]

III. Theoretical Arguments for and against Funding Subnational Governments with Revenues from Natural Resources

This section considers the general issue of the suitability of oil revenue as a source of finance for subnational governments. Since on eq-

---

[2]For example, in Nigeria, about 82 percent of total public revenue is currently derived from oil, and in Venezuela more than 50 percent.

[3]In November 2000, the Congressional Economic Committee of Ecuador established a formula whereby the military would receive 45 percent of the royalties of state-owned Petroecuador's production (about US$127 million based on 1999 output), against a request from the military of 50 percent of all crude oil royalties. Furthermore, the formula limits the military share to a three-year period, ending the previous military's 30-year stake.

uity and efficiency grounds, producing areas have to be compensated for oil exploitation and production costs, the assignment of net, rather than gross, revenue is considered. These costs will be briefly addressed before analyzing the revenue assignment issue.

Additional Costs of Investment in Infrastructure

Although most investment for the exploitation of oil and other natural resources is made directly by the producing companies, additional investment in local infrastructure is usually needed. Roads to the producing fields have to be built; airports and ports may have to be upgraded; school, health, and social services have to be expanded to serve the growing population attracted to the area. If the demand for these services exceeds the level that would have prevailed in the absence of oil and natural resources extraction, the governments of the producing jurisdictions are entitled to have these additional costs funded. Since the oil rent is the income in excess of that required to cover the costs of all inputs necessary for production, both efficiency and equity considerations suggest that the costs faced by subnational governments are refunded before this rent is distributed. In other words, only the net rent has to be allocated.

In a way this amounts to applying the peak load pricing principle to oil exploration and production expenses (McLure, 1983). The principle says that the cost of expansion of the capacity has to be borne by those who make use of it. Those companies are the equivalent of peak-hours users of mass transportation. However, effective implementation of the peak load principle is far from easy, since the effective beneficiary of the expansion has to be determined, that is, oil-producing companies or the local population.

Compensation of Environmental Damages

The same arguments apply to environmental costs. These social costs have to be added to those borne by the producing companies to determine the total rent generated by a project and should be refunded to the concerned jurisdictions. Environmental damages caused by oil can be substantial and the cost of correcting them can be large. The most obvious example is environmental degradation caused by burning natural gas at the wellhead instead of exploiting it.

There are well-established techniques for assessing environmental damages; uniform national standards have to be used, so that environmental standards set up for oil-producing areas are not higher or lower than those set up for areas concerned with other economic activities. As in the case of infrastructure capacity costs, environmental damages require joint assessment and negotiation among different levels of government.

Assignment of Net Rent and Efficiency

Possible distortions can arise from the way oil resources are spent. In this sense, revenue from natural resources is similar to that from any other tax base. Unequal access to revenue allows governments to spend it inappropriately. As shown in the literature (Boadway and Flatters, 1982; McLure, 1983), unless beneficiary subnational governments spend these revenues for "country building policies"— such as the provision of purely national public goods, the construction of truly national infrastructure, or portfolio investments in financial assets made according to the same principles followed by private investors—labor and capital allocation distortions are inevitable. This is because energy-rich subnational governments can apply lower tax rates, or grant higher subsidies, to suppliers of labor and capital. Since the location of individuals (and capital) would be dictated by after-tax and subsidy income, the migration of production factors would not be related to factor productivity, or to the living amenities of oil-producing areas, thus potentially leading to efficiency losses.[4]

Substantial efficiency losses can also derive from misspending of oil revenue in oil-rich jurisdictions. In turn, misspending can derive from insufficient absorption capacity and/or from corruption; this problem is exacerbated by the regional concentration of oil rents. While the central government is not inherently superior in administering funds, the sheer size of oil revenue constitutes a larger challenge for smaller gov-

---

[4]The magnitude of the loss depends on migration elasticities, that is, on region-specific factors. For example, migration elasticities in Alaska are surely much lower than in other U.S. states. They can, however, be substantial in developing countries, where employment opportunities are scarce nationwide, especially when oil is discovered in nonremote and hospitable areas.

ernments, especially in developing countries with recent traditions of local self-administration.[5]

Similar arguments apply regarding the evaluation of the likely impact of corruption. The prevalence of corruption depends, among other things, on the level of information, political system, administrative traditions, homogeneity of local jurisdictions, and sectoral composition of expenditure at the national and local levels. However, concentration of resources within a small jurisdiction may weaken the constraints on corrupt behavior. In a number of countries, access to oil revenue has produced corruption and a generalized weakening of public institutions. However, empirical evidence refers almost exclusively to central governments, because until recently oil rents were reserved to the center, as noted above (for example, Bergesen, Haugland, and Lunde, 2000; Oxfam, 2001).

Assignment of Net Revenue and Constitutional Arrangements

Constitutional arrangements cannot be invoked in setting equity criteria for the intergovernmental allocation of oil rents, apart from the case of confederations, where oil and its revenue are property of the members of the confederation and not of the confederation itself. This is because the primary allegiance of citizens is to the confederated states, and nothing is due to the confederation that does not derive from a decision of each distinct confederated state.[6] In the more common case of federations, their nature does not help per se to settle disputes over property rights. In other words, while the constitution of a federal state may attribute property rights to its states, the constitution of another one may actually mandate the reverse. Furthermore, constitutions can be amended and be subject to contrasting interpretations.

---

[5]A World Bank study on the oil-producing department of Casanare in Colombia illustrates the risk of wasting oil revenues when they reach sizable levels in a short period of time. Casanare, created in 1991, is one of the newest departments in Colombia. Oil royalties were negligible until 1994, then reached 73 percent of the department total income by 1997. According to the law, local governments must invest 100 percent of royalties in high-priority projects in the sectors of education, public health, sewage systems, and water supply. However, in 1996 only 40 percent of the royalties had been spent in those high-priority sectors (Davy, McPhail, and Sandoval Moreno, 1999).

[6]Even when simple majority vote is required, confederated states still have a vetoing power that can ultimately be exercised through secession.

Canada and Nigeria provide good examples of the latitude of possible interpretations of constitutional arrangements and of the conflicting views about possible amendments. Canadian non-oil-producing provinces have traditionally adhered to the principle that Canada is a single nation and a single community. If so, natural resources belong to the federal government and should be shared among all provinces, and/or used for country-building purposes. Oil-producing provinces held the opposite view, stressing the primacy of provincial communities; national majorities should not be entitled to take natural resources away from where they are produced.[7]

In Nigeria, interregional conflict on oil has originated secessions, civil wars, and the frequent demise of democracy. Oil-producing federated states have traditionally taken on the view that "equitable federalism" implies the adoption of the derivation principle (resources stay where they are produced). Producing states have brought forward the principle that equitable federalism means redistribution (Ikein and Briggs-Anigboh, 1998).

Assignment of Net Revenue and Principles of Distributive Justice

Theories of distributive justice are useful for understanding the evolution of constitutional arrangements concerning the allocation of rents from natural resources, rather than for setting up specific criteria for revenue assignments.

An example is offered by a positive interpretation of the Rawlsian approach. When little or nothing is known about oil reserves and their value, a proponent of Rawls' theory of justice would suggest that these revenues should be centralized because of the large uncertainty concerning the distribution of oil reserves among the various areas of the country. In other words, every individual would vote for centralization, if he or she had to decide under a "veil of ignorance" and faced with the possible risk of receiving no revenue, if it turns out that his or her region has no reserves at all and oil property rights are decentralized. Experience shows that, when the vast potentials associated with

---

[7]It should has also to be noted that the Canadian provinces situated on the Atlantic coast shifted gradually from the nation-building to the province-building approach when their prospects of oil discoveries became brighter (Simeon, 1980; and McMillan, 1982).

oil discoveries became common knowledge, but the actual distribution among regions remained unknown because no exploration had yet been made, constitutional provisions about property rights on natural resources became more detailed and ownership and control of natural resources were vested to the central government.[8]

However, when the veil of ignorance about the effective location of oil disappears, as happened in some Latin American countries in the early 1990s, constitutions adopted in that period showed a shift toward the explicit recognition of subnational government entitlement to oil revenue (for example, in Argentina and Colombia). This is because resource-rich jurisdictions exerted increasing pressures on the writers of those constitutions to see that their property rights were recognized.

The same rich jurisdictions would not appeal to Rawlsian principles of justice, which would protect the right of the less endowed areas, but rather to Nozick's criteria of justice. Specifically, they would argue that oil reserves and the benefits from their exploitation are legally acquired property rights and that there is no way of dispossessing the jurisdictions that benefit from these rights.

On the basis of countries' current social and redistribution policies, it is hard to imagine a country's social welfare function that would assign the entire oil revenue to producing jurisdictions. At the same time, it would be hard to imagine a social welfare function that would totally disregard the claims of the producing jurisdictions to have a share of net oil rents. In other words, present-day political orientations are for redistribution of wealth, but not for total equalization, which translates into centralized assignment of most net oil rent and recognition of a small share to the producing jurisdictions. This recognition is also attributable to political expediency, as it can be essential for keeping countries together and for fostering nation building. To this end, national and local shares should be negotiated and subject to continuous renegotiation, while no party holding a stake should have a veto power concerning the allocation.

In any negotiation, the result depends on the distribution of bargaining power among contestants. In the case of natural resources, the central government has plenty of instruments to bend negotiations to its favor, or to correct their result. This is clearly shown by the

---

[8]Before then, when very little was known about oil, constitutions ignored the issue or left oil to subnational government property.

moves of the federal government in Canada after the first oil shock (McLure, 1983). To counteract the excessive shift of resource in favor of Alberta, Canada resorted to a few but quite effective decisions, including

- holding domestic prices below market prices. This system benefits consumers (but has efficiency and equity costs);
- levying export taxes on foreign sales of oil, reducing room for subnational taxes;
- eliminating deductions for subnational taxes and royalties in the calculation of central income (company) tax liability; and
- modifying the formula used for equalization in a way that penalized producing and too tax-prone subnational governments.

IV. Sharing Oil Revenue Among Levels of Government

Three systems are used for sharing revenue from natural resources among the central and the subnational levels of government.

Tax base sharing. In this system, subnational governments can levy specific taxes on natural resources situated within their jurisdiction. Subnational governments can determine the tax bases and the tax rates freely, as found mostly in old federations. In otherwise decentralized systems, tax rates are set within the limits imposed by the central government. In a number of countries, there is an overlapping of tax bases, that is, more than one level of government has access to the same oil-tax base.

Tax revenue sharing. In this system, tax bases, tax rates, and revenue shares accruing to the producing and/or transporting subnational governments are determined by the central government.[9] This is now the most common system. Examples are provided both by federal countries, such as Australia, Brazil, Argentina, Russia, and Canada (in the case of the "Atlantic Accord" concerning the Newfoundland and Labrador provincial government) and by nonfederal countries, such as Colombia, Bolivia, Papua New Guinea, and Italy (a more complete list

---

[9]In lieu of taxation, two alternative systems for diverting to the public sector a share of revenue from natural resources are presently used. Revenue can arise from bidding for the rights to exploit resources and from holding equity in oil companies. In these cases, the central government conducts the bidding and shares its results, or it acquires a share of equity in producing companies and then transfers part of it to subnational entities.

of these arrangements is provided in Table 10.1). A recent trend shows that revenue from offshore oil, which is everywhere property of the central government, is being shared also among neighboring subnational governments. This is the case of Canada, Australia, Brazil, and Italy. Since there are much lower infrastructure costs and almost no externalities from offshore exploration and production, sharing with subnational governments shows the intensity of their pressures and the difficulties of resisting them.[10]

In a number of countries, such as Bolivia and Colombia, a part of revenue from natural resources is kept in separate equalization funds and then used for allocations to nonproducing local jurisdictions. Well-structured fiscal equalization systems for subnational governments, such as the Australian and Canadian ones, include revenue from natural resources in the determination of the fiscal capacity of beneficiary jurisdictions. An implication of this is that, even in nonproducing jurisdictions, subnational government revenue is somehow determined by the availability of natural resources and their fluctuating trends.

In-kind revenue sharing. According to this system—which plays a minor role in the allocation of oil revenue—the producing and/or transporting subnational governments have access to a share of natural resource revenue generated within their jurisdiction via the provision of infrastructure by the companies that exploit these resources and on the basis of an explicit national regulation. The most quoted example is provided by the "Infrastructure Tax Credit Scheme" of Papua New Guinea, whereby up to 2 percent of a developer's total tax obligation can be spent on infrastructure within the province in a given year, providing the infrastructure is approved by the department of mining and petroleum, the provincial government, and the taxation office (Andrews-Speed and Rogers, 1999). This system is not to be confused with the common practice by producing companies of providing, on a voluntary basis, infrastructure and services to the areas concerned by their operations. This is done to alleviate the problems created by their activity and to promote better relations with local communities and local governments (see, for illustration, Davy and McPhail, 1998; Filer, 1995; and Labonne, 1995).

---

[10]Ahmad amd Mottu (Chapter 9 in this volume) present a summary ofthe most relevant revenue-sharing schemes

These three systems are not mutually exclusive. For example, in Papua New Guinea the Infrastructure Tax Credit Scheme coexists with the sharing of revenue from royalties on oil, while in other countries tax-base sharing coexists with revenue sharing. An evaluation of the three systems is provided in Box 10.1.

V. Oil Revenues and Equalization Systems

Disparities in the revenues from oil, and the problems arising from them, can be attenuated through equalization mechanisms, especially when the constitution, or previous agreements that are not easily renegotiable, grant a large share of oil revenues to producing jurisdictions.

Equalization of Net Against Gross Revenues

To the extent that oil revenue represents a compensation for environmental damages and a refund of industry-specific infrastructure costs, it does not constitute additional resources. As noted above, only revenue in excess of those compensations and costs should be subject to equalization.

Netting revenues is not usually done for nonnatural resource taxes. Equalization systems assume that there are no collection costs for the taxes they include in the equalization process. This is a reasonable and simplifying assumption, when all the concerned subnational government units have access to the same tax bases, as collection costs should be broadly similar across the various areas. However, in the case of oil and other natural resources this may not be the case. Hence, including gross revenues in equalization schemes without any consideration of what producing jurisdictions have spent for generating the tax base amplifies the revenue capacity from natural resources compared with other tax bases, or to the same tax base in other jurisdictions.

Canada has partly solved this problem by scaling back by 30 percent the natural resource revenue subject to equalization. This offset provision applies only to those provinces that have 70 percent or more of the total tax base from a revenue source (Courchène, 1998). An alternative solution, much fairer but more difficult to implement, would be to equalize effective net revenues, by itemizing infrastructure costs, as broadly done in Australia.

Box 10.1. *Evaluation of Oil-Revenue-Sharing Systems*

Sharing Tax Bases

From the point of view of local governments, natural resources would provide an optimal tax base for the following reasons:

- the tax base is immobile, so the imposition of the tax does not affect its location;
- to a large extent, the burden of natural resource taxes is borne outside the producing jurisdictions; this avoids the political pressure that is usually associated with the imposition of taxes;
- local jurisdictions can fully exploit the favorable location of natural resources.

However, the need for choosing efficient systems of taxation, administration difficulties, and the relevance of national interests in energy policy weigh against revenue assignment to subnational governments. For example, a tax on the actual cash flow of producing firms (also called the rent resource tax)[1] has a complex design, and its administration is exceedingly difficult for subnational governments. General (or oil-industry-tailored) income taxes also present problems, due to their complex information requirements and the need for a sophisticated tax administration to deal with large international companies.[2] Moreover, the application of cash flow or income taxes implies that tax liabilities will be negative at the start of new projects. Thus, tax collections will flow in only after the project is operational, a burden that subnational governments are unlikely to be able to bear (particularly considering their need to build the infrastructure before the start of production).

Consequently, the choice of tax instruments comes down to production-based taxes, such as royalties and severance taxes.[3] These are in fact the

---

[1]Garnaut and Clunies Ross (1975 and 1983); Boadway and Flatters (1993); Otto (1995); Emerson (2000); Sunley and Baunsgaard (2001).

[2]For example, apportioning of collections among different jurisdictions may be difficult when the same company operates across different jurisdictions.

[3]These are excise taxes levied on oil production by states in the United States.

Systems for Equalization

There are two main equalization systems, based on

- bringing oil revenue within the general equalization framework, as in Australia and Canada; and
- using a distinct equalization system for oil and other natural resources, as in Bolivia and Colombia.

most common instruments used for obtaining a share of rents by subnational governments (Otto, 2001, and Table 10.1). They present clear advantages for subnational governments over the previous instruments, mainly by ensuring steadier revenue flows.[4] However, they still pose policy coordination issues in the energy field. In other words, the choice of the tax rates will impinge on energy policy—determining the flow of production—which is clearly a national policy priority, especially in oil-specialized economies.

Based on this discussion, a locally collected unit royalty (with a ceiling on the total amount of collections) may be advisable, to ensure subnational governments that their oil-determined needs—for environmental protection and infrastructure building—are sheltered against the vagaries of national coalitions and their appetites.

Revenue-Sharing Schemes

This system may not be recommended as a general instrument for financing subnational governments, as these governments would not be responsible for the determination of their tax rates. However, in the case of oil revenue, it can actually provide a better alternative to tax-base sharing, because tax rate setting should be better left to the central government.

Infrastructure Tax Credit Schemes

These schemes are suited to very small governments and local informal communities with insufficient administrative capacity. Infrastructure credit schemes help to establish working relations between producing companies and local stakeholders. Higher levels of government should still be involved in the decision-making process, particularly in monitoring the execution of projects.

---

[4]Some of the present schemes use regressive tax rates to ensure that collections do not skyrocket during periods of rapid increases in oil prices.

The main advantage of general equalization systems is to bring together revenues from oil and non-oil and hence increase the equity content of equalization. In principle (and also in practice if there are sufficient resources), general equalization systems could entirely compensate for the vagaries of the geographic distribution of natural resources. However, when oil is vastly concentrated, (i) full compensation may no longer be feasible because either it exerts an excessive strain on central government resources, or it has to severely reverse preequalization agreed subnational shares—which would be politically unacceptable; and (ii) the implementation of the system has to solve a few difficult technical problems, that are illustrated in the next section.

There are two versions of equalization mechanisms: the vertical equalization model, such as the Australian and the Canadian systems, whereby grants are paid by central to the subnational governments; and the horizontal equalization model, such as the German one, whereby grants are paid from relatively richer jurisdictions to relatively poorer jurisdictions, without central government funding.[11]

In the vertical model the skewness of the distribution of the revenues to be equalized influences the total amount of the grant.[12] More precisely, in open-ended systems, such as in Canada in the early days, with no upper limit to the total amount disbursed by the federal government, whenever the standard tax base—the tax base of the jurisdictions with reference to which revenues are equalized—increases, the total amount of the grant is bound to increase also, other things being equal. Thus, central government resources may be subject to such a severe strain as to require a change in the formula, as happened in Canada with the first oil shock. The large increase in oil prices at that time bloated the revenues of Alberta, where almost all Canadian oil production was taking place. The standard tax base (then the national average) took off, requiring, other things being equal, a similar expansion of grants. Since the federal government had access to only 10 percent of oil revenues, sticking to the formula would have implied equalization payments to be financed with its own tax revenues, thus having to face the choice of either incurring deficits or squeezing its own expenditure. Furthermore, the gap between Alberta and the other provinces became so large that even the rich provinces, such as Ontario, became beneficiaries of

---

[11]For simplicity, the paper focuses on fiscal capacity equalization, leaving aside consideration of expenditure needs.

[12]A simple look at the Canadian formula (the calculation of tax capacity is almost the same in Australia) illustrates the point:

$TT = \Sigma T_i$ and

$T_i = t_s \, (TB_s/P - TB_i/P_i) \, P_i$,

where TT is the total grant; T is the grant to individual provinces; t is the tax rate; TB is the tax base; P is the population; s is the standard (it may be the national average, or the average of a selected group of provinces above the average, as in Canada); and i stands for beneficiary provinces, that is, those for which the difference in the expression between brackets is positive.

equalization transfers (although in the end they were financed through the use, by the federal government, of the tax base located in their jurisdiction).

Over the years Canadian governments have made basic corrections to the formula, including: (i) the exclusion of Alberta's tax base from the equalization standard; (ii) the exclusion from equalization payments of those provinces, such as Ontario, with a non-oil tax base above the national average; (iii) the exclusion of a share of the oil-tax base from the equalization system; and (iv) the introduction of a ceiling to the total amount paid for equalization. Obviously, these changes implied a curtailment of the equalizing impact of the mechanism.[13]

Vertical closed-ended equalization systems such as the Australian one—where, starting from the year 2001, the equalization system is funded by the Goods and Services Tax collections—do not by definition put severe strains on the federal finances. However, when distribution of oil revenues is highly skewed, their equalizing capacity faces the same problems as the open ended systems.

Horizontal models do not by construction have the same difficulties. The degree of equalization is written in the formula. It is not imperiled by sudden changes in the total amount of oil revenue and/or in the skewness of their distribution. Moreover, strains on central government finances cannot arise because, if the standard is set at the national average, the total grant from net paying jurisdictions is equal to the total grant received by beneficiary jurisdictions.[14]

The strain is rather put on the oil-producing jurisdictions, particularly if they represent a minor share of the total national population. More specifically, the share of oil revenue they can retain is directly re-

---

[13]These measures can be and have been variously combined, and they do not exhaust the range of instruments needed to dampen the impact of exceptional circumstances on the sustainability of equalization mechanisms.

[14]A typical formula based on the equalization of tax capacity—that is, on standardization of revenues—would be:

$$TT_J = \alpha \left[t_s(TB_J - TB_s) \right] \text{ and}$$

$$TT_I = \alpha \left[t_s(TB_s - TB_I) \right],$$

where, in addition to the previously mentioned symbols, J stands for paying jurisdictions; and I stands for the beneficiary jurisdictions. Thus, TT_J is the total grant paid by the contributing jurisdictions; TT_I is the total grant received by the beneficiary jurisdictions; and α is the degree of equalization attained by the mechanism, varying from 0—no equalization at all—to 1, meaning perfect equalization (that is, equal per capita revenues).

lated to the share of their population on the total national population. If equalization is geared to fully equalize per capita revenues, then the share of retained revenues for the producing jurisdictions is equal to the share of their population.[15]

The two systems—vertical and horizontal—could be combined, as proposed by Courchène (1979). For example, the vertical system could be reserved to non-oil revenue, while oil revenue would be subjected to a horizontal system. However, the basic properties and difficulties of implementing equalization would be essentially unaltered.

Separate equalization systems are generally funded only by oil revenue and do not include other sources of revenue. They amount basically to reserving a share of total national revenue from oil to the non-producing, or little-producing jurisdictions, and to distributing it according either to the difference between their resource revenue and the national average (as in Bolivia[16]), or to other needs, or to revenue capacity-related indicators. In Colombia, for example, the *Fondo Nacional de Regalías* (National Royalties Fund) is allocated on the basis of development projects presented by subnational jurisdictions. The idea is to allow nonproducing jurisdictions to share some of the growth opportunities created by the exploitation of oil and natural gas resources.

The equalizing impact of separate mechanisms derives, as in the case of the general equalization systems, from the relative shares of natural resource revenue granted to producing and nonproducing jurisdictions and their relative shares in the total population. The effectiveness of equalization is imperiled by the exclusion of non-oil sources of revenue. Thus, a rich (with high non-oil tax revenue) department can receive, as in the Bolivian case, the same amount of resources as a poor department, if the difference between oil revenue and the national average happens to be the same in both departments.

---

[15]A simple example illustrates the severity of the constraint on the share of the producing jurisdictions. Suppose that there is only a producing region, which represents 5 percent of the national population. If total oil revenue is 10,000 units and total national population is 100, then the national average is 100. To get a level of equalization similar to the German one, where per capita revenue of the less endowed regions is brought to 0.9 times the national average, the share of the producing region should be equal to 14.5 percent of the total. In fact, if per capita equalization payment is 90, that has to be paid to 95 persons. Total payment is thus 8,550, leaving 1,450 units to the producing jurisdiction. The share is far below the sharing rates presently accorded to the producing jurisdictions in all the countries reviewed in Table 10.1.

[16]To this aim revenue from natural resources is supplemented by appropriations from the central government budget. The Bolivian model is thus not a pure version of a separate equalization system. Moreover, it is not restricted to revenues from oil, but it refers to all natural resources.

In industrial countries with a well-developed national statistical system, separate systems have practically no raison d'être. In developing countries, however, where equalization systems have to rely mostly on rapidly obsolete population figures for the allocation of funds, separate systems may be considered on a temporary basis because of their greater simplicity.

Technicalities of Natural Resource Equalization Schemes

The implementation of natural resource equalization schemes presents some difficulties, particularly when natural resources are concentrated in one or in a few provinces. First, it has to be decided if natural resources must be considered separately for equalization purposes. Second, a common criterion for the determination of the tax base has to be found.

When a single resource is concentrated in only one subnational jurisdiction, the equalization of the tax capacity is transformed into a simple revenue equalization. This is because only a single tax rate is applied. By definition, then, actual collections are equal to tax capacity.

The second problem relates to the use of common criteria for the determination of the tax base. When the distribution of mines and oil fields is geographically concentrated,[17] and/or when subnational governments use different taxes and/or different criteria for the determination of the tax base, then a common tax base has to be used. Australia is presently using a value-added approach to calculate the comparable revenue base from natural resources for each state. The revenue base is currently calculated as the value added by the whole mining industry, including oil and gas, less: (i) some exploration expenditure and (ii) some allowance for future capital expenditure.[18]

---

[17]In Australia, gold and oil are extracted in Western Australia, while coal is extracted in New South Wales and Queensland.

[18]A number of issues have arisen in measuring these two deductions. In the first case, in order to allow mining sectors to continue exploration (at least on operating leases), the value of exploration has to be netted from value added. However, getting comparable data on exploration is problematic, particularly for companies that have both operational and speculative leases. In the second case, the Australian system also deducts from value added a ten-year average of capital expenditure in each jurisdiction. An additional issue has been how to deal with the practice in one state (which owns the rail freight network) of charging much higher freight rates instead of higher royalties on black coal. This quasi-royalty has been added to the value added of the mining industry in that state as it is recorded as an industry expense only because of the unusual freight arrangements. The assumption made in this respect is that the excess freight expense is equivalent to a royalty payment, and therefore should be treated as such (Commonwealth Grants Commission, 2002).

VI. Conclusions

This paper has explored methods, merits, and drawbacks of assigning net oil and natural gas revenue to subnational governments. There are two main arguments against local assignment, namely the usually vast geographical concentration of this revenue and its volatility. Recent international experience shows, however, a growing trend to share oil revenue among all levels of government. In addition, offshore oil revenue tends to be shared, although there are very few theoretical arguments in favor of this policy.

These trends are to be explained mainly in terms of political expediency. Decentralization, that is, devolution of powers to subnational governments, increases the weight of these governments and institutionalizes their demand for a (growing) share of natural resources located in their jurisdiction.

Concerning the instruments used for revenue assignments, the paper has argued that revenue sharing is the most appropriate one, while local taxes on oil can be problematic. This is because of the complexity of administration and collection and because locally determined taxes will impinge on energy policy, which is mainly a central government responsibility.

When oil revenue is shared with subnational governments, equalization is needed to attenuate disparities and to alleviate problems. There are, however, limits to the intensity of equalization, when oil revenue is large and highly concentrated in spatial terms.

Bibliography

Andrews-Speed, Philip, and Christopher D. Rogers, 1999, "Mining Taxation Issues for the Future," *Resource Policy*, Vol. 25, pp. 221–27.

Bergesen, Helge Ole, Torleif Haugland, and Leiv Lunde, 2000, *Petro-States— Predatory or Developmental?* (Dundee: Fridtjof Nansen Institute and Econ Centre for Economic Analysis).

Boadway, Robin W., and Frank R. Flatters, 1982, *Equalization in a Federal State* (Ottawa: Economic Council of Canada).

———, 1993, "The Taxation of Natural Resources: Principles and Policy Issues," World Bank Policy Research Working Paper No. 1210 (Washington: World Bank).

Clark, Allen L., and Jennifer Cook Clark, 1999, "The New Reality of Mineral Development: Social and Cultural Issues in Asia and Pacific Nations," *Resources Policy*, Vol. 25, No. 3, pp.189–96.

Commonwealth Grants Commission, 2002, "Update Report on State Revenue Sharing Relativities," Working Papers, Vol. 2 (Canberra).

Courchène, Thomas J., 1979, *Refinancing the Canadian Federation: The 1977 Fiscal Arrangements Act* (Toronto: C.D. Howe Research Institute).

———, 1998, "Renegotiating Equalization: National Polity, Federal State, International Economy," C.D. Howe Commentary, No. 113 (Toronto: C.D. Howe Research Institute).

Daniel, Philip, Keith Palmer, Alistair Watson, and Roland Brown, 2000, *Review of Fiscal Regimes for Mining and Hydrocarbons* (Independent State of Papua New Guinea: Asian Development Bank).

Davy, Aidan, and Kathryn McPhail, 1998, "Integrating Social Concerns into Private Sector Decisionmaking: A Review of Corporate Practices in the Mining, Oil, and Gas Sector," World Bank Discussion Paper No. 384 (Washington: World Bank).

———, and Fabián Sandoval Moreno, 1999, "BPXC's Operations in Casanare, Colombia: Factoring Social Concerns into Development Decisionmaking," World Bank Social Development Paper No. 31 (Washington: World Bank).

Emerson, Craig, 2000, "Mining Taxation and Mineral Processing Policies," in *Resource Tax Policy in Countries of the Asia Pacific Region*, ed. by Terry Dwyer (Canberra: Australian National University).

Filer, Colin, 1995, "Participation, Governance and Social Impact: The Planning of the Lihir Gold Mine," in *Mining and Mineral Resource Policy Issues in Asia-Pacific: Prospects for the 21st Century*, ed. by Donald Denoon, Chris Ballard, Glenn Banks, and Peter Hancock (Canberra: Australian National University).

Garnaut, Ross, 1995, "Mining Dilemmas of Governance," in *Mining and Mineral Resource Policy Issues in Asia-Pacific: Prospects for the 21st Century*, ed. by Donald Denoon, Chris Ballard, Glenn Banks, and Peter Hancock (Canberra: Australian National University).

———, and A. Clunies Ross, 1975, "Uncertainty, Risk Aversion and the Taxing of Natural Resource Projects," *Economic Journal*, Vol. 85, No. 338, pp. 272–87.

———, 1983, *Taxation of Mineral Rents* (Oxford: Clarendon Press).

Government of Australia, Department of Industry, Tourism and Trade (ISR), 2001, "Competitive Australia. Petroleum Taxation" (Canberra). Available via the Internet: http://www.isr.gov.au.

Government of Canada, 1985, "The Atlantic Accord. Memorandum of Agreement between the Government of Canada and the Government of Newfoundland and Labrador on Offshore Oil and Gas Resource Management and Revenue Sharing" (Ottawa). Available via the Internet: http://www.gov.ns.ca/fairness/pdf/aa_mou.pdf.

Gray, Dale F., 1998, "Evaluation of Taxes and Revenues from the Energy Sector in the Baltics, Russia, and other Former Soviet Union Countries," IMF Working Paper 98/34 (Washington: International Monetary Fund).

Ikein, Augustine A., Confort Briggs-Anigboh, 1998, *Oil and Fiscal Federalism in Nigeria: The Political Economy of Resource Allocation in a Developing Country* (Aldershot: Ashgate).

Labonne, Beatrice, 1995, "Community and Mineral Resources: from Adversarial Confrontation to Social Development through Participation, Accountability and Sustainability," in *Mining and Mineral Resource Policy Issues in Asia-Pacific: Prospects for the 21st Century*, ed. by Donald Denoon, Chris Ballard, Glenn Banks, and Peter Hancock (Canberra: Australian National University).

McLure, Charles E., Jr., 1983, "Fiscal Federalism and the Taxation of Economic Rents," in *State and Local Finance: the Pressure of the 1980's*, ed. by George Break (Madison: University of Wisconsin Press), pp. 133–60.

———, 1994, "The Sharing of Taxes on Natural Resources and the Future of the Russian Federation," in *Russia and the Challenge of Fiscal Federalism*, ed. by Christine Wallich (Washington: World Bank), pp. 181–217.

McMillan, Melville, 1982, *Natural Resource Prosperity: Boon or Burden for Canadian Federalism* (Canberra: Australian National University).

Mieszkowski, Peter, and Eric Toder, 1983, "Taxation of Energy Resources," in *Fiscal Federalism and the Taxation of Natural Resources*, ed. by Charles E. McLure Jr. and Peter Mieszkowski (Lexington, Massachusetts: Lexington Books), pp. 65–91.

O'Faircheallaigh, Ciaran, 1998, "Indigenous People and Mineral Taxation Regimes," *Resource Policy*, Vol. 24, pp. 187–94.

Otto, James M., ed., 1995, *The Taxation of Mineral Enterprises* (London: Graham & Trotman).

Otto, James M., 2001, *Fiscal Decentralization and Mining Taxation* (Washington: World Bank Group Mining Department).

Oxfam America, 2001, *Extractive Sectors and the Poor*, Global Policy Forum (New York).

PricewaterhouseCoopers, 1998, "Comparative Mining Tax Regimes." Available via the Internet: www.pwcglobal.com.

Rodgers, Barry, 1998, "Canada's Experience in Attracting and Managing Upstream Petroleum Investments in the Offshore," a paper presented at the Seminar on Attracting & Managing Upstream Petroleum Investments in Russia Sponsored by the International Energy Agency and the Ministry of Fuel and Energy of the Russian Federation. (Calgary: Canadian Institute of Resources Law). Available via the Internet: http://www.iea.org/nmc1/russia/4-can.htm.

San Miguel, Diego Nicolás, 1999, "Is Mining a Model of Fiscal Federalism in Argentina? A Comparative Study with Canada and Australia," CEPMPL

Annual Review 3. Available via the Internet: http://www.dundee.ac.uk/ccpmlp/car/html/car3.htm.

Scott, Anthony, 1980, "Comments on Simeon, Courchène and Melville papers," in *Canadian Public Policy*, Supplement, pp. 206–10.

Simeon, Richard, 1980, "Natural Resource Revenues and Canadian Federalism: A Survey of the Issues," in *Canadian Public Policy*, Supplement, pp. 182–91.

Sunley, Emil, and Thomas Baunsgaard, 2001, "The Tax Treatment of the Mining Sector: An IMF Perspective," background paper prepared for the World Bank Workshop on the Taxation of the Mining Sector, Washington, April.

United Nations Economic and Social Commission for Asia and the Pacific, Committee on Environment and Natural Resources Development, Note by the secretariat, 2001, "Selected Issues Relating to the Work of the Committee on the Environment and Natural Resource Development: Policy Issues in Decentralizing the Management of Mineral Resources Development to Benefit Local Communities" (Bangkok). Available via the Internet: http://www.unescap.org/55/e1126e.htm.

Part III.
Institutional Arrangements for Dealing with Oil Revenue Instability

11

Stabilization and Savings Funds for Nonrenewable Resources: Experience and Fiscal Policy Implications

JEFFREY DAVIS, ROLANDO OSSOWSKI, JAMES A. DANIEL, AND STEVEN BARNETT[1]

I. Introduction

A country with large exhaustible resources such as oil can benefit substantially from them, but the revenues from exploiting these resources can pose challenges. Fiscal policymakers need to decide how expenditures can be planned and insulated from revenue shocks arising from the volatility and unpredictability of resource prices. Decisions also need to be made on the extent to which resources should be saved for future generations.

In some countries that are dependent on the export of oil and other nonrenewable resources, governments have established, or are considering setting up, nonrenewable resource funds (NRFs) to help in the implementation of fiscal policy. Recent volatility in oil prices has lent importance to this discussion in several countries.

NRFs can take various forms, ranging from separate institutions with discretion and autonomy to funds that in practice amount to little more than a government account. The general justification for such funds is

[1]This paper is a shortened and revised version of the paper initially published as IMF Occasional Paper No. 205 (Davis and others, 2001). An earlier version was also included in a volume published by the University of Alberta (Ossowski, 2002).

that some share of government revenues derived from the exploitation of a nonrenewable resource should be put aside for when these revenues decline, because the price of the resource has fallen, or the resource has been depleted or both. *Stabilization* funds aim to reduce the impact of volatile revenue on the government and the economy. *Savings* funds seek to create a store of wealth for future generations.

The operational implications and effectiveness of NRFs are considered in the following sections. Section II discusses some key fiscal policy implications of reliance on nonrenewable resource revenues. Section III considers the rationale for funds and discusses their main design characteristics. Section IV examines the operational aspects of funds, including their relationship with the budget; asset-management issues; and governance, transparency, and accountability. Section V provides a preliminary assessment of the effectiveness of funds, using both econometric evidence and country case studies. Section VI concludes.

II. Nonrenewable Resource Revenues: Policy Implications

A country with large fiscal revenues derived from exploiting a nonrenewable resource such as oil typically faces two main problems—that the revenue stream is uncertain and volatile, and that it will eventually dry up. NRFs are sometimes proposed to deal with both these problems. First, a fund may be seen as able to stabilize budgetary revenues. When the resource price is "high," the fund would receive resources, which it would then pay out to the budget when the price is "low." Second, a fund may be seen as a way to save some of the revenue generated by exploiting the finite stock of the resource, which can then provide income after it has been exhausted. Funds may also be set up for other reasons: to counteract real exchange rate volatility and "Dutch disease," [2] for liquidity and political economy purposes, and to enhance governance and transparency.

Volatility and Uncertainty of the Revenue Stream

A volatile and uncertain fiscal revenue source renders fiscal management, budgetary planning, and the efficient use of public resources

---

[2]"Dutch disease" refers to the tendency for large resource revenues to appreciate the real exchange rate, which then damages the nonresource tradable sector.

Table 11.1. *Indicators for Selected Countries with Nonrenewable Resource Funds (NRFs)*

Country[1]	Nonrenewable Resource Revenue[2] (In percent of total government revenue)	Nonrenewable Resource Exports[2] (In percent of GDP)	Average Size of Nonrenewable Resource External Shock[3] (In percentage points of GDP[4])
Chile	8.6	10.1	1.7
Kuwait[5]	59.3	39.7	5.9
Norway	14.4	12.1	1.6
Oman	77.3	35.9	5.3
Papua New Guinea	11.4	27.9	3.4
Venezuela	58.2	19.1	4.9

Sources: IMF, *World Economic Outlook* (various issues); and authors' estimates.
[1]The nonrenewable resource for Kuwait, Norway, Oman, and Venezuela is oil; for Chile, copper; and for Papua New Guinea, gold, copper, and oil.
[2]1985–99.
[3]1975–99.
[4]Average absolute value of the annual difference in the ratio of nonrenewable resource exports to GDP.
[5]Excludes 1991–93.

difficult. This is particularly the case when it makes up a large share of total revenue. The nonrenewable resource sector is an important source of foreign exchange and fiscal revenues in many countries, making them vulnerable to external variables largely beyond the control of policymakers and domestic agents (Table 11.1). The uncertainty and volatility of nonrenewable resource revenues is typically greater than for other kinds of revenue, mainly as a result of unpredictable and frequently large fluctuations in international commodity prices.

When revenue falls sharply and unexpectedly, expenditure often falls sharply too, which is typically costly. Cutting current expenditures can be notoriously difficult and unpopular, and it may be socially damaging, especially if not done in the context of a medium-term comprehensive strategy of expenditure adjustment. Cutting capital spending might involve the abandonment of viable projects, where the return on some additional expenditure may be high. As a result, the productivity of public investment could be affected. But if expenditure is not reduced in the face of large permanent negative shocks, fiscal sustainability could be questioned.

Dissaving to smooth the downward adjustment of spending in response to a negative revenue shock or to completely insulate spending from such a shock should reflect the extent to which the revenue shock is permanent or temporary. If temporary, the government could dissave until revenue recovers (the scope of financing permitting). If permanent, dissaving should be used to smooth the downward adjustment in spending, but not to prevent expenditure adjustment. Spending that is not adjusted to a permanent shock could be unsustainable, with the government continuously dissaving and eventually being forced to adjust. In particular, catastrophic negative price shocks that prompt major solvency reassessments (as in the case of oil in 1986) may require large adjustments even in the presence of smoothing mechanisms.

In practice it is often difficult to distinguish, ex ante, between permanent and temporary nonrenewable resource revenue shocks. Assuming the revenue shock is due to a change in the price of the resource,[3] the decision whether the shock should be treated by the government as permanent or temporary should reflect the following three considerations.

First, oil prices would appear to have no well-defined and time-invariant averages. Barnett and Vivanco (Chapter 5 in this volume) discuss the statistical properties of oil prices and conclude that a given oil price change may not convey much information about oil prices over the long run. In particular, the evidence suggests that oil prices display significant mean reversion, especially since the 1980s, but that the mean being reverted to may not be constant over time. Moreover, there may also be periodic permanent, or at least more long-lasting, shocks, such as those in 1973 and 1986.

Second, prudence would suggest that a negative shock should be seen as permanent, and a positive shock as temporary, until proven otherwise. The stronger a government's financial position, the less it needs to heed this advice because it can better afford to delay cutting expenditures. Also, the less costly expenditure is to adjust, the quicker it should be adjusted.

Third, there may be exceptional reasons why the current price of a resource is not likely to be its price in the future. For example, global production may be known with reasonable certainty to increase or decrease. Where resources have forward markets, however, this information should be largely reflected in the resource's forward price. For example, the spot price of oil rose sharply after the Iraqi invasion of Kuwait in 1990, but the forward price of oil rose significantly less, because financial markets expected the situation to be temporary.

---

[3]It is usually easier to assess whether volume shocks are temporary or permanent.

In fiscal management, a distinction should be made between countries that rely heavily on revenue from nonrenewable resources and those that have a broader fiscal revenue base. For countries that have a relatively diversified production structure and alternative sources of fiscal revenue, the impact of resource price volatility would be less severe. As discussed in Section V, this distinction has important implications for NRFs.

Exhaustibility of the Revenue Stream

Government revenue derived from exploitation of nonrenewable resources differs from other revenue in that it partly represents a depletion of wealth. When a significant share of government revenue is derived from the exploitation of such resources, intergenerational equity and fiscal sustainability require consideration of the finite nature of the resources and of the prospective evolution of government net wealth, since analysis based solely on indicators of fiscal balance could be misleading. In particular, government wealth can be seen as the sum of net financial wealth and resource wealth. Thus, if all the revenue from nonrenewable resources were to be consumed, this would leave less wealth and lower consumption opportunities for future generations. This would generally be considered undesirable on intergenerational equity grounds.

Exactly how much revenue from nonrenewable resources should be saved rather than consumed is a complex question that has been the subject of substantial research.[4] In general, sustainable government consumption is related to the permanent income out of government net wealth (inclusive of resource wealth). This relationship would need to take into account factors such as population growth and technological change. It is also difficult to estimate in practice, with any degree of confidence, such variables as the future price of the nonrenewable resource, the amount of the endowment, and the cost of extracting it, especially when these factors may vary substantially and frequently.

Nevertheless, considerations of long-run fiscal sustainability would generally imply saving a portion of today's nonrenewable resource revenue, and setting normative limits on the nonresource fiscal

---

[4]See, for example, Tersman (1991), and Engel and Valdés (2000).

deficit.[5] This approach would both stabilize usable revenue and provide for the accumulation of financial resources that make up for the depletion of the natural resource, thereby helping to implement fiscal policies that are set within a longer-term framework. The factors that could help determine ranges for the sustainable level of the nonresource fiscal deficit are discussed by Barnett and Ossowski in Chapter 3 in this volume.

Savings with the objective of preserving net government wealth are different from the financial savings designed to smooth expenditure adjustment discussed in the previous subsection. The former represents an economic concept of saving—that is, the excess of current revenue over current expenditure—and the theory is mute whether it should be invested in public works or held as financial assets, and thus whether the government should run an overall surplus or deficit. Savings to smooth expenditure adjustment, however, relate to financial savings. For example, if a government runs high economic savings but spends massively on public investment during "good" times and fails to build up financial assets, this may not help it to finance expenditure adjustment during "bad" times.

Real Exchange Rate Volatility and "Dutch Disease"

Large revenues from volatile nonrenewable resources have implications for the economy as a whole, not just for the fiscal sector. Nonrenewable resource shocks can affect the level of the real exchange rate through several channels, including disposable income, wealth effects, procyclical government spending on nontradables, and short-run monetary disequilibrium. There is evidence that the volatility of the real effective exchange rate is damaging to the nonresource sector and capital formation (World Bank, 1993; Servén and Solimano, 1993). Moreover, an increase in resource revenues, particularly if perceived as permanent, may place upward pressure on the real effective exchange rate, with effects on the nonresource tradable sector (Gelb and Associates, 1988).

Fiscal policy can play a role in addressing these issues, particularly when the government receives substantial nonrenewable resource rev-

---

[5]Countries that have just discovered large nonrenewable resource endowments may be justified in consuming the initial revenue from the resource if it is below the estimated permanent income from the resource.

enue. The basic fiscal response should be to smooth spending on non-tradables when resource revenues vary. For the balance of payments as a whole, large resource current account receipts could be offset by capital account outflows. To the extent that nonrenewable resource receipts flow to the government, the government or the central bank could build up external assets or repay foreign debt.

Liquidity

In addition to addressing net debt and sustainability issues, governments also need to manage their gross assets and liabilities (see Section IV). Countries with heavy reliance on volatile resource revenues will generally need to have substantial financing available. During downturns, governments could either borrow or run down their financial assets; which one to rely upon is mainly an asset-management issue.

International lending to developing countries and primary commodity producers with heavy reliance on volatile resource revenues, however, tends to be procyclical (World Bank, 1994). Some of these countries may find it difficult to ensure financing when the price of the resource falls sharply, at a time foreign resources may be most needed. They may also find other limits on their capacity to tap international capital markets, which may be difficult to predict. Countries that face such constraints in their borrowing capacity may place a premium on liquidity as such, and may wish to maintain a large stock of liquid financial assets, ideally in the form of external claims to avoid merely passing on the shock to the domestic private sector.

Other Issues

Running fiscal surpluses is often politically difficult. Even though there may be an economic case for building up public financial savings, decision makers may be subject to pressures for additional spending when revenues are available (Eifert, Gelb, and Tallroth, Chapter 4 in this volume). As a means of helping to build political support for financial savings, governments often "earmark" the savings for certain types of high-priority public spending. Governments also earmark funds in the desire that the high-priority public spending plans will have the requisite financing.

High nonrenewable resource revenues may be misused or otherwise subject to poor governance. Stringent institutional measures to prevent such behavior may be required. Linked to the issue of governance is that of transparency. The more transparent the resources flowing to the public sector, the more difficult it will be to misuse them.

III. Funds and Their Rationale

Some countries have considered, or turned to, the use of NRFs to address some of the issues discussed above, such as the short-run stabilization and long-run saving challenges posed by nonrenewable resource revenues. The general characteristic of such funds is that they are public sector institutions, separate from the budget, that receive inflows related to the exploitation of a nonrenewable resource. Table 11.2 summarizes the main objectives and design features of selected funds.

Stabilization Funds

A stabilization fund is a mechanism designed to reduce the impact of volatile revenue on the government and the economy. Its objectives may also include supporting fiscal discipline and providing greater transparency in the spending of revenue.

Stabilization funds do not set formal restrictions to the conduct of overall fiscal policy. In particular, they do not directly affect spending. Moreover, stabilization funds on their own cannot reduce the revenue uncertainty and volatility facing the public sector as a whole. The objective of rendering budget revenue more predictable and stable is achieved by transferring the uncertainty and volatility (or a portion of them) to the fund. Changing the revenue stream accruing to the public sector as a whole might be achieved by using commodity risk markets (see "Alternative Approaches," below).

Contingent stabilization funds

Stabilization funds often take the form of price- or revenue-contingent funds. Such funds are designed to accumulate resources when the resource price or revenue is "high" (exceeding some threshold) and to pay out when the price or revenue is "low" (falling below a second threshold). The thresholds are usually preannounced.

These funds aim to smooth fluctuations in the recurrent resources available to the budget, by reducing or eliminating the uncertainty and volatility of resource-related revenues flowing into the budget. This could allow budgetary spending to be insulated from changes in the resource price—which is implicitly assumed to deviate only temporarily from its long-run average—or a more limited smoothing of expenditure adjustment to price shocks.

Contingent rules may determine that resources should be deposited in the fund if the export price or revenue exceeds some reference value. The reference value may be fixed in nominal terms, or it may be changed on a discretionary basis. Alternatively, the reference value may be calculated on the basis of a formula that may be linked to past observations, or may include forecasts of future prices. If prices or revenues are lower than the reference values used for determining withdrawals, the fund may use these resources to make transfers to the budget or for other purposes. In addition, the required accumulation and permissible depletion of resources may also be made dependent on the size of the fund at the time.

The accumulation of assets in the fund may be subject to a cap determining the fund's maximum size, particularly if the main objective is short-run stabilization. The rules would also need to specify whether the fund can borrow (typically this is not the case) or needs to keep a minimum balance, and whether its capital may be used as explicit collateral for government debt operations.

Contingent funds with fixed rules may prove difficult to design and operate.[6] As discussed in Section II, it may not be possible to specify long-run averages for prices or revenues with any degree of confidence, nor to determine whether a particular shock is likely to be permanent or not. Under such circumstances, a contingent fund could face the prospect of accumulating funds indefinitely or being rapidly exhausted. Indeed, shock persistence in commodity prices may explain why many domestic price stabilization schemes and international commodity stabilization agreements for producers collapsed or were terminated in the 1980s and 1990s owing to their financial unsustainability.

Even if a long-run average price could be established from historical data, this would not necessarily imply that deviations will be temporary in the future, that this average price will not change, or that the size of the shocks will not be overwhelming. Thus, the time-series

---

[6]See Claessens and Varangis (1994); World Bank (1994); and Hausmann (1995).

Table 11.2. *Objectives and Design Features of Selected Funds*

Country/State	Name	Stated Objective(s)	Date Established	Accumulation Rules	Withdrawal Rules	Compliance with Rules/Changes to Rules	Control
Alberta (Canada)	Alberta Heritage Savings Trust Fund	Savings (pre-1997, also economic and social development)	1976	30 percent of resource revenues until 1983. 1984–87: 15 percent. Transfers discontinued thereafter.	Discretionary transfers to the budget.	Yes/Yes	Oversight Committee (members of parliament) and provincial treasurer.
Alaska (United States)	Alaska Permanent Fund	Savings	1976	50 percent of certain mineral revenues (increased from 25 percent in 1980).	Principal (inflation-adjusted since 1982) invested permanently. Use of earnings decided by governor and legislature.[1]	Yes/Yes	Independent trustees, ultimately governor and[*] legislature.
Chile	Copper Stabilization Fund	Stabilization	1985, activated in 1987	Based on discretionary reference price determined by the government.[2]	Transfers to the budget (and extrabudgetary lending) based on discretionary reference price determined by the government.[2]	Yes/No	Ministry of finance, central bank, and state copper company (CODELCO).
Kuwait GRF	General Reserve Fund	Stabilization and savings	1960	Residual budgetary surpluses.	Discretionary transfers to the budget.	.../...	Minister of finance, central bank governor, and other officials.
RFFG	Reserve Fund for Future Generations	Savings	1976	10 percent of all government revenue.[3]	Discretionary transfers to the budget (with National Assembly approval).	.../...	Minister of finance, central bank governor, and other officials.
Kiribati	Revenue Equalization Reserve Fund	Stabilization and savings	1956[4]	"When surplus permits," later apparently changed to 25 percent of all phosphate receipts.	Discretionary transfers to the budget with parliamentary approval.	No/Yes	Minister of finance, secretary of the cabinet, and other officials.

Country	Fund	Type	Date	Source	Withdrawal rules	Yes/No	Management
Norway	State Petroleum Fund	Stabilization and savings	1990, activated in 1995	Net government oil revenues.	Discretionary transfers to the budget to finance the non-oil deficit (approved by Parliament).	Yes/No	Ministry of finance.
Oman							
SGRF	State General Reserve Fund	Savings	1980	Since 1998, oil revenue in excess of budgeted amount.	Discretionary transfers to the budget.	.../Yes	Autonomous government agency.
CF	Contingency Fund	Stabilization	1990, abolished in 1993	Residual oil revenue after budget and SGRF allocations.	...	.../...	...
OF	Oil Fund	Oil sector investment	1993	Since 1998, market value of 15,000 barrels per day.	...	.../...	Ministry of finance.
Papua New Guinea	Mineral Resources Stabilization Fund	Stabilization	1974, abolished in 2001	Government mineral revenues.	Government discretion, though based on estimates of long-run prices.	.../Yes	Government.
Venezuela	Macroeconomic Stabilization Fund	Stabilization	1998	Since 1999, 50 percent of oil revenue above reference values, set by decree for 1999–2004.[5]	Transfers to the budget and other state entities based on reference values; also discretionary transfers.[5]	No/Yes	Parliament and the executive.

Sources: National authorities; and IMF staff.

[1]Fixed portion of the earnings distributed as cash to Alaskans; also used to inflation-proof the principal (as required by the 1982 amendment) and to increase capital.

[2]If copper price is up to $0.04 per pound above reference price, no deposit; 50 percent deposit between $0.04 and $0.06 per pound, and 100 percent thereafter. Withdrawals symmetric.

[3]Received 50 percent of GRF assets when established.

[4]Phosphate stock became exhausted in 1979.

[5]Fifty percent (100 percent before 1999 change) of revenue above reference value to be deposited. Withdrawals, with congress approval, if (a) oil revenues in given year are lower than reference value or (b) the resources of the fund exceed 80 percent of annual average oil revenue in the five preceeding years. Withdrawals under (b) were initially earmarked for debt repayment and capital expenditure. After 1999, these withdrawals earmarked for social and investment spending and debt repayment. In late 2001, the rules were modified again, and the central government and the state oil company were exempted from depositing resources in the fund in the last quarter of 2001 and during 2002. Fund balance at the end of the fiscal year must not be less than one-third of that at the end of the preceding year.

properties of the resource price may change, making the fund unsustainable.[7] These factors may help to explain why in some funds with these characteristics the rules have changed over time, or why the actual operation of the fund has included an element of discretion not contemplated in the rules.

An approach based on a backward-looking formula would effectively change the nature of the fund. It would no longer be designed to prevent spending from being affected by the resource price cycle, but rather it would smooth budget revenue, thereby allowing time to adjust spending to changes in the resource price. Given the large fluctuations of nonrenewable resource prices, however, the fund's capital may experience large and protracted changes and may be quite sensitive to factors such as initial conditions.[8]

The accumulation and drawdown rules might be related to resource futures prices. Futures prices are, however, quite volatile (although somewhat less so than spot prices) and, like other forecasts of resource prices, contain large ex post errors.[9]

Contingent funds can render the recurrent resources available to the budget more predictable and stable by transferring uncertainty and volatility to the fund. This has implications for the liquidity that the fund may need to hold, in the absence of other financing sources, to function as a stabilization mechanism for the recurrent resources available to the budget (Arrau and Claessens, 1992).

Stabilization funds and the fungibility of resources

A distinction should be drawn between the operational objectives of stabilization funds and overall policy goals. The *operational* objective of stabilization funds is the stabilization of recurrent resources available to the budget, and funds may be helpful in shielding the budget from revenue uncertainty and volatility. But the fund's rules do not deal with spending or deficits at the government level. The basic *policy*

---

[7]For example, a technological change may alter the equilibrium demand or supply of the resource, or both.

[8]Simulations confirm the importance of the initial conditions for the results.

[9]Research indicates that crude oil futures prices provide forecasts that are, in general, superior to those obtained from alternative techniques for short-term horizons. For longer periods, their accuracy diminishes markedly; however, even for those horizons, the futures forecasts are no worse than, and are often better than, those obtained from alternative techniques (Kumar, 1992).

objective, however, is the stabilization of public finances. Therefore, the issue is whether the fund effectively constrains government spending or the nonresource deficit.

Since a stabilization fund does not directly affect spending and thus savings, the implicit mechanism whereby a fund would lead to higher savings during "good" times is via a liquidity constraint. By placing some of the resource revenue receipts out of reach of the budget, the government would not be able to finance more expansionary expenditure plans.[10]

In the absence of liquidity constraints, however, resources are fungible. The government could borrow or run down assets to finance higher expenditures, leaving government savings unchanged even if the fund were to operate in accordance with its rules and if budget revenue were stabilized. Thus, if there is insufficient control of expenditure or deficits outside the fund, the advantages of operating a fund that stabilizes resources available to the budget would be limited. Indeed, governments will probably find borrowing particularly easy when the resource price is high and the fund's assets are burgeoning.[11] The achievement of actual expenditure smoothing therefore requires *additional fiscal policy decisions* besides the operation of a fund.

Savings Funds

Savings funds seek to create a store of wealth for future generations. This would allow the latter to benefit from part of the revenue arising from the depletion of exhaustible natural resources in the current period (see Table 11.2).

Savings funds have frequently relied on noncontingent rules. In revenue-share funds, the accumulation rule may stipulate that revenues amounting to some prespecified share of resource revenues or of total revenues be deposited in the fund independently of resource market and overall fiscal developments. Alternatively, a fixed nominal contribution to the fund may be specified. The aim is to put away some resources to gradually build up a store of wealth so that future generations might benefit from part of the proceeds of nonrenewable re-

---

[10]If the government did not raise its expenditure plans when the resource revenue rose, savings would increase automatically and there would be no need for a fund.

[11]If the fund were allowed to spend directly or to lend, this would further impair any ability of the fund to generate financial savings.

sources extracted in the current period. An ancillary aim may be to reduce the reliance of the budget on a particularly volatile source of receipts.

Revenue-share savings funds may also have stabilization objectives. When withdrawals are allowed to finance the budget, for instance during resource price downturns, recessions, or catastrophic events, the fund's operations also include short-term purposes.

The case for a savings fund is subject to conceptual issues analogous to those discussed in the context of stabilization funds. In particular, in the absence of liquidity constraints, savings funds would not necessarily lead to higher savings, as the government can finance spending in other ways. As long as the government can borrow to finance its transfers to the fund, the usefulness of placing floors on how much the fund should save on a gross basis would be limited because net indebtedness would not be constrained. The problem of determining a long-run average price also remains.

If a savings fund spends on investment items, financial savings are reduced. A fund dedicated to this end and managed separately from other public sector spending decisions could also lead to inefficiency. This is related to the issue of revenue earmarking, which is discussed in Section IV.

Financing Funds

In a financing fund the operational rules are designed so that it effectively finances the overall budget balance. The Norwegian State Petroleum Fund operates on this basis (Skancke, Chapter 12 in this volume). Under the rules in place, the budget is required to transfer to the fund net oil revenues. In turn, the fund finances the budget's non-oil deficit through a reverse transfer. In practice, this amounts to the fund financing the overall budget balance. If the budget is running an overall surplus, the latter is transferred to the fund; if the budget is in deficit, the latter is financed by the fund. The assets held in the account may be managed according to separate investment guidelines (as in Norway), or jointly with other resources of the treasury.

A financing fund provides an explicit and transparent link between fiscal policy and asset accumulation, and addresses fungibility issues. Changes in the assets held by the fund correspond to those in the overall net financial asset position of the government, which is driven by the overall fiscal balance. The fund accumulates assets to the extent that there are actual surpluses in government finances. Thus, net allocations to the fund, together with the income earned by the fund's assets, give an indication of the trajectory of financial wealth, because this arrangement rules out financing the accumulation of resources in the fund through borrowing. Fiscal surpluses are required, however, for a financing fund to become operational if its initial funding is not to be financed through borrowing.

The establishment of a financing fund, effectively little more than a government account, may be related to political economy considerations. The fund may help to make explicit the intertemporal implications of expenditure choices without the potential cost of budget fragmentation (see Section IV). For example, an increase in expenditure would automatically lead to lower deposits into the fund, or a greater withdrawal from the fund, with computable consequences for fiscal solvency and the returns on government assets in future years. At the same time, this type of fund may provide little "disciplining" effects, since the flows in and out of the fund depend on resource revenue and policy decisions of the authorities embodied in the nonresource fiscal stance.

Additional Arguments for Funds

A fund might dampen real exchange rate volatility and the effects of Dutch disease insofar as it might facilitate the placement of resources abroad during booms. This could also be achieved by the government or the central bank using the current receipts to increase, respectively, foreign deposits or foreign exchange reserves.

Similarly, a fund could help to increase the government's stock of liquid assets, thereby providing an element of self-insurance. Again, the government could, in principle, hold liquidity for precautionary purposes without recourse to a formal fund.

A fund may seek to achieve greater transparency. For example, if the fund's assets largely represent the net financial wealth of the government, and information about the fund is easily and frequently made available, a fund may be a useful vehicle to improve the transparency with which the government manages nonrenewable resource revenues.

Another potential transparency benefit of an NRF is that, by removing part of resource revenues from the budget, the reported budget balance could be more representative of the underlying budget position. For example, if revenues were higher than budgeted (owing to a higher resource price) and the excess were to be deposited into a fund, the reported budget balance would not improve. Moreover, if budget expenditures were to overrun, for example, financed by higher borrowing, the recorded budget balance would deteriorate. This transparency benefit could be similarly achieved, however, by an appropriate fiscal reporting system, for example, through inclusion of a nonresource balance.

Establishing a fund could also reduce transparency. For example, a fund's assets may be claimed to be the government's savings from resource revenues. But if the government borrows from elsewhere to finance its deposits into the fund, the gross assets held in the fund would provide a misleading indication of the government's net wealth. Moreover, adding institutions and extra accounts to a fiscal system may in practice hamper transparency and budget management. These issues are discussed further in Section IV.

If governance were a major problem in existing institutions, a separate institution could, in principle, be created that would have better governance. The establishment of an institution with large gross assets, however, may pose major risks, even if it were initially expected to be well run. In particular, there is a danger that the fund may become infected with the poor governance practices already existing elsewhere in the public sector. Increases in the amount of public gross assets may widen the scope for losses to the public purse. The preferred solution may well be to tackle the governance issues directly, rather than set up new institutions.

Alternative Approaches

The objectives of stabilization, saving for the future, or investing abroad to sterilize large foreign exchange inflows could be achieved through implementation of a sound fiscal policy within the context of an overall budget strategy (Barnett and Ossowski, Chapter 3 in this volume). If the appropriate fiscal response to a higher nonrenewable resource price was to increase public savings, the government could achieve it in the context of such a framework, and with any financial saving comprising part of the total financial resources available to the government. Similarly, when prices fall and the appropriate response is to dissave, this can be done by borrowing or running down total financial assets. An overall fiscal policy could also be geared toward saving for the future or placing resources abroad to sterilize large foreign exchange inflows.

The formulation of an overall fiscal policy may be aided by a medium-term expenditure framework that can help to limit the extent of short-run expenditure responses to rapidly changing resource revenues. Multiyear expenditure planning can also allow a better appreciation of the future spending implications of present policy decisions, including the recurrent costs of capital spending (Potter and Diamond, 1999).

Stabilization funds on their own cannot reduce the uncertainty and volatility of nonrenewable resource revenues facing the public sector as a whole. In this context, however, there may be a role for the use of contingent financial instruments such as options and futures contracts to deal with the external exposure and transfer risk to international financial markets. Recourse to contingent markets might permit prices (or price ranges) for nonrenewable resource deliveries in future periods to be "locked in." As a result, budgeting could become more realistic and certain. Hedging could also provide some protection against substantial price falls. In practice, however, there may be limitations to the extent to which future production might be hedged. In addition, the undertaking of hedging operations requires an appropriate institutional framework, to minimize possible governance and transparency risks (Daniel, Chapter 14 in this volume).

Funds and the Political Economy of Government Spending

The establishment of NRFs may be justified on political economy grounds. Funds have been seen as potentially helpful instruments when governments have difficulty in maintaining stable expenditures.

First, governments, even if they see the case for increased financial savings when nonrenewable resource revenues are high, often face substantial political pressures to spend the higher revenues. This case argues for funds to play a role in mitigating the pressures on governments, but not necessarily to place any additional constraints on fiscal policy.

Second, politicians may not fully appreciate the need to save in such circumstances, they may be short-sighted, or they may not be rewarded for thinking about long-term issues. In such cases, it could be argued that they should be constrained to do so. This situation could suggest the placement of additional constraints on fiscal policy (for instance, in the form of binding fiscal rules) to ensure more "responsible" behavior.[12]

Third, governments may actually find it politically difficult to issue gross debt to finance spending and transfers to an NRF. For example, parliaments may be opposed to further issues of debt. In all these cases, by formally limiting the resources available, funds could help to prevent large increases in spending during revenue upswings.

However, large (or rapidly growing) NRFs may themselves give rise to domestic spending pressures and exacerbate the problem of rendering longer-run saving abroad politically acceptable. This could happen, for example, if there is public perception that some of the resources in the fund could be better used to increase domestic expenditure or to reduce taxation.

IV. Operational Aspects of Funds

The establishment of an NRF requires decisions about its integration within the fiscal framework and its asset-management strategy. Governance, transparency, and accountability issues also need to be addressed.

The Fund and the Budget

Consideration needs to be given to the integration of the fund within the budget process and to the consequent institutional arrangements.

Integration with the budget

If a decision is made to establish a fund, it should be integrated within the budget process in a coherent manner. Proper integration of the fund and the budget helps to maintain a unified control of fiscal policy and avoid problems in expenditure coordination, such as duplication of expenditure or capital spending decisions made without taking into account their impact on future recurrent spending. It also facilitates a consistent prioritization across all government operations.

---

[12]Fiscal rules may constrain expenditure, the deficit, or they may restrict the ability to borrow. As discussed in Kopits and Symansky (1998), fiscal rules can have both advantages and disadvantages.

This would suggest preference for institutional arrangements that maintain a unified control over expenditure, avoiding the emergence of two "budgets," namely the traditional budget and a separate expenditure program financed by the fund. The separation of spending programs could lead to fiscal management problems. In practice, it may not be clear how spending priorities would be set, or which expenditures would be financed by the fund and which by the budget. Therefore, to address the risks that funds might pose in terms of fragmentation of policymaking and loss of overall fiscal control, it would be important to ensure that spending decisions are taken within the context of the budget and that expenditure is included in the budget in a comprehensive way.

The need for legitimacy and contestability of budgetary resources provides additional reasons why it would be preferable for the resources in the fund to be spent through the normal budgetary approval process. Public resources should be raised and spent in accordance with public demands and for the highest (marginal) value. The legitimacy of the budget is enhanced by legislative approval of the annual appropriation law. This therefore suggests that any off-budget spending that is allowed should remain subject to parliamentary scrutiny and consideration.

Institutional arrangements for the fund

Three institutional arrangements may be distinguished that vary according to the degree of integration with the budget.

The virtual fund

The existence of a fund need not imply the creation of a new institutional mechanism. A nonrenewable resource "fund" may be a fund in name only. This accounting-only design is referred to as a "virtual fund" because there is no separate institutional structure for the management of the fund, and all revenues and expenditures are on-budget. Certain resources would be identified as belonging to the fund. These resources could be held in the government's main account or in a separate government account. Restrictions in line with the objectives of the fund would be placed on drawing down the fund's resources for expenditure. Any drawdown of government deposits, including the fund account, would appear as deficit financing. The assets that "belong to the fund," however, would be managed like other government assets.

Under a virtual fund arrangement, there would be no earmarking of the fund's resources for certain items of expenditure. Expenditures would continue to be executed by the relevant line ministries and agencies and would be included in the budget. Correspondingly, allocative decisions at budget time would be taken by the parliament. Thus, a virtual fund design need not hamper fiscal management, and it would be consistent with transparent policy decisions, accountability, and control of expenditures through normal budgetary procedures—provided it is supported by adequate accounting, reporting, and audit procedures (see "Governance, Transparency, and Accountability," below).

A virtual fund could strengthen the political feasibility and support for saving nonrenewable resource revenues. It could also help to strengthen the incorporation of sound economic principles within the budget process by focusing attention on the nonresource balance and by highlighting that nonrenewable resource revenues are not like other revenues and should, in general, be saved rather than spent.

All resources pass through the budget

Under this approach, transfers to and from the fund's account could be explicit line items in the budget. All revenues would be included in the budget, and the amount that is to be saved in the fund would be shown as a transfer to the fund. If there is a need to dissave, or drawdown on the fund, this would be shown in the budget as a transfer, and all spending would be done by appropriation. This approach would preserve the unity of the budget, without the restrictive rules implicit in the virtual fund.

The resources transferred to the budget could be earmarked for particular expenditures. Earmarking may be seen as making it easier to resist political pressures to use windfalls for less appropriate purposes. However, earmarking would result in resources being placed outside the allocative budget process and might lead to inefficient expenditure and the misuse of resources.[13] The impact of earmarking is also uncertain insofar as budgetary resources are fungible.

Off-budget expenditure

An extrabudgetary fund may be set up as a separate entity with authority to undertake off-budget expenditures. Arrangements may also

---

[13]These risks would likely be increased when earmarking takes place for off-budget expenditures.

Box 11.1. *Oil Funds and Extrabudgetary Spending in Nigeria and Venezuela*

Nigeria

Before 1995, Nigeria had various types of extrabudgetary funds that were financed by oil revenues and used for off-budget expenditure. Spending from these funds expanded from 4 percent of GDP in 1990 to close to 12 percent of GDP in 1994—more than one-third of the federal budget. Serious problems were experienced as a result of the nontransparent use of off-budget funds. Expenditures were mainly undertaken in various types of investments in the oil sector and other "priority" development projects for which project selection criteria and procedures were lax. Moreover, implementation capacity to manage investment expenditure was inadequate. As a result, a number of large investment projects have required large and costly financing and have had low ex post rates of return.

Venezuela

The Venezuelan Investment Fund (VIF) was established in the mid-1970s to act as the repository of the oil windfall. Its resources were soon diverted toward equity stakes in public enterprises (including in the manufacturing sector), many of which turned out to be loss makers. In recent years, a share of the VIF's resources has been used to provide cash injections to state companies in the electricity sector. These companies have registered deficits and relied on transfers from the central government and the VIF to finance capital expenditure and meet debt-service obligations. In effect, subsidies have been provided off-budget through the use of VIF resources.

---

include the fund having its own direct sources of revenue. A rationale for this design is the notion that potential overspending might be prevented by keeping resources off-budget. Also, such an approach may be justified as one means to "get around" an inefficient or corrupt system and to deliver more effectively the desired spending policies.

This approach may lead to coordination problems with the budget. Moreover, if spending is undertaken without parliamentary approval and adequate oversight, it could result in nontransparent off-budget practices and give rise to governance concerns. In addition, it remains doubtful on practical grounds whether, if the overall budget system is poor, a better subsystem can be established to deal with windfall proceeds. As illustrated in Box 11.1, in a number of cases the oversight of a fund's spending has been inadequate, and public resources have been misallocated.

If a separate NRF with spending authority is considered, a separate appropriation bill for the fund should be submitted for parliamentary approval. Budget formulation and reporting should focus on a consolidated presentation (inclusive of the operations of the fund), and all the expenditures should be executed by the treasury.

Asset Management Issues

An NRF could, over time, hold an important share of the public sector's financial assets. The management of the fund's capital is therefore a key component of the strategy for the fund. Strategies for managing NRF assets have varied greatly among countries (Table 11.3).

Asset management strategy

An asset management strategy would need to be defined for the fund, including prudential investment rules targeting desired levels of risk, liquidity, and return. The fund's financial operations should be designed to avoid disrupting financial markets and macroeconomic stability. Equally important, the strategy would need to take into account the main objectives of the fund, and in particular the relative emphasis placed on stabilization and savings, in the government's overall asset management strategy.

Consideration would need to be given to the appropriate time horizon. For example, the liquidity and maturity of "risk-free" assets would be a relevant consideration. A fund with mainly a stabilization objective that might need to draw down its assets at short notice, for instance during sharp commodity price downturns, would not necessarily view high-quality long-term bonds as "risk free." Similarly, decisions whether to hold equities in the portfolio might depend on whether the fund's objectives are seen as mainly related to long-term savings or short-term stabilization. The currency composition of the assets would also be important.

The asset management strategy should reflect a consolidated portfolio of the government. In addition, the fund's short-term asset operations should be consistent with, and coordinated with, the debt management operations of the ministry of finance, the treasury's management of the government's cash flow, and the financial assets already held as part of the government's balance sheet. In some cases, difficult

Table 11.3. *Asset Management of Selected Funds*

Country/State	Foreign/Domestic Asset Split	Operational Management	Level of Assets[1] (In percent of GDP)
Alberta (Canada)	Mainly domestic	Treasury's Investment Management Division	8
Alaska (United States)	Mainly non-Alaskan, including foreign	Alaska Permanent Fund Corporation (special private corporation)	98[2]
Chile	Mainly foreign	Central bank	…
Kuwait[3] GRF	Domestic and foreign	Kuwait Investment Authority (since 1982), autonomous government body	…
RFFG	Mainly foreign	Kuwait Investment Authority (since 1982), autonomous government body	…
Kiribati	Foreign	Reserve Fund Investment Committee	897
Norway	Effectively foreign. Held as local currency account at central bank, which manages a counterpart portfolio of foreign assets	Central bank, partly using private investment managers	41
Oman[3] SGRF	Almost entirely foreign	Autonomous government agency	23
OF	Mostly foreign	Ministry of Finance	4
Papua New Guinea	Held as local currency account at central bank	MRSF Board[3]	0
Venezuela	Foreign	Central bank	5

Sources: Data provided by the authorities; and IMF staff.
[1]End-2001.
[2]In percent of gross state product, end-2000.
[3]For names of funds, see Table 11.2.

choices may need to be made between assets held in the fund and outstanding gross government debt.

A strong case may exist for placing the fund's accumulated resources abroad. Investing them in domestic nongovernmental financial assets would transmit resource revenue volatility to the economy. In downturns, the liquidation of domestic financial assets (such as domestic deposits) could have a contractionary effect on the economy (unless offset by open market operations), while investment in domestic financial assets and monetization of the fund's flows during upturns could fuel aggregate demand.[14] Also, the protection of the competitiveness of the nonresource tradable sector may be a policy objective, which could be helped by the sterilization of savings.

In general, the fund should not invest in the government's own domestic or foreign liabilities as part of its asset allocation. From a portfolio perspective, such a strategy would make little sense. It would amount to the government issuing debt to itself—with potential costs in terms of transaction fees paid to intermediaries and liquidity of the domestic debt market. Moreover, arrangements whereby the fund holds its own government's debt could lack transparency.

The fund should not be permitted to borrow or to lend. For the transparent and effective conduct of fiscal policy, it is best for borrowing and lending decisions to be centralized at the ministry of finance, in collaboration with the central bank. Also, the fund's capital should not be used as collateral for government borrowing.

Domestic investment issues

The fund's resources might be used to undertake domestic investment in physical assets rather than be sterilized abroad. Countries with pressing infrastructural needs or with perceived opportunities for productive domestic investment are particularly likely to consider this option. Such a strategy could also aim at enhancing the competitiveness (and promote the growth) of the nonresource tradables sector; in effect, part of the resource wealth would be given up for the prospect of higher nonresource wealth. There is, however, a danger that such spending may rise to an unsustainable level, or that too quick an increase may result in poor-quality projects.

There are a number of reasons to suggest that an NRF should not undertake domestic capital expenditure directly. First, investment should be guided by overall policy considerations (including medium-term recurrent implications), rather than by the availability of resources in the fund. Second, a perception that resources are readily available for do-

---

[14]These arguments, however, may not apply in the case of perfect capital mobility and highly developed domestic financial markets, and when the operations of the fund are small relative to the size of the domestic financial market.

mestic uses could create incentives for rent seeking and make the fund prone to abuse. Third, it may be difficult to assess the effects of the domestic use of resources on aggregate demand and competitiveness if the spending is off-budget. Finally, an NRF with stabilization objectives may need to build up liquid assets to preserve its precautionary objective for budget financing.

Operational management of assets

Specific operational asset-management guidelines should govern the allocation of the fund's resources. The guidelines should be publicized to allow performance of the fund to be measured relative to them. They should be unambiguous regarding the desired risk-return combination, the proportions to be invested in various types of assets, the geographical mix of assets, and the desired currency composition of the portfolio. There should be clear responsibility for the establishment and implementation of the guidelines. This might rest with the ministry of finance since it is responsible for the overall management of public resources.

There are several options regarding the operational management of the fund's assets. The ministry of finance could be responsible, or this may be delegated to the central bank. A board, comprising representatives from the government or legislature or both, could be established to manage the fund or to advise the government on the management of the fund. Responsibility for managing the fund's assets could be assigned directly to an independent board of trustees that answers to the cabinet and the parliament but is not a political organization. The management of the fund's assets could be subcontracted to private investment managers, with their selection decided in the same way as procurement for any other government service.

Whichever model is chosen, a clear allocation of responsibilities would be important to ensure that those who manage and oversee the operations of the fund are held accountable. Provisions would need to be drawn up stipulating who is in charge of, and accountable for, setting the fund's overall investment policy, drawing up operational guidelines, managing the fund's resources, and evaluating performance (see below). There should be an unambiguous assignment of accountability for the performance of the fund, preferably with one individual answering to parliament. More broadly, the division of responsibilities among the ministry of finance, the monetary authority, and the fund should be clearly specified.

Governance, Transparency, and Accountability

The rules and operations of an NRF should be transparent and free from political interference. To facilitate this objective and performance evaluation, the law creating the fund should clearly state its rules, purposes, and objectives. Lack of transparency would hamper legitimacy and undermine public support for the fiscal policy objectives related to the fund's operations. It would also allow incentives for lobbying for resources, and pressures to increase spending with positive nonrenewable resource shocks. Therefore, stringent mechanisms should be put in place to ensure accountability and prevent the misuse of resources.

This requires regular and frequent disclosure and reporting on principles governing the fund, its inflows and outflows, and the allocation of assets. Regular interyear reporting should be submitted to the legislature and made widely available to the public, for example, by posting on the Internet, as done by Norway and Alaska. In addition, a detailed annual report should be provided to the legislature on the flows into and out of the fund during the year and the allocation of the resources under the fund's supervision. The report should contain a summary of the asset allocation of the portfolio, summary statistics on the performance of the portfolio during the year, and a critical retrospective on the activities of the fund during the year.

To ensure propriety in the fund's activities, it will be important to have the fund's activities audited by an independent agency to supplement the internal audit of the fund. Such an audit should include both financial and performance audits and, if relevant, the procedures for the choice of external managers for the fund. Audit and reporting should cover evaluation of the fund's performance. Such evaluations should be done by an independent professional company with no financial interest in the outcome.[15]

V. How Effective Are NRFs?

This section evaluates the effectiveness of NRFs in two ways. First, it considers the effect of NRFs on government expenditure and its rela-

---

[15]Performance evaluation should be distinguished from financial compliance assessments: the latter aims to ensure that all resources are accounted for, while the performance evaluation aims to assess whether resources were used in the best possible way, and adhered to investment guidelines.

tionship to resource export receipts. The empirical evidence draws on econometric estimates, using data for a number of countries with NRFs.[16] Second, it provides a review of selected country experience with NRFs to assess whether, and in what way, the rules of the NRF may have constrained government behavior.

Empirical Results

The experiences of selected nonrenewable resource-producing countries with and without NRFs are examined below; for a given country with an NRF, pre- and post-fund performance results are compared.

A sample of 12 countries is examined, including 5 countries that have had NRFs for a significant period and 7 others that are used as a comparator group (Table 11.4). The statistical analysis focuses on central government expenditure and nonrenewable resource export earnings, both in real per capita terms. The use of export earnings may be preferable to government resource revenue because the latter may accrue with a lag and could even be endogenous.[17]

In some countries with NRFs, expenditure has tended to be less correlated with changes in the price of the resource. Three of the five countries with an NRF surveyed (Chile, Kuwait, and Norway) share some distinctive characteristics. Along with the United Kingdom, these are the only countries in which nonrenewable resource export earnings do not bear a statistically significant positive relationship to expenditure (see Table 11.4). In Chile the relationship is actually negative, which could be due to the procyclicality of copper export earnings (Spilimbergo, 1999) combined with a countercyclical fiscal policy. Similar results, although not statistically significant, are found for Norway.

The case of Oman is more difficult to assess. Over the longer run, the relationship between oil export earnings and expenditure appears similar to that in Bahrain and Saudi Arabia, two comparable countries without an NRF (Figure 11.1). Moreover, among the countries in the sample, nonrenewable resource export earnings have the

---

[16]Davis and others (2001) provide more details on the data, methodology, and results.

[17]A forward-looking government would alter spending on the basis of anticipated revenue. Thus, even if the revenue from higher resource export earnings does not reach the budget for some time, government spending could respond immediately. The endogeneity could arise if profit transfers from the state resource enterprise are determined at least in part by the level of expenditure.

Table 11.4. *Selected Countries:*
Relationship Between Nonrenewable Resource Export Earnings and Central Government Expenditure

Country	Sample Period	Fund Start	Ratio of Average Nonrenewable Resource Export Earnings to Government Expenditure (In percent)	Percent Change in Government Expenditure Associated with a 50 Percent Nonrenewable Resource Price Increase	Impact of Nonrenewable Resource[1] Lagged	Impact of Nonrenewable Resource[1] Contemporaneous
Countries with nonrenewable resource funds						
Chile	1969–99	1986	31.4	-6.2	–	ns
Kuwait	1965–90	1976	141.0	-0.2	+	–
Norway	1976–99	1991	30.7	-1.7	ns	ns
Oman	1965–99	1980	73.2	24.2	+	+
Papua New Guinea	1974–99	1974	71.4	3.0	+	ns
Countries without nonrenewable resource funds						
Algeria	1979–99	–	68.2	8.7	+	ns
Bahrain	1965–99	–	79.3	9.9	+	ns
Mexico	1980–99	–	16.4	10.2	ns	+
Saudi Arabia	1965–99	–	83.0	11.5	ns	+
United Arab Emirates	1980–99	–	101.0	9.3	+	+
United Kingdom	1983–99	–	5.0	2.8	ns	ns
Venezuela[2]	1965–98	–	86.2	10.3	+	ns

Source: Davis and others (2001), Tables A2.1 and A2.2.

[1] Based on preferred equations, as described in Davis and others (2001); "ns" indicates that the variable is not statistically significant at the 10 percent level. A "+" or "–" indicates the sign on the estimated coefficient, if statistically significant.

[2] Venezuela introduced an NRF in late 1998.

Figure 11.1. *Nonrenewable Resource Export Earnings and*
Central Government Spending
(*In local currency, real per capita*)[1]

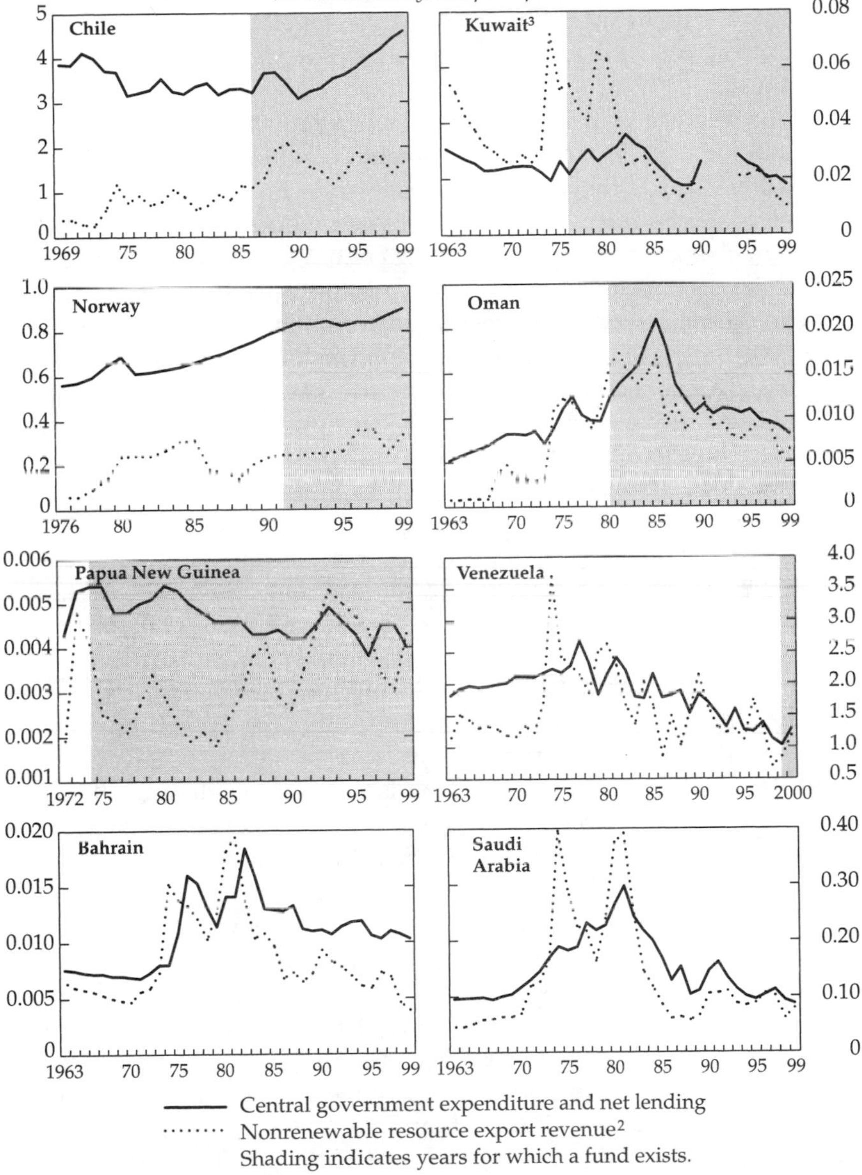

——— Central government expenditure and net lending
·········· Nonrenewable resource export revenue[2]
Shading indicates years for which a fund exists.

Sources: IMF, *World Economic Outlook*, various years; and IMF staff estimates.
[1]In thousands of local currency per capita; deflated by the CPI, 1995 = 100.
[2]For Chile, copper; for Papua New Guinea, copper, gold, and oil; for other countries, oil.
[3]Excludes information for 1991–93 owing to regional conflict and subsequent
reconstruction period.

strongest influence on spending in Oman. Inspection of the data, however, suggests that expenditure may have been driven less by revenue availability in recent years, although formal tests do not find evidence of a change in the relationship. Finally, Papua New Guinea exhibited a small but positive response of spending to resource export earnings.

The empirical evidence suggests that the establishment of the NRF did not have an impact on government spending. This result is quite robust and holds for the four countries in which tests could be performed.[18] Tests were performed to assess whether: (i) there was a significant change in the process driving central government expenditure after the establishment of the NRF; (ii) the specific relationship between central government expenditure and nonrenewable resource export earnings changed after the establishment of the fund—for example, a stabilization fund might be expected to reduce the sensitivity of expenditure to resource export earnings; and (iii) the establishment of the NRF coincided with a downward shift in the path of expenditure, as might be expected from a savings fund. For all four countries, none of the three tests suggested that creation of the fund had a statistically significant impact on expenditure.

While the empirical results are quite strong, their interpretation should be qualified. The results are constrained by limitations on the availability and quality of data and the small sample. A particular concern is that government spending, including possibly direct spending by the NRF itself, may not be fully captured in the expenditure data— this would tend to bias the results in favor of finding a positive effect of NRFs on fiscal policy. Moreover, it is difficult to determine the optimal relationship between nonrenewable resource export earnings and expenditure, and, in comparing the results across countries, the size of nonrenewable resource export earnings relative to the economy (or expenditure) should not be ignored. For example, developments in nonrenewable resource exports are more important to Venezuela than to Chile.

The empirical evidence points toward two general results. First, it suggests that some of the countries with an NRF had a more limited expenditure reaction to changes in resource revenues than those without such funds—expenditure is found not to have been positively re-

---

[18]Papua New Guinea had an NRF throughout the sample period and thus could not be included.

lated to resource export earnings in the former. In Oman, however, prior to the 1990s, government expenditure was sensitive to oil export earnings despite the existence of a fund, and this has also been the case, to a lesser extent, in Papua New Guinea. Second, the evidence suggests that the relationship between government spending and resource export earnings was not affected by the establishment of NRFs in the four cases considered. This may suggest that countries with more prudent expenditure policies tended to establish an NRF, rather than that the NRF itself led to more prudent expenditure policy, though in some cases the fund may have helped maintain cautious policies.

Selected Country Experience

The rest of this section examines the specific historical experience of selected countries with NRFs.[19] Particular attention is paid to how the design and implementation of funds have addressed the uncertainties underlying nonrenewable resource prices and the extent to which funds may have constrained overall fiscal policy. The main characteristics of some more recent oil funds are discussed in Box 11.2.

Norway's State Petroleum Fund (SPF)

The Norwegian government established the SPF in 1990 (Skancke, Chapter 12 in this volume). However, the fund was not activated until 1995, following the achievement of overall budget surpluses. The fund is designed to manage accumulated budgetary surpluses and does not have specific rules for the accumulation or withdrawal of resources, making its operation flexible. Specifically, the budget transfers to the SPF net oil revenues. In turn, the SPF finances the budget's non-oil deficit through a reverse transfer (provided there are enough resources in the SPF).[20] Thus, the SPF effectively finances the overall budget balance. An overall budget surplus would be transferred to the fund; a budget deficit would be financed by the fund. The accumulation of assets in the SPF, which include returns on the fund's capital, thus repre-

---

[19]See also Fasano (2000).

[20]The overall budget balance is calculated with oil investments made on behalf of the state direct financial interest in the oil sector.

Box 11.2. *Some Recent Oil Funds*

Several countries have set up new oil funds in the last few years. Creation of these funds may have been prompted in part by the large oil price volatility observed in recent years.[1]

Algeria. An oil stabilization fund was established in 2000. Oil revenues in excess of budgeted amounts are to be deposited in the fund. Withdrawals are permitted to finance the budget and lower the stock of outstanding public debt. In practice, the authorities have decided to accumulate in the fund a reserve to finance expenditures in case of a shortfall in hydrocarbon revenue below the amount projected in the budget, and to use the balance to amortize the public debt. At end-2001, the resources in the fund amounted to about 6 percent of GDP.

Iran. An oil stabilization fund was created in late 2000 to insulate the budget from fluctuations in oil prices. The fund receives oil revenues in excess of the budgeted amount. If by the end of the eleventh month of the fiscal year the realized crude oil export revenue is less than the budget figure, the treasury may draw from the fund the amount required to compensate for the shortfall. Up to 50 percent of the fund's accumulated assets may be lent out domestically in foreign currency to eligible firms in the private sector. In fiscal year 2002/03, in addition to these provisions, a substantial one-time withdrawal from the fund was envisaged to compensate for the exchange rate unification costs.

---

[1]The funds recently created in Azerbaijan and Kazakhstan are discussed in detail by Wakeman-Linn, Mathieu, and van Selm in Chapter 13 of this volume.

---

sents government net financial savings. The amount actually saved depends on oil prices and the fiscal stance as embodied in the non-oil fiscal deficit. SPF assets are under the control of the ministry of finance and are managed by the central bank, with a high level of transparency and accountability. The size of accumulated funds is increasing rapidly, and reached 41 percent of GDP at end-2001.

A key reason for establishing the SPF was the desire to make more transparent the intertemporal policy choices available to the country, related to the expected secular decline in oil and gas output and increase in pension outlays. In this context, the SPF has helped to provide a long-term framework for the annual process of setting the non-oil budget deficit. There is currently a wide-ranging debate in Norway on

Mexico. An oil stabilization fund was established in 2000. According to the fund's rules, a proportion of total federal government revenue (which includes oil revenue) in excess of budgeted amounts is to be deposited in the fund. Originally, the resources accumulated in the fund could only be used to compensate the budget for oil export revenue shortfalls due to a price decline of more than US$1.5 a barrel below the budget reference price; total withdrawals from the fund were capped at 50 percent of accumulated assets at the end of the previous year. In March 2002, however, the fund's rules were amended to allow for full compensation of shortfalls, and during the course of the year the resources that had been accumulated through end-2001 (equivalent to 0.2 percent of GDP) were fully drawn.

Trinidad and Tobago. The Revenue Stabilization Fund has been operational since 2001. If oil revenue is higher than budgeted by at least 10 percent, two-thirds of the excess revenue must be placed in the fund. Withdrawals can be made from the fund if oil revenue is lower than budgeted, up to the revenue shortfall or 25 percent of the accumulated fund balance at the end of the previous year (whichever is the lowest).

In several of the funds described above, the trigger for accumulation/withdrawal of resources is budgeted oil revenue. Therefore, the objective of these funds would seem to be the stabilization of budget revenues as the budget is executed during the year. This design could provide incentives for strategic setting of oil revenue in the budget—budgeting a relatively high level of oil revenues would increase the likelihood of being able to draw from the fund during the fiscal year. Moreover, if the budget is in deficit, higher-than-budgeted oil revenues could lead to the paradoxical situation of having to borrow in order to place resources in the fund.

the proper use of the rapidly growing assets in the SPF, which focuses on both long-term and cyclical considerations.[21]

The SPF is effectively a government account rather than a fund. Its features ensure integration into a unitary fiscal system and address fungibility issues. The fund does not attempt to deal directly with the problems posed to the budget by the volatility of oil prices—the latter are addressed in the context of the standard budgetary process. The

---

[21]Under guidelines for a new macroeconomic policy framework adopted in 2001, for each year the structural non-oil budget deficit should approximately correspond to the expected return on the SPF at the start of the year. The expected real rate of return is estimated at 4 percent.

lack of restrictions posed by the SPF has worked well, since Norway has typically followed sound fiscal and macroeconomic policies. Moreover, for a country like Norway, with a highly diversified production structure and a broad fiscal revenue base—oil revenues have typically accounted for less than 15 percent of government revenue—the challenge posed by oil price volatility to fiscal management is significantly less than for other oil producers.

Chile's Copper Stabilization Fund (CSF)

The CSF was established in 1985 following a sustained increase in the international copper price. The CSF's accumulation and withdrawal rules are based on a reference copper price determined annually by the authorities. No explicit formula is used to calculate the reference price. In practice, however, the reference price followed a ten-year moving average until the mid-1990s; more recently, the reference price has been set somewhat lower than the moving average. When the price of copper exceeds the reference price by between US$0.04 and US$0.06 a pound, 50 percent of the resulting state copper company's revenues is deposited in the CSF; above US$0.06 per pound, 100 percent. The rules for withdrawals are symmetric.

The resources of the CSF are understood to have grown substantially after 1987.[22] However, significant withdrawals took place beginning in 1998, mainly due to a sharp downturn in copper prices, and CSF resources were also used to subsidize domestic gasoline prices through credits to the Oil Stabilization Fund. By 2002, the resources of the CSF had been exhausted, and the fund had to be replenished.

The impact of fluctuations in copper exports on Chile's public finances is significantly less than in the case of many major oil producers. Copper revenues in Chile have typically amounted to less than 10 percent of total government revenues. In addition, the volatility of copper prices has been lower than that of oil prices.

Fiscal and macroeconomic policy has generally been sound in Chile. From a political economy perspective, operation of the CSF may have helped the government to resist expenditure pressures during upswings in copper prices in the late 1980s and mid-1990s, a fact consistent with the negative correlation between copper price increases and government spending reported above. On the other hand, the CSF did

---

[22]Information on the fund's assets is not publicly available.

not constrain expenditure, since the government would have been able to borrow.[23]

Oman's State General Reserve Fund (SGRF)

The SGRF was established in 1980 with the objective of saving oil revenue for future generations. In addition, the Contingency Fund was established in 1990 to smooth the budgetary oil revenue stream, but this was replaced in 1993 by the Oil Fund, which finances investments in the oil sector.

Oman's long experience with funds illustrates the difficulties that the behavior of oil prices and integration with overall fiscal policy can pose. At inception, the SGRF received 15 percent of oil revenues. However, the rules for the operation of the SGRF have since been changed frequently. Since 1998, the SGRF has received oil revenue in excess of the reference oil price set in the annual budget. In any given year, the government may withdraw from the SGRF up to the amount of the budgeted deficit; special procedures exist, however, for additional withdrawals in excess of the budgeted deficit. Under this arrangement, the SGRF accumulates resources when oil revenues in excess of the budgeted reference oil price are larger than SGRF financing of the budget deficit.[24]

Because resources of the SGRF can effectively be withdrawn at the discretion of the government, the SGRF's balance has been determined in part by overall budgetary needs. Mainly as a result of withdrawals from the SGRF to finance the budget, the fund does not seem to have been able to fulfill its objective of accumulating resources for the time (probably only 15 to 20 years away) when oil reserves are exhausted.

Kuwait's Reserve Fund for Future Generations (RFFG)

The RFFG was established in 1976. The objective of the fund is to save in order to provide a stream of income for future generations. The accumulation rule of the fund requires the government to deposit 10 percent of total government revenue, irrespective of oil or budgetary developments. In addition, the fund accumulates the return on its as-

---

[23]In 2001, a fiscal rule was introduced in Chile. The rule targets a central government structural fiscal surplus of 1 percent of GDP.

[24]The Oil Fund receives oil revenues equivalent to the market value of a fixed volume of oil production. In 1998, the government borrowed from the Oil Fund to finance the budget; this was repaid in 1999.

sets. The fund's capital is understood to be invested mainly in foreign assets.[25] There are no precise rules governing the withdrawal of assets, although drawing on the fund requires approval by the national assembly. Use of the fund's resources in the aftermath of the Gulf War helped to finance a large part of the reconstruction effort.

On the basis of available information, Kuwait has followed relatively prudent fiscal policies. Over the past two decades, the consolidated fiscal position has generally been in strong surplus (excluding the reconstruction period in the early 1990s), and expenditure policy has not generally been driven by revenue availability.

Papua New Guinea's Mineral Resources Stabilization Fund (MRSF)

The MRSF was established in Papua New Guinea in 1974, with the objective of stabilizing revenue to the budget from mining and oil sources. The inflows into the MRSF's account were the revenues from mineral resources. The MRSF could make transfers to the general treasury account, based on a combination of rules and discretion. The MRSF Board, which was made up of government officials, had to project average annual mineral resource revenue over the next eight years, with price forecasts constrained by long-run historical average prices. On this basis, a transfer, considered by the board to be sustainable over the next five years, was made.

Performance of the MRSF was mixed. First, despite its stated objectives, transfers from the MRSF varied significantly from year to year, almost as much as the resource revenues themselves. This was due to the instability of revenue forecasts—itself a reflection of underlying resource price volatility, but also of budgetary needs. An initial provision restricting the amount transferred to the budget in any one year to no more than 20 percent higher than the previous year was found to be unduly restrictive and was relaxed in 1986. Second, the fund does not appear to have been well integrated with overall fiscal policy or to have helped stabilize budget expenditure, which was partly financed with debt operations outside of the MRSF.[26] The fund was recently wound down.

---

[25]Partly in reflection of the desire to insulate the fund from spending pressures, provision of public information on the fund's assets is prohibited by law.

[26]The government concluded in the 2000 budget that the performance of the MRSF had not been as originally envisaged, and that the stabilization objectives of the legislation setting up the fund had not been achieved in the face of the fiscal decision makers' willingness to issue excessive volumes of government debt (Morauta, 2000).

Venezuela's Macroeconomic Stabilization Fund (MSF)

The MSF, established in late 1998 with the objectives of insulating the budget and the economy from fluctuations in oil prices, initially had relatively rigid rules for transfers to and from the fund. Contributions to the fund were specified as the oil revenues above a reference value corresponding to the five-year moving average. Resources could only be drawn from the fund if oil revenues in a given year were below the reference values, or resources in the fund exceeded 80 percent of the five-year moving average of oil export revenues; in the latter case, excess resources were to be used to amortize government debt.

The rules of the MSF were substantially modified in May 1999. The reference values triggering accumulation or withdrawal of resources were fixed (based on an oil price of US$9 per barrel). The resources to be deposited in the fund were limited to only half of every dollar over the new reference value, and discretionary withdrawals from the fund with government authorization and legislative approval were allowed. In late 2001, the MSF was modified again and the government and the state oil company were exempted from having to deposit resources in the last quarter of 2001 and during 2002. Further changes to the rules are currently under discussion.

The experience with the MSF in recent years has been disappointing, as it has not resulted in an improved fiscal performance, and has led to high-cost borrowing to meet its rules. The integration of the fund's operations with central government operations has proven especially problematic. Because the central government remained in deficit in 1999–2000 despite the strong recovery in oil prices, it could only make deposits into the fund with recourse to other financing. In particular, the buildup of gross assets in the fund was financed in part by domestic borrowing. Moreover, operation of the MSF did not prevent the implementation of an expansionary expenditure policy as oil prices recovered from their low levels in 1998 and early 1999.

Summary of country experience

These country experiences highlight some of the practical difficulties posed by the operation of funds. NRFs have been associated with a variety of operating rules and fiscal policy experience. In some cases where the underlying fiscal policies were generally sound to begin with (such as Norway), funds have been better able to address the problems posed by the behavior of nonrenewable resource prices and fungibility issues. At the same time, however, their operation may not have provided significant restrictions to government behavior. In many other cases, however, the funds' rules have been frequently bypassed or changed, effectively incorporating an element of discretion. In most funds, the rules allow discretionary withdrawals to be made. As a result, often they do not seem to have constrained government spending or the nonresource deficit.

NRF performance appears to be related in part to the size of the volatility faced by governments. In particular, in Chile and Norway the share of volatile resource revenue in total government revenue is significantly lower than in other countries with NRFs. In these countries, the problems that revenue volatility poses for fiscal management are less severe than for countries that have a heavier reliance on revenues from nonrenewable resources. Conversely, the experiences of Venezuela and Oman suggest that where volatile resource revenues are large, funds (and contingent funds in particular) may be difficult to operate, and their effectiveness may be limited.

VI. Conclusions

Fiscal policy in countries with a high degree of dependence on oil and other nonrenewable resources is complicated by the uncertainty and volatility of revenues, as well as by the fact that the resources are exhaustible. NRFs have been suggested as a way of dealing with the effects of price variability, making it easier to put revenues aside when prices are high so that they can be made available to maintain expenditures when prices are low. Funds may also serve as mechanisms to allow part of the nonrenewable resource wealth to be shared by future generations.

NRFs are, however, not an easy—nor necessarily an appropriate—solution to the fiscal policy problems faced by these countries. Statistical evidence suggests that the prices of nonrenewable resources such as oil may not have an average that is constant over time; shocks can be persistent, and it may not be possible to distinguish clearly between transitory and permanent components. This means that there is no simple signal for determining when resources should be put aside and in what amount. It is also important to focus on the overall stance of fiscal policy: if a fund accumulates resources while the budget runs substantial deficits, there may be little effective contribution to stabilization or savings.

An NRF cannot substitute for effective fiscal management in the short run or for a measured intertemporal approach to fiscal policy in the longer term. The issue then becomes whether the establishment of an NRF might contribute to such policies. In some circumstances, this could be the case. Thus, an NRF might facilitate political acceptance of the idea of saving part of a windfall. Similarly, it might focus attention on the fact that the resources are limited. Large or rapidly growing NRFs, however, may themselves give rise to spending pressures.

There are additional risks and possible disadvantages to establishing an NRF. In the absence of liquidity constraints, an NRF may not constrain the overall stance of fiscal policy. Moreover, a fund does not reduce the volatility of prices, which might, in some cases, be too severe for it to handle. An NRF may itself spend excessive amounts of the resources it receives, or use them inappropriately. More generally, if the NRF is not well integrated with the budget, it can complicate fiscal management, lead to an inefficient allocation of the government's total resources, and contribute to lack of transparency and governance problems. Therefore, if a decision is made to establish an NRF, it is crucial that the fund be designed appropriately.

An NRF should be coherently integrated within the budget process. This can be achieved by identifying certain resources as belonging to the fund, but maintaining these revenues in identified accounts within the overall budget. A separate institutional structure might be argued, particularly where budget management of resources has been poor. Governance problems can, however, emerge just as easily in the NRF. Even with a separate institutional structure, it would be preferable for all spending and transfers to go through the budget. In any event, budget formulation and reporting should focus on a consolidated presentation, and expenditure should best be executed by the treasury.

An NRF may receive large amounts of resources, lending importance to its asset-management strategy. This should be effectively coordinated with other government financing operations. A strong case may exist for placing the NRF's assets abroad, since investment in domestic nongovernment financial assets could transmit resource revenue volatility to the economy.

Similarly, the rules and operations of an NRF should be transparent, with stringent mechanisms to ensure accountability and prevent the misuse of resources. This requires regular and frequent disclosure and reporting on the principles governing the fund, its inflows and outflows, and the allocation and return on assets. The NRF's activities should be audited by an independent agency, and investment performance should be periodically evaluated.

The limited number of cases, and problems with data, complicate the evaluation of the operations of existing NRFs. In some countries with NRFs, expenditure has tended to respond less to changes in resource prices than in those without funds, although this experience is not uniform. Moreover, the data suggest that these countries followed similarly prudent expenditure policies both before and after the establishment of a fund. It could, however, be argued that establishment of a fund helped these countries to maintain cautious policies in the face of ongoing revenue volatility.

More detailed evaluation of country experience suggests that NRFs have been associated with a variety of operating rules and fiscal policy experience. In several cases, rules have been bypassed or changed and do not themselves seem to have effectively constrained spending, and the integration of the fund's operations with overall fiscal policy has often proven problematic. Although flexible transfer rules may not formally restrict government behavior, they could still make expenditure restraint more politically acceptable. There is evidence that NRFs have been more difficult to operate when reliance on resource revenues was greatest.

Whether the political economy arguments for an NRF outweigh the potential disadvantages will need to be considered on the basis of the situation in each country. This decision should reflect two strong results that emerge from this study. First, NRFs should not be seen as a simple solution to a complex problem. Second, if an NRF is established, then it should be designed appropriately; otherwise it may well do more harm than good. Key features of a well-designed fund would include coordination of the fund's operations with those of the rest of the public sector, in the context of a sound fiscal policy; effective integration with the budget, which would best be achieved by not imposing rigid rules on fund operations; an appropriate asset-management strategy; and mechanisms to ensure full transparency and accountability.

Bibliography

Alier, Max, and Martin Kaufman, 1999, "Nonrenewable Resources: A Case for Persistent Fiscal Surpluses," IMF Working Paper 99/44 (Washington: International Monetary Fund).

Arrau, Patricio, and Stijn Claessens, 1992, "Commodity Stabilization Funds," World Bank Policy Research Working Paper No. 835 (Washington: World Bank).

Auerbach, Alan J., Jagadeesh Gokhale, Laurence J. Kotlikoff, and Erling Steigum Jr., 1994, "Generational Accounting in Norway: Is Norway Overconsuming Its Petroleum Wealth?" Ruth Pollak Working Papers Series on Economics, No. 24 (Boston: Boston University).

Basch, Miguel, and Eduardo Engel, 1993, "Temporary Shocks and Stabilization Mechanisms: The Chilean Case," in *External Shocks and Stabilization Mechanisms*, ed. by Eduardo Engel and Patricio Meller (Washington: Inter-American Development Bank and Johns Hopkins University Press).

Chalk, Nigel, 1998, "Fiscal Sustainability with Nonrenewable Resources," IMF Working Paper 98/26 (Washington: International Monetary Fund).

Claessens, Stijn, and Jonathan Coleman, 1991, "Hedging Commodity Price Risks in Papua New Guinea," World Bank Policy, Research, and External Affairs Working Paper No. 749 (Washington: World Bank).

Claessens, Stijn, and Sweder van Wijnbergen, 1993, "1990 Mexico and Venezuela Recapture Clauses: An Application of Average Price Options," *Journal of Banking and Finance*, Vol. 17 (June), pp. 733–45.

Claessens, Stijn, and Panos Varangis, 1994, "Oil Price Instability, Hedging, and an Oil Stabilization Fund: The Case of Venezuela," World Bank Policy Research Working Paper No. 1290 (Washington: World Bank).

Davis, Jeffrey, Rolando Ossowski, James A. Daniel, and Steven Barnett, 2001, *Stabilization and Savings Funds for Nonrenewable Resources: Experience and Fiscal Policy Implications*, IMF Occasional Paper No. 205 (Washington: International Monetary Fund).

Engel, Eduardo, and Patricio Meller, eds., 1993, *External Shocks and Stabilization Mechanisms* (Washington: Inter-American Development Bank and Johns Hopkins University Press).

Engel, Eduardo, and Rodrigo Valdés, 2000, "Optimal Fiscal Strategy for Oil Exporting Countries," IMF Working Paper 00/118 (Washington: International Monetary Fund).

Fasano, Ugo, 2000, "Review of the Experience with Oil Stabilization and Savings Funds in Selected Countries," IMF Working Paper 00/112 (Washington: International Monetary Fund).

Gelb and Associates, Alan, and Associates, 1988, *Oil Windfalls: Blessing or Curse?* (New York: Oxford University Press for the World Bank).

Hausmann, Ricardo, 1995, "Dealing with Negative Oil Shocks: The Venezuelan Experience in the Eighties," IADB Working Paper No. 307 (Washington: Inter-American Development Bank).

International Monetary Fund, *World Economic Outlook* (Washington, various years).

Kopits, George, and Steven Symansky, 1998, *Fiscal Policy Rules*, IMF Occasional Paper 162 (Washington: International Monetary Fund).

Kumar, Manmohan S., 1992, "Forecasting Accuracy of Crude Oil Futures Prices," *Staff Papers*, International Monetary Fund, Vol. 39 (June), pp. 432–61.

Liuksila, Claire, Alejandro García, and Sheila Bassett, 1994, "Fiscal Policy Sustainability in Oil-Producing Countries," IMF Working Paper 94/137 (Washington: International Monetary Fund).

Morauta, Hon. Sir Mekere, 2000, "Economic and Development Policies," *2000 Budget of Papua New Guinea*, Vol. 1 (Department of Finance and Treasury). Available via the Internet: http://www.treasury.gov.pg/treasury/treasury.nsf/pages/budget2000.

Ossowski, Rolando, 2002, "Oil Funds: Conceptual Framework and Selected International Experience," in *Alberta's Volatile Government Revenues: Policies for the Long Run*, ed. by L.S. Wilson, Western Studies in Economic Policy No. 8 (Edmonton: University of Alberta), pp. 73–96.

Potter, Barry H., and Jack Diamond, 1999, *Guidelines for Public Expenditure Management* (Washington: International Monetary Fund).

Servén, Luis, and Andrés Solimano, eds., 1993, *Striving for Growth after Adjustment: The Role of Capital Formation* (Washington: World Bank).

Spilimbergo, Antonio, 1999, "Copper and the Chilean Economy, 1960–98," IMF Working Paper 99/57 (Washington: International Monetary Fund).

Steigum, Erling, Jr., and Øystein Thøgersen, 1995, "Petroleum Wealth, Debt Policy, and Intergenerational Welfare: The Case of Norway," *Journal for Policy Modeling*, Vol. 17 (August), pp. 427–42.

Tersman, Gunnar, 1991, "Oil, National Wealth, and Current and Future Consumption Possibilities," IMF Working Paper 91/60 (Washington: International Monetary Fund).

United Nations Conference on Trade and Development, 1996, *Price Risk Management in the Fuels Sector: A Manual* (New York, Geneva).

Varangis, Panos, Takamasa Akiyama, and Donald Mitchell, 1995, *Managing Commodity Booms—and Busts* (Washington: World Bank).

Varangis, Panos, and Don Larson, 1996, "Dealing with Commodity Price Uncertainty," World Bank Policy Research Working Paper No. 1667 (Washington: World Bank).

Warrack, Allan A., and Russell R. Keddie, 2000, "Alberta Heritage Fund versus Alaska Permanent Fund: A Comparative Analysis," paper presented at the Thirty-ninth Annual Meeting of the Western Regional Science Association, Poipu, Kauai, Hawaii, February.

Weiner, Robert J., 1996, "Petroleum Fiscal Dependence: Revenue Forecasting and Oil Price Volatility," George Washington University School of Business and Management Working Paper 96-44 (Washington: George Washington University).

Wickham, Peter, 1996, "Volatility of Oil Prices," IMF Working Paper 96/82 (Washington: International Monetary Fund).

World Bank, 1993, "Venezuela, Oil and Exchange Rates: Historical Experience and Policy Options," World Bank Report No. 10481-VE (Washington).

———, 1994, "Nigeria—Macroeconomic Risk Management: Issues and Options," World Bank Report No. 11983-UNI (Washington).

12

Fiscal Policy and Petroleum Fund Management in Norway

Martin Skancke

I. Introduction

One of the challenges of policymaking is to illustrate complex ideas in a way that is easy to understand. Mundane as this may seem, it really goes to the core of policymaking. No policy can ever be implemented if it does not have public support, and no policy can build public support unless it is communicated in a clear and powerful way.

When I worked on fiscal policy and Petroleum Fund issues for the Norwegian Ministry of Finance, efforts were made to help the minister build support for a prudent and sustainable fiscal policy. Advocating fiscal restraint is not easy when the general government budget surplus is around 15 percent of GDP. Norway's fiscal policy challenges were illustrated in a number of ways; Figure 12.1 below had the greatest impact. In the years since it was developed, it has become a standard feature of fiscal policy documents in Norway.

Of course, a graph that shows only one income component and one expenditure component for government cannot by itself give a meaningful picture of the sustainability of fiscal policy. But there are still two important lessons to be learned from this graph. One is that oil revenues are extremely volatile, so there is a need for some sort of mechanism to decouple government spending from oil revenues in the short term. The second is that the compounded effect of rising pension expenditures and declining oil revenues over the next decades will be

Figure 12.1. *Net Cash Flow from Petroleum and Pension Expenditure*
(In percent of GDP)

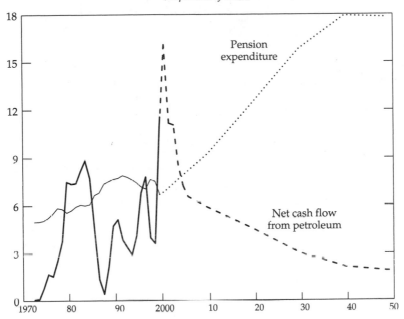

Source: Government of Norway, Long-Term Program, 2002–05.

considerable, so there is also a need for a mechanism to soften this blow to public finances.

In short, the Petroleum Fund is the mechanism to address both of these concerns. It has the twofold purpose of smoothing out spending of oil revenues and at the same time acting as a long-term savings vehicle to let the Norwegian government accumulate financial assets to help cope with expenditures associated with the aging of the population.

This chapter will expand both on the guidelines for fiscal policy and on the guidelines for the Fund itself. It should be stressed, however, that while the accumulation of a petroleum fund probably is a necessary condition for coping with the challenges of an aging population, it is certainly not a sufficient condition. Several policy measures are required, the most obvious of which are:

- encouraging people of working age to remain in the labor force through measures to reduce inflow into the disability pension scheme and by raising the average age of retirement;

- improving the productivity of the labor force, inter alia by improving the quality of education; and
- ensuring a high return on investments in the public and private sectors through attention to governance issues in the public sector and through an active policy to promote competition.

An interesting observation in this context is that the total value of Norway's petroleum wealth (around 200 percent of GDP) corresponds only to around 6–7 percent of total national wealth. In comparison, the value of human capital is around 80 percent of total wealth. So reducing the size of Norway's labor force by 10 percent through longer vacations, shorter working hours, reduced retirement age, etc., will reduce its future consumption possibilities by the same amount as a drop in the value of Norway's oil wealth to zero. Clearly, maintaining the size of the labor force is the key economic policy challenge in the years ahead and the key lever to ensuring a sustainable fiscal policy.

II. The History of the Fund

The Norwegian Government Petroleum Fund was formally established in 1990 when the Norwegian parliament (Stortinget) adopted the Act on the Government Petroleum Fund (Act of June 22, 1990, No. 36).

However, the Fund mechanism (which will be discussed in greater detail below) entails that money will only be allocated to the Fund when there is a budget surplus. In the first half of the 1990s there were budget deficits due to the strong recession. Only in 1995 was the budget back in surplus, and the first transfer from the state budget to the Petroleum Fund was made in 1996 for fiscal year 1995. After that, however, the Fund has grown strongly. At the end of 2001 the Fund amounted to NOK 613.7 billion (about US$80 billion), or around 45 percent of GDP. Projections indicate that the Fund will grow to 120 percent of GDP at the end of 2010. Given the present guidelines for fiscal policy, the Fund is expected to stabilize at a level of around 160–170 percent of GDP in the years after 2030.

Until 1997, the entire Fund consisted only of fixed income assets. In the Revised National Budget 1997, the government put forward a proposal to allow the Fund to also invest in equities beginning in 1998. New guidelines were adopted providing for an investment of 30–50 percent of the Fund in equities. The background for this decision was

Figure 12.2. *Cumulative Return on Subportfolios in the Petroleum Fund*
(The Fund's currency basket at December 31, 1997 = 100)

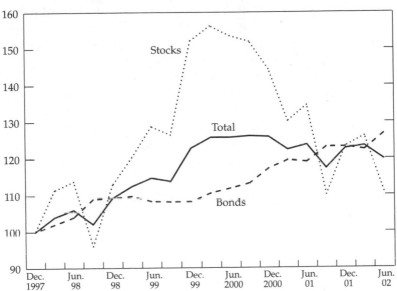

Source: Norges Bank.

that new estimates of the development of government finances indicated that more money would be allocated to the Fund, and that it would take longer before it would be necessary to start drawing on the Fund. This suggested that the investment universe should be expanded to also include equities.

In 2000, the investment universe was further expanded to include investments in emerging markets.

The Petroleum Fund's average real annual return in the period from January 1998 to December 2001 was 3.6 percent.

Figure 12.2 shows cumulative rates of return for the whole Petroleum Fund since the beginning of 1998. The return up to June 2002 was 20 percent. Figure 12.2 also shows cumulative rates of return from January 1, 1998 for the fixed income and equity portfolios separately. In the 18 quarters since then, the cumulative nominal return on equity instruments has been somewhat lower than the return on fixed-income investments, particularly due to losses in the equity portfolio in the second quarter of 2002. The return on the equity instruments has also varied a lot more during the period.

III. The Fund Mechanism

The Petroleum Fund can also be seen as a fiscal management tool to ensure transparency in the use of petroleum revenues. In the work preceding the act establishing the Fund, it was emphasized that the Fund's resources must be included in a coherent budgetary process. When the Fund was established it was therefore emphasized that the accumulation of assets in the Petroleum Fund should reflect actual budget surpluses. This reflects an important point: running a budget surplus is the only way a government can accumulate financial assets on a net basis. If a fund is set up with an allocation rule that is not linked to actual surpluses, the accumulation of assets in the fund will not reflect actual savings.

Consider, for instance, a fund with allocations based on an actuarial calculation of pension liabilities in a situation with government budget deficits. As there is no link between allocations and actual savings, the accumulation of assets in this fund would not reflect an improving net asset base for the government. In fact, the government would be forced to borrow money to cover the allocations to the fund. From an asset management point of view, this would hardly make sense.

From a political economy point of view, the issue is more complex. Funding a pension system in the absence of a budget surplus means that more protection is given to future pension payments than to other public outlays. If future economic growth and government revenues are lower than expected, the burden of adjustment will fall primarily on public consumption. With a fund that is not earmarked for any specific purpose, there is more flexibility in fiscal policy, and more room to maneuver when coping with the effects of unexpected shortfalls in future revenue. Of course, it could be argued that even if pensions have a special protection through funding, that effect can always be counteracted through taxation if needed. But that would still leave inefficiencies, as high transfers from government to the private sector would have to be offset with correspondingly higher tax rates. On the other hand, it could be argued that pension payments for various reasons deserve special treatment, and that these payments should have some sort of special protection. In any case, it is probably useful to distinguish between the legal obligations the government has as an employer and the more political commitments that have been made to protect the benefits of the general pension system.

Another line of argument is that funding of pension liabilities or other ways of keeping a fund outside the direct reach of politicians in-

Figure 12.3. *The Fund Mechanism*

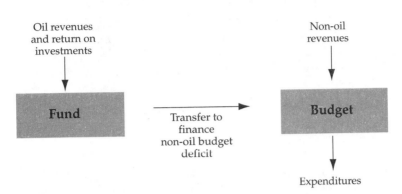

creases legitimacy and public support for protection of the fund's assets. An often-cited example is the high public support for protection of the assets in the Alaska Permanent Fund, which hands out real returns on the fund directly to the citizens of Alaska. True as this may be, the real issue is whether there is any higher public support for net, as opposed to gross, asset accumulation. It does not help much to protect the oil fund if debt is being accumulated elsewhere. Besides, if oil revenues are to be passed on to the private sector, it seems better to do this by reducing distortionary taxes rather than giving direct handouts. This requires oil revenues to be spent over government budgets to cover increasing non-oil deficits.

A full treatment of this issue would fall well outside the scope of this paper. Suffice it to say that there is no correct answer to the question of whether oil funds or other kinds of stabilization funds should be earmarked for special purposes. The main concern to economists should be to give a full account of the consequences of the various options. The Norwegian solution has—thus far—been not to earmark the Petroleum Fund to pensions or any other purpose, although the justification for building up the Fund is of course closely linked to the future development of pension expenditure.

The interaction between the Petroleum Fund and the fiscal budget is illustrated in Figure 12.3 below. The Fund's income is the central government net cash flow from petroleum activities, and the return on Fund investments is added to the Fund. The Fund's expenditure consists of an annual transfer to the Treasury corresponding to the amount of petroleum revenues used in the fiscal budget, to cover the non-oil deficit. In this way, money is accumulated in the Fund if, and only if, there is a government budget surplus including oil revenue.

The Fund mechanism is designed to provide a strong link between the accumulation of assets in the Petroleum Fund and fiscal policy, as described above. To understand the dynamics of asset accumulation, it is therefore necessary to turn to the guidelines for Norwegian fiscal policy.

IV. Guidelines for Fiscal Policy

In the past, Norway has generally pursued a relatively prudent fiscal policy, with general government budget surpluses in the range of 2–4 percent of GDP. Only in the deep recession of the mid-1990s did the fiscal budget slip into deficit for a few years, as illustrated in Figure 12.4. These were actually the only years after World War II when Norway had budget deficits on a general government basis.

Looking ahead, there are substantial challenges in formulating and implementing fiscal policy in Norway, although the starting point is advantageous compared to that of other countries. The Long-Term Program for 2002–2005 presents macroeconomic projections illustrating these challenges.

The so-called baseline scenario describes a path for the Norwegian economy where growth in public employment is limited to achieve sustainable and balanced growth over the long term. This path provides room for growth in public employment that is largely consistent with maintaining current public welfare standards and coverage, including approved reforms. With a continuation of the current social security regulations, unchanged tax rates, and user fees for public services, the projections show a relatively small increase in the use of petroleum revenues, as measured by the structural, non-oil fiscal budget deficit in the period to 2020. However, the deficit shows a strong increase in the period between 2020 and 2040 as a result of an increase in pension expenditures and other expenditures associated with the aging of the population.

In this scenario, there is no room for any new reforms or enhancement of public welfare services. The baseline scenario illustrates that if policy is not revised in a way that contributes to increasing public sector efficiency or strengthening general government budgets, there will be no scope for using more petroleum revenues in the coming years than what follows from approved reforms. This result is in keeping

Figure 12.4. *Fiscal Budget and Petroleum Fund Surplus*
(In billions of Norwegian kroner)

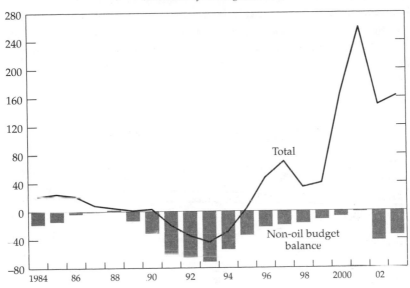

Source: Norwegian Ministry of Finance.

with the generational accounts, which are now approximately in balance.

Figure 12.5 compares developments in the baseline scenario with the developments in the "crowding-out" scenario and a scenario where the use of petroleum revenues over the fiscal budget is set equal to the expected real return on the Government Petroleum Fund. These scenarios are also presented in the Long-Term Program for 2002–2005. The crowding-out scenario looks fairly extreme, but it illustrates the consequences of continuing to increase public service employment in pace with actual growth over the past ten years, while continuing to pursue today's policy in key areas such as the pension system and taxation.

Spending the real return on the Government Petroleum Fund over the fiscal budget implies a gradual increase in the use of petroleum revenues up to 2020. The projections in the Long-Term Program are based on the assumption that these revenues are used partly to increase public sector employment and partly to reduce taxes.

Figure 12.5 shows developments in the use of petroleum revenues over the fiscal budget and in public sector employment. Employment

Figure 12.5. *Non-Oil Budget Deficit and Local Government Employment under the Three Long-Term Program Scenarios*

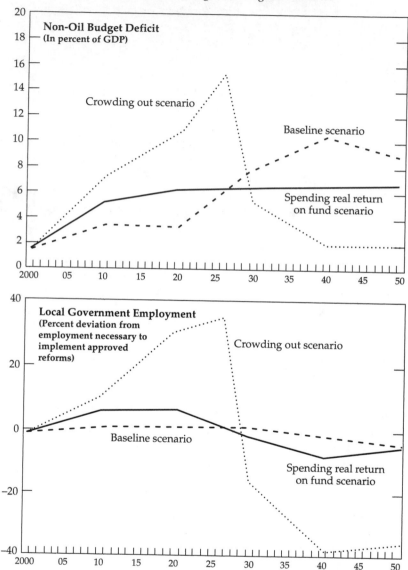

Source: Norwegian Ministry of Finance.

developments are illustrated by the difference between public employment in the various scenarios and the employment level necessary to
implement approved welfare reforms and otherwise maintain current
standards and coverage for public welfare services. The chart illustrates some of the mechanisms associated with the phasing in of petroleum revenues:

- By allocating sufficient capital to the Petroleum Fund to meet future expenditure growth associated with the aging of the population and future pension expenditures, it is possible to ensure a
  steady growth in public welfare services without the need for
  tightening spending in other areas; refer to developments in the
  baseline scenario. This scenario implies that the use of petroleum
  revenues increases relatively slowly over the next 20 years, followed by a sharp increase.
- With a continuation of growth in public sector employment in line
  with that of the 1990s, the non-oil deficit will increase rapidly and
  necessitate a sharp tightening in public finances some time ahead.
  This is reflected in the crowding-out scenario. Higher real-wage
  growth and a scaling back of exposed sectors will match the rapid
  increase in the use of petroleum revenues. This deterioration in
  competitiveness will subsequently have to be reversed. The petroleum revenues will in this case to a large extent have been spent
  over the next 20 years, and imports of goods and services must
  again be financed primarily through exports from the mainland
  economy.
- Use of the expected real return on the Government Petroleum Fund
  implies a steady phasing-in of petroleum revenues. This scenario
  ensures that this part of government wealth is not depleted, while
  providing room for some expansion of welfare services and/or
  some reduction in taxes. However, such a phasing-in will also require the implementation of measures that contribute to limiting
  growth in general government spending or increasing revenues.
  The scale of the necessary tightening ensuing from this scenario is,
  however, substantially smaller than in the crowding-out scenario.

The points above illustrate that the question is not really whether to
use more petroleum revenues over government budgets, but when this
should take place. In the assessment of how petroleum revenues
should be phased in over the years ahead, the following considerations
are central:

- The need for steady growth in public services implies, in isolation,
  substantial restraint in the use of petroleum revenues over the

next two decades. The petroleum revenues saved can then be used to cover higher future expenditures, particularly after 2020. A strong increase in the use of petroleum revenues in this period could, however, lead to strong price and cost inflation during these years and to considerable restructuring problems for the internationally exposed sector in this period.

- The need to achieve stable economic developments over time, both before and after 2020, points to a fairly steady phasing-in of petroleum revenues. The more the use of petroleum revenues is increased over the next ten years, the greater the need will be to strengthen government budgets at a later stage in order to achieve steady growth in public services.

- The aim of maintaining an internationally exposed sector and avoiding wide-scale restructuring in the economy is of particular importance. Increased use of petroleum revenues may increase economic activity. In a situation with high-capacity utilization, this could lead to a weakening of internationally exposed industries. When phasing in petroleum revenues, particular emphasis must be placed on maintaining a strong internationally exposed sector with a view to promoting long-term balanced growth in the Norwegian economy. Both Norway's experience and that of other countries show that an excessive use of petroleum revenues can result in substantial restructuring costs and unemployment problems. (This is the so-called Dutch disease. We should not forget the lesson the Dutch learned in the 1970s, even if they were later generally very successful in their economic policies.)

- The uncertainty associated with future petroleum revenues suggests that considerable caution should be applied to their use.

- Norwegian economic policy should probably not be based on further tax increases. Tax levels are generally high by international standards, and there seems to be agreement—at least in principle—that some of the room to maneuver coming from an increased use of petroleum revenues should be used over time to reduce taxes and excise duties to increase the efficiency of the mainland economy.

Where does all of this leave us? It turns out that using the annual expected real return on the Petroleum Fund over the fiscal budget neatly balances these considerations—it is in a way a "middle road" between the baseline and crowding-out scenarios. This, it might be added, is pure coincidence, and not a general result that can be applied indiscriminately to other countries. But the use of the annual expected real return on the Fund is an attractive option for several reasons:

- It is a simple rule, which is easy to communicate.
- It provides a reference for the budget process.
- It guarantees sustainability of fiscal policy under oil revenue volatility since the use of revenues is based on realized revenue flows from petroleum activities, and not on uncertain future revenues.
- It provides a commonsense solution to the intergenerational distribution question, since all generations will "harvest" their share of oil revenues through spending the real return of the Fund while the real value of the Fund itself will be protected. (But since GDP is growing over time, the real return of the Fund will of course constitute a lower share of total income in the future.)

In 2001, the use of petroleum revenues over the fiscal budget is close to 2 percent of GDP, as measured by the structural, non-oil budget deficit.[1] The guideline for fiscal policy implies an estimated increase in the use of petroleum revenues over the fiscal budget of about 0.4 percent of mainland GDP in each year up to 2010, taking the non-oil budget deficit to about 5 percent of mainland GDP in 2010. At this point, the capital in the Government Petroleum Fund will be around 120 percent of GDP.

V. Organization of the Fund

The Petroleum Fund law states that the Ministry of Finance is responsible for the management of the Petroleum Fund. When setting up the system for management of the fund, there were three major requirements to be met:

Professionalism. In practice, this implied the need to ensure full use of the capabilities of Norges Bank (the Norwegian central bank), while also building skills and capabilities in the Ministry. It also implied extensive use of external fund managers for those assets that Norges Bank previously had little experience with.

Accountability. A system of checks and balances was set up to ensure accountability and a clear division of responsibilities between the Ministry and Norges Bank.

---

[1]Adjustments have been made for variations in tax revenues associated with economic activity, accounting factors, and some extraordinary, temporary revenues and expenditures.

Transparency. This is a key issue. If there is a need to build a consensus around saving over 100 percent of GDP in financial assets, policymakers should be prepared to tell the public exactly how they are going to invest the money, and what the returns on the investments are.

As the formal owner of the fund, the Ministry is responsible for defining the long-term investment strategy. This includes the strategic choices made in the management of the Fund regarding currency and country distribution and the distribution between asset classes and between securities in different market segments.[2]

These strategic choices are reflected in a benchmark portfolio. This portfolio is a "virtual" fund, consisting of equity and bond indices for the various markets in which the Fund is invested. The benchmark serves two purposes:

- The Ministry has defined limits for the maximum variations permitted relative to the benchmark portfolio. The limit is defined as a maximum expected tracking error of 1.5 percent.[3] The benchmark is thus an integrated part of the risk control system for the Fund.
- The benchmark is also used to assess Norges Bank's performance. Actual returns are compared with returns on the benchmark portfolio and performance differences are reported and explained in the Fund's reports.

Within the strategic guidelines set by the Ministry, the operational management of the Fund has been delegated to Norges Bank. In addition to the Ministry of Finance's guidelines for the Petroleum Fund, an agreement has been drawn up that regulates the relationship between the Ministry and Norges Bank in connection with management of the Fund.

Formally, the Petroleum Fund is a deposit account denominated in Norwegian kroner at Norges Bank, owned by the government. As such, it is a liability for Norges Bank. However, the guidelines state that Norges Bank is to acquire foreign securities in its own name for a value corresponding to the krone bank account. The return on these foreign investments, less Norges Bank's management fee, is defined as the return on the Petroleum Fund.

Norges Bank delivers detailed annual reports on the management of the Petroleum Fund. These public reports describe how the Fund is managed and include a list of the companies in which the Fund's capital has been invested. The reports provide figures on total return,

---

[2]The investment guidelines for the Fund are in the Appendix.
[3]The tracking error is defined as the standard deviation of the difference between the benchmark and the actual portfolio.

Figure 12.6. *Organization of the Fund*

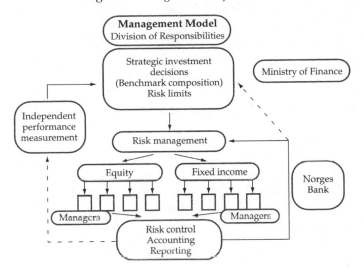

benchmark return, attribution of the excess return, and management costs. The annual reports also contain articles on the investment philosophy behind the operational management, information on the process of selecting external managers, and so on.

In addition, Norges Bank submits quarterly reports to the Ministry of Finance containing the main return and cost data. Norges Bank also reports to an independent company hired by the Ministry to make calculations of Fund returns and attribution analysis of differences between actual and benchmark returns. The reports from this company are public and are published on the Internet, as are the reports from Norges Bank.

The management system outlined above is illustrated in Figure 12.6. In addition to the structure illustrated in this figure comes the auditing of the Fund and its management, which is done by the Office of the Auditor General. The Auditor General is appointed by and reports directly to Parliament, ensuring parliamentary control on Fund operations.

VI. Managing the Fund—Operational Issues

Until 1998, Norges Bank had no experience in managing portfolios of international equities. Drawing on the bank's expertise in managing large portfolios in international government bonds, a project group started in spring 1997 to prepare for investing part of the Petroleum Fund in equities. A new department, Norges Bank Investment Management (NBIM), was established in January 1998. The board of the bank delegated to NBIM the operational management of the Petroleum Fund (€14 billion at that time), the long-term portfolio of the foreign exchange reserves (€12 billion), and the Norwegian Petroleum Insurance Fund (€1.2 billion). At the end of 2001, the combined assets under management were over €100 billion.

NBIM is organized with Chinese walls to the ordinary central bank functions. The head of NBIM reports to the governor of Norges Bank but takes no part in the internal discussion on monetary policy. All investment decisions are delegated to NBIM according to clearly defined guidelines, and NBIM reports to the governor and his staff on a monthly basis. Within NBIM, investment decisions are delegated to three front office units: Equities, Fixed Income, and Tactical Asset Allocation. The head of NBIM defines investment mandates and sets risk limits for each front office unit. There are no committees making investment decisions.

The staff of NBIM has grown from 71 at year-end 1998 to just over 100 now. During the first half of 1998, the portfolio of the Petroleum Fund was transformed from 100 percent fixed-income instruments in 8 countries to a diversified portfolio of 60 percent fixed income and 40 percent equities in 21 countries. Four external index managers carried out all investments in equities. Since autumn 1998, NBIM has also farmed out external mandates for active equity management. In 1999 NBIM started with internal active equity management, and in 2000 small portfolios for indexing and enhanced indexing were also put in place. By spring 2001 large external index mandates were transformed to internal enhanced index portfolios. About 50 percent of the equity portfolio is now managed in-house, while 15 external managers oversee the rest. The external active managers do the bulk of active risk taking.

The primary goal of Norges Bank's management of the Petroleum Fund is to outperform the benchmark portfolio defined by the Ministry of Finance. The strategy for surpassing the performance of the benchmark portfolio was presented in the annual report for 1999. The following are vital components of the strategy: spreading active management over several types of positions, combining external and internal management, and specializing internal management in areas where there is a good chance of predicting price movements better than the average market participant. Special emphasis is also placed on risk management, portfolio analysis, and efficient trading in the market. By spreading active management over a large number of independent decisions, NBIM seeks to make effective use of the clearly defined risk limits set out by the Ministry of Finance.

Distinguishing between index management and active management is an important aspect of the management strategy. The risk limits defined by the Ministry of Finance state that management of the Fund must, by and large, closely follow the benchmark portfolio. A number of effects are achieved by "earmarking" a portion of the portfolio to closely follow the benchmark portfolio. Management costs for this portion of the portfolio are kept low since this type of management can be achieved using simple techniques. This also results in a sharper focus on the portion of the portfolio that can be managed actively. A broader overview is obtained, which makes it possible to assess the merits of the different types of management, and to make use of the special strengths of the various managers.

An important means of keeping costs low is to allow the active managers, who cost more, to invest only in what they specialize in. In the contracts entered into with active managers, a target area is established for minimum and maximum risk relative to the benchmark indices. Part of the fees of most managers is based on how successful they are in achieving an excess return. This provides them with an incentive to use their own expertise to take active positions. If, alternatively, NBIM had delegated the entire equity portfolio to external active managers, the total management fee would have been considerably higher than that resulting from a division into index and active management.

A common feature of the equity managers selected up to the present is that, in general, their investment strategy is to analyze and choose from among individual companies with the aid of a range of valuation models, and without any restrictions on country or sector positions. This means that their results (excess or deficit return) will normally show less covariation with more general market trends than if the strategy had placed most of its emphasis on analyses at a macro-level. On the allocation side, the emphasis has been on achieving a low correlation among the external managers.

It is not only the number of independent decisions that is of importance, but also how wide price-trend variations are among the securities from which selection has taken place. There were very large differences in the performances of comparable companies in the autumn of 1999. There was a broad spread between the price trends of companies that performed well and those that fell behind, particularly in the technology and IT sectors. Under such conditions, the potential for excess return is greater for managers who select individual equities than it is in periods of substantial covariation in the return on individual equities. This suggests that the degree of risk taking may vary over time as the potential for excess returns changes. In other words, it is also important to predict risk, not just prices and returns.

Another important element of the strategy for keeping management costs down is a keen focus on transaction costs. Over time, transaction costs will be of considerable importance for the net return, particularly for the Petroleum Fund, which enters the market each quarter with large amounts of new capital. The question of which transaction pattern will result in the lowest overall transaction costs is considered each time.

When purchasing external services, NBIM has attempted to create as much competition as possible between potential suppliers, for example by placing an invitation for tenders on the Internet. The activities of Norges Bank's own management are subject to its internal budget and accounting regulations, and are monitored by the bank's control system in the same ways as the other departments in Norges Bank.

In summary, in setting out to achieve an excess return, a fundamental choice has been made to take many small positions against the benchmark index rather than a few large positions. The strategy reflects that spreading active management over many different types of positions (diversification of risk taking) can result in a more robust excess return in the face of general fluctuations in the market. Unless one is particularly skilled at forecasting market trends, a conscious strategy of spreading risk in position taking results in the best trade-off between excess return and risk.

VII. Some Policy Conclusions

The main message of this paper is that the first priority for fiscal authorities in any country should be developing a prudent and sustainable long-term strategy for fiscal policy. Only if that fiscal policy strategy entails the accumulation of government funds should rules for a "Petroleum Fund" be developed. It will usually not make much sense to accumulate government capital in a fund while debt is being built up in other parts of government. The rules for allocation of capital to the Fund should reflect this.

Successful implementation of a fiscal policy strategy that implies large-scale accumulation of government funds requires a high degree of consensus, transparency, and accountability. In the case of Norway, it was possible to build on an existing and well-functioning institutional framework when the Petroleum Fund was established. The central bank already had extensive experience in managing its ordinary currency reserves, and systems of reporting and control were well established. Furthermore, there was a long tradition of transparency, both with respect to the government's fiscal policy strategy and the operations of the central bank. The guidelines for management of the Petroleum Fund draw up a clear division of responsibilities between the Ministry of Finance as "owner" of the Fund and Norges Bank as manager.

Some oil-producing countries may still have to make substantial progress with respect to governance and transparency before a Norwegian-style petroleum fund can be established. These countries should focus on building democratic institutions with transparency, accountability, and good budget procedures if attempting to implement a fiscal policy strategy that implies a substantial accumulation of government funds.

Appendix. Investment Guidelines

The main elements of the current investment guidelines are:
- equity portion: 30–50 percent;
- regional distribution: Europe 40–60 percent, the Americas 20–40 percent, Asia/Oceania 10–30 percent;
- investment area: 28 countries (of which 7 are emerging markets as of January 31, 2001);
- maximum ownership share in any one company: 3 percent;
- benchmark portfolio for bonds and equities: based on well-defined market indices (FTSE All World Index for equities and Schroder Salomon Smith Barney's World Government Bond Index); and
- duration of the fixed-income portfolio: 3 to 7 years.

The single most frequent question about the investment guidelines is how Norway "calculated the optimal equity share of the Fund." The answer is: "This cannot be done." Up to a certain point, of course, moving from a 100 percent bond portfolio—as Norway did—to a mixed portfolio of equity and bonds will give a diversification gain that will offset the isolated effect of taking on more equity risk. So expected returns can be increased and risk can be reduced at the same time by including some equities in the portfolio. But this effect is depleted once about 5 or 10 percent equity share is reached, depending on the time horizon and how risk is measured. Beyond that, higher expected returns are being traded off for higher risk.

No economist or analyst can tell what the "correct" equity share is—apart from stating that, to the extent that higher expected returns and lower risk can be obtained at the same time, this is an offer that should not be refused. Nor could civil servants tell their politicians what the "correct" equity share for the Petroleum Fund would be. What was done in Norway was to illustrate the trade-off in the best possible way by answering questions like "What is the probability of negative return in one year for different equity shares?" and "What is the accumulated effect of x percent higher average return on the Fund over the next y years?" Of course, typical equity ratios for international institutional investors were also looked at as references. But in the end, the choice of equity share in the Fund is a political decision, reflecting the subjective trade-off between risk and expected return that the politicians have made on behalf of the people they represent.

The second most frequent question is why the Petroleum Fund is only invested outside Norway. There are several reasons for this:

- *The need to stabilize the Norwegian economy.* The corollary to substantial surpluses on the current account will be a considerable outflow of capital in the years to come. If the private sector were to contribute to this capital outflow to any considerable extent, interest rates in Norway would have to be lower than abroad in order to entice private investors to invest abroad rather than at home. Norway would then risk financial market bubbles in periods of high oil revenues. By investing the Petroleum Fund directly abroad, the central government will contribute to the substantial capital outflow and thereby shelter the domestic economy from the effects of high petroleum revenues more effectively.
- *The need for a varied industry structure.* This is closely linked to the argument above. The investment of the Petroleum Fund abroad helps to avoid excessive real exchange rate appreciation, which in turn would lead to an industry structure that cannot be sustained when oil revenues start to decline.
- *The need to use the Petroleum Fund as a buffer.* For the Fund to function as a financial buffer that can be drawn on to finance budget deficits, it is important that the size of the buffer can vary without

affecting the rest of the economy to any extent. Substantial and strongly fluctuating central government financial claims on domestic sectors would not satisfy such a requirement.

- *Domestic investments could result in a lower Fund return.* The optimal level of domestic real investments for a country as a whole is given by the return on these investments compared with the return on alternative financial investments. Since a country as a whole can only save financially by accumulating claims on other countries, it follows that the relevant interest rate in this case is the international rate. The optimal level of real investments should then be independent of the income level. Of course, if a country faces an effective credit constraint this argument will not hold, but for Norway it probably does.
- *Diversification.* The risk of the Fund's investments would be greatly increased if one did not take full opportunity of the diversification gains of international investments.
- *Domestic investments could undermine the fiscal budget as a management tool.* The Petroleum Fund consists of that part of petroleum revenues that are not used in the fiscal budget, and the return on this capital. In the budgetary deliberations, Parliament decides the extent of central government expenditure. If, in addition, the Petroleum Fund were used to finance domestic investments in, for example, infrastructure, the Fund would effectively become fiscal budget number two. This would weaken the position of the fiscal budget as a political management tool.

When the original currency distribution of the Petroleum Fund was determined, emphasis was placed on the need to maintain the international purchasing power of the Fund. On this basis, Norway's import weights were used to determine the Fund's currency distribution.

However, as the Fund grew in size and it became apparent that the Fund's investments would probably have a very long time horizon, the question was raised as to whether import weights provide the most appropriate currency distribution:

- Investments in line with import weights may mean that the Fund becomes too dominant in small markets where Norwegian imports are considerable (e.g., Sweden and Denmark).
- Import patterns can change over time.
- For some countries, real import weights may be higher or lower than the level implied by direct trade between Norway and the country. This will be the case if, for example, Norway's imports from third countries contain substantial factor inputs from the re-

spective country or if the country itself imports considerable factor inputs from third countries.

- The long time horizon of the Fund's investments increases the risk that recessions, and at worst war, disasters, etc., will at some point have an impact in market countries. Such events often affect a number of countries in the same region. Investments based on import weights may thus result in excessive exposure to regional shocks in Europe.
- For equity investments in major enterprises, it is meaningless to talk about a distribution of investments in different markets. The global operations of large, international companies are often more extensive than their national activities, and their profitability is therefore primarily linked to global economic trends.
- The use of import weights as the basis for the currency distribution of the Petroleum Fund was aimed at reducing the exchange rate risk associated with changes in exchange rates between the currencies in which the Fund has invested. This exchange rate risk, however, is usually reduced in the long term. By investing in different currencies, the total real return (when exchange rate movements and differences in interest rates and price inflation between countries are taken into account) will have a tendency to converge over time. Empirical studies provide some support for this mechanism, but primarily in the long term.

So it seemed reasonable to make a "compromise" between import weights and global GDP weights. From January 1, 1998, the share of Asian currencies was set to 10–30 percent, American currencies to 20–40 percent, and European to 40–60 percent. This implied a shift out of European currencies compared with what pure import weights would have given.

When it was decided that portions of the Petroleum Fund could be invested in equity instruments, a choice had to be made between strategic investments in the form of large investments in individual companies on the one hand, and financial investments on the other, which involve smaller investments in a large number of equities.

Several factors indicated that the Petroleum Fund should be exclusively invested as financial investments:

- The Petroleum Fund is a fiscal policy instrument devised for the purpose of promoting the long-term objectives of fiscal policy. Based on the purpose of the Fund, it is natural that the Fund's capital be invested in a way that best safeguards the considerations linked to state finances. This means that the guiding principles should be to safeguard government resources and to ensure a maximum return at an acceptable level of risk.

- By spreading the investments on a number of equities, the Fund will achieve a diversification of the portfolio. If the Fund were instead to purchase large stakes in selected companies, it would be assuming a company-specific risk. This risk does not increase the expected return on the investment. Such strategic investments result in a less favorable portfolio diversification.
- Empirically, only a broadly diversified portfolio will yield an excess return when investing in equities. There is little reason to believe that strategic investments over time yield a higher return than financial investments.
- An important purpose of the Fund is to serve as a buffer against economic downturns that affect state finances and/or the external account. This requires a certain degree of liquidity of the investments. Strategic investments are long term and cannot easily serve as a buffer.
- Strategic investments abroad, e.g., in the form of purchases of distribution channels to secure markets for Norwegian products, may from an economic viewpoint be viewed as tantamount to providing financial support to enterprises that benefit from such investments. The Petroleum Fund is not a suitable instrument for providing support of this nature.
- If the Fund acquires large equity stakes in foreign companies that subsequently are confronted with financial problems, the Norwegian government may come under substantial pressure to help find solutions to enable the enterprise to continue operations. This could easily conflict with the guideline that the Fund's capital shall be invested on the basis of commercial considerations.
- If the Fund were to act as a strategic investor, it would be much more difficult to evaluate management performance because it may be difficult to find an adequate basis of comparison. For example, it would be difficult for the authorities to criticize the performance of a manager who has been instructed to invest in a company whose results subsequently deteriorate. By acting as financial investor it is in principle easier to assess whether the return is satisfactory based on comparison with observable benchmark portfolios. For purposes of transparency and control, it is essential that the results can be properly assessed.
- Strategic investments require a completely different budget procedure, tighter control by the authorizing agency, a specified divi-

sion of political responsibility, and a completely different type of expertise and evaluation than in the case of financial investments. It was thus concluded that the Petroleum Fund should exclusively act as a financial investor so that the ownership stakes in individual companies are small. The Fund's investments in equities shall be composed to yield a return that is in line with broadly diversified portfolios of equities listed on various international stock exchanges.

Bibliography

The best sources for reading more about the Norwegian Petroleum Fund are the Ministry of Finance and Norges Bank websites:

- http://www.odin.dep.no/fin contains material on the history of the Fund, formal guidelines, and all public documents relating to its management. It also contains material on the guidelines for fiscal policy and the Long-Term Program.
- http://www.norges-bank.no/ contains information on Norges Bank's management of the Fund, including all annual reports, letters from the bank to the Ministry of Finance, and various articles on fund management issues.

Also highly recommended is the book written by professor Rögnvaldur Hannesson at the Norwegian School of Economics and Business Administration on experiences with oil funds in various countries: Hannesson, Rögnvaldur, 2001, *Investing for Sustainability* (Boston: Kluwer Academic Publishers).

13

Oil Funds in Transition Economies: Azerbaijan and Kazakhstan

JOHN WAKEMAN-LINN, PAUL MATHIEU, AND BERT VAN SELM[1]

I. Introduction

The challenge of economic transition—of transforming an economy from a system of command and control to a free market—is a daunting one. Countries facing the challenge of transition in the 1990s had little proven economic theory and few relevant historical precedents to guide them. Even today, more than ten years after the collapse of the Soviet Union, economists continue to debate how best to advance the process of transition.[2]

The challenge of managing oil wealth has proven similarly daunting for many countries. Numerous studies (for example, Hausmann and Rigobon, Chapter 2 in this volume, and Sachs and Warner, 1995) have shown that resource-rich—particularly oil-rich—countries have experienced slower economic growth over time than resource-poor countries. While a variety of explanations have been proposed for this empirical fact (e.g., Dutch disease, the adverse economic effects of price volatility, the political economy effects of the struggle

---

[1]We would like to thank John Dodsworth and Peter Keller, as well as the participants in the IMF's June 2002 Conference on Fiscal Policy Formulation and Implementation in Oil-Producing Countries, for helpful comments and suggestions.

[2]For a discussion of these debates, see the special issue of the *IMF Staff Papers* on transition economies (Volume 48, 2001).

for economic rents), numerous countries appear to be worse off as a result of their oil endowments than they would have been without the oil.

Countries confronted with both challenges—transforming their economy to a free market, while managing an oil boom—face a potentially overwhelming task. As noted by Rosenberg and Saavalainen (1998), the problems of managing a resource boom greatly complicate the difficulties facing a transition economy. This paper assesses the approach taken by two such countries—Azerbaijan and Kazakhstan—to address these serious challenges.

Despite an ambiguous track record of oil funds in other countries (see Davis and others, Chapter 11 in this volume), both countries have created oil funds to assist in managing their new petroleum wealth. In what follows, we assess the reasons why these countries have opted for oil funds, as well as the prospect that these funds may assist them in better managing their oil wealth and economic transition. Section II describes the current situation and prospects for oil and gas production in Azerbaijan and Kazakhstan. Section III explores their reasons for creating oil funds. Section IV focuses on the operational aspects of these oil funds and evaluates their design features in seeking to assess the prospects for their success. Section V concludes.

II. Oil and Gas Sector Prospects in Azerbaijan and Kazakhstan

Azerbaijan's and Kazakhstan's oil and gas prospects have improved substantially in recent years. In both countries, important new discoveries were made, and there has been considerable progress in the construction of new pipelines to bypass the Russian oil and gas pipeline monopolies and to link these countries to world energy markets.[3] Proven reserves will allow Azerbaijan to increase oil production to about 1.3 million barrels per day (bpd) by 2010, while Kazakhstan's production could exceed 3 million bpd by about 2015.

---

[3]For a more complete discussion of these issues see Dodsworth, Mathieu, and Shiells (2002) and Mathieu and Shiells (2002).

Figure 13.1. *Azerbaijan: Oil Production and Exports*
(*In millions of barrels per day*)

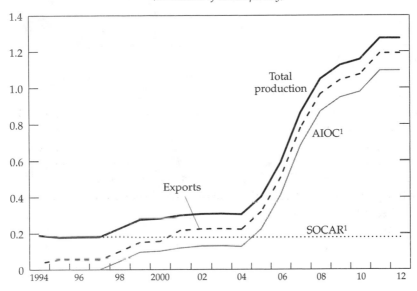

Sources: Azerbaijan authorities; and authors' estimates and projections.
[1]SOCAR – State Oil Company of the Azerbaijan Republic; AIOC = Azerbaijan
International Operating Company.

Azerbaijan

Oil and gas production in Azerbaijan decreased sharply in the final years of the USSR and the first years after the Soviet Union's breakup. Gas production has continued to decrease, but oil output has increased in recent years (Figures 13.1 and 13.2). In 1995, Azerbaijan International Operating Company (AIOC), a consortium of international oil firms, was formed to operate Azerbaijan's most promising oil field, Azeri-Chirag-Guneshli (ACG), with production starting in 1998. AIOC's oil production is projected to reach 1 million bpd by 2010. Oil and gas already constitute over 90 percent of Azerbaijan's exports and will contribute over half of government revenue by 2005 (Figure 13.3).

Azerbaijan's proven oil reserves have been estimated at 7 billion barrels, and possible reserves at twice that amount. Proven gas reserves increased sharply when drilling at Shah Deniz yielded positive results; at 870 billion cubic meters (bcm), this is one of the

Figure 13.2. *Azerbaijan: Gas Production and Exports*
(In billions of cubic meters per year)

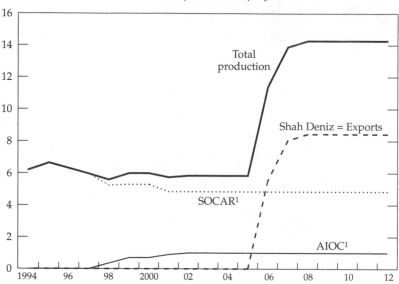

Sources: Azerbaijan authorities; and authors' estimates and projections.
[1]SOCAR = State Oil Company of the Azerbaijan Republic; AIOC = Azerbaijan
International Operating Company.

biggest gas fields in the world. Drilling at other fields has not yet
produced major finds, and a few production-sharing agreements
(PSAs)[4] have been dissolved. However, due to limited rig availability,
many promising fields remain untested, and the State Oil Company of
Azerbaijan Republic (SOCAR) remains confident that more oil and gas
will be found.

Huge oil and gas sector investments are planned in the coming
years. Investment in the development of ACG is projected at more than
US$3.8 billion over 2002–5. The cost of the new export pipeline (Baku-
Tbilisi-Ceyhan, or BTC) needed to transport the oil from this field is estimated at US$3 billion. The first phase of expenditures for the
development of Shah Deniz is estimated at US$1.4 billion; full field de-

---

[4]Azerbaijan has used PSAs as the main tool for attracting foreign investment into the
oil and gas sector. Once signed, PSAs are ratified by parliament and have the force of
law.

Figure 13.3. *Azerbaijan: Oil and Gas Sector Exports and Fiscal Revenues*
(In percent)

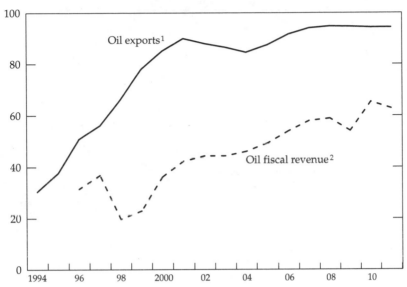

Sources: Azerbaijan authorities; and authors' estimates and projections.
[1]As a percentage of total exports, based on March 2002 IMF *World Economic Outlook* price projections.
[2]As a percentage of total fiscal revenue, based on March 2002 IMF *World Economic Outlook* price projections.

velopment would cost an additional US$3 billion. The South Caucasus Pipeline that will bring Shah Deniz gas to Turkey is expected to cost about US$1 billion. To put these figures in context, Azerbaijan's GDP in 2001 was about US$5.7 billion, or less than half the combined cost of these investments.

Kazakhstan

In the Soviet era, Kazakhstan's considerable petroleum endowment was underexploited, due to a scarcity of capital resources and the more easily accessible reserves in the Volga basin. Exploration and development have accelerated since independence, as international firms have been attracted by the favorable prospects in the Caspian basin. A mix of traditional projects, PSAs, and joint ventures with the state oil and gas company, Kazmunaigas, have been used.

Figure 13.4. *Kazakhstan: Oil Production*
(In millions of barrels per day)

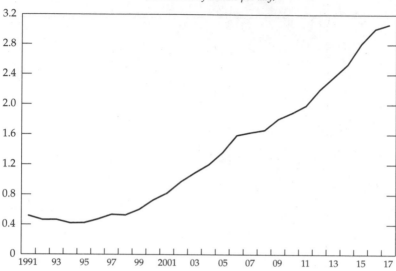

Sources: Kazakhstan authorities; and authors' estimates and projections.

Oil and gas producers are investing heavily to expand production from just 800,000 bpd in 2001 to around 3.1 million bpd in about 15 years, which would put Kazakhstan among the top ten oil producers in the world (Figure 13.4). Since independence some US$7 billion has flowed into the sector, and it is expected that around US$3–4 billion will be invested in the petroleum sector annually through the medium term. Gas production of about 15 bcm per year, largely oil-associated gas, is also expected to rise strongly over the medium term to perhaps 50 bcm per year (Figure 13.5). The petroleum sector accounted for an estimated 25 percent of GDP in 2001 and crude petroleum exports reached US$4.5 billion, about one-half of exports. Fiscal receipts from the sector have surged with rising output and the recovery in prices since 1998, to about one-quarter of general government revenue in 2001 (Figure 13.6).

Three large projects dominate the petroleum sector. The onshore Tengiz field has recoverable reserves estimated in the range of 6–9 billion barrels. Production is expected to double to around 500,000 bpd in five years and rise further in the long term. The Karachaganak gas and gas condensate field is expected to more than double production to 230,000 bpd of condensate and to link up to the Caspian Pipeline Consortium (CPC)

Figure 13.5. *Kazakhstan: Oil Exports and Fiscal Revenues*
(In percent)

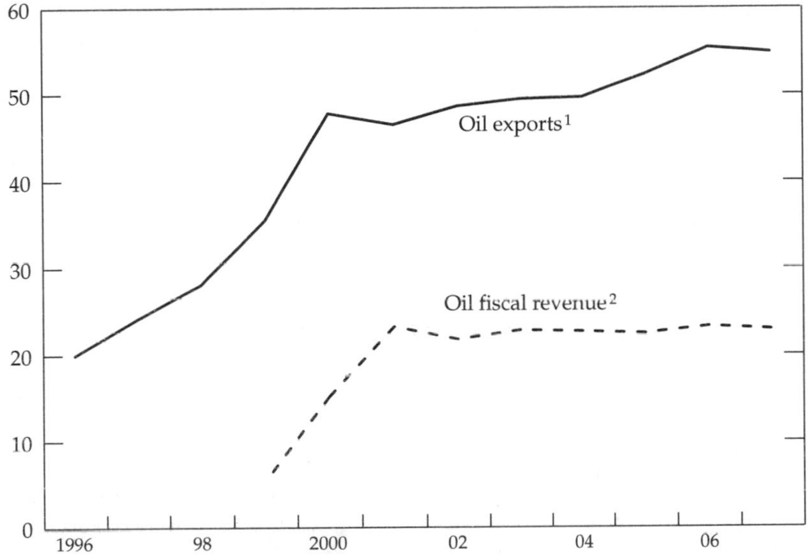

Sources: Kazakhstan authorities; and authors' estimates and projections.
[1]As a percentage of total exports, based on March 2002 IMF *World Economic Outlook* price projections.
[2]As a percentage of total fiscal revenue, based on March 2002 IMF *World Economic Outlook* price projections.

pipeline by mid-2003.[5] The size of the recently discovered Kashagan field has been estimated at 8–13 billion barrels of recoverable reserves. Kashagan, the largest find in the past 30 years, will not begin production before 2005, but output could reach well over 1 million bpd by 2015.

III. The Rationale for Oil Funds in Azerbaijan and Kazakhstan

Large oil and gas revenues, and the prospect of much more to come, led both Azerbaijan and Kazakhstan to create special natural resource

---

[5]The CPC pipeline linking the Tengiz field with the Black Sea was officially opened in late 2001. The 1,500-km line is the first private international joint venture in the region. The line had an initial capacity of about 600,000 bpd and cost US$2.6 billion to construct. It is estimated to have cut export transport costs in half.

Figure 13.6. *Kazakhstan: Gas Production*
(*In billions of cubic meters*)

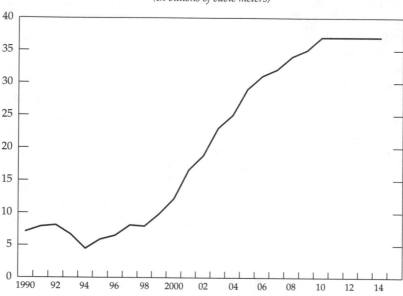

Sources: Kazakhstan authorities; and authors' estimates and projections.

funds to manage these revenues. While the effectiveness of this instrument has not been established unambiguously either in economic theory or in international practice, Azerbaijan's and Kazakhstan's unfinished transitions from planned to market economy provide additional reasons to separate oil and gas revenues from regular government revenues.

Political Economy Rationale

Oil funds in general, and those in Azerbaijan and Kazakhstan in particular, can be thought of as having two primary objectives and two secondary, and related, objectives. The primary objectives are stabilization—insulating fiscal and monetary policy, and the economy, from swings in oil and gas revenues—and savings for future generations. The secondary objectives are maintaining fiscal discipline, which requires that oil money not be available to close any gaps in the budget resulting from poor tax collection performance or excessive expenditures, and avoiding monetary expansion and pressures for excessive appreciation of the exchange rate, which requires strict limits on expenditures of oil and gas revenues, with any unspent revenues being saved outside the country.

From the perspective of economic theory, it is difficult to make a case for an oil fund. As argued by Davis and others (see Chapter 11 in this volume), "The policy objectives of [oil funds] could, in principle, be achieved through implementation of a sound fiscal policy within the context of a medium-term budget framework." In other words, any fiscal policy decision that can be made in the context of an oil fund—for example, to target a particular path of the non-oil deficit—can also be made without an oil fund. Similarly, an oil fund is not required for a government to save oil-related revenues abroad, thereby preventing exchange rate pressures from these revenues and easing the task of the monetary authorities. The rationale for the creation of an oil fund must thus be based on political economy arguments, rather than purely economic arguments.

Annual budget debates are typically short-run exercises, focused on political and economic pressures over the next year (or, where medium-term expenditure frameworks are used, the next three years) (Schick, 2002). However, planning for sound use of oil and gas revenues requires a longer horizon, one that is well beyond normal political horizons. A long-term political compact, detailing how oil- and gas-related revenues are to be used not just this year, but for years to come (i.e., an agreement on an oil fund), can protect some portion of oil revenues, thereby allowing larger fiscal surpluses in the short run, and a more desirable path of expenditures over the medium to long run, than would otherwise be politically feasible.[6] By allowing larger surpluses, oil funds can also improve coordination between monetary and fiscal policy, since this fiscal sterilization of oil revenues means that the monetary authority has less of a sterilization task confronting it (and its often very limited intervention tools).

These political economy arguments clearly applied—or were thought by the authorities to apply—in Azerbaijan and Kazakhstan. In both countries, the government was worried about political pressure to

---

[6]The Norwegian Petroleum Fund, for example, is designed as a "tool for coping with the financial challenges connected to an aging population and the eventual decline in oil revenues, by transferring wealth to future generations" (Norwegian Ministry of Finance).

spend oil wealth rapidly and inefficiently. As a result, and reflecting political realities in the two countries, Azerbaijan and Kazakhstan created oil funds subject only to presidential control, bypassing parliament. By taking control over oil revenues—excluding SOCAR oil revenues from Soviet-era oil fields in Azerbaijan and a baseline level of oil revenue in Kazakhstan—away from parliament, they sought to insulate these revenues from short-term pressures for expenditures. As discussed below, however, it is not clear that this objective has been achieved.

In Azerbaijan, prior to the establishment of the oil fund significant portions of oil-related receipts were used to close gaps in the state budget, undermining expenditure and tax discipline, while the funds and their expenditures were often not accounted for in a transparent manner.[7] Creation of the oil fund was thus motivated in part by a desire to improve both fiscal discipline and transparency. In Kazakhstan, prior to the creation of the National Fund for the Republic of Kazakhstan (NFRK), significant oil revenues were kept off budget and held in undisclosed offshore accounts, beyond the purview of both Parliament and the Chamber of Accounts.[8] At the time, keeping these funds in such accounts was viewed as necessary for maintaining financial discipline. The creation of the NFRK thus led to improved transparency in the management of petroleum revenues.

Oil Funds and Economic Transition

The Commonwealth of Independent States (CIS) countries confronted a wide range of economic and political challenges following the collapse of the Soviet Union. Two of those challenges had particular relevance for the decisions facing Azerbaijan and Kazakhstan over how to deal with their growing oil and gas revenues. Those challenges related to the need to develop the institutions for conducting economic policy in a market economy and the need to develop new industries and services to replace inefficient Soviet-era enterprises, which would not be viable in a market economy.

---

[7]In 1998 and 1999, oil bonus financing of the state budget amounted to 1.8 and 3.7 percent of GDP, respectively. Off-budget use of oil bonus money included payments related to the purchase of one Tupolev 154 and two Boeing 757 aircraft in 1998.

[8]In 1996 the authorities sold a 25 percent stake in the Tengiz field to Mobil for about US$1.1 billion, with an up-front payment of about US$500 million and performance-based tranches through 2000. On April 4, 2002, the prime minister revealed that a significant portion of these funds had been kept in undisclosed offshore accounts. Some US$300 million was repatriated to the NFRK in mid-2002.

At independence, Azerbaijan and Kazakhstan lacked many of the institutions vital to the conduct of economic policy in a market economy. In particular, they lacked both a modern tax policy and administration and institutions for budget preparation and execution. All CIS countries have struggled since independence to create a modern tax policy and a tax administration capacity capable of shifting "from handling the taxation transactions of a highly controlled state sector to dealing with the more challenging compliance activities of the emerging private sector and increasingly autonomous state-owned firm" (Ebrill and Havrylyshyn, 1999). This has proven to be a difficult task for all these countries, as is clearly demonstrated by the low levels of tax collection and tax compliance in these countries.

But for Azerbaijan and Kazakhstan, an easily available alternative source of money—oil revenue—has made the challenge of developing market-oriented tax policy and tax administration that much more difficult. While no one would argue for the exclusive use of depletable oil revenue in lieu of tax revenue, when faced with the need for additional revenue it is certainly easier—both administratively and politically—to use oil money rather than strengthen tax administration and enforcement or revise tax policy. Thus, if they were to be successful in developing a sound tax policy and administration, these countries needed to find a way to insulate tax-related decisions from the easy availability of oil money.

Similarly, all CIS countries faced the need to develop market-oriented systems for budget preparation and execution (Potter and Diamond, 2000). Carefully prioritizing and controlling expenditures, in an environment of rapidly falling revenues (Ebrill and Havrylyshyn, 1999), was a high priority, as was redirecting expenditures away from commercial activities and toward those activities more consistent with government expenditures in a market economy.[9] Again, this has proven very difficult for CIS countries, as the inability to keep expenditures in line with available revenues and financing has repeatedly led to budgetary expenditure arrears (World Bank, 1996).

As with tax policy and administration, the availability of oil money has made the challenge of expenditure prioritization and control even more difficult in Azerbaijan and Kazakhstan. Political pressures to in-

---

[9]Oil revenue has eased the problem of revenue availability, as declining tax revenue was offset by rising oil revenue. To this extent, the existence of oil revenue eased the transition process for Azerbaijan and Kazakhstan, relative to other countries. But that did not eliminate the need to develop a modern tax system or reduce the importance of containing expenditures to sustainable and manageable levels.

crease spending to unsustainable levels, or levels both beyond the absorptive capacity of the economy and beyond those that the governments could efficiently and effectively control, needed to be resisted. Again, this called for some way of insulating oil receipts from the political debate over expenditures.

The second major challenge facing the CIS countries, which was made even more difficult for the oil-producing countries of Azerbaijan and Kazakhstan, was the need to develop new businesses, often in new industries, to replace large, inefficient, and failing Soviet-era enterprises. While all CIS countries faced this challenge, the task was made more difficult for Azerbaijan and Kazakhstan. If they wanted to avoid being entirely dependent on oil and gas, they needed to develop new non-oil businesses and industries. And to do that, one prerequisite was to manage their oil and gas revenues so as to avoid an excessive real appreciation of their exchange rate and the consequent Dutch disease. This called for controlling the rate of expenditures of oil and gas revenue, targeting those expenditures primarily toward investments that would enhance productivity of non-oil sectors, and ensuring that any unspent funds were held abroad (where they would not have an impact on liquidity or the exchange rate).[10] And, in the views of these governments, this called for some special treatment of oil and gas revenues, some mechanism for isolating these resources from the normal budget debates.

Declared Objectives

The declared objectives of the oil funds of both Azerbaijan and Kazakhstan include the primary objectives of desiring to insulate the economy from oil price volatility (stabilization function) and to save part of the wealth generated from natural resource exploration for future generations (savings function). In practice, in Kazakhstan the oil fund makes an important contribution to stabilizing budget revenues, as accumulation in the oil fund is contingent on the oil price, while the flow of oil-related revenues to the budget is independent of the actual price. In Azerbaijan, the source of the revenue determines whether it is treated as state budget revenue (taxes on SOCAR's production from Soviet-era fields) or as oil fund revenues.[11] This choice of accumulation

---

[10]This applies in the case of finite oil supplies. If the oil revenue continues indefinitely, it will eventually be impossible to contain the real appreciation. However, there would still be an argument for targeting expenditures on enhancing productivity in the non-oil sectors.

rule reflects the fact that in Azerbaijan, the government views the oil fund primarily as a savings fund.

In the case of Azerbaijan, diversification of the economy beyond the oil sector is another important oil fund objective. The oil fund can contribute to non-oil sector development in two ways. First, by saving a part of oil and gas sector revenue in the form of foreign currency-denominated assets, the real exchange rate appreciation associated with a natural resource boom is mitigated. This helps maintain the competitiveness of the non-oil and non-gas sectors of the economy. Second, the declared purpose of oil fund spending is to build the infrastructure needed for the development of the non-oil sector. In Kazakhstan, diversification of the economy is not an explicit part of the oil fund's rationale and the authorities have indicated they do not intend to spend any oil fund resources for the next three years at least.

In Azerbaijan, a final declared objective of the oil fund is to help avoid excessive spending. By making the oil fund subject to presidential control only, government and parliament spending of oil fund assets is precluded.[12] Denying the state budget access to easy oil money, as was the case prior to the establishment of the oil fund, means that any shortfalls in the state budget must be made up through improved tax administration or reduced expenditures.[13] Hence, in the case of Azerbaijan, secondary objectives played an important role in the decision to create an oil fund.

IV. Oil Fund Design

General Oil Fund Design Criteria

Even where the political economy case can be made for an oil fund, it does not follow that any oil fund is desirable. To be effective—

---

[11]In 2001, government revenue related to SOCAR's output was 52 percent of overall oil- and gas-related government revenue. This share will decline over time, as production from Soviet-era fields declines and output from new fields increases.

[12]However, presidential spending of these funds is not effectively controlled. To date, four presidential decrees have called for spending from the oil fund in Azerbaijan. Three called for spending to improve the living conditions of refugees and internally displaced persons, while one called for spending to finance SOCAR's share of the BTC equity costs.

[13]The government of Azerbaijan is cash-constrained; access to domestic or international capital markets is very limited.

that is, to contribute to improved macroeconomic policymaking—there are certain features that must be reflected in the design of the oil fund.

First, the oil fund must be fully integrated with overall fiscal policy and the government's macroeconomic objectives. This can best be assured by having the oil fund serve as a financing mechanism for the state budget. Where this approach is not followed, as in Azerbaijan, it is essential that the government adopt and enforce procedures to ensure the consistency of the oil fund with the state budget and the government's economic objectives.

Second, the money in the oil fund must be managed with transparency and accountability, both so that the money is not wasted and so that parliament and the public can have confidence that oil fund assets are being protected. Without this confidence, the political compact that allowed the creation of the oil fund will not be sustainable.

Third, the oil fund must be subject to sound asset management. The assets must be invested abroad (to avoid monetary and exchange rate pressures) in highly rated assets. Domestic investments—particularly in commercial activities—must be precluded. Oil- and gas-exporting countries that have attempted to diversify their economies by investing petroleum wealth in domestic commercial activities have not been very successful.[14]

Fourth, oil fund rules need to be consistent over the long term. This means, among other things, that the rules should not lead to an excessive buildup in oil fund assets. If there is an excessive accumulation of assets in the oil fund, it may eventually be impossible to resist political pressures to spend those assets, perhaps rapidly and unwisely. This would be the case for an oil fund whose rules called for too little expenditure of oil revenues or, in other words, a lower than desirable (from a political or economic perspective) non-oil deficit. The rules should also effectively preclude "raiding" of the fund—expenditures outside the agreed purposes and/or procedures of the fund—which would again call into question the long-term sustainability of the political compact.

---

[14]Amuzegar (1999) offers a wealth of examples of misguided investment decisions in OPEC countries. Mumey's (1994) study of Alberta's natural resource fund makes it clear that similar problems can occur in developed market economies.

The Oil Funds in Azerbaijan and Kazakhstan Relative to the Above Design Criteria

Box 13.1 summarizes the main features of the two funds. The Kazakh NFRK is clearly consistent with the first design criterion: Kazakhstan has a unified budget, with all baseline revenues and any eventual expenditures as part of the state budget, ensuring an integrated fiscal policy consistent with the government's overall macroeconomic objectives.[15] In Azerbaijan, as noted, the oil fund budget is separate from the state budget. To overcome the problems that can be caused by implementing two separate budgets, Azerbaijan has adopted rules designed to ensure the planning, execution, and monitoring of a consolidated government budget (consisting of the state and oil fund budgets).

Thus, the two budgets are to be prepared in tandem, on the basis of the same economic projections and targets, by the Ministry of Finance. The president approves the consolidated budget. When parliament approves the state budget, it also approves the consolidated budget expenditure ceiling, as well as the deficit of the consolidated budget excluding oil fund revenue. All oil fund expenditures (except its operational expenditures) are executed through the treasury, and quarterly reports on the execution of the consolidated budget are made public. It remains to be seen whether this (of necessity more cumbersome) approach will be effective in ensuring a coherent overall fiscal policy consistent with the government's macroeconomic objectives. The signs are encouraging, as the preparation of the 2003 budget started with the Ministry of Finance producing a consolidated budget, which was then "divided" into oil fund and state budgets.

Both oil funds meet the second design criterion. They are both subject to annual external audits, the results of which are supposed to be made public.[16] In addition, in Azerbaijan the oil fund is subject to audit by parliament's supreme audit institution. In Kazakhstan, the NFRK is managed by the central bank, with the balance in the fund regularly

---

[15]As noted above, revenues above the baseline assumption are "off budget," although they are recorded in the treasury accounts. NFRK investment earnings are not recorded in the treasury or the budget.

[16]The first annual audit has been conducted in Azerbaijan, the results of which are available on the oil fund's website (www.oilfund.az). The first annual audit of Kazakhstan's fund was completed in March 2002, but has not been released to the public. Information on the Kazakh government's own annual report on NFRK operations was made public in May 2002 and quarterly reports on asset totals and their allocation are available on the NFRK website (www.nationalfund.kz).

Box 13.1. *Operational Aspects of Azerbaijan's and Kazakhstan's Oil Funds*

	Azerbaijan	Kazakhstan
Oil Fund Inflows	All PSA-related revenues: profit oil, oil bonuses, transit fees for managing the Baku-Supsa pipeline, acreage fees, rental fees.	Three sources: (i) The saving function: 10 percent of baseline revenues from nine oil fields and three mineral companies, projected at an annually set baseline price assumption; (ii) a stabilization function: all revenues from the nine companies above the baseline revenue target; and (iii) ad hoc inflows (e.g., bonuses and privatization receipts).
Expenditures	Off state budget, but through the treasury; oil fund budget and state budget prepared on a consistent basis; consolidated budget approved by the President; Parliament approves the consolidated budget expenditure ceiling, as well as the deficit of the consolidated budget, excluding oil fund revenue.	Stabilization reflows to the budget (for oil revenue shortfalls, subject to an overall revenue shortfall). President can be spent through the budget approved by parliament.
Foreign/Domestic Asset Split	100 percent foreign.	100 percent foreign.

---

published in the central bank balance sheet. In Azerbaijan, quarterly reports on the revenues, expenditures, and balance in the oil fund are published in the press.

Similarly, both oil funds are subject to sound asset management rules (the third criterion). In both cases, the funds are invested abroad, in highly rated assets, subject to strict investment guidelines. Kazakhstan

	Azerbaijan	Kazakhstan
Operational Asset Management	Oil fund; external managers can be hired.	National Bank of Kazakhstan and external portfolio managers.
Portfolio Composition	Fixed rate instruments (state securities, bank deposits); external managers may invest in equity.	Two portfolios: a short-term stabilization portfolio and a longer-term savings portfolio. Each has separate investment benchmarks and guidelines.
Legal Basis	Presidential decrees, with key rules reflected in the Budget Systems Law.	Laws, presidential decrees and government decisions.
External Audits	2001 external audit (Ernst & Young) has been completed and published.	Information on the internal 2001 annual report was published. The 2001 external audit (Ernst & Young) remains confidential.
Reporting	Quarterly publication of oil fund revenues and expenditures in the context of the consolidated budget.	Asset balance is regularly published in the balance sheet of the National Bank.
Supervisory Board	Appointed January 2002, with rotating six-month chairmanship; approved 2001 audit and amended 2002 budget in July 2002.	Executive board chaired by the President.

uses independent, offshore professional asset managers, while Azerbaijan is in the process of contracting with such managers.

There is some concern as to whether the oil fund rules in these countries meet the final criterion of being consistent over the long term. Pressures to spend on ad hoc projects are building and—absent the development of medium-term expenditure strategies, which do not yet exist in either country—may become irresistible. The development of such a medium-term expenditure strategy, including a prioritized public investment program, and the linkage of oil fund expenditures to that strategy, is urgently needed in both countries.

V. Conclusions and Policy Agenda

Both these funds are new, so any judgments about their success in meeting their stated objectives must, of necessity, be preliminary. On balance it seems likely that these funds—if operated in accordance with existing rules—will contribute to improved management of oil and gas wealth. In both cases, the limitations on expenditures and the requirements for investment abroad should help avoid excessive real appreciation. Both sets of rules should ensure substantial savings for future generations (if they can resolve the concerns about long-term consistency). Kazakhstan's rules should insulate fiscal policy from oil revenue instability. While stabilization is a secondary objective in Azerbaijan, over time, as the Soviet-era oil fields become less important, the degree of stabilization resulting from the operations of Azerbaijan's oil fund will grow. Finally, both sets of oil fund rules should support fiscal discipline. However, in the case of Azerbaijan this effect is only partial, since wide swings in oil prices would lead to similar swings in revenues from Soviet-era oil fields, which go directly to the state budget.

Preliminary evidence suggests that both funds have contributed to improved transparency and accountability. In Azerbaijan, prior to the creation of the oil fund, no regular reporting took place on the use of oil bonus receipts. With the creation of the oil fund, quarterly reporting of oil fund revenues and expenditures and annual external audits have been put in place. Similarly, in Kazakhstan, before the establishment of the NFRK oil revenues were administered in an ad hoc, nontransparent manner. Now, any future expenditures of the oil fund will pass through the state budget, all inflows will pass through the treasury, and its portfolio balance will be published monthly.

However, these oil funds are works in progress, and there are some causes for concern. In Azerbaijan, revising the accumulation rule could strengthen the stabilization element of the oil fund. And the completion of a medium-term expenditure framework (MTEF) and a public investment program (PIP), in the context of which oil fund spending can take place, is a high priority. In Kazakhstan, it is important to ensure that all transactions of the NFRK are effectively controlled by the central treasury, including the recording of investment returns. Finally, in both countries there is a need to develop a coherent long-term spending strategy, in order to address short-term pressures for potentially unwise expenditures, avoid excessive buildup of oil fund assets, and ensure that the funds are spent efficiently. In particular, it is important that these strategies do not call for the use of oil funds as development banks.

Of even greater concern is Azerbaijan's tendency to ignore existing rules and Kazakhstan's reluctance to publish the external audit. The above assessment of the likely contribution of these oil funds to the conduct of economic policy is based on the assumptions that the rules will be adhered to and transparency will be assured. If, on the other hand, the rules are merely guidelines to be ignored when they are inconvenient, these oil funds will not serve as the long-term political compact discussed above, but instead could be even more subject to short-term pressures than the annual budget. And without full transparency, confidence in these funds will not last. Therefore, the oil funds should be given a stronger legal basis by submitting all rules governing the fund to parliament for approval, and these rules should require full transparency. Such a step would ensure that, before the rules could be changed, there would first have to be a public discussion and amendment of the law. In Azerbaijan, significant progress in this direction has recently been made, as amendments to the Budget Systems Law have now incorporated the oil fund rules into that law.

Oil and gas government revenues are set to surge over the medium term in both countries. Now is the time to firmly establish the institutions needed to deal with the expected boom, and the authorities of both Azerbaijan and Kazakhstan have taken encouraging steps to do so. If well managed, Azerbaijan's and Kazakhstan's natural resource wealth can play an important role in facilitating the transition from plan to market. The oil and gas sector brings in foreign capital and expertise and supplies these countries with the means to improve the non-oil business climate in the form of better infrastructure, education, and public health. However, many countries have found themselves cursed by the availability of oil and gas riches. Mismanagement of these assets can easily turn them into liabilities. While the oil funds in Azerbaijan and Kazakhstan have the potential for contributing to improved macroeconomic management in those countries, for that potential to be realized a further strengthening of these oil funds, as discussed above, is urgently needed.

Bibliography

Amuzegar, Jahangir, 1999, *Managing the Oil Wealth: OPEC's Windfalls and Pitfalls* (London and New York: I.B. Tauris & Co. Ltd.).

Dodsworth, John, Paul Mathieu, and Clinton Shiells, 2002, *Cross-Border Issues in Energy Trade in the CIS Countries*, IMF Policy Discussion Paper 02/13 (Washington: International Monetary Fund).

Ebrill, Liam, and Oleh Havrylyshyn, 1999, *Tax Reform in the Baltics, Russia, and Other Countries of the Former Soviet Union*, IMF Occasional Paper No. 182 (Washington: International Monetary Fund).

International Monetary Fund, 2001, "Transition Economies: How Much Progress," *IMF Staff Papers*, Vol. 48, Special Issue (Washington).

Mathieu, Paul, and Clinton Shiells, 2002, "The Commonwealth of Independent States' Troubled Energy Sector," *Finance and Development*, Vol. 39, No. 3, pp. 34–38.

Mumey, Glen, 1994, "The Alberta Heritage Fund in 1993," Western Centre for Economic Research Bulletin No. 20 (Edmonton: University of Alberta).

Norwegian Ministry of Finance, "The Norwegian Government Petroleum Fund." Available via the Internet: http://www.odin.dep.no/fin/engelsk/p10001617/ index-b-n-a.html.

Potter, Barry, and Jack Diamond, 2000, *Setting Up Treasuries in the Baltics, Russia, and Other Countries of the Former Soviet Union—An Assessment of IMF Technical Assistance*, IMF Occasional Paper No. 198 (Washington: International Monetary Fund).

Rosenberg, Christoph B., and Tapio Saavalainen, 1998, "How to Deal with Azerbaijan's Oil Boom? Policy Strategies in a Resource-Rich Transition Economy," IMF Working Paper 98/6 (Washington: International Monetary Fund).

Sachs, Jeffrey D., and Andrew Warner, 1995, "Natural Resource Abundance and Economic Growth," Harvard Institute of Economic Research Discussion Paper No. 517 (Cambridge, Massachusetts: Harvard Institute for Economic Development).

Schick, Allen, 2002, "Budgeting for Fiscal Risk," in *Government at Risk: Contingent Liabilities and Fiscal Risk*, ed. by H.P. Brixi and A. Schick (Washington: World Bank), pp. 79–97.

World Bank, 1996, *World Development Report: From Plan to Market* (Washington).

14

Hedging Government Oil Price Risk

JAMES A. DANIEL[1]

I. Introduction

Oil price risk is the risk that oil prices may change rapidly, substantially, and unpredictably. Governments are subject to this risk in two main ways. Governments of oil-producing countries often rely heavily on revenue from oil production. Governments that administratively set oil-related product prices will suffer financially when the input price rises if they do not raise output prices (Gupta and others, see Chapter 15 in this volume). And, in both cases, governments will be very aware of the social, political, and economic costs of volatile oil prices. Governments have tried to deal with the problem of their oil price risk exposure in a variety of ways, for example, stabilization funds. But these methods are, to a greater or lesser extent, flawed, as the government is still bearing oil price risk that it is inherently ill-suited to bear.

Oil price risk markets seem a possible solution, at least theoretically. The principle is quite simple. Governments could either lock in the price of their future production or consumption now or insure against large oil price moves, or both. In this way, rather than trying to cope

[1]An earlier version of this paper was presented at the International Research Center for Energy and Economic Development (ICEED) conference in April 2000 in Boulder, Colorado, and published as ICEED Occasional Paper 35 and as an article in the *Journal of Energy and Development*, Vol. 27, No. 2. I would like to thank Steven Barnett, Juan Pablo Córdoba, Jeffrey Davis, Alan Gelb, Rolando Ossowski, Panos Varangis, Alvaro Vivanco, and Peter Wickham for comments on earlier versions of this paper. Alvaro Vivanco also provided excellent research assistance. All remaining errors are mine.

with a volatile and unpredicable revenue stream, the revenue stream itself is made more stable and predictable. This paper aims to explore whether this simple theoretical solution to managing government oil price risk might be able to work in practice and if it can, what is preventing governments from doing it.

II. Why Oil Price Risk Matters to Governments

Governments typically bear two kinds of oil price risk. First, and foremost, many governments obtain substantial revenue from oil production and exports. Second, many governments also try to smooth domestic oil product prices to mitigate the social, economic, and political impacts of large and frequent changes in these prices. In both cases, the fiscal position of the government depends substantially on the oil price.

Such oil price risk is difficult for governments to bear. In the absence of financing opportunities, when prices go down (or up for oil consumers[2]) governments have to cut expenditures or raise other revenue. This is difficult to do quickly and especially difficult to do efficiently. It is also likely to make fiscal policy procyclical, put a heavy burden on the private sector and the poor, and lead to macroeconomic instability (e.g., monetary financing, exchange rate fluctuations, debt rescheduling, and variable economic growth) and social and political unrest. Increasing spending when prices rise is easier, but difficult to do efficiently. More generally, reliance on oil revenue often leads to stop-go fiscal policy. Other problems include the difficulty of planning, for example, basing a budget on oil price assumptions that could turn out to be very wrong. And when price assumptions do turn out to be wrong, governments immediately feel the revenue impact as their revenue depends on the spot price of oil.

To help deal with oil price risk, some governments have established oil stabilization funds. In the case of oil producers, the idea is that a stabilization fund would smooth out the fluctuations in the international price of oil and stabilize the stream of government oil revenue. This would work by the fund's accumulating resources when the international spot price is above its reference price and vice versa. For oil con-

---

[2]The emphasis in the paper is on governments heavily dependent on oil revenue rather than governments that smooth domestic oil-product prices. However, most of the arguments apply to both.

sumers, the fund would work in reverse: the fund would subsidize domestic consumption when the spot price is above its reference level and vice versa.

But stabilization funds are inherently flawed.[3] Because the international oil spot price does not have a well-defined time-invariant "equilibrium" value to which it reverts, funds based on rigid transfer rules are likely to be overwhelmed by oil price shocks, as such shocks are often large and long-lasting. More generally, funds do not stabilize government finances unless accompanied by other policy actions, such as expenditure restraint, as resources are fungible. For example, government expenditure is not directly affected by stabilization funds as governments can typically borrow to finance expenditure while still meeting their obligations to the stabilization fund during times of "high" oil prices. Moreover, stabilization funds will likely create duplications, overlaps, and inefficiency in the management of public resources; complicate fiscal policymaking; and may foster poor governance and damage transparency.

Instead of setting up an explicit stabilization fund, governments can borrow (or run down assets) abroad when the international price goes against them. (Domestic financing would just pass on the shock to the domestic private sector.) Provided such financing is used to buy time to ride out temporary shocks or to adjust to permanent oil price shocks, this approach is attractive in theory. The problem is that just when a country needs the financing, it is likely to be least able to obtain it. For example, an oil exporter will find it hardest to raise financing when the oil price plummets. Also, many countries do not have access to significant foreign assets. Further, it is politically difficult to generate the corresponding surplus to repay the debt when the situation is reversed, leading to solvency problems.

The size of the oil price risk borne by governments can be very large and not necessarily linked to the global importance of a country's oil exports (Table 14.1). For example, oil revenue accounted for 51 percent of GDP in 2000 for Angola (90 percent of total revenue and grants). However, Angola accounts for less than 1 percent of global crude plus petroleum exports. In contrast, oil revenue in Norway, one of the world's most important oil exporters, accounted for only about 13 percent of GDP in 2000 (29 percent of total revenue). Moreover, the change in oil revenue from year to year for governments highly dependent on

---

[3]Davis and others, Chapter 11 in this volume.

Table 14.1. *Oil Revenue Dependence for Selected Major Exporters, 2000*

	Government Hydrocarbon Revenue		Crude Exports (1998)	
	In percent of total revenue	In percent of GDP	In percent of world exports	In millions of barrels per day
Angola	90	51	1	0.7
Equatorial Guinea	88	25	0	0.1
Oman	85	40	2	0.9
Nigeria	82	38	4	1.9
Saudi Arabia	79	29	14	7.9
Qatar	78	26	1	0.7
Algeria	77	30	2	1.2
Congo, Republic of	77	22	0	0.3
Yemen	76	33	1	0.3
Kuwait[1]	68	45	4	2.0
Libya	67	29	2	1.3
Gabon	67	23	1	0.3
Iran[2]	67	22	5	2.7
Bahrain	64	18	0	0.2
United Arab Emirates	60	23	4	2.4
Venezuela	58	17	5	2.9
Azerbaijan	37	8	0	0.2
Ecuador	36	11	1	0.3
Mexico	31	7	3	1.8
Cameroon	30	6	0	0.1
Russia[3]	30	5	7	3.7
Norway	29	13	6	3.2
Syria	28	9	1	0.3
Trinidad and Tobago	26	7	0	0.2

Sources: IMF staff estimates; and U.S. Energy Information Administration.
Note: The definition of oil and government revenue may vary across countries.
[1]Fiscal year 1999/00.
[2]Fiscal year 2000/01 (estimates).
[3]The estimate of government oil revenue is particularly imprecise due to classification issues.

oil revenue can be massive. For example, Yemen's oil revenue increased from 18 percent of GDP in 1999 to 33 percent of GDP in 2000.

III. Why Oil Price Risk Markets Could Be a Solution

The basic problem for oil-dependent governments is that they are exposed to large oil price risk that they are ill-suited to bear. The answer could be to transfer this risk outside the country to those better able to bear it. This can be done, in theory at least, via oil price risk markets.

Figure 14.1. *Illustrative Hedging Strategies*
(In U.S. dollars per barrel)

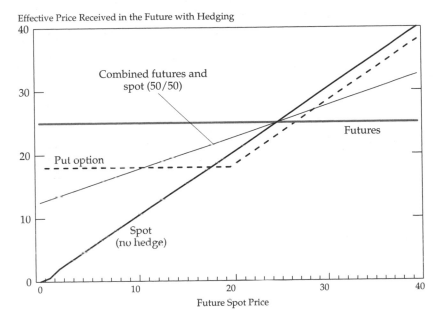

Source: Author's calculations.

There are two main ways to do this (for an oil producer): selling oil forward or buying insurance against large price falls. Such hedging could make the government's revenue stream both more stable and more predictable. In other words, not only would the government's oil revenue vary less, the government would have time to foresee any change and thus to adjust smoothly.

A futures strategy would lock in now the oil price the government will receive in the future. For example, assume in drawing up a budget for 2004 a government knows for certain that it will receive oil revenue equivalent to 100 million barrels of crude oil multiplied by the price it receives per barrel. Without hedging, the government may project an oil price, say US$25 a barrel, but it would actually receive whatever the spot price turns out to be in 2004 (i.e., the thick 45-degree line in Figure 14.1). This future spot price cannot be predicted with significant certainty and may well be very different from the current spot price. Under a futures hedging strategy, the government would sell crude futures for 100 million barrels of crude at the 2004 futures price, say

US$25, which would then be the effective[4] price the government will receive in 2004 (resulting in the horizontal line in Figure 14.1).

An options strategy would set a minimum price that the government could be sure of receiving in the future. In the example above, the government may decide that it could cope with a 2004 oil price as low as US$20 but any price below this would cause major difficulties. The government could then buy options to sell ("put" options) crude in 2004 at US$20 a barrel. If the spot price in 2004 were then to fall below US$20, the financial gains on the options would bring the effective price up to US$20 minus the premium (resulting in the dotted kinked line in Figure 14.1). In contrast to the futures strategy, the options strategy involves the up-front cost of the option premium. In effect, the government is buying insurance against a sharp fall in the oil price.

Hedging strategies can be made very complex to suit the needs of the particular hedger. A simple example illustrated in Figure 14.1 is the combined futures and spot strategy in which half the output is sold on the futures market and the other half on the spot market. Compared to the option strategy, this combined strategy would still provide some protection against spot price falls but would not involve paying a premium. Compared to the pure futures strategy, the combined strategy would allow the government to benefit from part of higher spot prices in the future, though at the cost of bearing part of any fall. Another common hedging strategy that may be attractive to oil producers is a no-cost collar whereby the cost of buying a premium to protect against sharply lower spot prices in the future is offset by selling an option whereby the oil producer would give up the benefit of sharply higher spot prices. This would thus limit the range of prices the government would receive in the future to a band between the two strike prices. A no-cost collar can also be combined with the purchase of an out-of-the-money call to enable the oil-producing government to take advantage of large price spikes that would be politically costly to miss out on.

Hedging Simulations

How would these theoretical hedging strategies have worked in the real world? The simplest simulation of a hedging strategy is to assume

---

[4]It is the "effective" price in that the price received is actually a combination of two operations: the sale of oil on the spot market and the gain/loss on the futures contract. These two operations net out to give a price equal to the futures price.

Figure 14.2. *West Texas Intermediate Crude*
12-Month Futures vs. Spot Prices by Contract Month
(In U.S. dollars per barrel)

Source: NYMEX.

that a government has a fixed amount of crude oil to sell every month and that the type of crude it has to sell is exactly the type that is traded on the world's largest oil risk market (New York Mercantile Exchange (NYMEX)). Using historical data for futures and options from NYMEX for the period 1990–July 2001,[5] simple hedging strategies can be simulated.

A simple futures strategy would be for the government to sell its oil via 12-month futures rather than on the spot market. The government would then receive the 12-month futures price rather than the corresponding[6] spot price. This would result in a much less volatile revenue stream and a slightly lower average price (see Figure 14.2) for the sam-

---

[5]Data on futures are available back to 1984, but continuous data on 12-month futures only go back to 1990.

[6]Corresponding in the sense that the average spot price for the month of June 2001 is compared to the average price of the 12-month futures contract that has the same delivery month (June 2001).

Figure 14.3. *Average Crude Oil Futures Prices Grouped*
by Spot Price, 1983–2001
(In U.S. dollars per barrel)

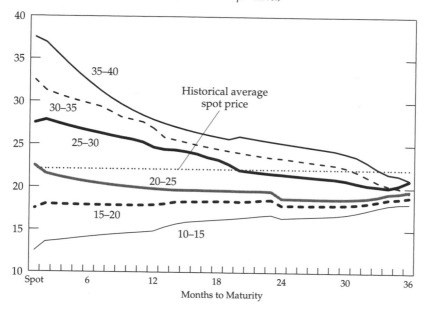

Source: Author's calculations based on NYMEX data.

ple period. The standard deviation of the average monthly spot price between January 1990 and December 2000 was 4.9, whereas the standard deviation of the corresponding 12-month futures was only 2.0. Or in other words, the mean absolute change in the monthly spot price in this period was US$1.33 compared to US$0.51 (a reduction of 61 percent) for the 12-month futures contract that expired in the same month. For only one year (1992) out of the ten is this volatility higher for the futures price, and then only by a very small margin as in this year spot prices were comparatively stable.

The reason behind the lower volatility of futures prices can be seen from the shapes of the futures curves for different spot prices. Figure 14.3 groups historical oil crude futures curves by their spot price ranges. Thus the bottom line in Figure 14.3 is the average oil futures curve for all futures curves with a spot price of between US$10 and US$15. These curves show that when the spot price is above its historical average, futures prices tend to converge to its historical average, and do the same thing when the spot price is below its historical average. In other words, while the spot price may not be mean-reverting, the futures price tends to be, and the farther forward the futures price, the greater the mean reversion. The rationale is probably that market participants believe there is an equilibrium price to which the spot price will eventually return. Often, market participants see the spot price as influenced by certain clear temporary factors, for example, the weather, an oil accident/pipeline interruption, or the Gulf War.

Over the sample period, the mean average monthly futures price was slightly (9 percent) lower than the mean spot price. This would imply that on average an oil producer would have had slightly lower revenue over this period using a futures hedge (and an oil consumer would have had slightly lower cost). However, this result may apply only to the specific sample period. Studies indicate that the futures price is an unbiased estimate of the future spot price (e.g., Kumar, 1992). Indeed, using all 12-month futures data from NYMEX over the sample period computed on a daily basis, the difference in the mean prices is trivial (less than 1 percent). However, this could also reflect the tendency of the forward oil prices to be in backwardation (prices fall farther into the future).

An options strategy also looks able to deliver greater stability at little cost. Simulating an options hedging strategy is more complicated than a futures strategy, reflecting the greater number of choice variables (e.g., strike price) and the frequent lack of observations (e.g., a 12-month put is not always quoted). Figure 14.4 illustrates a simple strategy: buying 6- to 18-month puts at a strike price of US$18 whenever they are available in the sample period 1990–2001 (options longer than a few months only became available in the early 1990s). Compared to the spot price, the options strategy results in a slightly lower effective price than the spot price for most of the period (reflecting the premium), but large gains for a few periods when the spot price fell sharply (1994, 1998).[7] In fact, the options strategy resulted in a slightly higher effective price than the spot price over the sample period. Because of the missing observations, it is not possible to compare the volatility of the two series, but it seems reasonable to assume that the

---

[7]The options strategy simulated assumes that the options are European, that is, can only be exercised at maturity. In fact, NYMEX options are American, that is, can be exercised at any time up to maturity, and hence the gains from the options strategy are probably underestimated in this simulation.

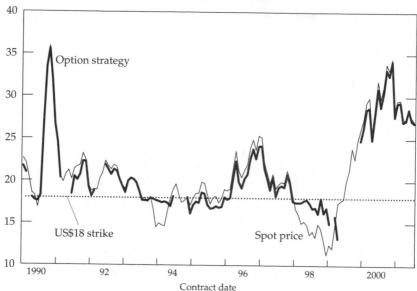

Figure 14.4. *Spot Price vs. Options Hedging Strategy*
(6- to 18-month Puts at a Strike of US$18 a barrel)
(In U.S. dollars per barrel)

Sources: NYMEX; authors' calculations.

volatility of the options strategy is lower as it removes two periods of large price movements.

Hypothetical Hedging Simulations for Mexico

The previous hedging simulation assumed that the type of oil produced by a country is exactly the same as that underlying the type of oil traded on NYMEX. This is not a realistic assumption. Mexico, for example, produces various types of crude that are significantly different from the light, sweet crudes traded on NYMEX.[8]

---

[8]Mexico produces three grades of crude oil: heavy Maya-22, which accounts for more than half of total production; light, low-sulfur Isthmus-34, accounting for less than one-third of total production; and extra-light Olmeca-39, which is about one-fifth of total production. Nevertheless, the coefficient of correlation between the Mexican export price and West Texas Intermediate for the period January 1983–March 2001 is a relatively high 0.95.

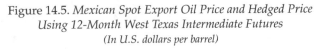

Figure 14.5. *Mexican Spot Export Oil Price and Hedged Price*
Using 12-Month West Texas Intermediate Futures
(In U.S. dollars per barrel)

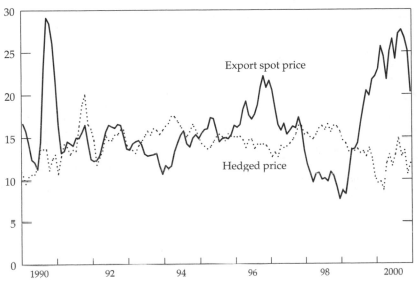

Sources: Author's calculations; Pemex, and NYMEX.

Thus, to realistically test whether hedging could produce real benefits, hedging strategies should be simulated for countries, such as Mexico, that produce oil types significantly different from those traded on NYMEX.

Simulating some hypothetical basic strategies for Mexico in the period 1990–2000 shows that hedging could have significantly reduced oil price volatility. The simplest strategy is to buy 12-month West Texas Intermediate (WTI) futures. The return from the hedging strategy is then the Mexican spot price plus the gain/loss from holding the corresponding 12-month WTI futures contract. Figure 14.5 shows the results from such a hedging strategy and the unhedged strategy (i.e., the Mexican spot price). The standard deviation falls by 58 percent, from 4.5 to 1.9. For the sample period, however, the mean price received under the hedging strategy is slightly lower than the spot price. As the difference between the two prices is the gain/loss on the WTI futures contract, and as this gain/loss can be assumed to be unbiased (see above), the lower average price for the hedging strategy presumably reflects the limited sample period.

The Over-the-Counter (OTC) Market

The futures and options traded on an exchange described above will probably not be the most appropriate instrument for hedging government oil price risk, especially for governments (or state-owned oil companies) with less developed institutional capacity for executing hedging strategies. For these entities, the most appropriate instrument may well be a tailor-made arrangement directly with a financial intermediary. For example, a government may agree with a financial intermediary that the latter would make up to the government any fall in the country's specific crude price below, say, US$15 a barrel, and that the government would pay over to the intermediary any increase in the spot price above, say, US$35 a barrel for a fixed volume of output for the next five years. Such an arrangement would not be traded on an exchange (though the intermediary might lay off some of the risk via an exchange) and is thus an OTC instrument.

OTC instruments come in many shapes and forms (see Box 14.1). Their benefits are largely that they remove basis risk,[9] can be available in very large volumes for single transactions, are often for longer periods of coverage, and do not usually involve initial deposits or margin calls. However, OTC instruments are usually less transparent and less liquid (and are thus not easily reversed) than exchange-traded instruments and often have higher legal fees than exchange-traded instruments. Because OTC transactions are not guaranteed by an exchange, both parties also take greater credit risk. OTC instruments may also involve lower overheads (one OTC instrument can cover hedging needs for years), while exchange instruments require setting up trading operations such as establishing broker accounts, managing and paying margins, analyzing and monitoring the market in question, ensuring compliance with the exchange's regulations, and, crucially, hiring and supervising traders. Thus, for a country looking to hedge its oil price risk for a long period of time in a one-off operation that can be tailored to fit its own risk preferences without establishing a trading operation, an OTC transaction may well be most appropriate.

---

[9]Basis risk refers to the risk that the spot price of the object being hedged may move differently than the price of the instrument used to hedge it.

Box 14.1. *Main Over-the-Counter Commodity Risk Instruments*

Forward contracts are agreements to sell or buy a certain product at a certain future time at a preset price. Forward contracts generally give rise to physical deliveries. A forward contract is like a futures contract, except it is made directly between a buyer and a seller and is usually an OTC instrument. While a commodity forward has certain benefits in common with other OTC instruments (e.g., elimination of basis risk), the much greater liquidity in the futures market makes futures contracts more relevant.

Commodity swaps are agreements between two parties to buy or sell a commodity at a fixed price for many periods in the future. Basic ("plain vanilla") commodity swaps involve one party exchanging a fixed price for a floating price. Whereas a futures contract or a forward relates to the price of one transaction in the future, a swap relates to many transactions, often for much longer into the future. For example, a producer could agree on the price of its output (e.g., 1 million barrels per quarter) with a financial institution for the next ten years. If the actual spot price were to fall below the agreed price, the financial institution would make payments to the producer and vice versa. Swaps thus give substantial certainty to future income streams and are often used in the context of project finance, but involve considerable credit exposure for both parties in the transaction.

Commodity bonds and/or loans are bonds or loans with payments (of principal and/or interest) linked to commodity prices. The link can be in two major forms: first, as a loan or bond type whereby a repayment is made with the financial equivalent of a fixed amount of a commodity (e.g., a coupon holder receives the market price of a barrel of oil) and second, as an option type, in which the investor can choose whether to receive a fixed financial sum or the financial value of a fixed amount of a commodity. These types of bonds and loans are usually linked to investment projects or to debt rescheduling. Such instruments give investors more confidence about the debtor's ability to pay and allow access on better terms to financial markets for firms or countries to which access might otherwise be difficult.

Hybrids are combinations of other instruments, for example, a swaption, which is an option to buy or sell a swap.

IV. Why Governments Are Not Using Oil Price Risk Markets

Information on actual use of commodity risk markets by emerging market governments (or their state-owned oil-exporting enterprises) with large commodity revenues is patchy and largely anecdotal. This understandably reflects client confidentiality and an unwillingness of

---

Box 14.2. *Mexico's Oil-Hedging Strategy*

According to press reports, in late 1990 and during the first half of 1991, Mexico used financial risk management tools to protect its earnings from crude oil exports against a price drop. The strategy reportedly involved selling about 100 million barrels of oil and covered a significant part of its export earnings over this period. Mexico's overall strategy was to ensure that it received at least US$17 a barrel, the price used as the basis for its 1991 budget. The strategy was quite successful since oil prices fell significantly in early 1991. Thus, not only did Mexico achieve more certainty ex ante about its oil earnings, it also profited ex post as the gains from having ensured a minimum price exceeded the initial costs of buying the put options.

A senior Mexican official said regarding their hedging program: "We said, listen, given the uncertainty and given the volatility, it can go to US$40 (a barrel) or it can drop to US$10. We have a budget here, a budget that we have to cover [. . .] We didn't do it to be ahead. The government does not speculate in that sense. Doing nothing is speculative. It does look good now that we are ahead compared to doing nothing. Some days we do not do as well. But we sleep well."

Source: *Washington Post*, March 27, 1991.

---

producers to reveal market-sensitive information. A few cases have been reported. The most notable was the Mexican use of oil risk markets during the Gulf War (see Box 14.2). However, market participants generally agree that developing country producer use of risk markets is small in relation to its potential. For example, the World Bank reported in 1999 that "developing countries are estimated to account for only 5 percent of open interest."[10,11] In contrast, a number of developed country producers (and users) have used commodity risk markets extensively. For example, the state of Texas has hedged its oil revenue with the government executing collar spreads (buying put options and selling call options) to narrow the range in which its revenue stream fluctuates.[12] What accounts for this lack of use?

---

[10]See World Bank (1999).

[11]Open interest is the number of outstanding contracts, both futures positions that have not been offset and option contracts that have not expired or been exercised.

[12]Texas Senator Teel Bivens said about the hedging program in 1991 that "As long as Texas relies so much on oil revenue, there will always be the chance the state will lose its bet. The state clearly needs a way to hedge its bets."

The Politics of Hedging

While it is difficult to be sure, probably the most important constraint on government hedging is political. For an individual finance minister (or head of a state oil producer), the political costs of hedging may outweigh the benefits, even if the economic case is clear. In the case of a fall in the spot price, any financial gains from a hedging program may be seen as speculative returns. If the minister had not hedged, it would be easy to blame the international oil markets for any budgetary problems. In the case of the spot price of oil rising, a hedging strategy may well result in the government "missing out" on higher revenue, which would be politically costly. If the government were to use a pure insurance hedging strategy, it might be politically difficult to use scarce resources to pay an option premium rather than, say, build a hospital. Further, the political cost of any operational failure in the hedging program, for example, a rogue trader making massive losses, would be high.

A good illustration of this type of constraint is provided by the political costs suffered by the Ecuadoran authorities in early 1993.[13] The government, through the central bank and the monetary board, purchased two three-month and six-month put options at a strike price of US$14.9 per barrel. The total premium payments for both options amounted to almost US$12 million. The government also entered into a six-month swap operation for 5 million barrels under which any excess of the spot price above US$14.9 per barrel had to be paid by the government. Spot prices turned out to be significantly higher than US$14.9 per barrel and the government had to let the options expire and pay about US$6 million on the swap arrangement. Members of the opposition, and even a deputy of the governing party, harshly criticized the operations, citing the high losses to the country. Congress also appointed a special committee to investigate "allegations of corruption" against the head of the central bank and the president of the monetary board.

Overcoming the political constraints to hedging will not be easy, but some steps could be taken. In the international arena, international agencies and research organizations could do more to promote awareness and understanding of hedging opportunities. Individual oil-dependent countries could explore the scope for hedging their oil price

---

[13]See Platt (1993).

risk with help not only from private sector companies but also from official and nonprofit agencies like the World Bank or the International Task Force on Commodity Risk Management. When hedging strategies are adopted, they should be right for the country, operated in a reliable and transparent manner, and presented as insurance against risks rather than as a separate source of revenue. For example, when presenting a budget, the hedging strategy should be presented at the same time. Hedging strategies should also be designed with the political costs in mind, which would enable sharing in the benefits of higher prices (for oil producers), such as the no-cost collar plus out-of-the-money call strategy described earlier.

Market Volume

Volume limits will constrain large oil producers from hedging, especially beyond six months, but volume does not seem a major constraint for other producers (or consumers). NYMEX and International Petroleum Exchange (IPE) crude oil open interest in futures and options beyond six months has recently averaged about 300 million barrels.[14] OTC crude oil open interest beyond six months is not known, but a rule of thumb suggested by some market participants is that OTC volume is about twice that of exchange-traded instruments. In sum, there may well be open interest of about 1 billion barrels for crude oil price risk beyond six months.

The annual exports of about half the 24 heavily oil-dependent countries in Table 14.1 would account for less than a third of the estimated volume currently available. Moreover, the full amount of the exports need not be hedged, and once producers start using the market, this may well stimulate further increases in volume. Because of the lower exposure to oil price risk for developing consumer governments, volume would be less of a constraint. Indeed, if both consuming and producing governments were to use the market, they would create their own volume. The execution of hedging strategies will also need to be carefully timed to minimize liquidity problems.

---

[14]NYMEX open interest in futures contracts beyond six months is known. Total NYMEX options open interest is known, but is not broken down by maturities. We assume the same maturity profile as for futures. IPE open interest for futures contracts beyond six months is known. However, not even total option open interest is known. We assume the same ratio for the IPE of option open interest to futures open interest as for NYMEX.

Creditworthiness and Use of Reserves

Governments with a poor credit standing may find their access to certain hedging instruments constrained. For example, a swap transaction would require a financial intermediary to assume the risk that the government would honor its obligations under the swap in the event market prices move against it for a period of many years. Access to other instruments, such as futures or the purchase of options, would not likely be constrained. Even for the instruments for which credit could be a constraint, it need not be binding. Many oil-dependent countries already have international credit extended to them in the form of bonds or bank loans, and producing countries will bear costs from their hedging operations when they will most likely be able to afford it (i.e., when the spot price is high). Other forms of credit enhancement could also be available, for example, some part of the oil export earnings could be escrowed or official financing might be available. More generally, however, hedging operations should enhance a country's creditworthiness as the countries become less vulnerable to oil price movements.

Risk market transactions, especially for less creditworthy countries, often involve significant up-front premiums and margin calls. The use of futures requires the deposit of margins[15] (usually 5–10 percent of the value of the underlying commodity), and the purchase of options requires payment of a premium. Other commodity derivative instruments also require the use of capital for purchasing the instruments or for collateral to cover performance risk. However, given the leverage derivative transactions can allow, the cost of hedging may well be lower than obtaining similar levels of risk protection through other forms, such as by issuing debt to build up foreign exchange reserves.[16]

Fairness of Futures Prices

Producers might well consider that market prices for future production are unreasonably low and thus would not be willing to sell their

---

[15]These margins do earn interest, however.

[16]For example, if a country wanted to keep a buffer in foreign exchange reserves equal to the reduction in one year of oil exports if the oil price fell from US$25 to US$15 a barrel and the country exported 40 million barrels a year, this would imply foreign exchange reserves of US$400 million. If, however, the country were to sell the oil forward at US$25, then it would not lose any revenue if the oil price went to US$15, and the amount of capital tied up in margin requirements would be about US$100 million. In other words, futures allow the same amount of protection but at a quarter of committed foreign exchange resources.

output forward at those prices. These views amount to a belief that commodity-producing governments are better at forecasting the future spot price than the market. For countries with substantial market-moving ability or important insider information, this may be true. But for other governments, it is unlikely to be true, as the historical record of budget forecasting shows.[17] Also, as discussed previously, past prices are no indication of future prices, and while the current spot price is an indicator of future spot price, futures market prices are somewhat more accurate and are probably the best estimate available. It is thus difficult, in an ex ante sense, to make the case that futures prices are "unfair."

Institutional Capacity and Operational Risk

The personnel (and cost) implications of implementing and monitoring hedging operations can be significant. Risk management activities require considerable knowledge of financial instruments and an appropriate institutional framework within which to carry out hedging operations. Expertise is required to understand the risk structure of the company or public sector, identify appropriate risk management instruments, and engage in and supervise hedging transactions. The institutional framework should also ensure adequate reporting, recording, monitoring, and evaluation mechanisms and establish internal control procedures that can protect against speculative transactions and execution errors. Hedging operations are often complex and, without the appropriately developed institutional capacity, can lead to less transparency and foster poor governance.

Not all hedging strategies are equally institutionally demanding. A strategy of continually trading a range of exchange-traded instruments is much more demanding than a single swap transaction. Substantial technical assistance is also available from many sources, for example, from the International Task Force on Commodity Risk Management and the World Bank.[18] It should also be borne in mind that many countries already undertake complex financial transactions

---

[17]See Weiner (1996).

[18]The United Nations, under the auspices of the United Nations Conference on Trade and Development (UNCTAD) has developed and implemented an energy price risk management training program for developing countries. Exchanges such as NYMEX and private sector firms can also provide substantial technical assistance.

that differ little from oil hedging programs (e.g., central bank hedging of foreign exchange or interest rate exposure) and the state-owned oil company may already be involved in short-term oil price risk hedging.

Basis Risk

Exchange-traded instruments may well be only weakly correlated with government revenue. However, this does not necessarily remove the ability to hedge. As the hypothetical example of Mexico described above shows, substantial hedging can still be achieved even if the crude produced differs substantially from the crude traded. Indeed, research[19] suggests that for crude oil exports, about 80 percent of the short-term (less than six months) price risk could be eliminated, and at least 70 percent of the price risk in excess of six months could be eliminated, for most crudes. Moreover, OTC instruments can be tailored to eliminate, or at least greatly reduce, basis risk (at a cost).

Market Impact

Forward sales by a large exporter may prompt a disproportionate market reaction, even for a small volume of sales. The possibility of a massive supply and a sea change in the use of risk markets by producers might well push prices down lower than justified purely by the size of any one transaction. If the producer is a member of a cartel, for example OPEC, the effect might be even larger. And while confidentiality is possible, it cannot be guaranteed.

Clearly, a large producer cannot try to sell all its output forward well into the future. But that is very different from a modest-sized producer gradually using a wide range of hedging instruments to protect a part of its oil revenue. The experience of Mexico during the Gulf War also indicates that even large producers can successfully execute substantial hedging transactions. Moreover, if futures prices do fall, this may bring forward greater demand by consumers to take advantage of low future prices.

---

[19]See Claessens and Varangis (1994).

V. Relevance for IMF-Supported Programs

The issue of oil-dependent-country use of oil price risk markets is relevant for the IMF. Any actions to reduce oil-dependent-country vulnerability to oil price shocks is of general relevance to the IMF, but more specifically, oil price risk hedging could help IMF-supported programs. If the oil price falls without hedging, programs can go off track: government deficit targets are overshot, growth falls, and external reserve and monetary targets are missed. Programs then either fail or have to be renegotiated from a worse position. Also, to help prevent such events, IMF-supported programs require larger net foreign asset targets, which are difficult to meet and costly to maintain.

Hedging may help address these problems. If oil revenue (and/or exports) were hedged, the program and the economy might not be so heavily affected by changes in the oil price, at least not immediately, and the government would have time to adjust in an orderly fashion to long-lasting changes in the oil price. Also, lower amounts of foreign exchange reserves might need to be kept so that when the oil price falls there would be an immediately offsetting increase in foreign exchange inflows from the hedge. The use of private sector tools and capital to solve macroeconomic problems also helps prevent crises and promotes private sector involvement. This suggests that the IMF could consider recommending that oil-dependent countries, especially those with IMF-supported programs, should explore the scope for hedging their oil price risk in conjunction with the World Bank and other agencies with specialized knowledge in this field. The IMF should clearly be careful not to align itself with a specific hedging transaction or institution.

VI. Conclusions

- Many governments are highly exposed to oil price risk that they are ill-suited to bear.
- Traditional methods of dealing with oil price risk are flawed.
- Oil price risk markets may be a way to deal with oil price risk. Simulations show that hedging strategies can substantially reduce oil price volatility without significantly reducing return and with the added benefits of greater predictability and certainty.
- Governments so far have not substantially used oil price risk markets. There are probably a number of reasons why, most impor-

tantly the political economy of using these markets and a lack of institutional capacity. Large oil producers are also constrained by market size.

- Except for very large oil producers, these constraints seem surmountable. For institutional capacity, there are many sources of technical assistance and many operations can be easily outsourced and monitored. Political economy constraints require a greater understanding of the markets by the countries, but would also benefit from greater attention from major international economic institutions and research groups.
- The IMF should consider recommending that oil-dependent countries, especially those with IMF-supported programs, explore the scope for hedging their oil price risk, in conjunction with the World Bank and other agencies with specialized knowledge in this field. The IMF should not, however, align itself with a specific hedging transaction or institution.

Bibliography

Arrau, Patricio, and Stijn Claessens, 1992, "Commodity Stabilization Funds," World Bank Policy Research Working Paper No. 835 (Washington: World Bank).

Basch, Miguel, and Eduardo Engel, 1993, "Temporary Shocks and Stabilization Mechanisms: The Chilean Case," in *External Shocks and Stabilization Mechanisms*, ed. by Eduardo Engel and Patricio Meller (Washington: Inter-American Development Bank and Johns Hopkins University Press).

Cashin, Paul, Hong Liang, and C. John McDermott, 2000, "How Persistent Are Shocks to World Commodity Prices?," *IMF Staff Papers*, Vol. 47, No. 2, pp. 177–217.

Cashin, Paul, C. John McDermott, and Alasdair Scott, 2002, "Booms and Slumps in World Commodity Prices," *Journal of Development Economics*, Vol. 69 (October), pp. 277–96.

Claessens, Stijn, and Sweder van Wijnbergen, 1993, "1990 Mexico and Venezuela Recapture Clauses: An Application of Average Price Options," *Journal of Banking and Finance*, Vol. 17 (June), pp. 733–45.

Claessens, Stijn, and Panos Varangis, 1994, "Oil Price Instability, Hedging, and an Oil Stabilization Fund: The Case of Venezuela," World Bank Policy Research Working Paper No. 1290 (Washington: World Bank).

Engel, Eduardo, and Patricio Meller, eds., 1993, *External Shocks and Stabilization Mechanisms* (Washington: Inter-American Development Bank and Johns Hopkins University Press).

Engel, Eduardo, and Rodrigo Valdés, 2000, "Optimal Fiscal Strategy for Oil-Exporting Countries," IMF Working Paper 00/118 (Washington: International Monetary Fund).

Hausmann, Ricardo, 1995, "Dealing with Negative Oil Shocks: The Venezuelan Experience in the Eighties," IADB Working Paper No. 307 (Washington: Inter-American Development Bank).

Kumar, Manmohan S., 1992, "Forecasting Accuracy of Crude Oil Futures Prices," *IMF Staff Papers*, International Monetary Fund, Vol. 39 (June), pp. 432–61.

Platt's *Oilgram News*: May 4, 1993, Vol. 71, No. 86, p. 6; and May 20, 1993, Vol. 71, No. 98, p. 4.

Spilimbergo, Antonio, 1999, "Copper and the Chilean Economy, 1960–98," IMF Working Paper 99/57 (Washington: International Monetary Fund).

United Nations Conference on Trade and Development, 1996, *Price Risk Management in the Fuels Sector: A Manual* (New York; Geneva).

Varangis, Panos, Takamasa Akiyama, and Donald Mitchell, 1995, *Managing Commodity Booms—and Busts* (Washington: World Bank).

Varangis, Panos, and Don Larson, 1996, "Dealing with Commodity Price Uncertainty," World Bank Policy Research Working Paper No. 1667 (Washington: World Bank).

Weiner, Robert J., 1996, "Petroleum Fiscal Dependence: Revenue Forecasting and Oil Price Volatility," The George Washington University School of Business and Management Working Paper 96–44 (Washington: George Washington University).

Wickham, Peter, 1996, "Volatility of Oil Prices," IMF Working Paper 96/82 (Washington: International Monetary Fund).

World Bank, 1993, "Venezuela—Oil and Exchange Rates: Historical Experience and Policy Options," World Bank Report No. 10481-VE (Washington).

———, 1994, "Nigeria—Macroeconomic Risk Management: Issues and Options," World Bank Report No. 11983-UNI (Washington).

———, 1999, "Dealing with Commodity Price Volatility in Developing Countries: A Proposal for a Market-Based Approach," Discussion Paper for the Roundtable on Commodity Risk Management in Developing Countries, Washington, September.

Part IV.
Designing Policies for
Domestic Petroleum Pricing

15

Issues in Domestic Petroleum Pricing in Oil-Producing Countries

Sanjeev Gupta, Benedict Clements,
Kevin Fletcher, and Gabriela Inchauste[1]

I. Introduction

Petroleum product prices are often heavily regulated. Domestic price controls are prevalent, especially in countries that are net exporters of oil. Governments often keep prices well below international levels, resulting in the implicit subsidization of oil consumption. However, as these subsidies are typically not recorded in government budgets as expenditures, their economic cost, as well as the incidence on different income classes, is often poorly understood. The lack of readily available estimates of the size of these implicit subsidies has thus precluded a fuller discussion of their costs and benefits. Good fiscal policy management requires that the cost of all government activities, including such quasi-fiscal ones, be made transparent.[2]

The purpose of this paper is to shed light on subsidies for oil consumption in oil-producing countries. The paper first assesses the mag-

[1]We are grateful for helpful comments from Muhammad Al-Jasser, Ulrich Bartsch, Philippe Callier, Juan Pablo Córdoba, Ramón Espinasa, Mangal Goswami, Eliot Kalter, Vladimir Klyuev, Jean Le Dem, Edouard Maciejewski, Edouard Martin, Melhem F. Melhem, Rakia Moalla-Fetini, Bright Okogu, Stephen Schwartz, Nicola Spatafora, Siddarth Tiwari, Bert van Selm, John Wakeman-Linn, and participants in the IMF Conference on Fiscal Policy Formulation and Implementation in Oil-Producing Countries, June 5–6, 2002. Shamit Chakravarti and Erwin Tiongson provided invaluable research assistance. The usual disclaimer applies.

[2]For a general discussion of quasi-fiscal activities, see Mackenzie and Stella (1996). For a discussion of quasi-fiscal activities in the energy sector specifically, see Petri, Taube, and Tsyvinski, Chapter 18 in this volume.

nitude of the costs stemming from such subsidization. In addition, the discussion addresses the consequences of these subsidies for economic efficiency, income distribution, and fiscal policy.

The paper is organized as follows. Section II describes petroleum-pricing policies in oil-producing countries and estimates the implicit subsidy on petroleum products in a wide sample of countries. Section III discusses the effects of pricing policies, including economic efficiency, equity, and macroeconomic performance, with a view to characterizing optimal pricing policy. Section IV then addresses issues in reforming pricing policies and eliminating implicit subsidies, including the preconditions for successful reform, the appropriate pace of reform, and the use and development of countervailing measures. Section V concludes.

II. Current Petroleum Pricing Policies

Description of Current Pricing Polices

Currently, a broad range of petroleum pricing policies exists across the world. In most Organization for Economic Cooperation and Development (OECD) countries, prices are market determined, although high excise taxes are usually levied on petroleum consumption. For example, total taxes on gasoline among the Group of Seven (G-7) countries range from US$0.10 per liter in the United States to US$0.81 per liter in the United Kingdom.[3]

In developing countries that are net importers of oil, prices are in some cases fixed by the government or by state-owned enterprises. In these cases, as well as in countries that have market-determined prices, excise taxes on petroleum are common; thus, the after-tax retail prices of petroleum products are typically higher than they would be in the absence of any taxes or government intervention.

In developing countries that are net exporters of oil, however, governments typically maintain domestic petroleum prices well below the free-market level. In most of these countries, the petroleum sector is dominated by a few large, state-owned enterprises, and the govern-

---

[3]Data refer to November 2001 *Monthly Price Statistics* (International Energy Agency, 2001b). As a comparison, the tax-exclusive price of gasoline in the United States was US$0.21 per liter.

ment typically controls both the wholesale and retail prices of petroleum products, either directly or indirectly, through export restrictions or other such measures. For example, in Kuwait in 1999, the after-tax price of gasoline was set at a level that was only 5 percent of the price that prevailed in the United States.[4] These below-market prices result in the implicit subsidization of petroleum consumption; by selling petroleum domestically at a lower price than could be obtained abroad, the government forgoes revenue.

Quantifying the Implicit Subsidies/Taxes

Several studies have attempted to quantify the magnitude and importance of implicit petroleum subsidies in oil-producing and other countries (Rajkumar, 1996; International Energy Agency, 1999; Metschies, 1999; and Gürer and Ban, 2000). However, these studies either focus on only selected countries or petroleum products or are dated. In this study, we attempt to provide an update on petroleum subsidies for a wide spectrum of countries and products. In addition, we propose a methodological improvement over most earlier estimates by including implicit tax subsidies that might be granted in the form of exemptions from value-added taxes (VAT) or other consumption taxes.

Subsidies can be defined broadly as the difference between the reduced price of a good with government support and the price of the good in the absence of such support (World Bank, 1997; Schwartz and Clements, 1999; and Gupta and others, 2000). Implicit subsidy for petroleum product i in country j in time period t ($S_{i,j,t}$) can then be defined as the difference between the "free-market price" ($M_{i,j,t}$) and the after-tax retail price ($P_{i,j,t}$) times the volume of consumption ($C_{i,j,t}$):

$$S_{i,j,t} = (M_{i,j,t} - P_{i,j,t})C_{i,j,t}. \tag{1}$$

The free-market price is defined as the price that would prevail if there were no government interventions to affect the relative price of the product in question. In other words, the free-market price is the competitive market price plus the level of taxation typically levied on consumption goods. For net oil-importing countries, this free-market price should equal the cost of importing another unit of petroleum. This is calculated as the sum of the world wholesale spot price for the

---

[4]Energy Information Administration (various years).

refined product $(W_{i,j,t})$, domestic distribution and marketing costs $(D_{i,j,t})$,[5] and all general consumption taxes $(V_{i,j,t}$—general sales taxes, VAT, and so on). General consumption taxes are included because, as a first approximation, these taxes do not distort most relative prices[6] and so should be included if the objective is to determine what the price of a petroleum product would be if it were given the same treatment by government policies as any other good. Thus, the free-market price is as follows:

$$M_{i,j,t} = W_{i,j,t} + D_{i,j,t} + V_{i,j,t}. \qquad (2)$$

For net oil-exporting countries, the free-market price is calculated in the same manner as for net oil importers, except that the cost of transporting petroleum from one country to another $(T_{i,j,t})$ is subtracted from the free-market price in equation (2) (since net oil exporters often do not import petroleum from other countries). Thus, for oil-exporting countries, the free-market price should represent the cost of consuming oil domestically, which is the opportunity cost of not selling the refined petroleum on the world wholesale market $(W_{i,j,t} - T_{i,j,t})$ plus the domestic distribution and marketing costs incurred $(D_{i,j,t})$ plus the general consumption taxes paid $(V_{i,j,t})$.

Data on all of the components in equation (1) for 86 countries were gathered for 1995–2000 from different data sources, including the Energy Information Administration and *Datastream*, and subsidies for major petroleum product types were calculated. The detailed methodology for these calculations is described in the Appendix. Once the subsidy for each subproduct was calculated, the total petroleum subsidy was simply calculated as the sum.

Several caveats to this methodology should be noted. First, the estimates only measure the subsidy due to underpricing. Substantial subsidies may also arise from nonpayment of bills by consumers to state-owned oil-producing or -supplying enterprises, a practice that is especially prevalent in transition economies. The subsidy estimates in this paper do not include these nonpayments, and thus they may in some cases understate the total petroleum subsidy. Second, the domestic prices on which the subsidy estimates are based are in some cases

---

[5]This includes the cost of transporting the product from the world wholesale market to the importing country.

[6]Because some goods, notably leisure, are often excluded from consumption taxes, some distortion of relative prices is still likely to occur, especially to the degree that goods are complements to, or substitutes for, the excluded goods.

the average for only a month or quarter rather than an entire year. Thus, the subsidy estimates in these cases should be viewed as a "snapshot" measure of the subsidy that is then annualized over the year.[7]

Finally, due to data limitations and in order to simplify the calculations, a constant average amount for domestic marketing and distribution costs is taken for each type of petroleum product based on data from G-7 countries. Similarly, a constant average amount for international transport costs is assumed for all destinations. These considerations introduce some measurement error since both types of costs will vary across time and country. However, previous studies have estimated that domestic marketing and distribution costs in developing countries are remarkably similar, on average, to domestic marketing and distribution costs in developed countries (Bacon, 2001), so the assumption of constant domestic costs should not introduce a significant bias. The assumption of constant international transport costs should not in general bias the results since these costs represent only about 2 percent of the retail price of petroleum products. However, it could understate the bottlenecks faced by some oil exporters in supplying additional petroleum output. For example, ice-blocked ports and pipeline capacity constraints can significantly increase marginal shipping costs of some oil producers.

Nonetheless, it should be noted that, using this methodology, the average estimate for net oil taxes is 1.6 percent of GDP for non-major oil-exporting developing countries and 2.7 percent of GDP for non-major oil-exporting OECD countries. These estimates are similar to other directly measured estimates of petroleum taxation (Gupta and Mahler, 1995), again indicating that the methodology in this paper uses broadly correct reference prices in estimating net taxes/subsidies.

Table 15.1 shows the average calculated subsidies for 1999 for various groups of countries.[8] The results indicate that major oil-exporting countries are typically net subsidizers of petroleum products, whereas oil-importing countries are net taxers (negative subsidies). Moreover, the subsidies in major oil-exporting countries

---

[7]This may be relevant, for example, in Ecuador in 2000. In this case, the domestic price was measured in January 2000 but prices were adjusted significantly later in the year. Thus, the large subsidy estimate for Ecuador shown in Table 15.2 represents the annualized subsidy in January 2000, which may be different from the actual subsidy for 2000 as a whole.

[8]1999 is the latest available year for most countries; the world oil price in that year was also near the average for recent years (US$18 per barrel).

Table 15.1. *Domestic Petroleum Price Subsidies, 1999*
(Median values in parentheses)

| | Average Oil Subsidies[1] | | | |
	(In percent of GDP)		(In percent of government expenditure)	
Major oil exporters[2, 3]	3.5	(2.5)	15.2	(8.6)
Of which:				
Subsidizing oil exporters[4]	4.4	(3.7)	18.7	(10.8)
Other oil exporters[5]	−1.9	(−1.8)	−7.0	(−7.0)
Net oil importers[6]	−2.2	(−2.1)	−8.3	(−8.6)
Of which:				
Countries not producing oil[7]	−1.7	(−1.6)	−7.0	(−6.4)
Memorandum items:				
Subsidy rate by type of product (in percent) for subsidizing oil exporters				
Gasoline	9	(8)		
Diesel	48	(46)		
Residential light fuel oil	71	(78)		
Number of countries per category:				
Major oil exporters[2,3]	15		15	
Of which:				
Subsidizing oil exporters[4]	13		13	
Other oil exporters[5]	6		6	
Net oil importers[6]	41		40	
Of which:				
Countries not producing oil[7]	20		19	

Source: IMF staff estimates. Based on exchange rates taken from IMF, *International Financial Statistics*.

[1]Negative figure indicates net taxation of petroleum.

[2]Based on a comparison of domestic production and consumption volumes.

[3]Includes Algeria, Ecuador, Indonesia, Iran, Kazakhstan, Kuwait, Libya, Mexico, Nigeria, Norway, Qatar, Russia, Saudi Arabia, the United Arab Emirates, and Venezuela.

[4]Comprises 13 countries with positive subsidies—all countries included in footnote 3 except Mexico and Norway.

[5]Includes Argentina, Bolivia, Canada, Colombia, Denmark, and the United Kingdom.

[6]Includes Austria, Barbados, Brazil, Chile, France, Germany, Greece, Guatemala, Hungary, India, Italy, Japan, the Netherlands, New Zealand, Peru, Poland, Romania, Spain, Suriname, Turkey, the United States, Belgium, Costa Rica, the Czech Republic, Dominican Republic, El Salvador, Finland, Grenada, Guyana, Haiti, Honduras, Ireland, Jamaica, Luxembourg, Nicaragua, Panama, Paraguay, Sweden, Switzerland, and Uruguay.

[7]Includes Belgium, Costa Rica, the Czech Republic, Dominican Republic, El Salvador, Finland, Grenada, Guyana, Haiti, Honduras, Ireland, Jamaica, Luxembourg, Nicaragua, Panama, Paraguay, Sweden, Switzerland, and Uruguay.

tend to be large, relative both to GDP and to government spending recorded in the budget.[9] In 1999, the average subsidy in major oil-exporting countries was 3.5 percent of GDP and 15.2 percent of budget government expenditure.

The degree of subsidization in oil-exporting countries varies significantly across products, countries, and time. As Table 15.1 shows, residential fuel oil and diesel fuel are subsidized more heavily than gasoline. Across countries, positive subsidies vary from 16.6 percent of GDP in Azerbaijan in 2000 to less than 1 percent of GDP in Libya in 1999 (Table 15.2). Across time, average petroleum product subsidies tend to rise when world crude oil prices are high and fall when crude oil prices are low. This occurs because governments tend to adjust domestic prices slowly in response to changes in world prices. For example, between January 1998 and January 2000, the spot price of refined gasoline rose by over 40 percent, yet the after-tax retail price of gasoline in Venezuela increased by less than 5 percent.[10]

III. Economic Effects of Petroleum Subsidies and Taxes

Is this subsidization appropriate? It depends on the effects of subsidies on economic efficiency and equity, the fiscal costs of these subsidies, and whether they contribute to or dampen cyclical fluctuations in economic activity.

Efficiency

In general, economic efficiency requires marginal cost pricing. This implies that, in the absence of market imperfections and other price distortions, it would be most efficient to set the domestic price of petroleum equal to the net price that could be received on the world market.[11] As noted earlier, the latter equals the sum of the wholesale

---

[9]Much of the subsidy here does not appear in government expenditure—only in the case that an explicit government subsidy was provided to an oil producer would these outlays be reflected in total government spending.

[10]Energy Information Administration (various years).

[11]A similar result holds in an intertemporal context where the first-order condition for optimization requires that the marginal revenue from exporting today be equal to the discounted marginal revenue from exporting tomorrow. Thus, the domestic price would be set equal to the marginal revenue from exports in each time period.

Table 15.2. *Domestic Petroleum Price Subsidies*
in Main Oil-Exporting Countries, 1996–2000
(In percent of GDP)

Country	1996	1997	1998	1999	2000
Algeria	3.0	2.2	...	2.5	...
Azerbaijan[1]	...	...	...	...	16.6
Ecuador	...	3.3	1.4	–1.5	12.6
Indonesia	...	...	7.7	6.5	...
Iran					
Official exchange rate	10.0	...	...	4.2	...
Weighted average exchange rate[2]	13.2			12.6	
Kazakhstan	...	4.3	...	6.8	...
Kuwait	5.1	5.1	...	4.8	...
Libya	...	5.8	...	0.7	...
Mexico	...	1.0	–0.9	–0.9	–0.4
Nigeria	...	...	...	2.5	...
Norway	–4.5	...	–4.8	–3.9	–4.5
Qatar	3.9	3.2	...	2.4	...
Russian Federation	...	5.0	–5.0	8.0	...
Saudi Arabia	7.4	7.0	...	5.9	...
United Arab Emirates	1.9	1.4	...	1.7	...
Venezuela	...	5.9	2.9	3.7	4.9
Average subsidy	4.2	4.0	0.2	3.5	7.9
Sample size	7	11	6	15	5
Memorandum item:					
Average price of crude oil					
(US$ per barrel, U.K. Brent)	20.5	19.1	12.7	17.7	28.3

Sources: Energy Information Administration (various years); IMF, *International Financial Statistics*; and authors' estimates.

[1]Based on IMF staff estimates using a different methodology (Wakeman-Linn and others, 2002). The figure includes only the subsidy due to underpricing; if the effects of nonpayment are also included, the effective subsidy in 2000 is estimated at 21.3 percent of GDP.

[2]Based on a trade-weighted average of the official and market exchange rates.

spot price for the refined petroleum product (minus any international transport costs) plus the marketing and distribution costs that are saved by not consuming the good domestically. This is also the price that would result from a perfectly competitive free market, as it would eliminate arbitrage between domestic and world prices.

In reality there are several imperfections in this market. First, governments impose taxes in order to raise revenue. Taxation of petroleum may help minimize the efficiency losses of taxation in general, since the revenue collected allows taxes on other products to be lower. While the theoretically optimal rate of taxation on petroleum depends on many factors, a neutral hypothesis would be to assume that petroleum should be taxed at the same rate as other products.[12] Under this taxation rule, the most economically efficient policy would be to set the price of petroleum equal to the opportunity cost of selling the product on the world market plus domestic distribution and marketing costs and any general consumption tax, which is the "free-market price" in equation (2).

Second, petroleum consumption is typically associated with several negative externalities, including air pollution and traffic congestion. These externalities generally argue for higher taxation of petroleum products in order to ensure that the price reflects these extra costs to society. How high should these taxes be? The answer depends on how large the externalities are, which is a subject of significant debate and uncertainty. However, a recent review of the research on this issue has estimated that the total environmental and congestion cost of gasoline consumption in the United Kingdom is between US$0.25 and US$0.40 per liter (Parry, 2001), an amount that would imply taxation equal to at least 100 percent of the free-market price. For developing countries, it is likely that the externality costs will be somewhat lower, since incomes are lower and people are therefore less willing to pay as much to reduce the environmental and congestion costs. Nonetheless, the externalities in these countries are still likely to be significant.

Finally, the domestic price of petroleum in some countries is likely to be influenced by their monopoly pricing power in world oil markets. In this case, the marginal revenue lost from not selling another unit of petroleum on the world market is not simply the free-market price; it also depends on the resulting change in the world price and the effect this has on the country's existing oil export revenues.

To see this, note that the revenue from exporting refined petroleum, R, is equal to the world wholesale spot price of petroleum, W, plus the domestic distribution and marketing costs saved, D,[13] minus the costs of international transport, T, times the quantity of exports, X:

$$R = (W + D - T)X. \tag{3}$$

---

[12]It has been shown that, under some conditions, it is most efficient to tax all commodities at the same rate (e.g., Atkinson and Stiglitz, 1976). A more general rule would be to tax goods so that the percentage tax-induced change in the quantity demanded (measured along the compensated demand curve) is the same for each taxed good (Ramsey, 1927).

[13]The distribution and marketing costs of domestic consumption are "saved," since these costs are not incurred if petroleum is exported instead of consumed domestically.

Thus, the marginal revenue from exporting another unit of petroleum is the following:

$$\frac{dR}{dX} = W + \frac{dW}{dX}X + D - T = W\left[1 + \left(\frac{1}{\eta_{X,P}}\right)\left(\frac{X}{X_W}\right)\right] + D - T, \qquad (4)$$

where $\eta_{X,P}$ is the price elasticity of demand for world petroleum and X_W is the total demand for petroleum on the world market.

For countries with a small share of the world market, the second term in brackets in equation (4) will be insignificant. For these countries, the opportunity cost of not exporting is simply equal to the world wholesale spot price plus the saved marketing and distribution costs minus international transport costs, as noted above. However, for countries that have a sizable share of the world market, the latter term in brackets is likely to be significantly negative so the opportunity cost of not exporting would be lower than the world price. If all other things are equal, this implies that it would be economically efficient to sell petroleum domestically at a lower price.[14]

How important might this consideration be in reality? Table 15.3 calculates the marginal revenue from exporting another unit of petroleum for the largest oil producers, using equation (4). Different long-run oil price demand elasticities are assumed,[15] and each country's oil exports as a share of world consumption are taken as given. It is further assumed that distribution, marketing, and international transport costs equal 75 percent of the wholesale price.[16,17] Table 15.3 also presents marginal revenue for the Organization of Petroleum Exporting Countries (OPEC) as a whole under the assumption that the cartel could make pricing and production decisions collectively and enforce a single domestic pricing rule among all members. The marginal revenue is expressed as a fraction of marginal revenue in the no-market-power (small exporter) case.

---

[14]The argument for creating a wedge between export and domestic prices is essentially identical to the classic terms-of-trade rationale for protectionism. This argument notes that trade tariffs may benefit a country if the changes in world supply or demand induced by the tariff positively affect the country's terms of trade.

[15]Golembek, Hagem, and Hoel (1994) estimate price demand elasticities of around –0.9 for OECD countries and –0.75 for non-OECD countries. Hwang and Yang (2001) find somewhat lower elasticities (around –0.25) in their study of U.S. data.

[16]In other words, equation (4) is evaluated at the point at which $D - T = .75W$.

[17]This number represents an average of distribution, marketing, and international transport costs in OECD countries observed over a period of time. If these costs were lower, the marginal revenue estimates would be somewhat lower. For example, if these costs were 50 percent of the wholesale price, then marginal revenue for Saudi Arabia would be 86 percent (rather than 88 percent) of the small exporter case when $\eta = -0.50$.

Table 15.3. *Marginal Revenue from Exporting for Largest Oil Exporters*

	Exports as Share of World Consumption[1]	Marginal Revenue[2]		
		($\eta = -0.25$)	($\eta = -0.50$)	($\eta = -0.75$)
All OPEC	32.7	0.25	0.63	0.75
Saudi Arabia	10.8	0.75	0.88	0.92
Russia	5.1	0.88	0.94	0.96
Norway	4.3	0.90	0.95	0.97
Venezuela	4.0	0.91	0.95	0.97

Sources: Energy Information Administration (various years); and authors' estimates.
[1]For 1998 (Energy Information Administration, 2001).
[2]As fraction of small exporter (no-market-power) case; assumes domestic distribution and marketing costs minus international transport costs are 75 percent of the wholesale price; η refers to the price elasticity of demand for world petroleum.

If each country determines its prices independently, marginal revenue is significantly less than in the no-market-power case only for the largest exporter, Saudi Arabia; in the case of that country, marginal revenue is still 75 percent of the no-market-power case, even assuming a demand elasticity as low as −0.25. If, however, OPEC is able to successfully coordinate pricing and export decisions across all members, then the marginal revenue from exporting may be as low as 25 percent of the no-market-power case, which, all other things equal, would argue for lower domestic prices in these countries.

Some caveats to this monopolistic pricing/terms-of-trade argument for lower domestic pricing should be noted. First, this monopoly pricing is only optimal from the viewpoint of the oil-exporting country. From a worldwide viewpoint, welfare is maximized by eliminating differences in prices among countries. Second, the calculations in Table 15.3 ignore the reactions of large oil-importing countries that may have monopsonistic power in world markets. These countries may have a symmetric incentive to influence the world price of oil by taxing consumption in their domestic markets. If monopolistic pricing behavior by large oil exporters encourages large oil importers to engage in retaliatory monopsonistic behavior, this will reduce the incentive to price in a monopolistic manner.

In sum, various considerations enter into the efficient pricing of petroleum products.[18] Precise calculations are therefore difficult, as there is significant uncertainty regarding key parameters such as the envi-

[18]Gupta and Mahler (1995) survey the reasons behind petroleum taxation policies.

Table 15.4. *Deadweight Loss from Subsidies in Selected Countries, 1999*[1]

Country	Actual Subsidy Rate (In percent)	Assuming Environmental Externalities of US$0.10/Liter		Assuming No Environmental Externalities	
		Optimal subsidy (tax) rate (In percent)	Deadweight loss[2] (In percent of GDP)	Optimal subsidy (tax) rate (In percent)	Deadweight loss[2] (In percent of GDP)
Algeria	37	−57	1.4	−10	0.4
Ecuador	−14	−65	0.5	−10	0.0
Indonesia	78	−62	5.4	−10	2.8
Iran[3]	87	−64	12.4	−10	6.9
Kazakhstan	46	−65	4.4	−10	1.5
Kuwait	95	−71	6.0	−10	3.5
Libya	10	−65	0.8	−10	0.1
Nigeria	22	−61	1.7	−10	0.3
Qatar	32	−57	1.3	−10	0.4
Russia	51	−58	4.9	−3	1.6
Saudi Arabia	53	−44	3.0	4	1.0
United Arab Emirates	30	−81	1.5	−10	0.3
Venezuela	72	−55	2.7	−5	1.3
OPEC as a unit	62	−22	2.2	31	0.4

Sources: Energy Information Administration (various years); and authors' estimates.

[1]Assumes an optimal, nondistortionary uniform consumption tax of 10 percent, $\eta = -0.5$, and market power effects as estimated in Table 15.3. Negative numbers imply optimal net taxation.

[2]Calculated as area C in Figure 15.1, using an assumed constant compensated elasticity of demand function ($Q = P^{\eta}X$, where η is the compensated elasticity of demand and X is a constant calculated for each country using the observed Q and P).

[3]Based on the trade-weighted average exchange rate.

ronmental effects of oil consumption and the long-run elasticity of oil demand. However, for countries with no market power, the negative externalities and the need for government revenue clearly indicate it is most efficient to tax petroleum at a rate that is *at least* equal to that imposed on other consumption goods. For the very largest oil exporters, the most efficient rate of taxation (from the country's viewpoint) may be slightly lower than in other countries, but it is likely to still be significantly positive, as the estimates discussed earlier indicate that the factors favoring taxation (negative externalities and the need for government revenue) will still outweigh the factors favoring subsidization (market power/terms-of-trade arguments for protection). For example, Table 15.4 presents optimal subsidy/tax rates for major oil exporters, based on assumed environmental externalities of US$0.10 per liter, an optimal uniform consumption tax of 10 percent, and a price elasticity

Figure 15.1. *Deadweight Loss from a Subsidy*

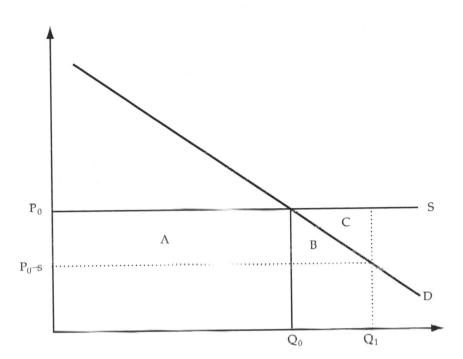

of demand of –0.5. It can be seen that net taxation is optimal under these assumptions even if one considers OPEC as a unified producer and seller.[19] Table 15.4 also estimates optimal subsidy (tax) rates excluding all environmental externalities. In this extreme case, significant net subsidization would be optimal only for OPEC as a unified producer and seller; however, the optimal rate of subsidization (31 percent) would still be only half the level of subsidization that actually prevailed in 1999.

Despite the apparent optimality of net taxation of petroleum, few oil-exporting countries pursue such a policy, resulting in significant economic losses. Rather, as Table 15.1 indicates, they typically subsidize consumption. This deviation from efficient pricing results in a deadweight welfare loss. This can be seen in Figure 15.1, where the loss in

---

[19]Domestic oil consumption would also fall in oil-exporting countries if prices were increased, leading to pressures to increase exports. Given the small share of world oil consumption accounted for by these countries, the impact on world prices would be small.

government/exporter revenue from subsidization (area ABC) is greater than the increase in domestic consumers' surplus (area AB). Table 15.4 presents estimates for the magnitude of this deadweight loss (area C in Figure 15.1) as a percentage of GDP for several major petroleum exporters. For 1999, these losses ranged from 0.5 percent of GDP in Ecuador to 12.4 percent of GDP in Iran.[20] High levels of domestic consumption resulting from these price distortions can even turn net exporters into net importers, as some analysts forecast may eventually happen in Iran.[21]

Equity

Subsidies are not the most efficient means of redistributing income or of improving the poor's access to energy. The impact of subsidies on equity can be evaluated by their relative efficacy—whether they reach those for whom they are intended—and the ease of administration, particularly given the incentives for smuggling and corruption. This section attempts to assess subsidies in each of these respects.

The available evidence shows that higher-income households consume larger quantities of petroleum products and electricity in oil-producing countries and thus benefit relatively more from subsidies.[22] For example, in the mid-1990s in Mexico and Ecuador, over 30 percent of household electricity consumption was accounted for by the top quintile (Table 15.5). Outside Latin America, Saboohi (2001) finds that in Iran the energy consumption of a poor household was 44 percent of that of a rich household. Similarly, in Venezuela, the richest 20 percent of the population received 6½ times more in subsidies per person than the poorest 33 percent of the population; while 38 percent of electricity subsidies went to the top 20 percent of the population, only 16 percent accrued to the bottom third (World Bank, 1995). In Ecuador, the more expensive energy products (electricity and liquefied petroleum gas (LPG)) received the highest subsidies, while household kerosene (kerex), which poor households considered convenient and versatile, was not subsidized (UNDP/World Bank, 1994).

---

[20]Note that the deadweight loss in Table 15.4 is in some cases larger than the subsidy in Table 15.2. This is because the deadweight loss also takes into account the externality costs (from pollution and congestion), whereas the subsidies in Table 15.2 are calculated relative to the "free-market price."

[21]See Dinmore (2002).

[22]Oil is a major input for electricity production.

Table 15.5. *Mexico and Ecuador: Share of Total Expenditures by Quintile*
(In percent of total spending)

Quintile	Electricity	Gasoline[1]	Gas/LPG	Petrol/Kerex	Others[2]
Mexico					
1	5.4	0.9	6.7	15.1	26.1
2	10.2	3.9	13.8	18.3	24.0
3	15.9	9.3	18.5	20.2	20.4
4	21.6	19.4	25.1	21.7	17.4
5	46.8	66.5	35.9	24.8	12.1
Ecuador					
1	9.2	...	15.2	43.2	...
2	15.3	...	23.2	20.6	...
3	16.2	...	20.1	13.8	...
4	26.4	...	22.1	7.6	...
5	32.9	...	19.4	14.8	...

Sources: UNDP/World Bank (1994); and IMF staff calculations based on the 1996 Mexican Income and Expenditure Household Survey (INEGI, 1996).
[1]Gasoline refers to gasoline, diesel, or gas purchased as fuel for vehicles.
[2]Includes coal, firewood, heating oil, candles, and other items such as paper or cardboard.

Relatively better-off groups also benefit more when quantities well above what the poor need are subsidized. In Yemen, for example, the lifeline electricity rate was set at a level of consumption that covered more than 75 percent of the population (Barnes and Halpern, 2000).

The pro-rich bias of subsidies is further compounded by smuggling and corruption. Subsidies create the incentive for smuggling petroleum products to markets where prices reflect market conditions. In Nigeria, for example, petroleum prices are a third of those prevailing in neighboring Niger or Cameroon, leading to widespread smuggling and chronic fuel shortages in many parts of the country.

Despite their pro-rich bias, the sudden removal of subsidies can have adverse social effects in the short run. This is particularly the case when a country lacks adequate mechanisms for shielding poor households from the resulting higher prices. Poor households may spend a significant share of their incomes on energy, and in the absence of compensating mechanisms, the ensuing loss in their consumption could be large. For example, in Ghana kerosene, diesel, and gasoline prices rose in real terms by 161, 214, and 156 percent, respectively, from 1983 through 1987. Since kerosene was a major fuel for the poor (as shown by the expenditure shares), estimates of the loss in consumer surplus for different magnitudes of price elasticity show that households in the bottom two quintiles lost the most (Hope and Singh, 1995).

Fiscal Costs

Subsidies also have substantial fiscal costs for oil-producing countries. In many such countries, the cost of subsidies exceeds the overall fiscal deficit, which averaged 2.1 percent of GDP in the second half of the 1990s in subsidizing oil-exporting countries. Given high levels of public debt in these countries (61 percent of GDP, for the four countries for which data are readily available), the potential gains (in terms of reduced fiscal vulnerability) from further fiscal consolidation could be sizable.[23]

If fiscal consolidation is not required, the revenue forgone by governments through the subsidization of petroleum consumption could be used to reduce tax rates or increase more productive spending, such as that for infrastructure and human capital formation.[24] For example, if subsidizing oil-exporting countries eliminated petroleum subsidies, they could increase spending on health, which is low in relation to the average in middle-income countries (Figure 15.2 and Table 15.6). This should contribute to boosting indicators of health status in oil-producing countries, which in some cases are below those in other countries with similar or lower per capita income.[25] In Venezuela, for example, immunization rates are below the level achieved by lower middle-income countries, despite per capita income that is about double the average for this group. Education spending is also low in some oil-producing countries (e.g., Nigeria).

Cyclicality

The policy of maintaining below-world-market prices for petroleum products has important implications for macroeconomic management.

---

[23]To the extent that subsidies are implicit, removing them may not automatically increase government revenue. Changes in tax policy may be required to capture higher profits of domestic oil-supplying or -producing enterprises. In addition, corruption in state oil companies (SOCs) may result in the government's effectively having less than a 100 percent claim on the SOC's profit, thus reducing the fiscal benefits of subsidy reform (see McPherson, Chapter 7 in this volume).

[24]For a related discussion of unproductive spending, see Chu and others (1995).

[25]See Gupta, Verhoeven, and Tiongson (2001) for an examination of the impact of public spending on health care and the health status of the poor.

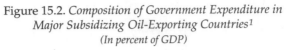

Figure 15.2. *Composition of Government Expenditure in Major Subsidizing Oil-Exporting Countries[1]*
(*In percent of GDP*)

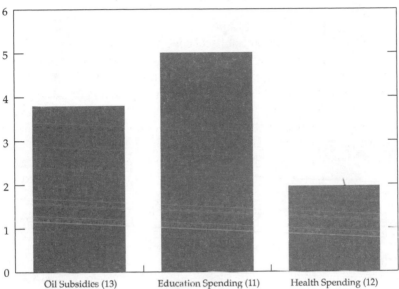

Source: IMF country documents.
[1]Unweighted averages for subsidizing oil-exporting countries. Oil subsidies are for 1999; expenditure data reflect averages over the period 1997–99. Number of countries in parentheses.

As noted earlier, many oil-exporting countries tend not to adjust domestic prices fully in response to changes in world prices. For net oil exporters, this means that implicit subsidies will be procyclical—subsidies will increase when world oil prices increase, which also tend to be periods of economic expansion for these countries. The procyclicality of subsidies will thus exacerbate the effects of oil price shocks on economic volatility.

Available data suggest that subsidies have a substantial procyclical bias. Figure 15.3 plots the changes in subsidies against real GDP growth per capita across countries. The coefficient implies that a 1 percentage point increase in per capita GDP growth is associated with an increase in oil subsidies of 0.6 percent of GDP.

One way to eliminate the procyclicality of oil subsidies is to tie domestic petroleum prices to fluctuations in international markets. This can, however, lead to wide swings in domestic prices, thereby

Table 15.6. Social Indicators and Social Spending in Subsidizing Oil-Exporting and Other Countries, 1997–99

	Life Expectancy	Illiteracy Rate (In percent of adult population)	Infant Mortality Rate (Per 1,000 live births)	Under 5 Mortality Rate (Per 1,000 live births)	Immunization Rate Against Measles (In percent of children aged less than 12 months)	GDP Per Capita (Constant 1995 US$)	Education Spending (In percent of GDP)	Education Spending (In percent of total expenditure)	Health Spending (In percent of GDP)	Health Spending (In percent of total expenditure)
Subsidizing oil-exporting countries (13)[1]	69	20	26	36	88	3,259	5.0	15.7	2.0	5.8
Of which:										
Algeria	71	35	35	39	76	1,534	8.8	28.0	1.5	4.9
Ecuador	69	9	29	37	87	1,521	3.1	15.6	0.9	4.8
Indonesia	65	14	43	54	80	1,025	...	...	0.6	3.3
Nigeria	49	39	82	149	48	253	1.4	7.6	0.7	3.8
Saudi Arabia	72	25	19	26	92	6,841	8.8	23.1	2.9	7.6
Venezuela	73	8	21	24	79	3,451	3.8	19.7	1.4	7.0
Low-income countries (56)[1]	55	41	75	126	67	423	4.0	15.0	2.0	6.8
Lower-middle-income countries (42)[1]	68	16	33	44	86	1,642	4.8	16.6	2.3	7.5
Upper-middle-income countries (26)[1]	71	11	18	26	90	5,306	4.7	14.4	3.3	9.7

Sources: World Bank, 2001, World Development Indicators. Expenditure data from IMF staff reports.

[1]Numbers in brackets refer to the numbers of countries in the different groups in 1999.

Figure 15.3. *Change in Subsidy and Real GDP Per Capita Growth*[1,2]

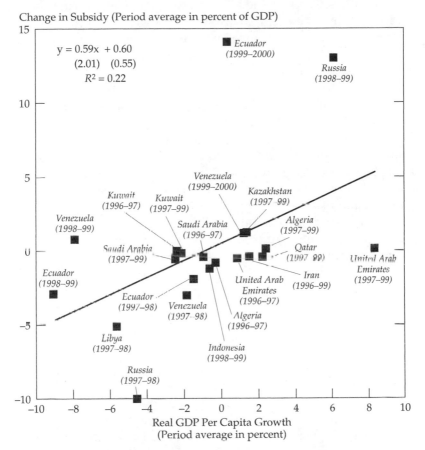

Change in Subsidy (Period average in percent of GDP)

$y = 0.59x + 0.60$
$(2.01) \quad (0.55)$
$R^2 = 0.22$

Real GDP Per Capita Growth
(Period average in percent)

Sources: IMF country documents; and authors' calculations.
[1]Excludes one outlying observation when real GDP growth per capita was in excess of 20 percent. Robust White (1980) *t*-statistics in parentheses of regression.
[2]Dates provided in parentheses indicate the period over which the change in subsidy was calculated.

increasing uncertainty about government revenue and investment decisions. Under these circumstances, governments could adopt partial pass-through rules and use financial hedging instruments.[26]

---

[26]See Federico, Daniel, and Bingham, Chapter 17 in this volume, and Daniel, Chapter 14 in this volume, for a more extensive discussion.

Partial pass-through rules can help smooth out the path of domestic petroleum prices. These include moving-average rules (which base retail prices on a moving average of past spot prices), trigger rules (which update only if spot prices change by a predetermined trigger amount), or max-min rules (which place a ceiling and a floor on the level of retail petroleum prices). For example, Chile has a max-min price stabilization law under which reference prices are updated weekly.

Hedging instruments can also mitigate oil price fluctuations. For example, the state of Texas hedges its heavy reliance on oil revenue by buying and selling options in order to narrow the range within which its revenue stream fluctuates. Oil-producing countries do not disclose whether they use hedging instruments because this is market-sensitive information; however, it is believed to be a common practice in a number of countries. Since risk management activities require considerable knowledge of financial instruments and an appropriate institutional framework, the human and institutional requirements to implement and monitor hedging operations are significant. In particular, if institutions in a country are weak, there may be scope for rent seeking. It is important that government officials be held accountable for their hedging decisions.

IV. Reforming Petroleum Pricing Policies

Petroleum price subsidy reform entails reducing generalized subsidies by raising prices and targeting subsidies to the poor and vulnerable population groups. Subsidy reform has not been easy for most countries because of the opposition from losers of subsidization, the likely impact of higher prices on the poor and on production costs, and the inability of the government to protect the poor because of weak administrative capacity.

What lessons does the past provide for successful subsidy reform? In particular, what are the preconditions for successful reform and what are the appropriate timing and sequencing of reforms? What countervailing measures could be adopted to address any adverse distributive consequences of reform, and how might poverty and social impact analysis be useful? This section addresses each of these questions in turn.

Preconditions for Reform

The decision to liberalize the petroleum market, if met with strong protest and social unrest, can undermine reform efforts. For example, in June 2000 Nigeria increased petroleum prices by 50 percent, leading to a general strike and riots, followed by a subsequent reversal of government policy. In Indonesia, an attempt to limit the fuel subsidy in 1998 was met with violent protests, forcing the government to partially roll back planned price increases. Similar protests have occurred in Venezuela and Ecuador.

The risk of political disruption is highest when rapid reform is attempted without credible social protection mechanisms in place and without adequate attention to building political consensus on the need for reform. To assess the political risks associated with price-subsidy reform and inform its design, policymakers could, to the extent feasible, do the following:

- Identify winners and losers in price-subsidy reforms. This can be done by examining the benefits of existing subsidies for different income classes and then identifying the characteristics of winners and losers.[27]
- Assess the political strength and the magnitude of the losses or gains of each group.
- Assess the feasibility and cost of alternative measures to protect the consumption of the poor or politically vocal groups.
- Generate political support.

Subsidy reductions should be embedded in a reform program that engenders broad support and yields widespread benefits. This stakeholder approach (Graham, 1994) implies that governments should avoid reforms that impose an unfair burden on a narrow group of socioeconomic or ethnic categories. Compensatory measures for the poor can help to gain the support of an important constituency. For example, Indonesia was able to reduce fuel subsidies in October 2000 and April 2001 after earlier failed attempts by compensating poor consumers through a combination of public works programs, microcredit, and cash assistance. This process was helped in part by growing acceptance among the population that fuel subsidies were not well targeted. In the longer term, sustained support for reforms should be crafted in a consultative process, with adequate poverty and social impact analysis (PSIA) to inform policy choices (see below).

Finally, publicity campaigns to discuss the trade-offs involved in providing subsidies can be useful in fostering support for reform. Successful reforms have often been accompanied by effective government

---

[27]See Gupta and others (2000).

communication to the population regarding the trade-offs and rationale for reform. This includes presenting the cost of subsidies in concrete terms and/or explaining how the reform package affects real
household income.[28] For example, in Egypt the budgetary burden of
subsidies was compared with revenues from the Suez Canal.

Timing and Sequencing of Petroleum Pricing Reforms

The optimal speed of subsidy reform depends on several factors.
First, the government must take into account fiscal considerations.
There is a trade-off between rapidly cutting budget-financed subsidies
and avoiding an adverse impact on the poor. Although a one-time adjustment of prices to eliminate subsidies can yield immediate budget
savings and quickly correct distortions in resource allocation, it can
also result in a sudden and significant decline in household consumption, especially for low-income households. Although there may be a
potential for rapid budgetary savings from the elimination of implicit
subsidies, a sustainable reform will also require substantial outlays to
protect the poor.

A second consideration regarding the speed of reform is the availability of social protection instruments. Such instruments require not
only resources, but also a system to deliver compensation to those who
need it. In general, if existing social protection instruments can be
adapted to the needs of the poor during reform, then reform can be
rapid. However, if new social safety net instruments need to be established, then the speed of reform will be affected by the administrative
capacity to design and implement adequate and well-targeted social
protection. In this regard, gradual adjustment may minimize the adjustment costs faced by businesses and individuals. A sudden increase
in prices of petroleum products can affect the viability of businesses,
potentially leading to job losses.

Third, governments must consider their political constraints. Rapid
reform is feasible only when governments are politically strong
and social disruption from implementing reforms is unlikely. Gradual
adjustment has the benefit of giving the government time to assess

---

[28]In this respect, increased transparency in the management of public finances is critical for gaining public support for higher petroleum prices. It would demonstrate that resources realized from reducing or eliminating implicit price subsidies would be used for
the benefit of the population in need.

and react to unintended consequences, including adverse political repercussions. Furthermore, insufficient institutional and administrative capacity to protect the poor can weaken political support for reforms.

Finally, the external environment may also affect the pace of reform. Specifically, more rapid reform may be possible under favorable external circumstances, such as low international prices. For example, in Guinea, prior to the adoption of an automatic adjustment mechanism for the retail prices of petroleum products, the price of gasoline at the pump was reduced in 2001 to reflect the decline in international oil prices.

Despite these advantages, a gradual pace of reform also has drawbacks. First, it extends the time frame for reaping budgetary gains and, by slowing the adjustment of prices, it diminishes the incentive for the private sector to rapidly switch to energy-efficient technology. It may also lead to policy reversals, especially if it is adopted to postpone politically difficult reforms.

In the absence of a formal price-setting mechanism, subsidies can quickly reemerge regardless of whether reform is rapid or gradual. For example, in Ecuador one-time adjustments were undertaken, but no automatic adjustment mechanism was put in place, leading to the reemergence of subsidies (Box 15.1). Exchange rate changes can also lead to the reemergence of subsidies when domestic prices are fixed. For example, in Indonesia, the resurgence of massive fuel subsidies was due to the large depreciation of the exchange rate coupled with the lack of an automatic price-setting mechanism.

The problem of policy reversal with gradual reform can be overcome by adopting and making public a detailed timetable of reform measures. For example, in Cameroon the authorities decided to phase out the petroleum subsidy by cutting it in half in 2001/02 and completely eliminating it in 2002/03.

Distributive Considerations and Countervailing Measures

The adverse social effects of reforming energy subsidies noted earlier can be mitigated through appropriate social protection mechanisms. Poverty and social impact analysis (PSIA)—which aims to assess the ex ante, during, and ex post consequences of policy interventions on the well-being of the poor—can help weigh the costs and benefits of alternative strategies prior to implementation and therefore inform the

---

Box 15.1. *Ecuador: Experience with Energy Price Subsidy Reform*

Ecuador provides a good case study of how the lack of a formal price-setting mechanism can hinder the implementation of lasting reforms of petroleum subsidies. Traditionally, Ecuador has granted subsidies to consumers for cooking gas, electricity, and some other commodities (mainly fuels and other utilities) and subsidies have continued to reemerge. The government grants these subsidies by fixing consumer prices below the opportunity cost—sometimes even below the cost of production—of these goods and services. In September 1998, the government decreed an increase of more than 400 percent in the price of cooking gas, thereby eliminating the existing subsidy. However, the new price was fixed in sucres and the subsidy quickly reappeared as the price of petroleum increased with exchange rate depreciation. In May 2000, the government introduced price increases of 65–92 percent for diesel and gasoline and of 90–333 percent for other derivatives. This sharply lowered the subsidy on fuels from an average of 35 U.S. cents per gallon to an average of 8 U.S. cents per gallon, but it left unchanged the subsidy on cooking gas. The government also implemented several increases in electricity prices: in September 1998, in January 1999, and in May 2000, when prices were raised by an average of 70 percent (combined with 4 percent monthly adjustments thereafter). The direct subsidy to small consumers was replaced with a system of cross-subsidies between large and small consumers. This increase was intended to allow electricity companies to cover their own operating costs, but prices were still significantly below long-term marginal cost. In 2001, a decree doubling the price of cooking gas and increasing petroleum prices was reversed—following massive protests in February of 2001—and instead the government agreed to freeze petroleum prices for a year and cut cooking gas prices.

Source: Offerdal and others (2000).

---

design of the reform program itself.[29] Such an analysis could help evaluate the timing and the sequencing of reforms as well as the need for countervailing measures.

For example, an ex ante social impact study for Iran (Saboohi, 2001) estimated that an increase in energy prices with the aim of eliminating energy subsidies would have a serious impact on household consump-

---

[29]See PSIA concept note (http://www.imf.org/external/np/exr/facts/sia.htm) and the recent Poverty Reduction and Growth Facility (PRGF) review (http://www.imf.org/External/NP/prgf/2002/031502.htm) for an assessment of recent experience on PSIA.

tion and inflation. However, estimates showed that if part of the additional resources obtained through the elimination of energy subsidies were allocated to strengthen the budgetary balance (thus containing inflation) and the rest of the resources were allocated to targeted programs for the poor, then rural populations and the poorest three deciles of urban households would be better off.[30]

Countervailing measures that can be implemented to minimize poverty and social impacts include cash transfers or limiting subsidies to a subgroup of the population. Cash compensation, in some cases, has taken the form of a separate benefit in lieu of the subsidy. In 1998, for example, Ecuador eliminated the cooking-gas subsidy and instituted a cash transfer program for poor families and the elderly. In the wake of the 1999 financial crisis, this cash transfer program became the backbone of the government's safety-net strategy. In other cases, cash benefits have been merged with existing social benefits.

Cash transfers have several advantages: they allow for consumer choice, their cost to the budget is explicit and known with greater certainty than generalized subsidies, and they can be targeted to the poor. However, their real value may erode quickly during periods of high inflation and they are prone to corruption. For example, although the safety-net program in Ecuador has been quite successful in providing relief to a large segment of the poor population, more than a quarter of the current recipients are not eligible (World Bank, 2000a). In addition, since these transfers are disbursed through the banking system, which is far better developed in cities and urban areas than in rural areas, the distribution tends to favor the urban population. The coverage of these transfers is, therefore, well below target in rural areas.

Other countervailing measures include limiting price subsidies to a subgroup of the population. For example, in Ecuador, the cash transfer program was complemented by targeted electricity subsidies to poorer consumers financed through higher prices charged to wealthier consumers. A more common approach among oil producers is to tax relatively inelastic products such as gasoline and subsidize so-called "social products" such as kerosene and diesel. This practice is common

---

[30]As another example, an ex post social impact analysis for an oil-consuming country—Armenia—showed that reforms in the energy sector had led to a more reliable electricity supply, improved the financial viability of energy companies, reduced cross-subsidization, and improved payment discipline. However, the poor cut consumption more (relative to the nonpoor), partly because the elimination of the increasing block tariff raised the average price of electricity more than expected (Lampietti and others, 2001).

in Algeria, Egypt, Iraq, and Syria (Al-Faris, 1997). In Yemen for example, gasoline prices were increased every year from 1996 through 1999, so that by 1998 they were 80 percent above world market prices. This allowed for cross-subsidies for diesel and, to a lesser extent, for fuel oil and kerosene. This policy, however, added to the discrepancy between domestic and border prices and suffered from the efficiency problems discussed earlier; furthermore, it provided incentives for industries and the nonpoor to shift their consumption to the subsidized products.

V. Conclusions

This paper finds that major oil-exporting countries tend to be net subsidizers of petroleum, while oil-importing countries tend to be net taxers. Implicit subsidies in major oil-exporting countries are large, equaling 3.5 percent of GDP and 15.2 percent of explicit government expenditure, on average, in 1999. Subsidies in major oil-exporting countries vary over time, with a marked procyclical bias. With respect to variation by product, residential fuel oil and diesel are subsidized more heavily than gasoline.

Subsidization does not appear to be a wise use of resources. From an efficiency point of view, it would be best for oil-exporting countries to set the domestic price of petroleum equal to the world market price (assuming no market imperfections). Taking into account market imperfections complicates the analysis but generally supports the notion that prices should be no lower than world market levels. From an equity point of view, subsidies tend to be an undesirable method of redistribution, either because they benefit all users (including the rich) or because they are indiscriminate, allowing for consumption well above what is needed by the poor. The pro-rich bias of subsidies can be further compounded by smuggling and corruption. From a fiscal perspective, the opportunity costs of these subsidies are substantial.

Despite the substantial costs of implicit petroleum subsidies, reform is difficult, as there is strong popular opposition to their elimination. Subsidy reform should be embedded in a reform program that engenders broad support and yields widespread benefits. This could include the use of countervailing measures and vigorous publicity campaigns to educate the population on the trade-offs involved in providing subsidies versus other social services. The speed of subsidy reform will depend on the required size of fiscal adjustment, the availability of social protection instruments, the strength of the government, and the administrative capacity to implement reforms. The adverse social and political effects of reforming energy subsidies can be mitigated by undertaking poverty and social impact analyses and establishing safety nets. These safety nets can include cash compensation for the most vulnerable, limiting price subsidies to a subgroup of the population, or tax exemptions for the poor. To inform the design, pace, and implementation of reform, PSIA should be undertaken prior to, during, and after a reform to ensure that appropriate mitigating measures are in place.

Appendix. Calculation of Implicit Subsidies

This appendix explains how implicit subsidies are calculated. Conceptually, the implicit subsidy for petroleum product i in country j in time period t ($S_{i,j,t}$) is defined as the difference between the "free-market price" ($M_{i,j,t}$) and the after-tax retail price ($P_{i,j,t}$) times the volume of consumption ($C_{i,j,t}$):

$$S_{i,j,t} = (M_{i,j,t} - P_{i,j,t})C_{i,j,t}. \tag{A.1}$$

To calculate this subsidy, data on each of these three variables are calculated as follows. Data on the after-tax retail prices of major petroleum products are obtained from various editions of the *International Energy Annual* (Energy Information Administration, various years). Data are obtained for gasoline,[31] motor diesel, residential light fuel oil, kerosene, residential liquefied petroleum gas (LPG),[32] industrial light fuel oil, and industrial heavy fuel oil.[33] Data are collected for the years 1995–2000. For most countries, however, data are available for only some years. Prices for each year come in various forms (either from a particular month, a quarter, or an annual average). There are 86 countries in the sample and all prices are expressed in U.S. dollars.

The data on consumption are obtained from the Energy Information Administration website.[34] These data are divided into gasoline, jet fuel,

---

[31]For most countries, prices are for premium gasoline; for a few, however, prices are reported for regular gasoline instead.

[32]LPG includes primarily residential propane or a mixture of propane and butane.

[33]Heavy fuel is also sometimes referred to as residual fuel oil.

[34]The website is http://www.eia.doe.gov/emeu/world/main1.html. This same information is published in the *International Energy Annual* (Energy Information Administration, various years).

kerosene, distillate fuel oil, heavy fuel oil, LPG, and other. For most countries, data are available for 1995–98. For some countries, data are also available for 1999. Missing consumption data for 1999 and 2000 are imputed by assuming that consumption grows at the rate of real GDP, measured in domestic currency. All GDP and exchange rate information are from *International Financial Statistics* (International Monetary Fund, various years).

The free-market price is defined as the price that would prevail if there were no government interventions to affect the relative price of the product in question. For net oil-importing countries, this free-market price should be equal to the cost of importing another unit of the good. This is calculated as the world wholesale spot price for the refined product ($W_{i,j,t}$) plus domestic distribution and marketing costs ($D_{i,j,t}$)[35] plus all general consumption taxes ($V_{i,j,t}$—general sales taxes, VAT, etc.). General consumption taxes are included because, as a first approximation, these taxes do not distort most relative prices[36] and so should be included if the objective is to determine what the price of a petroleum product would be if it were given the same treatment by government policies as any other good. Thus, the free-market price is as follows:

$$M_{i,j,t} = W_{i,j,t} + D_{i,j,t} + V_{i,j,t}. \tag{A.2}$$

Data on world wholesale spot prices are obtained from *Datastream*. For each of the following retail prices, the corresponding wholesale spot price is used: (i) premium gasoline—New York premium unleaded nonoxygen gasoline; (ii) regular gasoline—New York regular unleaded nonoxygen gasoline; (iii) motor diesel—New York low sulfur (0.5 percent) diesel fuel; (iv) light fuel oil (both residential and industrial)—New York No. 2 fuel oil; (v) kerosene—Singapore jet kerosene; (vi) LPG—Mount Belvieu propane; and (vii) heavy fuel oil—Northwest Europe heavy fuel oil (3.5 percent sulfur). There are four or five major world markets for each type of product (mainly New York harbor, the U.S. Gulf Coast, Los Angeles, Singapore, and Rotterdam). The choice of market is based on data availability from *Datastream*. However, prices in these markets usually do not differ widely for long periods of time, so the use of only one market should not introduce significant bias into the estimates. For each observation, the frequency

---

[35]See footnote 5.
[36]See footnote 6.

of the wholesale price (i.e., whether it is a monthly, quarterly, or annual average) is chosen so as to match the frequency in which the corresponding retail price is reported. All prices are in U.S. dollars.

For gasoline, motor diesel, light fuel oil, and heavy fuel oil, domestic distribution and marketing costs are measured as the difference between the average before-tax retail price across eight OECD countries taken from *Monthly Price Statistics* (International Energy Agency, 2001b)[37] and the wholesale price of each of these products in November 2001. For kerosene and LPG, costs are calculated as the difference between the average before-tax retail price to end users in the U.S. from the *Annual Energy Review* (Energy Information Administration, 2000) and the average annual wholesale price for 2000. The resulting estimates for domestic distribution and marketing costs in U.S. cents per gallon are 36.4, 44.3, 35.6, 19.8, 59.1, and 15.2 for gasoline, motor diesel, light fuel oil, jet kerosene, propane, and heavy fuel oil, respectively.

To simplify the calculations, these domestic distribution and marketing costs are kept constant over time and country for each product. This introduces some measurement error since these costs will vary across time and country. However, previous studies have estimated that domestic marketing and distribution costs in developing countries are remarkably similar, on average, to domestic marketing and distribution costs in developed countries (Bacon, 2001), so the assumption of constant costs should not introduce a significant bias.

Data on general consumption taxes are obtained for each country from *Corporate Taxes: Worldwide Summaries* (PricewaterhouseCoopers, various years) and internal IMF databases. The taxes include the standard rate of any VAT or general sales tax that is applied at the central government level.

For net oil-exporting countries, the free-market price is calculated in the same manner as for net oil importers, except that the transportation cost of shipping petroleum from one country to another ($T_{i,j,t}$) is subtracted from the free-market price since oil exporters need not import petroleum from other countries.[38] These transportation costs are estimated as US$9.71 per metric ton, which was the average for all

---

[37]The eight countries are Canada, France, Germany, Italy, Japan, Spain, the United Kingdom, and the United States. Data are missing for Canada for light and heavy fuel oil and for the United States for heavy fuel oil.

[38]Note that insurance costs are not taken into account, which could lead to an overestimation of the subsidy. However, these costs are likely to be very small and would not substantially change the results.

routes between 1996–2000, based on data from the *OPEC Annual Statistical Bulletin 2000* (Organization of Petroleum Exporting Countries, 2001). The assumption of constant international transport costs should not in general bias the results since these costs represent only about 2 percent of the retail price of petroleum products. In some countries and under some conditions, however, they may be substantially higher. In the former Soviet Union, for example, ice-blocked ports and pipeline capacity constraints may significantly increase marginal transport costs.

Another complication that arises in calculating subsidies is that available consumption data are divided into somewhat different categories than the price data. This problem is most pronounced for distillate fuels, which are lumped into one group in the consumption data but for which three different retail prices exist (motor diesel, residential light fuel oil, and industrial light fuel oil). For most OECD countries, however, the breakdown of distillate fuel consumption into the various subproducts does exist in the *Energy Statistics of Non-OECD Countries 1997–98* (International Energy Agency, 2001a).[39] Thus, it is assumed that all countries divide their consumption of distillate fuels into the three categories in the same proportions as the OECD average for 1998. Similarly, jet fuel and kerosene are provided as separate categories in the consumption data, whereas only data on kerosene are provided in the retail price data, and only data on jet fuel are provided in the spot price data. Thus, kerosene and jet fuel are lumped together as one consumption category, and the retail price for kerosene is compared to the market price for jet fuel. In addition, retail prices for some products are missing for many countries. In these cases, it is assumed that the subsidy rate on missing prices is equal to the subsidy rate on motor diesel. If the retail price of motor diesel is missing, it is assumed that the subsidy rate on missing prices equals the subsidy rate on residential light fuel oil.

Bibliography

Albouy, Yves, and Nadia Nadifi, 2000, "Impact of Power Sector Reform on the Poor: A Review of Issues and the Literature," Energy Sector Management Assistance Program Paper No. 002 (Washington: World Bank).

---

[39]Data taken from the table on page II.11.

Al-Faris, Abdul-Razak, 1997, "Energy Pricing Policies in Arab Countries: Impacts of Structural Adjustment Programmes," *OPEC Review*, Vol. 21 (December), pp. 245–60.

Asia Pacific Economic Cooperation Forum, World Bank, Asian Development Bank, Inter-American Development Bank, and IMF, 2001, "Social Safety Nets in Response to Crisis: Lessons and Guidelines from Asia and Latin America" (unpublished; Washington: International Monetary Fund).

Atkinson, A.B., and J.E. Stiglitz, 1976, "The Design of Tax Structure: Direct Versus Indirect Taxation," *Journal of Public Economics*, Vol. 6, No. 1–2, pp. 55–75.

Bacon, Robert, 2001, "Petroleum Taxes: Trends in Fuel Taxes (and Subsidies) and the Implications," Viewpoint Note No. 240 (Washington: World Bank).

Barnes, Douglas F., and Jonathan Halpern, 2000, "The Role of Energy Subsidies," in *Energy and Development Report: Energy Services for the World's Poor*, ed. by Penelope J. Brooke and Suzanne Smith (Washington: World Bank Energy Sector Management Assistance Program).

Chu, Ke young, and others, 1995, *Unproductive Public Expenditures: A Pragmatic Approach to Policy Analysis*, IMF Pamphlet Series, No. 48 (Washington: International Monetary Fund).

Dinmore, Guy, 2002, "Iran's Oil Crisis Threatens to Drain the Country's Lifeline," *Financial Times*, May 7.

"Economic Theory, African Reality," 2002, *Economist*, January 24.

"Ecuador Battles Over Cooking Gas," 2001, *Economist*, February 8.

Energy Information Administration, *International Energy Annual* (Washington: various years). Available via the Internet: http://www.eia.doe.gov/emeu/iea/contents.html.

———, 2000, *Annual Energy Review* (Washington). Available via the Internet: http://www.eia.doe.gov/emeu/iea/contents.html.

Freund, Caroline L., and Christine I. Wallich, 1995, "Raising Household Energy Prices in Poland: Who Gains? Who Loses?," World Bank Policy Research Working Paper No. 1495 (Washington: World Bank).

Golombek, Rolf, Cathrine Hagem, and Michael Hoel, 1995, "Efficient Incomplete International Climate Agreements," *Resource and Energy Economics*, Vol. 17, pp. 25–46.

Graham, Carol, 1994, *Safety Nets, Politics, and the Poor: Transitions to Market Economies* (Washington: Brookings Institution).

Gupta, Sanjeev, and Walter Mahler, 1995, "Taxation of Petroleum Products: Theory and Empirical Experience," *Energy Economics*, Vol. 17 (April), pp. 101–16.

Gupta, Sanjeev, and others, 2000, *Equity and Efficiency in the Reform of Price Subsidies: A Guide for Policymakers* (Washington: International Monetary Fund).

Gupta, Sanjeev, Marijn Verhoeven, and Erwin Tiongson, 2001, "Public Spending on Health Care and the Poor," IMF Working Paper 01/127 (Washington: International Monetary Fund).

Gürer, Nadir, and Jan Ban, 2000, "The Economic Cost of Low Domestic Product Prices in OPEC Member Countries," *OPEC Review*, Vol. 24 (June), pp. 143–83.

Harberger, Arnold, 1964, "Taxation, Resource Allocation, and Welfare," in *The Role of Direct and Indirect Taxes in the Federal Revenue System: A Conference Report of the National Bureau of Economic Research and the Brookings Institution* (Princeton, New Jersey: Princeton University Press).

Hope, Einar, and Balbir Singh, 1995, "Energy Price Increases in Developing Countries: Case Studies of Malaysia, Indonesia, Ghana, Zimbabwe, Colombia, and Turkey," World Bank Policy Research Working Paper No. 1442 (Washington: World Bank).

Hwang, M.J., and C.W. Yang, 2001, "Unstable Price Elasticity and High World Oil Prices," paper presented at the 52nd International Atlantic Economic Conference, Philadelphia, Pennsylvania, October 11–14, 2001.

International Energy Agency, 1999, *World Energy Outlook: 1999 Insights: Looking at Energy Subsidies: Getting the Prices Right* (Paris). Available via the Internet at http://www.iea.org/statist/index.htm.

———, 2001a, *Energy Statistics of Non-OECD Countries 1997–98* (Paris).

———, 2001b, *Monthly Price Statistics, November 2001* (Paris). Available via the Internet at http://www.iea.org/statist/index.htm.

International Monetary Fund, *International Financial Statistics* (Washington, various years).

Lampietti, Julian A., and others, 2001, "Utility Pricing and the Poor: Lessons from Armenia," World Bank Technical Paper No. 497 (Washington: World Bank).

Lovei, Laszlo, and Alastair McKechnie, 2000, "The Costs of Corruption for the Poor," in *Energy and Development Report: Energy Services for the World's Poor*, ed. by Penelope J. Brooke and Suzanne Smith (Washington: World Bank Energy Sector Management Assistance Program).

Mackenzie, George A., and Peter Stella, 1996, *Quasi-Fiscal Operations of Public Financial Institutions*, IMF Occasional Paper No. 142 (Washington: International Monetary Fund).

Metschies, Gerhard P., 1999, *Fuel Prices and Taxation* (Eschborn: Deutsche Gesellschaft für Technische Zusammenarbeit).

Offerdal, Erik, and others, 2000, *Ecuador—Selected Issues and Statistical Appendix*, IMF Staff Country Report 00/125 (Washington: International Monetary Fund).

Organization of Petroleum Exporting Countries, 2001, *OPEC Annual Statistical Bulletin 2000* (Vienna).

Parry, Ian, 2001, "Are Gasoline Taxes in Britain Too High?," *Challenge*, Vol. 44 (July), pp. 67–81.

PricewaterhouseCoopers, *Corporate Taxes: Worldwide Summaries* (New York: John Wiley and Sons, various years).

"Put Your House in Order," 1998, *Economist*, February 5, U.S. Edition, Survey.

Rajkumar, Andrew Sunil, 1996, "A Study of Energy Subsidies," Environment Department Background Technical Paper (unpublished; Washington: World Bank).

Ramsey, Frank P., 1927, "A Contribution to the Theory of Taxation," *Economic Journal*, Vol. 37, No. 145 (March), pp. 47–61.

Saboohi, Y., 2001, "An Evaluation of the Impact of Reducing Energy Subsidies on Living Expenses of Households," *Energy Policy*, Vol. 29, No. 3 (February), pp. 245–52.

Schwartz, Gerd, and Benedict Clements, 1999, "Government Subsidies," *Journal of Economic Surveys*, Vol. 13, No. 2 (April), pp. 119–47.

United Nations Development Program (UNDP), World Bank, 1994, *Ecuador: Energy Pricing, Poverty and Social Mitigation*, Report No. 12831-EC (Washington).

Wakeman-Linn, John, and others, 2002, *Azerbaijan Republic: Selected Issues and Statistical Appendix*, IMF Staff Country Report 02/41 (Washington: International Monetary Fund).

White, Halbert, 1980, "A Heteroskedasticity-Consistent Covariance Matrix Estimator and a Direct Test for Heteroskedasticity," *Econometrica*, Vol. 48 (May), pp. 817–38.

World Bank, 1995, "Venezuela: Efficiency Repricing of Energy," Sector Report No. 13581 (Washington).

———, 1997, "Expanding the Measure of Wealth: Indicators of Environmentally Sustainable Development," Environmentally Sustainable Development Studies and Monograph Series, No. 17046 (Washington).

———, 2000a, "Ecuador: Crisis, Poverty and Social Services," Sector Report No. 19920 (Washington).

———, 2000b, *Maintaining Utility Services for the Poor: Policies and Practices in Central and Eastern Europe and the Former Soviet Union* (Washington).

———, 2001, *World Development Indicators* (Washington).

World Bank Energy Sector Management Assistance Program, 1994a, "Ecuador: Energy Pricing, Subsidies and Interfuel Substitution," ESMAP Report No. 11798 (Washington).

———, 1994b, "Ecuador: Energy Pricing, Poverty and Social Mitigation," ESMAP Report No. 12831 (Washington).

16

The Impact of Gasoline Price Subsidies on the Government and the National Oil Company

RAMÓN ESPINASA[1]

One aspect seldom analyzed when discussing the distributive effects of gasoline subsidies in oil-exporting countries is the distribution of subsidy losses between the government and the national oil company (NOC).[2] It is usually assumed that losses are borne by the government and have a direct fiscal effect. However, it will be shown that when part of the subsidy is absorbed as an NOC profit loss, this share of the subsidy will have only an indirect effect on government finances with a time lag, as NOC investment is reduced, affecting production and income and resulting in lower government oil revenue in later periods.

A second aspect often missed in gasoline price subsidy analyses is the role played by domestic transportation and retail sale costs. Many studies compare the netback refinery gate price of export products with the domestic retail product price at the gas station. Such an analy-

---

[1]This paper is based on my experience at Petróleos de Venezuela S.A. (PDVSA), where I worked for 20 years and was chief economist between 1992 and 1999. It also reflects the experience I gained working on other Latin American countries over the past three years at the Inter-American Development Bank. I am grateful to Annalisa Fedelino and Rolando Ossowski for their accurate and useful comments. However, the responsibility of what is said in this paper is exclusively mine.

[2]In the first part of this paper, the NOC is assumed to be a fully vertically integrated commercial oil company, with a single taxation regime for the oil industry, consisting of royalty and income tax. The government is assumed to be the NOC's sole shareholder, with access to company profits as paid-in dividends. Later in the paper, the case involving private sector participation in distribution and retail is considered.

sis misses the local transportation and retail sale costs. These costs are not negligible and ignoring them can underestimate by a sizable amount the magnitude of the retail price subsidy.

In what follows, a simple oil sector accounting model is developed to study the distributive effects of price subsidies when they are shared between the government and the NOC as well as to assess the subsidy with respect to domestic transportation and retail sale costs. For the sake of simplicity, it is assumed that a state monopoly produces, refines, and markets crude oil and products—as is the case in a number of oil-exporting developing countries.

I. Revenue

It is assumed that the country produces a quantity Q of gasoline[3] that it sells either to the international (Q_x) or domestic (Q_d) market:

$$Q = Q_x + Q_d. \tag{1}$$

It is also assumed that the country always produces at capacity (which is assumed fixed in the short run), and therefore that an increase in domestic sales is at the expense of exports. Thus,

$$\Delta Q / \Delta t = 0 \text{ and} \tag{2}$$

$$\Delta Q_d = -\Delta Q_x. \tag{3}$$

Three prices are relevant in this framework:[4] two prices at the refinery gate for sales to the international[5] (p_x) and the domestic markets (p_d) and the retail price at the pump to the local final gasoline consumer (p_r).

The retail price at the pump is assumed to be the same as the domestic price at the refinery gate,[6]

---

[3]Gasoline is assumed to be the only crude oil product manufactured and traded, given its importance as the main oil product. For the sake of simplicity, it is also assumed that all crude oil produced is transformed into gasoline, and that there are no crude oil exports.

[4]For the sake of simplicity (and without loss of generality), both the international price at the refinery gate and the domestic price are assumed to be constant through time.

[5]The country is assumed to be a price taker in the international oil products market.

[6]This assumption is consistent with the fact that the NOC is assumed to be a fully vertically integrated company, which has a monopoly on production, transformation, transportation, distribution, and retail sale of crude oil and gasoline. The assumption will be relaxed later when private participation in domestic distribution and retail sale is introduced.

$$p_r = p_d.$$ (4)

The export price at the refinery gate will be higher than the domestic market price at the refinery gate,

$$p_x > p_d.$$ (5)

The revenue forgone or implicit subsidy (s) per unit sold to the domestic market is[7]

$$s = p_x - p_d.$$ (6)

Current revenue (Y) from a quantity (Q) of oil products sold to the international and domestic markets at refinery gate prices (p_x) and (p_d) is

$$Y = p_x Q_x + p_d Q_d.$$ (7)

The revenue forgone (ΔY) due to an increase (ΔQ_d) in domestic sales at the expense of (ΔQ_x) of export sales can be derived from (7) as

$$\Delta Y = -\Delta Q_d (p_x - p_d).$$ (8)

Thus, substituting (6) into (8), the forgone public sector revenue (ΔY) at the refinery gate can be expressed as the increase in the volume of products sold to the domestic market (ΔQ_d) times the unit subsidy (s),

$$\Delta Y = -\Delta Q_d s.$$ (9)

II. Operational Costs

Assuming that export terminals are next to the refineries, the operational costs of the NOC are those that result from producing and transforming each unit of export product (c_x) and producing, transforming, distributing, and retailing each unit of gasoline to the domestic market (c_d) times the respective quantities,

$$OC = c_x Q_x + c_d Q_d.$$ (10)

The retail cost of selling a unit of product on the domestic market (c_d) will be larger than the cost of selling it at the export terminal (c_x),

$$c_d > c_x.$$ (11)

---

[7]The domestic price of gasoline at the refinery gate (p_d) may be lower than the cost of producing it. In this case, the NOC would be facing not just an implicit loss in terms of revenue forgone but a direct cash loss.

The difference will be the costs of domestic distribution and retail sale, and they will be referred to generically as retail sale costs (c_r),

$$c_r = c_d - c_x. \tag{12}$$

This point needs to be highlighted because in many studies of domestic price subsidies the netback refinery gate price of export products is compared to the domestic retail product price at the gas station or to the final consumer. This comparison misses the cost of domestic marketing and retail costs, which can be large.[8]

Substituting (12) in (10), the increase in operational costs due to shifting output from the export market to the domestic market is

$$\Delta OC = \Delta Q_d c_r. \tag{13}$$

III. Operational Surplus

The operational surplus (OS) is defined as current revenue (Y) minus operational costs (OC),

$$OS = Y - OC. \tag{14}$$

Substituting (7) and (10) in (14), the operational surplus in terms of prices and costs is

$$OS = Q_x(p_x - c_x) + Q_d(p_d - c_d). \tag{15}$$

An increase in the supply to the domestic market brings about a squeeze in the operational surplus as the operational costs increase according to (13) and revenue is forgone according to (9). The reduction in operational surplus is derived from (15) and results from adding the lower revenue and the increase in costs times the change in domestic supply,

$$\Delta OS = -\Delta Q_d(s + c_r). \tag{16}$$

IV. Government Take

The forgone public sector revenue and the increase in operational costs affect the NOC and the government according to how the NOC's operational surplus is distributed between them.

---

[8]Marketing and retail costs in the United States are between one-fourth and one-third of the final retail price. These costs can represent between 1 percent and 2 percent of GDP in developing oil-exporting countries.

The government take (GT) from the operational surplus has three components: royalty payments (R), income tax (T), and paid-in dividends (D),[9]

$$GT = R + T + D. \tag{17}$$

The government take will be affected by subsidized sales to the domestic market depending on how each of the three components varies with such sales,

$$\Delta GT = \Delta R + \Delta T + \Delta D. \tag{18}$$

Royalty

Royalty payments are calculated as a royalty rate (r) applied to total production (Q) times the international f.o.b. price[10] (p_x),

$$R = rQp_x. \tag{19}$$

As the royalty payments are independent of domestic prices or volumes, this component of government take is independent of domestic product sales.

Income Tax

Government revenue from petroleum industry income tax (T) is calculated as a tax rate (t) applied to profits, taking royalty payments as a production cost. Assuming that there are only operational costs, the taxable revenue is the operational surplus minus the royalty payments,

$$T = t(OS - R). \tag{20}$$

The change in income tax from the petroleum industry due to changes in sales to the domestic market is the tax rate times the change in operational surplus given by (16), since there is no change in royalty payments,

$$\Delta T = t\Delta OS. \tag{21}$$

---

[9]The relative importance of these components varies from country to country and depends on the legal and institutional oil sector framework.

[10]The royalty payment is often made on the basis of the wellhead international crude oil price. For the sake of simplicity, in this model the royalty is calculated on the basis of the price at the refinery gate of the exported gasoline (the only exported product; see footnote 3).

Paid-In Dividends

Net profits after tax (Π) are the operational surplus shown in (15), assuming there are only operational costs, minus the royalty payments given by (19) and the income tax payment calculated in (20),

$$\Pi = OS - R - T. \tag{22}$$

The change in net profits due to changes in domestic sales amounts to the change in operational surplus given by (13) and the change in income tax shown in (19) since there are no changes in royalty payments,

$$\Delta\Pi = \Delta OS - \Delta T. \tag{23}$$

Substituting (21) in (23),

$$\Delta\Pi = (1 - t)\Delta OS. \tag{24}$$

As the sole shareholder of the NOC, the government is entitled to a fraction (α) of the net profits as paid-in dividends (D),

$$D = \alpha\Pi. \tag{25}$$

Paid-in dividends will fluctuate with net profits,

$$\Delta D = \alpha\Delta\Pi \tag{26}$$

Substituting (23) in (26),

$$\Delta D = \alpha(1 - t)\Delta OS. \tag{27}$$

V. Change in Government Take

Once the changes in the different components of the government take due to subsidies and the cost of sales to the domestic market have been measured, the change in the overall government take can be calculated, substituting (21) and (27) in (18),

$$\Delta GT = \Delta OS(t + \alpha - \alpha t). \tag{28}$$

Substituting (16) in (28),

$$\Delta GT = -\Delta Q_d(c_r + s)(t + \alpha - \alpha t). \tag{29}$$

Thus, for a given increase in the volume supplied to the domestic market, the change in government take due to higher subsidies and retail costs will be the total reduction in operational surplus multiplied by $(t + \alpha - \alpha t)$.

It can be shown that $(t + \alpha - \alpha t)$ is always positive and less than one, since

$$0 < t < 1 \text{ and } 0 < \alpha < 1, \tag{30}$$

$$0 < t + \alpha - \alpha t < 1. \tag{31}$$

Thus, given (29) and (31), the drop in government take is a fraction of the price subsidy plus retail costs fluctuating between zero and one. The rest of the subsidy will be absorbed by the NOC as reduced retained dividends.

It can be seen from (29) that the lower the oil income tax rate (t) and the lower the share of paid-in dividends (α), the lower the drop in government take due to petroleum products price subsidies and marketing and retailing costs associated with increases in domestic sales. On the other hand, the higher the income tax rate (t) and the government's share in the NOC's profit after tax (α), the higher the pass-through of those subsidies and costs to lower government take.

VI. Change in Retained Dividends

The retained dividends (RD) are the share of profits after tax not paid to the shareholder in (25),

$$RD = (1 - \alpha)\Pi. \tag{32}$$

The change in retained dividends due to changes in profits is

$$\Delta RD = (1 - \alpha)\Delta\Pi. \tag{33}$$

Substituting (24) in (33) it is possible to measure the change in retained dividends due to a reduction in operational surplus because of product price subsidies and retail sale costs, given an oil income tax rate (t) and a share (α) of paid-in dividends,

$$\Delta RD = \Delta OS(1 - t - \alpha + \alpha t). \tag{34}$$

Substituting (16) into (34),

$$\Delta RD = -\Delta Q_d(c_r + s)(1 - t - \alpha + \alpha t). \tag{35}$$

(ΔRD) will always be positive and a fraction $(1 - t - \alpha + \alpha t)$ of (ΔOS) since, given (31),

$$-1 < -t - \alpha + \alpha t < 0. \tag{36}$$

Table 16.1. *Distribution of Losses Between Government and NOC*[1]
(In percent)

	Oil Industry Fiscal Regime			
	I	II	III	IV
Fiscal regime				
Royalty rate (r)	30	30	17	—
Income tax rate (t)	34	50	67	80
Government share of net profits (α)	—	10	10	—
Breakdown of losses				
Government share	34	55	71	80
NOC share	66	45	29	20

Source: Author's calculations.
[1]Assumes a fully vertically integrated NOC.

From (36) it is clear that the lower the oil income tax rate (t) and the government's share in profits after tax (α), the higher will be the share of domestic product price subsidies and marketing costs ((Q_d ($c_r + s$)) absorbed by the NOC in the form of lower retained dividends.

VII. Breakdown of Losses Between the Government and the NOC

For a given oil industry tax regime, the breakdown of losses between the government and the NOC due to price subsidies and retail costs can be calculated. For illustrative purposes, Table 16.1 shows four hypothetical fiscal regimes, ranging from a combination of high royalty and low income tax rate to a regime with a high income tax rate and no royalty.

It can be seen that, since the royalty payment is independent of profits (losses) while the income tax is calculated on profits, under scheme I (high royalty and low income tax rate), the NOC bears the bulk of losses. Conversely, under scheme IV (high income tax rate and no royalty), the government absorbs the higher share of the losses.

In addition, it should be noted that retained dividends are likely to be the main source of financing for NOC fixed capital formation. Therefore, an increase in product subsidies and marketing costs would, through lower NOC investment, result in lower future production and revenue, thereby affecting government revenue in the medium term. How and when lower NOC investment will affect government revenue will depend on the magnitude of the losses and the characteristics of investment. The greater the share of investment devoted to the maintenance of productive capacity, the more immediate will be the effect on production, exports, and fiscal revenue from lower investment associated with reductions in retained dividends.

VIII. Private Retail and Excise Taxes

In countries with a state monopoly on crude oil production and refining, the domestic distribution and retail sale of gasoline may be carried out by private companies. In addition, excise taxes are often levied on domestic gasoline sales as a source of government revenue. These two cases will be discussed briefly below.

In some cases, private companies are allowed to buy gasoline from the NOC at the domestic refinery gate price (p_d) and sell it at a retail sale price (p_r), with both prices controlled by the government. The retail price will be higher than the domestic refinery gate price, thus relaxing the assumption in (4) and replacing it with

$$p_r > p_d. \tag{37}$$

The revenue of the private companies per unit of gasoline sold in the domestic market (y_r) is equal to the price differential,

$$y_r = p_r - p_d, \tag{38}$$

and their profit margin per unit (π_r), given unit distribution and retail costs (c_r), is

$$\pi_r = y_r - c_r. \tag{39}$$

From (39) it can be seen that the private companies' profit margin will depend on government policy regarding the price differential and on the private companies' productivity and ability to reduce distribution and retail costs. In particular, assuming costs increase due to inflation, the profit margin may be squeezed unless the government lowers the refinery gate price or increases the retail price.

In some instances, the government may introduce an excise tax on petroleum products. If the NOC acts as the collection agency, the new tax (T_g) will be added to the domestic price at the refinery gate (p_d), yielding a final retail price to the consumer (p_r) equal to

$$p_r = p_d + T_g + y_r. \tag{40}$$

Assuming the domestic price at the refinery gate is left unchanged, the private distributors and retailers would be squeezed if an excise tax were introduced and the retail price not fully adjusted.

IX. Conclusions

A few conclusions can be drawn from the simple accounting model presented in the previous sections. First, the fiscal regime applied to the NOC can have a significant bearing on how the subsidies on domestic gasoline sales affect government revenue. Oil tax systems with higher royalty rates and lower income tax rates make the NOC bear the bulk of the subsidy cost in the form of lower retained dividends. In turn, lower NOC investment as a consequence of reduced financial resources will affect government revenue with a lag.

Second, domestic marketing and retail sale costs—usually not accounted for when assessing gasoline price subsidies—can make these subsidies substantially larger than often recognized.

Third, in the case of a mix of government monopoly up to the refining stage and private distributors and retail sellers, if both the refinery gate and retail sale prices are controlled, the profit margins of the private companies will be squeezed if higher costs are not accompanied by price adjustments. Profit margins would also be squeezed if the refinery gate price for sales to the domestic market were increased without a corresponding increase in the retail price.

Finally, the introduction of an excise tax on refined oil products can generate fast cash for the government; however, as long as the domestic price at the refinery gate is not changed, it does not change the NOC subsidy to domestic petroleum product consumption. Furthermore, a fully vertically integrated NOC or the private companies distributing and selling gasoline could see their margins squeezed if an excise tax is introduced and the retail price is not fully adjusted.

17

Domestic Petroleum Price Smoothing in Developing and Transition Countries

---

Giulio Federico, James A. Daniel, and Benedict Bingham[1]

I. Introduction

This paper examines the case for smoothing retail petroleum prices in the face of volatile international oil prices in developing countries where petroleum prices are regulated by the government. This is an important policy question in many developing countries, given the high volatility of international oil prices, the potentially significant fiscal exposure of many governments to petroleum price changes, and the high political profile of petroleum prices.

In a competitive market economy the case for full and automatic pass-through of international price changes to domestic retail prices is strong, on both economic and institutional grounds.

Full pass-through allows for a correct price signal, which enhances efficiency and does not expose the government to undue fiscal volatility as a result of variable oil prices. However, most of the developing country governments that regulate petroleum prices do not implement automatic and full pass-through mechanisms when setting these prices. A survey of selected developing countries conducted for this paper reveals that most adopt a discretionary approach to changes in

---

[1]This is a revised and shortened version of "Domestic Petroleum Price Smoothing in Developing and Transition Countries," by Giulio Federico, James A. Daniel, and Benedict Bingham (2001).

petroleum retail prices, which commonly fails to pass through changes in international prices on a consistent basis. This suggests that, at least from a political economy perspective, full-cost pass-through is not a robust policy reform.

This paper seeks to explore whether, and under what conditions, petroleum pricing mechanisms—which provide a degree of insulation to the private sector from international oil price volatility—can offer welfare-enhancing and potentially more politically sustainable alternatives to full-cost pass-through mechanisms. The paper approaches this issue by first considering the consumer-welfare implications of volatile oil prices. It concludes that retail petroleum price volatility is likely to have a negative welfare impact on consumers, and that while the private sector in developing countries is probably able to manage routine variations in oil prices, there may be scope for efficient government intervention to insulate the private sector from sharp shifts in oil prices.

The paper then explores the case for government-managed retail price smoothing. We first consider a number of potential pricing rules that diverge from full pass-through and provide a degree of price smoothing. The price properties associated with these rules and the fiscal implications of implementing such rules for the government are assessed on the basis of historical oil prices. The paper concludes that there appears to be a sharp trade-off between retail price insurance and government fiscal stability in the face of volatile prices, and that most pricing rules leave the government overexposed to oil price risk, especially given the institutional difficulties associated with volatile fiscal revenues.

The paper also briefly considers possible hedging strategies for a government wishing to smooth domestic petroleum prices. This has the advantage relative to pricing mechanisms based on spot prices of relying directly on market-based mechanisms for price insurance. As such, it appears potentially able to deliver significant price smoothing with relatively limited fiscal exposure.

The paper concludes that full pass-through of international price changes may be suboptimal, especially in the face of large shocks. However, governments in developing countries are not well equipped to deal with the significant fiscal risk associated with price-smoothing activities. They should, therefore, introduce relatively limited partial pass-through mechanisms (e.g., short moving averages of past prices) or rely on market-based insurance mechanisms to reduce oil price risk.

II. Current Practice of Petroleum Pricing in Developing Countries

The level of petroleum product retail prices is an important economic variable for both the public and the private sectors in many developing countries, and decisions on the degree of pass-through of changes in international oil prices have significant economic impact on one or both of the sectors.

Domestic taxation of petroleum products is a large source of revenue for many developing countries: it generally accounts for about 7–30 percent of overall revenue, which corresponds to 1–3½ percent of GDP. This is achieved by relatively heavy taxation of petroleum products, which varies by region and petroleum product, reflecting oil availability and distributional and efficiency considerations.

Many developing countries are also significantly exposed to oil prices at a macroeconomic level. This can be illustrated by considering the net oil balance as a percentage of GDP for oil-importing countries. For a sample of 42 net oil-importing developing countries, most countries' exposure to oil price changes in 1999[2] was on the order of 1–4 percent of GDP.

The substantial economic impact of changes of both international and retail petroleum prices and of taxes on petroleum products implies that the adjustment of domestic prices to international oil prices is an important economic and political issue in many developing countries. If adjustment is complete (full pass-through) the government is relatively insulated from a fiscal point of view,[3] and the private sector bears the volatility in real income. If adjustment is partial, the government would bear some volatility. This trade-off between private and public income volatility poses a difficult policy question because of the high volatility of crude oil prices.[4]

In spite of often substantial policy focus on the issue, reforms of domestic petroleum pricing mechanisms toward systems of automatic and full pass-through have been slow, and frequently reversed in recent years. This can be seen from the survey of current country prac-

---

[2]The average crude oil price in 1999 was US$18.1 a barrel, close to the nominal average for the period 1987–2000. Exposure to oil is defined as the ratio of net oil exports to GDP.

[3]The nature of oil taxes (specific versus ad valorem) and the price elasticity of demand have a bearing on the degree of insulation. Fiscal stability is enhanced with specific taxation of oil products and low elasticities of demand.

[4]See Wickham (1996), and Barnett and Vivanco, Chapter 5 in this volume, for a detailed discussion of the volatility of oil prices.

Table 17.1. *Summary of Country Practices on Petroleum Pricing*

Area	Surveyed	Oil Importers	Regulate Retail Petroleum Prices	Have an Automatic Pass-Through Mechanism	Have Full Pass-Through	Have a Stabilization Fund
Africa	11	10	8	3	2	1
Asia-Pacific	7	5	4	1	1	1
Europe	7	5	3	0	0	2
Middle East	11	6	11	4	3	1
Western Hemisphere	9	5	7	3	2	3
Total	45	31	33	11	8	8
Percentage of total	100	69	73	24	18	18
Percentage of countries with regulated prices			100	33	24	24

Source: Authors.

tices on petroleum pricing, which shows that most of the 45 transition and developing countries in the selected sample[5] appear to both regulate petroleum pricing and use some form of partial and discretionary pass-through mechanism.

The findings of the survey are summarized in Table 17.1, which reveals three key stylized facts about current petroleum pricing policies in selected developing countries:

- *A significant majority of the countries surveyed regulate petroleum prices* (either at the retail or ex-refinery level). Even those governments that have deregulated prices exert pressure on oil companies to moderate their price increases (e.g., as in Thailand and the Philippines during the international price hike of 2000) and still play a role in the price-setting process.

- *Only a minority of countries have an automatic mechanism* for adjusting retail prices to changes in international prices. Of these, the majority currently operate a full pass-through mechanism, even though a number of these mechanisms stopped being implemented in the course of 2000, due to the pressure of high international prices.

---

[5]The countries surveyed were (Africa) Côte d'Ivoire, Guinea, Kenya, Mozambique, Nigeria, Senegal, South Africa, Tanzania, Togo, Uganda, and Zambia; (Asia-Pacific) China, Korea, Mongolia, Philippines, Papua New Guinea, Thailand, and Vietnam; (Europe) Armenia, Azerbaijan, Georgia, Kyrgyz Republic, Moldova, Russia, and Ukraine; (Middle East) Algeria, Egypt, Iran, Jordan, Mauritania, Morocco, Pakistan, Sudan, Tunisia, Turkey, and Yemen; and (Western Hemisphere) Argentina, Bolivia, Brazil, Chile, Colombia, Costa Rica, Mexico, Peru, and Venezuela.

- *Approximately one-quarter of countries that regulate prices run specific stabilization funds* to manage the price-smoothing process. Some countries have recently abolished their funds because of their fiscal implications.

III. Oil Price Volatility and Its Welfare Implications for Consumers

The economic literature on the welfare implications of price volatility shows that there exist three main drivers of cost and benefits to consumers from price instability: (i) arbitrage and substitution possibilities; (ii) risk aversion; and (iii) adjustment costs.

Arbitrage and Substitution

If consumers are able to vary the level of consumption of a good characterized by unstable prices, substituting away from it in high-price periods and consuming more in low-price periods, they may actually benefit from exogenous price instability. This insight is originally due to Waugh (1944), and has subsequently been generalized by others (e.g., Massell, 1969).

Risk Aversion

Risk-averse consumers may prefer stable to unstable prices, given that the marginal utility they gain from high-consumption periods (e.g., periods characterized by low petroleum prices) is lower than marginal utility from low-consumption periods (Newbery and Stiglitz, 1981). This effect works against the substitution effect highlighted above. Turnovsky, Shalit, and Schmitz (1980) examine the nature of this trade-off, combining risk aversion with the "Waugh" effect to show that with a high-income share of the good in question, high coefficients of risk aversion, and low elasticities (both income and price elasticity), consumers prefer price stability and reductions in price volatility.[6] As

---

[6]Turnovsky, Shalit, and Schmitz (1980) show that the sign of the benefit (loss) from price stability has the same sign as the following expression: $s(R - \eta)+e$, where s is the budget share of the good in question, R is the coefficient of relative risk aversion, η is the income elasticity of demand, and e is the price elasticity of demand (which is negative).

pointed out by Gilbert (1993), these conditions may yield an ambiguous answer as to whether petroleum price stability is desirable: the demand for petroleum products is relatively price-inelastic, and expenditure shares on petroleum tend to be high (both of which point to benefits from price stability) but income elasticities are also high, which suggests price instability may be welfare-improving.

Adjustment Costs

Consumers of petroleum products (both households and firms) may face costs of adjusting their economic activities (consumption and/or production) in the face of volatile petroleum prices.[7] This would cause them to prefer stable prices, which do not lead to volatile real incomes (for households) and costs (for firms) and which, therefore, do not require adjustment.

Moreover, depending on the nature of these adjustment costs, consumers will also prefer some unstable price profiles to others. For instance, if adjustment costs are convex (i.e., they display increasing marginal costs), they would prefer gradual price changes to sudden price changes.[8] If adjustment costs are mainly fixed, consumers will tend to react only to large and persistent price changes (adopting (S,s) types of rules[9]).

For both types of adjustment technology (convex and concave), the costs of adjusting may often be effectively sunk (i.e., they cannot be recovered once they have been incurred), which induces "wait and see" behavior by consumers, arising from the option value of deferring adjustment with a volatile price.[10]

---

[7]The precise nature of this effect is likely to differ between households and firms. Households may face costs in changing consumption bundles and in adapting to a new level of income. These may take place due to "learning-by-doing" effects and suboptimal changes in expenditure patterns when disposable income changes rapidly (e.g., expenditure cutting when income falls may hit items that are the easiest, rather than most appropriate, to cut). Firms, on the other hand, may face adjustment costs in the form of the investment required to adapt their production technology to the level of oil prices.

[8]This implies that, if they can, they will only partially adjust when hit by a price shock (see Nickell, 1985).

[9](S,s) rules describe behavior by which adjustment takes place when the underlying variable that determines the optimality of adjustment is below a given "floor" level (s) or above a "ceiling" level (S).

[10]See, for instance, Dixit (1992).

Optimal Consumption Behavior with Volatile Oil Prices

This brief review of welfare effects shows that consumers' preference for price stability relies crucially on the presence of risk aversion and/or adjustment costs. The high impact of consumption of petroleum products on households' and firms' budgets, the relatively low price elasticity of demand for these products, and the likely presence of both risk aversion and adjustment costs all seem to suggest that consumers would prefer to have stable petroleum prices.

In a regime of full spot-price pass-through with volatile oil prices, agents can, therefore, be expected to attempt to engage in risk-coping activities and to try to attain an optimal consumption path.[11] This, in turn, will depend on the nature of the price shocks they face, their attitude to risk, and their adjustment technology.

If a price shock is known to be *temporary*, risk-averse consumers and/or consumers with any kind of adjustment costs will try to *stabilize* consumption and consume at the permanent level of disposable income. Dissavings would, therefore, occur in low-income/high-oil-price periods, and savings would be made in high-income/low-oil-price periods.

If a shock is known to be *permanent* (or very long-lasting), optimal consumption behavior will vary with the characteristics of the consumer:

- A risk-averse consumer with no adjustment costs will adjust to it fully and immediately.
- A consumer with convex adjustment costs will adjust to it gradually, smoothing the path of consumption or investment (i.e., behaving as if the price path is smoother than it actually is).
- A consumer with fixed adjustment costs would fully adjust if the shock is large enough and not adjust if it is small, following an (S,s) type of rule.

Hence, given the nature of oil prices, consumers may wish to engage in partial or delayed adjustment behavior and attempt to prevent excessive volatility in consumption due to variable oil prices. This kind of consumption behavior needs to be managed and financed by consumers. For instance, if the oil price increases, a consumer attempting to smooth out consumption will have to increase overall expenditure

---

[11]For simplicity, we refer here only to households that consume petroleum products and to consumption-stabilization or smoothing activities. Similar arguments would apply to firms.

and will require additional funds to do so. Three options for the management of the consequences of oil price instability are available:

- *Credit markets.* Consumers can potentially use credit markets to smooth the path of consumption in the face of volatile oil prices and spread adjustment over time. That is, when prices rise sharply, agents could borrow to finance a gradual adjustment (in the case of convex costs) or no adjustment (in the case of concave costs and insufficiently large price changes) and gradually repay the debt. Conversely, if prices fall, agents could save, or repay old debts. Using credit markets may be an effective option to smooth consumption, but it is likely to be of limited availability, especially in developing countries.
- *Self-insurance.* Self-insurance can finance sluggish or impartial adjustment of consumption to current oil prices as an alternative to credit markets. Agents can self-insure by accumulating precautionary savings to draw down in times of "high" (or rising) prices and pay into when prices are "low" (or falling). This option essentially corresponds to the creation of a private stabilization fund and implements an optimal spending-and-saving rule (as derived, for instance, by Hausmann, Powell, and Rigobon, 1993) in the face of price volatility and adjustment costs. For self-insurance to occur it is important, however, that private agents be in a position to accumulate assets that are sufficiently remunerative and liquid. This implies that they need an appropriate macroeconomic environment where the value of liquid assets is not eroded by inflation and where they have access to adequate saving instruments. In many developing countries, the self-insurance option may, therefore, also be limited (Fafchamps, 1999).
- *Hedging.* A direct instrument for the management of oil price risk by consumers is provided by hedging markets. These markets provide contracting tools (such as futures and call options) buyers can use to lock in prices and insure against short-run fluctuations. The main limitation of the use of hedging instruments in developing countries for private-consumption-smoothing purposes is access. Small consumers do not have access to financial instruments, given the high transaction costs and the absence of intermediation in most developing countries. Private sector corporations may have better access to these instruments, even if this may still be limited by considerations of default risk and creditworthiness. Hedging instruments may, therefore, represent a "missing market" for many consumers in developing countries.

However, market-failure considerations may affect all three options for managing oil price risk, and therefore consumers may find it hard to finance, and thus implement, otherwise optimal risk-coping behavior.

IV. The Scope for Government Smoothing of Retail Petroleum Prices

It is useful to start the analysis of the case for government-managed petroleum price smoothing by reviewing the standard case for the full and immediate pass-through of changes in international prices.[12] This is based on two key considerations:

Efficient pricing. If the government engages in price-smoothing activities and only partially adjusts domestic oil prices to reflect international spot prices, it creates a wedge between consumer prices and the opportunity cost of oil. This entails a basic efficiency cost, that is, a *distorted price signal*, which creates a deadweight loss. Given the low price elasticity of demand for petroleum products, this loss may be relatively small. It may, however, be magnified by hoarding and smuggling activities[13] and should, therefore, not be underestimated.

Institutional considerations.[14] A full pass-through rule in the context of petroleum price regulation has a number of appealing institutional properties, such as its transparency and fiscal insulation properties.[15] Full pass-through minimizes both the government's exposure to fiscal

---

[12]Throughout this section, we assume that the government regulates the price level of petroleum products, which is the norm in developing countries. We briefly touch upon the issue of price deregulation and its potential role in allowing for retail price smoothing later in this chapter.

[13]The former may result if consumers expect that the government will eventually pass through a price increase. The latter may occur if price smoothing creates a price difference between petroleum products across neighboring countries, which consumers try to arbitrage. This would have the effect of increasing demand in the country that implements a partial pass-through rule when international prices rise and depressing demand when they fall.

[14]For a fuller discussion of the political considerations of price subsidy reform and the economics of price subsidy reform more generally, see Gupta and others (2000), and Gupta and others, Chapter 15 in this volume.

[15]We are assuming here, and throughout the rest of this section, that governments levy specific (rather than ad valorem) excises on petroleum products, which implies that the revenues from these excises are largely independent of the oil price (with an assumption of inelastic demand).

risk due to oil price variability and the risk of political interference in the price determination process, avoiding for instance the emergence of hidden price subsidies when prices rise or "stealth" taxes when prices fall.

Any case for government-run smoothing needs to address these positive efficiency and institutional properties associated with full pass-through and demonstrate compensating benefits deriving from partial pass-through. These benefits could result from a market failure deriving from the absence of some consumer risk-management instruments in developing countries, which does not allow private agents to smooth their consumption path adequately. Governments may, therefore, have a role in providing a profile of retail prices that allows consumers to smooth consumption more effectively than in a full pass-through environment and that avoids unnecessary fluctuations.

A second argument against a full pass-through rule based on spot prices is that this may be politically difficult in many countries and, therefore, unstable. Petroleum price rises are very visible government interventions and tend to attract considerable attention. There may, therefore, be "political adjustment costs," which justify price smoothing. This is particularly so at times of sharply rising international prices, when full pass-through rules can break down and degenerate into ad hoc price adjustments by the government. Such situations took place during the course of 2000 in a number of countries (e.g., Bolivia and Costa Rica).

Indeed, of the countries in our survey that regulate retail petroleum prices, only 24 percent adopt full pass-through rules for adjusting retail prices in response to changes in international prices. Alternative partial pass-through rules may prove to be more sustainable than full pass-through of spot price changes and may, therefore, deserve consideration on "political-economy" grounds, even if they may be second best to full pass-through rules in terms of economic efficiency.

The Scope for Partial Pass-Through of Spot Prices

Governments can smooth the profile of retail petroleum prices by only partially passing through changes in the international oil price. Governments that smooth retail petroleum prices can adopt a discretionary or rules-based mechanism. The survey results presented in Section II indicate that discretionary price adjustments are the dominant mechanism through which governments adjust petroleum prices.

The theoretical advantage of a discretionary approach to price smoothing is that it allows governments to decide when and how much to adjust domestic petroleum prices, without being constrained by a price formula. This gives governments the flexibility to determine the optimal path of retail prices as a function of general market conditions, which may not be fully reflected in the level of spot prices. For instance, if the government is faced with a price spike in the spot market, it can use its discretion to assess whether it should be seen as permanent (or, at least, long-lasting), and thus initiate adjustment in the retail price, or temporary and, therefore, not requiring retail price adjustment.

In practice, however, governments will find it hard to make these kinds of judgments, thus undermining the benefits that may derive from the discretionary approach. There is also a risk with discretionary price smoothing that it will be used for political purposes and prevent desirable adjustment to retail prices, both when international prices rise (to avoid the political cost associated with high domestic petroleum prices) and when they fall (to allow the government to accumulate additional fiscal resources). As a result, governments implementing discretionary price adjustments may tend to adjust prices rarely and, when they are forced to do so, by large amounts (e.g., as was the case in the Philippines during the operation of the now-terminated Oil Stabilization Fund). This is likely to be particularly harmful to consumers, by effectively magnifying both price shocks and price uncertainty.

Automatic price adjustment mechanisms are based on formulas that determine the level of the retail price at regular intervals, on the basis of international prices. The advantage of this approach is that it minimizes political interference in the price-setting process and can shield it from political pressures for low petroleum prices, which at times of rising international prices may have large fiscal implications. On these grounds, price adjustment rules seem superior to a discretionary approach. However, the distinction between the two can become blurred, and automatic mechanisms can collapse into a discretionary approach if they are not always implemented. To avoid this, rules need to be politically robust and, in particular, avoid sharp upward price adjustments when possible.

Partial pass-through rules

Governments can implement three types of partial pass-through rules to allow for domestic price smoothing:

- *moving average rules*, which base retail prices on a moving average of past spot prices;
- *trigger rules*, by which prices are updated only if spot prices change by more than a predetermined trigger amount; and
- *max-min rules*, which place a ceiling and a floor on the level of retail petroleum prices.

This paper's assessment of these rules is based on simulations of their impact on retail prices and on the government's fiscal position. Specifically, partial pass-through rules should

- complement rather than substitute for feasible private sector adjustment; and
- strike a balance between retail price variability and fiscal risk.

The first criterion implies that pass-through rules should be designed with the main purpose of helping consumers implement their optimal partial (or delayed) adjustment behavior. This means that partial pass-through rules should try to smooth large and sharp price shocks and not necessarily prevent small price shocks, against which consumers should be able to self-insure under most circumstances. By doing so, partial pass-through rules can reduce the negative impact of price volatility for both risk-averse consumers and consumers with adjustment costs and, therefore, enhance efficiency. This will also add to the political robustness of a partial pass-through rule, reducing the occurrence of large discrete price changes and potentially preventing the collapse of the price rule at times of rising prices.

Optimal partial pass-through behavior, however, also implies that the rules should not prevent adjustment to permanent (or persistent) price changes, which need to be passed through to allow consumers to adjust to them. Therefore, any subsidy paid out via the rule at times of high prices needs to be phased out gradually, if the high-price situation persists.

To capture the importance of price shocks for consumer welfare, the paper focuses on the short-run changes[16] of the price series simulated with the different partial pass-through rules, measuring both their overall volatility and the frequency of large price jumps relative to a full pass-through rule. This implicitly recognizes that sudden price changes are more costly to consumers than slow and persistent changes (which consumers can gradually adapt to) and should, there-

---

[16]We capture this by examining the first difference of the log of the monthly series.

fore, be the focus of attention when designing a partial pass-through rule.

The second design criterion recognizes that any price risk from which the pass-through rule shields consumers needs to be borne by the government. As discussed above, this in turn has fiscal implications and can lead to persistent surpluses or deficits associated with the pass-through mechanism. The simulations produce a measure of the magnitude of both the year-on-year fiscal shocks and the cumulative fiscal implications of the partial pass-through rules. These shocks are scaled in percentage of GDP for the typical net oil importer in the sample, based on the 1999 average ratio of net oil balance to GDP (i.e., approximately 3 percent of GDP).

The simulations carried out are based on spot crude prices for the January 1987–June 2000. The price properties and fiscal impact reported for each rule, therefore, abstract from the fact that countries may be importing petroleum products (whose price may be imperfectly correlated with the crude price).[17] This is, however, not unduly restrictive given that crude and petroleum product prices tend to move in line with each other except for short-term changes (which may reflect changes in capacity margins in the refinery industry and seasonal demand effects).

It should also be noted that by basing simulations on historical prices, the paper does not claim to be measuring structural properties of the partial pass-through rules. These simulations serve mainly as an illustration of the kind of retail price smoothing and fiscal risk partial pass-through rules can be expected to yield.

Moving average rules

Under a moving average rule, current retail prices are based on a moving average of past spot prices, starting from the current month and moving backwards. The longer the time horizon of the moving average, the more price smoothing this rule achieves.

The theoretical attractiveness of these price rules is that they "follow the market" and do not impose exogenous targets for the level of retail prices, which may prove to be inappropriate in the face of large and

---

[17]They also abstract from the presence of fixed margins in the final retail price, which reduce its variability relative to crude prices. It is, however, straightforward to gross up the price variability measures we report into retail price variability figures by making assumptions on the size of the various fixed margins in the value chain.

persistent shocks. Moving average rules with long enough time horizons can, therefore, provide substantial price smoothing, shielding consumers from transitory price spikes while gradually passing through persistent price changes. These rules, however, do not discriminate between large and small price shocks and do not directly seek to complement private sector self-insurance by focusing on the large shocks.

Simulations show that these rules can achieve substantial price smoothing, both in terms of reduction of the standard deviation of shocks and the frequency of large shocks. The effectiveness of price smoothing rises substantially with the length of the moving average, but even the three-month moving average can achieve a 30 percent reduction in standard deviation and a reduction by more than half in the frequency of monthly shocks in excess of 10 percent, relative to spot prices.

The substantial price smoothing the rules can achieve comes with a significant fiscal risk. For instance, the 12-month moving average leads to large fiscal shocks (on average 0.3 percent of GDP per year, for a typical oil importer) and can also bring about large cumulative deficits (0.6 percent of GDP by 2000, assuming the rule started in 1987). Shorter rules are less risky—the three-month moving average is associated with average shocks of less than 0.1 percent of GDP, and its cumulative impact broadly ranges between +/–0.1 percent of GDP.

Trigger or (S,s) rules

Under trigger rules, a price band is initially determined (e.g., plus or minus 10 percent of the current spot prices), and retail prices are updated to reflect the current spot price only when spot prices reach a level outside the band. When prices are changed, the price band shifts up or down, taking the current spot price as the new central point of the band.

The effect of this pricing rule is to avoid minor fluctuation in retail prices but pass through relatively large changes in international prices. This rule is, therefore, effective in shielding governments from having to bear large price shocks, but by doing so it exposes the private sector to these shocks. This would be optimal in the presence of fixed adjustment costs, but as argued in Section II, consumers with this type of adjustment costs should be able to autonomously implement their optimal adjustment behavior by self-insuring against small shocks. Trigger rules, therefore, do not appear to complement consumers' risk-coping measures and can only be justified on grounds that do not relate to price smoothing.[18]

Simulation results show that trigger rules are not effective at providing price smoothing. They actually increase the size and frequency of large price shocks and, in the case of the +/–30 percent trigger, they can increase the overall standard deviation too. This is matched by an overall beneficial fiscal risk profile, but also by large fiscal shocks. Implementing a trigger rule can actually lead to substantial fiscal receipts (as in the case of the +/–30 percent rule). This effect arises from the fact that oil prices are characterized by frequent small price decreases (which are not passed through under this rule and, therefore, lead to fiscal revenue) and less frequent, but large, price increases (which under a trigger rule are passed through).[19]

Given the poor (or even negative) contribution to retail price smoothing of trigger rules, the main justification for adopting this kind of rule (as opposed to a full pass-through rule) is that it minimizes the transaction costs of continuously updating domestic prices to reflect international spot prices, while insulating governments from excessive oil-related risk. It, therefore, can represent a convenient way of effectively implementing a full pass-through rule (as long as the width of the price band is not too large).

Both Costa Rica and Bolivia implemented trigger rules recently. Costa Rica has had a +/–5 percent trigger rule since 1990, although it has not always been consistently applied. Bolivia also adopted a +/–5 percent trigger mechanism, but it was suspended in July 2000, when retail fuel prices were temporarily frozen for a period of one year.

Max-min rules

Max-min rules specify a price band around a central price, which defines the maximum and minimum level retail prices can reach. If the cost-plus level of retail price is above the band's ceiling, the government absorbs the difference between the two prices by paying out a

---

[18]Moreover, by reducing the frequency of price adjustments and increasing their magnitude, trigger rules may be politically fragile and more likely to be violated than rules that allow for continuous adjustment.

[19]This is consistent with the findings of Deaton (1992) for non-oil commodities. This effect arises from the asymmetry in storage opportunities, resulting from the fact that negative storage is not possible, so that the constraint on large price increases is weaker than on large price falls. Cashin, McDermott, and Scott (2002) find a similar effect for oil.

subsidy. If the cost-plus retail price is below the minimum price set by the band, the government taxes away the difference and sets retail prices at the minimum level.

This price rule achieves directly the aim of complementing consumers' risk-coping activities, shielding them from large price shocks and passing through small shocks. It does not, however, automatically pass through large price changes if these are persistent and, therefore, require adjustment. For this to occur, and to avoid excessive fiscal risk to the government, a max-min rule needs to be complemented by a mechanism that updates the position of the max-min band or scales down the additional subsidy (tax) determined by the rule if the cumulative loss (gain) exceeds a given level. Chile recently adopted both of these measures (see Box 17.1) as part of the reform of the mechanism in place since 1991.

This paper simulates three kinds of max-min rules, all broadly based on the Chilean mechanism. These rules have a width of 12½ percent relative to the central price (like the Chilean rule); two of these have a fixed central price (at US$18.50 and US$20 a barrel, respectively), while one has a moving band, which is updated in accordance with the recent updating formula adopted by the Chilean energy regulator.[20]

The simulations show that fixed band rules are more effective than moving band rules in mitigating price volatility and reducing the impact of large price shocks. This is because the fixed bands, unlike the moving average band, do not move with current prices, which dilutes their shock-absorption properties.

The beneficial price-smoothing effects of fixed band rules are, however, reflected in the higher fiscal risk profile they generate. Both the US$18.50- and US$20-a-barrel rules lead to large absolute fiscal shocks. They differ radically, however, in their cumulative effect, with the US$20-a-barrel rule leading to a substantial surplus over the 1987–2000 period and the US$18.50-a-barrel rule leading to a deficit. This highlights the main weakness of a fixed band approach, that is, the need to estimate an expected level for prices (to set the central level of the band), which may prove to be inappropriate and lead to excess fiscal revenues or losses from price smoothing. The "Chilean"

---

[20]The current Chilean formula updates the max-min price band according to historical prices, short-term projections, and long-term forecasts. For the purposes of our simulation, we have assumed that the short-term projection component of the price band formula is equal to the current spot price and that the long-term forecast is US$20 a barrel.

Box 17.1. *Chile's Price Stabilization Mechanism*

Chile has operated a domestic petroleum price stabilization mechanism since January 1991 and has recently reformed it.[1] The original mechanism was based on a max-min price rule implemented by a Stabilization Fund initially capitalized with US$200 million. Under this mechanism, maximum and minimum prices for each petroleum product were set at +/–12½ percent of a reference price set by the energy authority on a discretionary basis to reflect medium- and long-term market trends. The max-min rule operated asymmetrically: if the (spot) import price was above the ceiling of the band, the fund would pay out a subsidy equal to the difference between the two prices; however, if the import price was below the floor of the band, 60 percent of the difference would be taxed away and deposited into the Fund.

Until mid-1999 this stabilization mechanism worked relatively effectively. The Fund accumulated resources, as import prices were more frequently below the price band than above it. However, the high prices of the second half of 1999 and 2000 led to financial problems for the Fund,[2] requiring a total additional injection of US$263 million (paid into the Fund in January and July 2000). The difficulties experienced by the Fund prompted a revision of the rules of the stabilization mechanism, which was passed into law in July 2000.

According to the new Price Stabilization Law, the reference prices that determine the position of the band for each petroleum product are updated weekly, on the basis of a formula that includes historical prices (a weighted average of prices from the past two years), short-term forecasts, and long-term forecasts. The asymmetry in the operation of the price band has been eliminated (so that 100 percent of the difference between the floor of the band and import price is now taxed away), and a contingent tax subsidy rule has been introduced. According to this rule, prices can rise (fall) above (below) the ceiling (floor) of the price band to prevent excessive depletion (accumulation) of the resources of the Fund. This ensures that the Fund never runs out of resources (i.e., as the Fund's resources converge to zero the subsidy paid out to consumers also converges to zero) and never accumulates more than a set maximum amount.

---

[1] The mechanism includes five petroleum products: gasoline, diesel, LPG, heating oil, and kerosene.

[2] This was exacerbated by the fact that in 1999 the reference prices for the max-min band were lowered (in spite of rising import prices) to avoid an increase in domestic prices.

---

moving band max-min rule, by contrast, led to substantially smaller fiscal shocks and a limited cumulative impact over the 1987–2000 period.

Table 17.2. *Summary of Properties of Partial Pass-Through Rules*

	Price-Smoothing Properties		Simulation Results	
			Reduction in standard deviation[1]	Average annual fiscal shock (In percent of GDP)[2]
	Temporary shocks	Persistent shocks		
Moving average	Smooths out all shocks	Full pass-through (with a lag)	30 to 70 percent	0.07 to 0.3 percent
Trigger	Smooths out only small shocks	Full pass-through (if large enough)	2 to 8 percent	0.05 to 0.26 percent
Max-min	Smooths out only large shocks	No pass-through (unless there is an updating rule)	27 to 45 percent	0.08 to 0.17 percent

Source: Authors' calculations.
[1]Relative to spot prices, based on first difference of the logs of the monthly price series, January 1987 to June 2000.
[2]Based on a 1999 typical oil importer.

Summary of assessment of partial pass-through rules

The main differences, summarized in Table 17.2, among the three types of rules are
- max-min rules are more effective at complementing private sector risk coping than both trigger rules (which do not provide price smoothing when the private sector is most likely to need it) and moving average rules (which smooth out all shocks);
- max-min rules need to be complemented by an updating rule for the position of the max-min price band to ensure that persistent shocks are passed through to the private sector; and
- the trade-off between retail price insurance and fiscal risk, as measured by historical simulations of the rules, appears sharp.

Given the findings from the simulations, it appears that the most effective partial pass-through rules, and those that strike an appropriate balance between retail price smoothing and fiscal shocks, are short moving-average rules (three-month and, possibly, six-month) and/or a max-min rule with an automatic updating of the max-min price band.[21]

More ambitious price-smoothing rules appear to leave the government overexposed to oil price-related fiscal risk, especially given the

---

[21]A hybrid of these two rules (i.e., a max-min rule for which the band is updated according to a relatively short moving average of past prices) may also be appropriate.

limited availability of effective risk-coping instruments for most developing country governments, as discussed in the next subsection. Therefore, while there is a case for government-led petroleum price smoothing, governments should not attempt to provide excessive price insurance to the private sector, given its fiscal implications. Governments may, on the other hand, find it relatively effective to rely on market-based insurance instruments to implement some retail price smoothing.

Managing the Fiscal Risk Deriving from Partial Pass-Through

It is clear from the historical simulations of partial pass-through rules that implementing a system of partial pass-through of oil price changes automatically transfers some financial risk to the government. The government faces a number of options for managing this risk.

The most immediate option for managing the risk associated with volatile oil revenues is for governments to use their budgets to absorb the shock, either adjusting expenditures or raising additional revenue. This is, however, unlikely to be an efficient option. Changing expenditures in line with oil prices is likely to entail fiscal adjustment costs, which implies that governments should attempt to smooth expenditures over time. Adjusting non-oil taxes is also likely to be inefficient for tax-smoothing considerations.

As in the case of the private sector, governments should try to smooth the budgetary shocks due to the partial pass-through of volatile oil prices. They can potentially do so by making use of credit markets. However, many governments are externally credit-constrained and may not be able to issue domestic debt because of the absence of developed domestic financial markets. Moreover, governments are most likely to be credit-constrained when they most need to borrow (i.e., when hit by negative terms-of-trade shock).

The most accessible risk-coping option for governments is to self-insure by engaging in precautionary saving behavior. The option of self-insurance is, however, not costless. The simulation results for partial pass-through rules presented above show that such saving or dis-saving may well be large and very long-lived. A deficit position, in particular, will need to be financed with up-front liquidity, which will have a cost. As shown by Deaton (1991), excessive price (or consumption) smoothing should not be attempted in the face of a combination of liquidity costs and persistent price shocks. Our simulations support this theoretical result. Saving or dissaving for long periods may also be hard to sustain politically.

One option for implementing a self-insurance mechanism in the face of oil-related fiscal risk is to set up a separate domestic oil price stabilization fund.[22] This has been a relatively popular option among oil importers. Of the countries in our survey that regulate prices, 24 percent currently run such funds, and a few have had funds for a number of years and only recently abolished them (e.g., Mauritania and the Philippines). In 2000, most of these funds were negatively hit by high oil prices and needed extra resources (Chile) or lost significant sums (Brazil). More generally, recent research indicates that such stabilization funds may complicate, rather than help, fiscal policy in responding to the challenge posed by oil price fluctuations (Davis and others, Chapter 11 in this volume).

Governments in developing countries, like private sector agents, do not seem to be suited to handle large fiscal variability due to oil price risk, given a lack of effective risk-coping instruments. Coupled with the high frequency and persistence of oil price shocks, this implies that any smoothing of spot price variability carried out by the government needs to be limited, and designed to minimize the fiscal shocks it implies for the public sector, as illustrated by the historical simulations presented above.

Hedging

Governments that wish to shield consumers from excessive petroleum price volatility can use financial hedging instruments to reduce oil price risk.[23] This has the advantage, relative to partial pass-through rules, of affecting the nature of the price process faced by the country's consumers directly, potentially removing or mitigating undesirable time-series properties of oil and, therefore, reducing the fiscal risk associated with partial pass-through of spot price changes. It also addresses a crucial market failure, namely the lack of access to hedging instruments for most consumers in developing countries.

---

[22]For a full discussion of oil savings and stabilization funds, see Davis and others, Chapter 11 in this volume.

[23]See Daniel, Chapter 14 in this volume.

Financial markets for oil products are very well developed and are used extensively by producers and consumers in industrialized countries. Crude oil and petroleum product financial contracts are heavily traded (both in New York, on NYMEX, and in London, on the IPE), especially for short maturities (up to 6–12 months).[24] This potentially offers substantial scope for risk management activities by oil-consuming countries, especially if they are relatively small oil purchasers.

The Scope for Private Sector Involvement in Petroleum Price Smoothing

Private oil companies may have an important role to play in facilitating or implementing a retail price-smoothing mechanism. The role of the private sector in relation to petroleum price smoothing is not the focus of this paper, but it is briefly discussed here to provide more comprehensive coverage of the subject and to highlight the implications of our analysis of the potential for government-led price smoothing for private sector involvement in this area.

In a regime of price regulation (e.g., in which the government sets a maximum price for petroleum products), the government may be able to delegate to private oil companies risk management activities relating to oil price variability and avoid bearing fiscal risk from price smoothing. It could do so in one of two ways:

- it could set retail prices according to a partial pass-through rule and fix petroleum excises. This would imply that domestic industry margins would fluctuate with international oil prices; or
- it could set retail prices on the basis of a "hedging" rule, whereby it presupposes that a given share of oil demand is purchased using financial instruments (e.g., traded futures) and fully passes through the notional purchase cost.

Under both mechanisms, private oil companies will seek to hedge or manage the oil price risk they face, using the range of instruments described above (e.g., financial instruments, credit markets, etc.). This may be superior to government handling of oil price risk, given the technical and political difficulties that may be associated with stabi-

---

[24]For instance, NYMEX crude oil open interest (the number of outstanding contracts that have not yet been closed) averages about one billion barrels a day, which is equivalent to 27 percent of global crude exports. Of this open interest, 75 percent is for six months forward or less, and about 5–10 percent for 24 months and beyond.

lization funds and the restricted access to financial and hedging markets governments may face. Private companies (especially if they are part of larger international groups) may have better access than governments to effective risk-coping measures.

These delegation mechanisms may, however, suffer from some limitations. In particular,

- they would render the price regulation of petroleum products harder to manage and require retail prices to take into account the higher cost of capital faced by private companies due to oil price risk;
- they may lead to suboptimal hedging behavior by the private sector if the government hedging rule is too rigid (or misspecified);
- governments may be unable to credibly commit to the price-stabilization formulas agreed to with private companies. For instance, in a situation of rising international prices, they may fail to raise retail prices to compensate private companies, even if the pass-through rule allows for a price increase; and
- given the nature of oil prices and the potential for chronic deficits or gains emerging from a partial pass-through rule, it is likely that there will be a need to renegotiate the risk-transfer arrangements between the government and the oil companies, and political pressure may build up not to compensate companies for low retail prices or to extract the rents from high retail prices. This political risk may, in turn, imply that private companies may be unwilling to manage the risk due to partial pass-through.

A contractually more straightforward alternative to the delegation of risk management activities to private oil companies would be to deregulate prices altogether. This has the advantage of letting market forces determine the appropriate level of retail price smoothing[25] and of being a more structural pricing reform than the introduction of partial pass-through rules and, therefore, less liable to be reversed or not adhered to. A number of countries in our survey have opted for deregulating petroleum pricing (27 percent of the countries in the survey).

Under some circumstances, price deregulation, however, may not be a viable strategy. If domestic market conditions are not sufficiently

---

[25]In countries where petroleum pricing is deregulated, private oil companies engage in some price smoothing. In the United States, for instance, the Department of Energy estimates that average gasoline retail prices fully reflect the variation in spot prices after three months, with 50 percent of the change passing through within four weeks (U.S. Department of Energy, 1998).

competitive (e.g., the market is too small to allow effective competition to emerge), price regulation may be necessary, which implies that the government needs to assume responsibility for price-smoothing decisions. If this is the case, governments should still consider the option of promoting the involvement of the private sector in managing price-smoothing activities.

V. Conclusions

The level of retail petroleum prices is an important economic variable in many developing countries, affecting both governments' fiscal revenues and consumers' disposable income. Consumers may suffer from petroleum price instability, due to risk aversion and adjustment cost considerations. Further, they may not be able to adequately mitigate the negative welfare impact of oil price volatility because of the absence of risk-coping instruments and limited self-insurance possibilities.

There appears, therefore, to be a case for government-led petroleum retail price smoothing in an environment where these prices are regulated. However, given the properties of international oil prices and, in particular, the persistence and high frequency of large price changes, petroleum price smoothing has significant fiscal implications for governments. The simulations of partial pass-through rules based on past international spot prices in this paper suggest that there is a sharp trade-off between price insurance and fiscal stability, and that only limited price smoothing (e.g., in the form of a short moving average rule or a moving max-min price band) is likely to be fiscally sustainable. Market-based price insurance appears to represent a superior alternative for smoothing retail prices—an alternative governments of oil-dependent countries should consider.

Private oil companies may also play an important role in facilitating or implementing a retail price-smoothing mechanism. Price deregulation, although sometimes politically difficult, remains the first-best solution, if competitive conditions are present in the domestic market.

Bibliography

Bevan, David, Paul Collier, and Jan Gunning with Arne Bigsten and Paul Horsnell, 1990, *Controlled Open Economies: A Neoclassical Approach to Structuralism* (Oxford: Clarendon Press).

Cashin, Paul, Hong Liang, and C. John McDermott, 2000, "How Persistent Are Shocks to World Commodity Prices?" *IMF Staff Papers*, Vol. 47, No. 2, pp. 177–217.

Cashin, Paul, C. John McDermott, and Alasdair Scott, 2002, "Booms and Slumps in World Commodity Prices," *Journal of Development Economics*, Vol. 69 (October), pp. 277–96.

Claessens, Stijn, and Panos Varangis, 1993, "Designing an Oil Import Risk Management: The Case of Costa Rica," in *Managing Commodity Price Risk in Developing Countries Using Financial Instruments: Case Studies*, ed. by Stijn Claessens and Ronald C. Duncan (Baltimore: Johns Hopkins University Press).

Deaton, Angus S., 1991, "Saving and Liquidity Constraints," *Econometrica*, Vol. 59, No. 5 (September), pp. 1221–48.

——, 1992, "Commodity Prices, Stabilization, and Growth in Africa," IPR Working Paper No. 40 (Washington: Institute for Policy Reform).

——, and Ron Miller, 1996, "International Commodity Prices, Macroeconomic Performance, and Politics in Sub-Saharan Africa," *Journal of African Economies*, Vol. 5, No. 3, pp. 99–191. Available via the Internet: http://www3.oup.co.uk/jnls/list/jafeco/hdb/Volume_05/Issue_03/05 0099.sgm.abs.html.

Dixit, Avinash, 1992, "Investment and Hysteresis," *Journal of Economic Perspectives*, Vol. 6 (Winter), pp. 107–32.

Engel, Eduardo, and Rodrigo Valdés, 2000, "Optimal Fiscal Strategy for Oil-Exporting Countries," IMF Working Paper 00/118 (Washington: International Monetary Fund).

Fafchamps, Marcel, 1999, "Rural Poverty, Risk and Development," FAO Economic and Social Development Paper No. 144 (Rome: Food and Agriculture Organization of the United Nations).

Federico, Giulio, James A. Daniel, and Benedict Bingham, 2001, "Domestic Petroleum Price Smoothing in Developing and Transition Countries," IMF Working Paper 01/75 (Washington: International Monetary Fund).

Gilbert, Christopher L., 1993, "Domestic Price Stabilization Schemes for Developing Countries," in *Managing Commodity Price Risk in Developing Countries*, ed. by Stijn Claessens and Ronald C. Duncan (Baltimore: Johns Hopkins University Press), pp. 30–67.

Gupta, Sanjeev, and others, 2000, *Equity and Efficiency in the Reform of Price Subsidies: A Guide for Policymakers* (Washington: International Monetary Fund).

Hausmann, Ricardo, Andrew Powell, and Roberto Rigobon, 1993, "An Optimal Spending Rule Facing Oil Income Uncertainty (Venezuela)," in *External Shocks and Stabilization Mechanisms*, ed. by Eduardo Engel and Patricio Meller (Washington: Inter-American Development Bank and Johns Hopkins University Press), pp. 113–71.

Kletzer, Kenneth M., David M. Newbery, and Brian D. Wright, 1991, "Smoothing Primary Exporters' Price Risks: Bonds, Futures, Options and Insurance," Economic Growth Center Discussion Paper No. 647 (New Haven, Connecticut: Yale University Press).

León, Javier, and Raimundo Soto, 1997, "Structural Breaks and Long-Run Trends in Commodity Prices," *Journal of International Development*, Vol. 9 (May–June), pp. 347–66.

Massell, Benton F., 1969, "Price Stabilization and Welfare," *Quarterly Journal of Economics*, Vol. 83 (May), pp. 284–98.

Mazaheri, A., 1999, "Convenience Yield, Mean Reverting Prices, and Long Memory in the Petroleum Market," *Applied Financial Economics*, Vol. 9 (February), pp. 31–50.

Newbery, David M.G., and Joseph E. Stiglitz, 1981, *The Theory of Commodity Price Stabilization: A Study in the Economics of Risk* (Oxford: Clarendon Press).

Nickell, Stephen, 1985, "Error Correction, Partial Adjustment and All That: An Expository Note," *Oxford Bulletin of Economics and Statistics*, Vol. 47 (May), pp. 119–30.

Paxson, Christina H., 1992, "Using Weather Variability to Estimate the Response of Savings to Transitory Income in Thailand," *American Economic Review*, Vol. 82 (March), pp. 15–33.

Turnovsky, Stephen J., Haim Shalit, and Andrew Schmitz, 1980, "Consumer's Surplus, Price Instability, and Consumer Welfare," *Econometrica*, Vol. 48 (January), pp. 135–52.

United States Department of Energy, 1998, *Assessment of Summer 1997 Motor Gasoline Price Increase.* Available via the Internet: http://www.eia.doe.gov/oil_gas/petroleum/info_glance/gasoline.html.

———, 2000, *A Primer on Gasoline Prices.* Available via the Internet: http://www.eia.doe.gov/emeu/plugs/plprimer.html.

Waugh, Frederick V., 1944, "Does the Consumer Benefit from Price Instability?," *Quarterly Journal of Economics*, Vol. 58 (August), pp. 602–14.

Wickham, Peter, 1996, "Volatility of Oil Prices," IMF Working Paper 96/82 (Washington: International Monetary Fund).

World Bank, 1999, "Dealing with Commodity Price Volatility in Developing Countries: A Proposal for a Market-Based Approach," Discussion Paper for the Roundtable on Commodity Risk Management in Developing Countries, Washington, September.

18

Energy Sector Quasi-Fiscal Activities in the Countries of the Former Soviet Union

Martin Petri, Günther Taube, and Aleh Tsyvinski[1]

I. Introduction

A decade into the transition, many of the successor states of the former Soviet Union (FSU) still struggle with adapting their energy sectors to the market economy model they have embraced. Across the FSU, energy sectors are still characterized by a high degree of government ownership, strong vertical integration within the energy sector, low and administratively set energy prices, cross-subsidization, and excessive operational losses. International and domestic barter trade can still be found in energy sector operations, and in many FSU countries, energy companies continue to function as quasi-fiscal institutions and social safety nets, providing large implicit subsidies to households and (state-owned) enterprises through low energy prices, preferential tariffs or free provision of services to privileged groups, the toleration of payment arrears, and noncash

[1]This is a revised and shortened version of "Energy Sector Quasi-Fiscal Activities in the Countries of the Former Soviet Union" by Martin Petri, Günther Taube, and Aleh Tsyvinski (2002). The case studies on Azerbaijan and Ukraine are based on data and information through end-2000. We thank the members of the IMF's Ukraine and Azerbaijan country teams, in particular Bogdan Lissovolik and Bert van Selm for helpful suggestions, and Alvaro Vivanco for research assistance. We are also grateful for comments from Jeffrey Davis, Rolando Ossowski, Annalisa Fedelino, Tom Richardson, and participants in IMF and World Bank seminars where the paper was presented. All remaining errors are ours.

arrangements.[2] For example, currently only Armenia, Georgia, and Moldova seem to charge electricity tariffs that are high enough to recover economic costs (i.e., including investment). As a result, energy sector operations across the FSU continue to give rise to large distortions and inefficiencies that hamper structural change and growth, while complicating fiscal policy and posing substantial risks to macroeconomic stability.

This paper seeks to analyze quasi-fiscal activities (QFAs) in the energy sectors of the countries of the FSU, especially those arising from low energy prices (mispricing) and the toleration of payment arrears. It does so by analyzing two case studies—one focusing on a net energy importer (Ukraine) and the other on an energy-rich country (Azerbaijan). These analyses are complemented by available information and data from other FSU countries. The paper is organized as follows. The next section discusses conceptual and methodological issues related to QFAs in general and those in the energy sector in the FSU in particular. Sections III and IV present the two case studies. In Section V, the paper draws some conclusions for policy reforms.

II. Quasi-Fiscal Activities (QFAs): Conceptual Issues

Public sector organizations and the central bank can play an important role as agents of fiscal policy through the use of QFAs, thus disguising the overall size of the government as conventionally measured (e.g., ratio of government spending to GDP) and the true extent of taxation. A broad definition would suggest that QFAs include all operations that "could in principle be duplicated by specific budgetary measures in the form of an explicit tax, subsidy, or other direct expenditure" (Mackenzie and Stella, 1996). In line with this definition, QFAs include multiple exchange rate regimes, exchange rate guarantees, nontariff trade barriers, credit rationing and directed lending at below-market rates, and below-market prices or cost recovery. While the general notion of these activities is well acknowledged and central bank QFAs and their amalgamation with budget deficits have been the subject of substantial debate and analysis, other types of QFAs have been less well researched, especially in transition

---

[2]For further background on the role of the energy sector in the Soviet economy, see IMF and others (1991). See EBRD (2001) for a comprehensive analysis of energy sector developments and reforms during the first decade of the transition.

Figure 18.1. *Energy Sector Quasi-Fiscal Activities (QFAs) and*
Budget Deficits in Selected FSU Countries, 2000
(In percent of GDP)

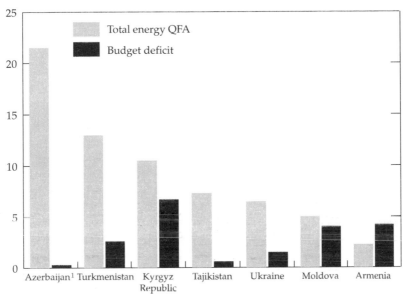

Source: Authors' estimates.
[1]The QFA estimate for Azerbaijan corresponds to 1999.

countries.[3] This is somewhat surprising considering their importance in these countries, but can probably be explained by the unavailability of data and complexity of undertaking quantitative analyses.

In the FSU, energy QFAs have become a source of large public sector financial imbalances and macroeconomic instability, primarily as a result of mispricing and the toleration of arrears. Among the FSU countries, Azerbaijan clearly stands out with by far the largest energy QFAs, estimated at over 20 percent of GDP in recent years (see the case study below for details). Energy QFAs are also large in Turkmenistan (above 10 percent of GDP), while they tend to range around 5 percent of GDP in most of the other FSU countries (Figure 18.1). Survey data (Appendix) suggest that resource-rich FSU countries tend to have significantly

---

[3]For a general discussion of QFAs, see Mackenzie and Stella (1996). QFAs related to the foreign exchange regime in Uzbekistan are analyzed in IMF (1998) and Rosenberg and de Zeeuw (2000).

larger energy QFAs because of the abundance of resources and the subsequently larger leeway to tolerate nonpayments and below-market
prices.[4] Additional channels of energy QFAs—barter and offset
arrangements—have also proven pervasive in many of the less reformed FSU countries.

Why Do (Energy) QFAs Matter?

QFAs can have a number of adverse economic effects, including the
misallocation of resources because of inappropriate price signals
and administrative restrictions that prevent more efficient market
solutions.[5] In the case of energy QFAs, below-market or cost recovery
energy prices and the failure to enforce payments (i.e., arrears) can
distort the allocation of resources, resulting in overconsumption,
insufficient investment, production inefficiencies, and crowding out
of the private sector. The implicit subsidies provided through
QFAs tend to be untargeted and assist all users of energy regardless
of their relative needs and profitability, thereby also helping enterprises avoid necessary restructuring. Inappropriately low energy
prices can also be viewed as an implicit tax that transfers resources
from the producers to the consumers of energy. Also, if energy tariffs
are set below cost recovery levels, profits of energy companies are
lower than they would otherwise be, which can result in underinvestment and a depletion of the capital stock. These, in turn, have tended
to cause blackouts and disruptions in energy deliveries, as observed in
recent years, for example, in Azerbaijan (despite its energy abundance) and Georgia. Lack of maintenance and failure to replace worn-
out machinery can also be dangerous for the population and the
environment, especially in the case of nuclear plants and gas or oil
pipelines.

Low energy prices and wasteful consumption were a key feature of
the central planning system of the Soviet Union. After the breakup of
the Soviet Union, its successor countries initially raised domestic
energy prices substantially. However, these increases have in recent
years often remained below what would be required to bring them in

---

[4]This is a common feature in resource-rich countries. For example, energy QFAs also
tend to be large in the petroleum producing countries in the Middle East and elsewhere.
See, for example, on Iran, Taube (2001).

[5]We are not aware of a case where QFAs were intended to correct market failures.

Figure 18.2. *Ratio of Total Primary Energy Consumption (in thousands of BTUs) to GDP (in PPP terms in current U.S. dollars) for 1999*

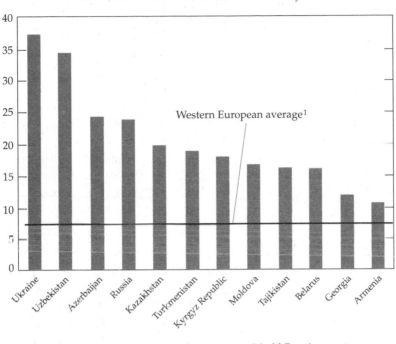

Sources: U.S. Energy Information Administration; World Development Indicators (2001); and World Bank.

[1]Includes Austria, Belgium, Denmark, Finland, France, Germany, Greece, Ireland, Italy, Luxembourg, the Netherlands, Portugal, Spain, Sweden, and the United Kingdom.

line with international prices or cost recovery levels. Moreover, de facto energy prices have been even lower as arrears have been tolerated. Energy efficiency actually deteriorated throughout the 1990s, because GDP fell faster than energy consumption. Meanwhile, in many FSU countries, per capita energy consumption has remained at stunningly high levels by international standards, especially if seen relative to per capita income levels (Figure 18.2), indicating that energy prices are "not right."

As far as the fiscal sector is concerned, QFAs can disguise the size of government involvement in the economy, affect the fiscal stance, and create lack of transparency. When measuring the fiscal (budgetary) stance, QFAs are usually not taken into consideration, which can result in a misleading interpretation of fiscal policy. For example, the government's intention to reduce the budget deficit by cutting subsidies to enterprises could be (more than) offset by the central bank stepping up directed lending to the very same enterprises. Similarly, sizable budgetary adjustment can be undermined if QFAs increase at the same time, resulting perhaps even in a deterioration in the underlying fiscal stance. Alternatively, if the change in the budget balance is only minimal while at the same time energy prices are adjusted substantially, the conventionally measured budget balance would disguise the true extent of the underlying fiscal adjustment.

Since QFAs, or the provision of implicit subsidies, are not discussed and decided upon by parliament, they create a lack of transparency and limit the power of the legislature in economic policymaking and the annual budget process. In addition, QFAs can increase the vulnerability of the government budget, for example if contingent liabilities are created through the provision of government guarantees on domestic- and foreign-currency-denominated borrowing by state-owned enterprises. Once called, these contingent liabilities, and the associated foreign exchange risk, can derail the intended fiscal policy stance.

Energy QFAs can contribute to the emergence of macroeconomic crises through a variety of channels. For example, if arrears to energy companies accumulate, and these enterprises in turn do the same vis-à-vis their suppliers and the budget (e.g., tax arrears), the central bank and/or the budget may be forced to extend large credits to the energy enterprises, which could fuel inflation. In addition, such bailout practices, even if they take place only once ("one-off arrears clearance"), condone the nonpayment culture and create moral hazard. Alternatively, arrears could be cleared through offsets, which tend to trigger further arrears, barter, and offsetting arrangements.[6] This could ultimately result in the government being unable to pay wages or interest because most of the revenue is noncash.

Methodological and Measurement Issues

Estimating energy sector QFAs generally depends on the quality of available data, which in many FSU countries remains a problem. In

---

[6]For detailed analyses of the nonpayment system in Russia and the electricity sectors in transition countries see Pinto, Drebentsov, and Morozov (2000) and Krishnaswamy (1999), respectively.

most cases, the main channel for QFAs is government-owned enterprises, and the data on their activities are often unavailable because the
companies involved claim that the data are commercially sensitive. In
some cases, the lack of data transparency may be motivated by rent
seeking. Moreover, available data could be inaccurate because companies lack technical expertise. Verification of the quality of available data
is further complicated by the fact that only a few energy companies un-
dergo audits by independent companies and most of them do not use
generally accepted accounting principles (GAAP).

Methodologically, energy sector QFAs related to arrears are relatively easy to estimate if payment data for enterprises and other end
users are available. Arrears to state-owned energy companies can conceptually be considered a QFA because their toleration is equivalent to
an implicit subsidy provided to energy consumers; arrears are effectively lost revenue for the energy enterprise and, through forgone
profit transfers or tax arrears, also lost revenue for the government. In
the case of private energy companies, arrears by end users could also
be considered as quasi-fiscal activities if the government does not
allow the energy companies to enforce payments. The quasi-fiscal activity would then be related to the implicit tax that firms face by being
forced to provide services.

QFAs on account of mispricing are considerably more difficult to estimate as they require determining a relevant benchmark price. In the
case of petroleum products, or coal, this is relatively easy because these
products are traded internationally at reasonably well defined and
comparable prices. For natural gas and electricity, however, there are
not always obvious market-based prices that could be used as benchmarks. Even in market-based economies, prices for these products are
often determined by cost recovery considerations because of limited
tradability and the existence of natural monopolies. As a result, in the
case of natural gas and electricity, estimating mispricing is necessarily
subject to greater uncertainty and judgment, as any quantitative analysis is based on hypothetical benchmark prices. The results of such
analyses tend to be quite sensitive to changes in these benchmarks. In
this regard, it would appear important to use reasonable assumptions,
especially on the benchmark prices, and undertake sensitivity analyses
with different assumptions to provide an indication of the range of
results.

Energy QFAs related to excessive losses or theft, noncash payments,
and government-guaranteed borrowing are even more difficult to estimate. Inefficiencies on account of poor management and state own-

ership can be considered a QFA because under a more market-friendly environment these enterprises would reduce or eliminate the losses, as they cannot be passed on to the government through reduced profit transfers and/or tax arrears. While it is difficult to estimate the extent of excessive losses or theft quantitatively, some estimates have become available, using reference values from other countries with more competitive environments (see the case study on Azerbaijan below). Estimating QFAs on account of noncash payments and government- guaranteed borrowing to energy companies is methodologically challenging and requires data that are difficult to obtain. No attempt has been made in the case studies for their quantification.

With these methodological remarks and caveats in mind, we have experimented with two different methodologies to compute energy sector QFAs in the two case studies as presented in the following two sections. In the Ukraine case study, dictated by the more limited availability of data, we used a relatively simple methodology that relies on relevant energy consumer prices or cost recovery prices as benchmarks, together with data on collection rates and consumption volumes ("end-product approach"). In the case of Azerbaijan, the availability of more detailed data allowed the estimation of energy QFAs on the basis of the consolidated financial accounts of enterprises involved in petroleum, electricity, and gas operations. As explained in detail in Box 18.1, the methodology allows the computation of QFAs related to the subsidized sale of petroleum products as an input into energy production and the calculation of QFAs related to the subsidized sale of energy (electricity and gas) to end users. The results of these calculations are then used to adjust the revenue and expenditure data from the financial accounts of the enterprises ("financial balance approach").

Quasi-Fiscal Activities Versus Quasi-Fiscal Deficit

Energy QFAs can be financed through various channels, which are fundamentally different in countries that are net energy importers or exporters. In the former, energy QFAs are mostly financed by reducing cash outlays through incurring domestic suppliers' arrears, external suppliers' arrears, tax arrears, or spending less on maintenance and investment than would be necessary under more market-related conditions. QFAs can also be financed through bank or

Box 18.1. *Two Methodologies to Estimate Energy QFAs*

End-Product Approach

Let: V be the quantity of energy product sold

$P(m)$ be the benchmark or cost-recovery output price

$P(a)$ be the actual price

c be the collection ratio

(1) Arrears at actual prices $= V P(a)(1 - c)$

= Value at actual prices minus collections

(2) Mispricing of output $= V[P(m) - P(a)]$

= Value at market prices minus value at actual prices

(3) Total quasi-fiscal activities $= VP(a)(1 - c) + V[P(m) - P(a)]$

= Arrears at actual prices + mispricing of products

$= VP(m) - VP(a)c$

= Value at market prices minus actual collections

Financial Balance Approach

Let: V' be the quantity of energy used as an input (e.g., petroleum)

$P'(m)$ be the market or cost recovery input price

$P'(a)$ be the actual input price

$P(c)$ be the cost recovery output price at actual costs (e.g., electricity)

Rev   be actual revenues

Cost   be the actual costs of the company

Under   be underinvestment

Arrears'   be arrears on inputs and taxes

For cost recovery to hold, the actual revenues of a company plus the mispricing of the output and its arrears have to equal its actual costs plus the mispricing of inputs plus the underinvestment plus arrears on inputs and taxes:

(4) $VP(c)$ $= V P(a)c + V[P(c) - P(a)] + VP(a)(1 - c) =$

Total revenues = actual revenues + mispricing of output + arrears on collections =

Total costs $= $ Cost $+ V'[P'(m) - P'(a)] +$ Under + Arrears'

= actual costs + mispricing of inputs + underinvestment + arrears on inputs and taxes

(5) Total QFA $= V[P(c) - P(a)] + VP(a)(1 - c)$

= mispricing of output + arrears on collections

$= $ Cost $+ V'[P'(m) - P'(a)] +$ Under + Arrears' $- VP(a)c$

= actual costs + input mispricing + underinvestment + arrears on inputs and taxes – actual revenues

---

Note that the financial balance approach implicitly includes excessive losses as part of the QFAs because the actual costs are equal to the sum of normal costs and excessive losses. By contrast, under the end-product approach excessive losses would need to be added to QFAs in equation (3).

nonbank borrowing, if energy companies experience cash deficits in their operations.[7]

In energy-exporting countries, it is easier to finance energy QFAs, which tend to waste and dissipate economic rents. In this case, it is also important to distinguish between quasi-fiscal *activities* and quasi-fiscal *deficits*. For example, an oil-producing country that sells oil domestically at prices below the export parity price but at a level sufficiently high to cover domestic costs would not incur a quasi-fiscal deficit. However, it would incur QFAs equivalent to the difference between the hypothetical value of domestically sold oil valued at the export parity price and the domestic revenue actually collected from these sales. This country would provide an implicit quasi-fiscal subsidy to its population equal to this difference, which represents the wasted economic rent. If domestic prices are set at a level below cost recovery, then the country incurs a quasi-fiscal deficit equal to the difference between the level of revenue necessary to reach cost recovery and the actual level of revenue from domestic oil sales. The quasi-fiscal activity in this case is larger, equal to the difference between the hypothetical sales value (sales volume valued at export parity price) and the actual sales value. It follows that QFAs tend to be larger than the quasi-fiscal deficits in countries that are net energy exporters.

Theoretically, there may also be a situation in which QFAs offset each other, so that net QFAs are smaller than gross QFAs. This is the case if there is cross-subsidization. In Ukraine, for example, electricity is sold at above-cost recovery prices to industrial consumers and at below-cost recovery prices to households. In this case there is a quasi-fiscal tax on industrial customers that helps to finance part of the implicit quasi-fiscal subsidy to households. Only the net QFA would contribute to the quasi-fiscal deficit in this case (see below).

III. Case Study: Ukraine

Background

Ukraine's economic performance during the first decade of transition has been mixed. Following the hyperinflation episode in the early

---

[7]Energy companies can also finance QFAs through tax exemptions. In the methodology used here this would not be considered a QFA because a tax exemption is a direct fiscal measure in the form of a tax expenditure.

1990s, inflation has been brought under control in recent years (e.g., consumer prices rose by 6 percent in 2001). However, the sharp output decline could not be arrested before 1999/2000, and strong real growth materialized for the first time only in 2000 and reached 9 percent in 2001. Ukraine was severely affected by the August 1998 crisis in Russia, which caused a sharp depreciation of the currency and a drop in export demand. The budget position has improved in recent years, with cash deficits of less than 2 percent of GDP in 2000 and 2001.

Ukraine has a large energy sector that accounts for about 25 percent of industrial output and 40 percent of imports. Since the sector has experienced a decline in output somewhat below that of overall GDP, its relative importance in the economy has increased during the 1990s. Per capita energy consumption has remained high—only slightly lower than in Russia, twice as high as in Poland, and about five times the average of Western European economies (see Figure 18.2). The energy sector has contributed importantly to the buildup of external debt, mostly because of gas imports financed by external payment arrears to Gazprom.[8] By January 2001, these arrears had reached US$1.5 billion, equivalent to 15 percent of Ukraine's total external debt.[9]

Energy QFAs

Energy QFAs are concentrated in the gas and electricity sectors. The market for petroleum products is fairly liberalized and hence offers little scope for QFAs.[10] In the coal sector, QFAs could be large, although in the absence of data this is difficult to verify. The government subsidizes the coal sector explicitly via the budget since average coal prices cover only about one-third of costs and coal miners are politically important.[11] However, the government also provides tax exemptions and tolerates the nonpayment of taxes by coal mines that also accumulate arrears toward state-owned enterprises. In addition, there are below-market-price sales to privileged consumer groups, and energy

---

[8]Ukraine is the world's third largest importer of natural gas (after the United States and Germany) and sixth largest consumer of natural gas. Annual consumption fell from a peak of 115 billion cubic meters in 1990 to around 80 billion cubic meters in 1999–2000.

[9]However, the Ukrainian government does not recognize these arrears as government debt.

[10]For an overview of Ukraine's oil sector see U.S. Department of State (2000).

[11]See Oxford Analytica (2001) and World Bank (1998).

generation companies are forced to buy from inefficient mines at above-market price.

We follow the end-product approach (see Box 18.1 above) to estimate energy QFAs in Ukraine, primarily for the year 2000, related to mispricing and arrears. The analysis is based on publicly available data (e.g., arrears data for different consumer groups as published by the Ministry of Energy). To arrive at estimates of mispricing, we compare the actual prices paid by different consumer groups with an approximate market price for gas and estimated cost recovery price for electricity. The third type of QFA—excessive losses, including through theft—is difficult to measure and we lack sufficient data to include it in the analysis. Activities such as theft may be important, especially taking into account the level of corruption and extent of the shadow economy in Ukraine. For example, according to some sources, transit gas with a value of US$1 billion (equivalent to about 3 percent of Ukraine's 2000 GDP) was stolen over the period to May 2000.[12]

Gas Sector QFAs

Naftogaz Ukrainy dominates the Ukrainian gas market. It is a state joint-stock company, almost fully owned by the government, and is structured as a holding company consisting of three specialized firms: wholesaler to domestic consumers, gas exploration and extraction company, and gas transportation and storage company. Domestic extraction covers only about 20 percent of consumption, and the remainder is imported from Russia and Turkmenistan: Naftogaz receives a transit fee paid in gas (about 30 billion cubic meters annually) that the Russian gas company Gazprom pays for using Ukrainian pipelines to export gas to Western Europe. Itera International, a private company with close links to Gazprom, handles the sale and transportation of Turkmen natural gas to Ukraine, supplying 20–30 billion cubic meters (bcm) per year on behalf of Naftogaz. In this study we estimate the QFA arising from the operations of Naftogaz.

Mispricing

During 1999 and 2000, three types of prices were used in the Ukrainian gas sector: (i) auction prices; (ii) contract prices; and (iii) prices set

---

[12]See Oxford Analytica (2001).

by the government. Auctions were introduced to reduce arrears and replace barter with cash transactions. Even though auctions covered only a very small part of transactions, they proved useful for the domestic extraction companies that received much needed cash. Contract prices form the broadest category; they vary based on the terms, volume, and forms of payment. The government sets retail gas prices for residential consumers (who consume 15–18 bcm) and budget organizations (1 bcm). Prices for residential consumers and budget organizations are, respectively, HRV 190 (US$35) and HRV 231 (US$43) per thousand cubic meters (tcm); they have remained unchanged since April 1999, despite considerable domestic inflation and rises in international energy prices.

In the case of gas, cost recovery pricing is not appropriate for the calculation of QFAs if there are economic rents involved in the production of low-cost gas. Therefore, even if the costs of production were known, these would not be a good estimate of market value. Moreover, production costs include exploration, extraction, and transportation, with the latter being a very large part of the cost. Thus gas sold close to the Russian border would have a different cost from gas sold elsewhere (and data on transportation costs are not available). For the same reason, it would not be obvious what international price to use as a benchmark. The price at the border with Russia may be very different from the one at the border with Poland due to transportation and storage costs, causing the price of gas to vary more in time and space than for other energy products. However, since Itera operates mostly on a commercial basis, its price for imported gas at the border with Ukraine (about US$70/tcm) could be considered the most relevant.[13]

To estimate the impact of mispriced gas supplied by Naftogaz, we chose prices for two reference groups as benchmarks: self-financing communal service enterprises ("communal enterprises") and independent traders. The operations of both groups are broadly in line with market principles and relatively free from government interference. The price paid by communal enterprises is probably closest to a "market" value, and comparable to the price charged by Itera.

---

[13]See Oxford Analytica (1999). Cost recovery would be an appropriate reference price for imported gas, but prices in the past were likely set higher than market value due to the nonpayment history of Naftogaz. For example, in 2000 the contract price for Naftogaz was US$80/tcm. See Oxford Analytica (2000).

Using the price charged by Naftogaz for supplies to communal enterprises as a benchmark, QFAs from gas mispricing are estimated at 3.3 percent of GDP in 2000, up from 1.5 percent of GDP in 1999, reflecting an increase in the reference price in line with those of international prices, while government-controlled gas prices remained essentially unchanged (Appendix). Using the price that traders pay as a benchmark reduces gas sector QFAs on account of mispricing to 1.3 percent of GDP in 2000, up from 0.2 percent of GDP in the previous year. Regardless of which benchmark price is chosen, the results show that most of the mispricing problem is related to regional administrations, which deliver gas to households, and therefore benefit the most from the implicit subsidy provided through inappropriately low gas tariffs.

Arrears

In addition to low prices, implicit subsidies are provided through the toleration of payment arrears. In 1999, average collection rates were low (40 percent on average), resulting in large arrears (4.1 percent of GDP). Due to government efforts and the improved macroeconomic situation, collection rates improved dramatically in 2000 (to 80 percent on average), reducing payment arrears to about 1 percent of GDP (Appendix).[14] While in 1999 the regional administrations and the Ministry of Energy were the largest contributors to arrears, in the following year regional administrations and traders were the major culprits. The payment record of regional administrations is linked to the payment performance of individual households (their customers).This suggests that private households have benefited not only from large implicit subsidies in the form of low gas tariffs but also from additional implicit subsidies from payment arrears.

In the gas sector, QFAs on account of arrears and mispricing are estimated at 5.6 percent of GDP in 1999 and 4.4 percent of GDP in 2000, based on the higher reference price (paid by communal enterprises); they are somewhat lower if the price paid by independent traders is used as a benchmark (Table 18.1). Arrears were the main component of energy QFAs in 1999, accounting for 73 percent of the estimated total. Reflecting sharply improved collection ratios in 2000, new arrears accounted for only 1.1 percent of GDP. However, since the reference

---

[14]Note, however, that the increase in cash payments is not known.

Table 18.1. *Ukraine: Gas Sector Quasi-Fiscal Activities, 1999–2000*
(In percent of GDP)

	1999	2000
Arrears	4.1	1.1
Underpricing	1.5 (0.2)[1]	3.3 (1.3)
Other, including theft[2]	...	...
Total quasi-fiscal operations	5.6 (4.3)	4.4 (2.4)

Sources: Naftogaz Ukrainy; and authors' calculations.
[1]Figures in brackets use the independent traders' price as the reference price.
[2]Not known, but presumed to be positive.

prices for gas rose in line with international energy prices, while government-controlled prices remained essentially unchanged, QFAs on account of mispricing gained in importance. In 2001, payment discipline improved further (to 87 percent), while reference prices declined moderately. As a result, quasi-fiscal activities likely declined further in 2001.

Electricity Sector QFAs

In 2000, Ukraine generated around 171 TWh of electricity, making it the sixteenth largest producer in the world. As indicated above, Ukraine's energy intensity is high by international standards, with wasteful consumption a major contributor to high electricity usage.[15] In 1996, the electricity sector was restructured by separating generation, transmission, and distribution and the creation of a wholesale market for electricity. Industrial enterprises have remained the main consumer, accounting for 50 percent of total electricity use in 2000, with the metallurgy and coal industry being the largest consumers within the industrial sector. Households consume 20 percent of the electricity, about the same share as budgetary organizations and communal services.

Mispricing

Electricity retail prices are regulated by the government and are adjusted infrequently. A major rise in tariffs took place during 1994–96,

---

[15]Electricity usage remains unusually high even when taking into account that Ukraine's shadow economy is very large.

when the average retail price tripled in U.S. dollar terms. Following that, however, there has been no further significant adjustment in electricity tariffs, with the exception of a 20 percent increase in the price of electricity retail (low-voltage) tariffs due to the imposition of the VAT in the year 2000 and in the context of privatizing six regional electricity distribution companies in 2001. However, reflecting substantial currency depreciation and increases in world energy prices, Ukraine's average electricity tariffs have remained well below cost recovery levels, and a large proportion of the population continues to benefit from preferential tariffs.

For the purpose of this study, we used cost recovery estimates for two different consumer groups: (i) *industrial users* (industrial enterprises, railroads, and agriculture); and (ii) *retail users* (communal services, budgetary organizations, and households). The transmission costs for the first group are relatively low because they mostly use the more efficient high-voltage grid. Cost recovery estimates by the World Bank for such consumers in other countries (e.g., Russia) are about US$20 per MWh, which is the benchmark we used for the calculations presented here, as precise estimates for Ukraine are not available. The second group consumes energy through more expensive low-voltage lines, where the cost recovery tariff has been estimated at US$39 per MWh.[16] In 2000, prices charged to industrial users were above cost recovery, implying an implicit tax of 1 percent of GDP and cross-subsidization of retail users, who received a quasi-fiscal subsidy of 1.4 percent of GDP. On a net basis, the QFA related to mispricing of electricity (0.4 percent of GDP) was thus relatively small (Table 18.2).

Arrears

According to one estimate, arrears to the electricity sector amounted to almost 5 percent of GDP in 1999. They were substantially smaller in 2000 (0.7 percent of GDP), reflecting improved collection rates and, to a minor extent, the collection of previously incurred arrears, helped by stronger enforcement of cutoff policies (Table 18.3). However, only a relatively small part of collections was in cash. In 2000, most of the arrears were incurred by the coal and metallurgy industries, the agricultural sector, and households (excluding those with privileged tariffs).

---

[16]See World Bank (2001) and Lovei (1998).

Table 18.2. *Ukraine: Mispricing in the Electricity Sector, 2000*

	Tariff	Cost Recovery	Cost Recovery	Mispricing
	(In U.S. dollars per MWh)		(In millions of HRV)	
Industry, of which:	25.40	20.00	5,140	–1,386
Coal	39.90	20.00	645	–641
Metallurgy	20.20	20.00	2,497	–30
Railroad	26.50	20.00	553	–179
Agriculture	28.00	20.00	496	–199
Total for users with tariffs above cost recovery (implicit tax)				–1,763 (1 percent of GDP)
Communal services	32.90	39.00	1,964	307
State budget organizations	32.04	39.00	589	105
Local budget organizations	32.67	39.00	497	81
Households (excl. those with privileged tariffs)	19.67	39.00	3,778	1,873
Total for users with tariffs below cost recovery (implicit subsidy)				2,365 (1.4 percent of GDP)
Net quasi-fiscal activity in electricity sector				602 (0.4 percent of GDP)

Sources: Authors' calculations; and Ministry of Economy of Ukraine.

Reflecting the collection of arrears accrued previously, collection rates for some user groups were actually above 100 percent in 2000, increasing from 49 percent in 2000 to 65 percent in 2001. Together with some tariff increases, this suggests a further reduction in quasi-fiscal activities in 2001.

Summary

The preceding analysis has shown that energy sector QFAs in Ukraine over the past few years were sizable and primarily caused by mispricing, especially in the gas sector (Table 18.4). Since no data for the coal subsector are available, and with detailed calculations for electricity sector QFAs only for the year 2000, it is difficult to judge if overall energy sector QFAs declined or not over the past few years. However, it is clear that energy sector QFAs remained sizable in 2000 (6.5 percent of GDP), even though significant progress was achieved in reducing arrears. With some progress on the arrears front for both gas

Table 18.3. *Ukraine: Electricity Sector Payment Arrears, 2000*

Consumers	Tariff in HRV per MWh	Collection Rate in Percent[1]	Arrears in Millions of HRV	Arrears as a Percent of Total
Industry, of which	137.1	88.6	746	67.1
Coal	215.5	65.6	442	39.8
Metallurgy	109.3	86.1	351	31.6
Agriculture	151.4	80.5	135	12.2
Households[2]	106.2	78.0	418	37.6
Subtotal (gross)			*1,299*	*116.9*
Railroad	142.9	102.9	−20	−1.8
Communal services	177.6	102.0	−32	−2.9
State budget organizations	173.0	124.5	−118	−10.6
Local budget organizations	176.4	104.3	−18	−1.6
Total (net)			*1,111*	*100.0*
			(0.7 percent of GDP)	

Sources: Ministry of Fuel and Energy of Ukraine; and Ministry of Economy of Ukraine.
[1]Collection rates can be larger than 100 percent due to repayment of arrears.
[2]Excluding those with privileged tariffs.

and electricity, the main contributing factor for energy QFAs was mispricing, especially in the gas sector where QFAs on account of mispricing rose to 3.3 percent of GDP, up from 1.5 percent of GDP in 1999, if measured at the higher benchmark gas price. This reflects the fact that domestic prices remained essentially unchanged while world energy prices increased.

The largest source of financing for energy sector QFAs in Ukraine has been the use of the in-kind transit gas that Naftogaz sells to domestic consumers.[17] The second form of financing is gas payment arrears to Russia, which have resulted in a buildup of significant contingent liabilities for the government since Naftogaz is a state-owned company. As it appears unlikely that Ukrainian consumers will pay for these arrears, Ukraine will need to settle the claims one way or another, for example, through special bilateral debt deals and/or by accepting a lower price upon privatization.[18] The third source of financing is the nonpayment of taxes by energy sector companies. Naftogaz,

---

[17]If Naftogaz transferred the proceeds to the budget as required by law, it would have to raise its tariffs or increase collections substantially.

[18]Ukraine has not recognized Naftogaz's debt to Gazprom as government debt, but Ukraine's public sector wealth is reduced by the accumulation of this debt.

Table 18.4. *Ukraine: Quasi-Fiscal Activities in the Energy Sector*
(In percent of GDP)

	1999	2000
Arrears	...	1.8
Gas	4.1	1.1
Electricity	...	0.7
Mispricing	...	4.7
Gas	1.5	3.3
Electricity (gross)	...	1.4
Gross quasi-fiscal activities	...	*6.5*

Source: Tables 18.1–18.3

for example, is one of Ukraine's largest tax debtors, and several electricity companies are also not current on their tax payments. The fourth most important source of financing is underinvestment and inadequate maintenance of the capital stock in the sector. However, after several years of neglect, this source of financing is becoming more limited and also more dangerous.

Some of the gross QFAs in the electricity subsector are financed through cross-subsidization, as explained above. Financing through the dissipation of economic rents is probably relatively small due to the limited domestic production of oil and gas. The last source of financing of QFAs is the incurrence of arrears to suppliers. This source of financing is also limited because independent suppliers would probably stop deliveries if they were not paid. Most of the sources of financing in Ukraine are declining and therefore the need to eliminate energy QFAs is becoming more urgent. Since economic rents are limited in Ukraine, the estimate of QFAs is approximately equal to the quasi-fiscal deficit, which will affect government finances eventually.

IV. Case Study: Azerbaijan

Background

Following the "transitional recession" in the early 1990s, which was exacerbated by the adverse impact of the war with Armenia, Azerbaijan has been able to stabilize its economy and achieve strong GDP growth. The country has been successful in lowering inflation. External current account deficits, while still high by international standards, have been much reduced from extraordinarily high levels.[19] In recent years, high GDP growth has been achieved mainly due to high oil prices and large foreign investments in the petroleum sector. Growth has thus been "unbalanced," with the oil sector expanding annually by around 20 percent in real terms in 1998 and 1999, while the rest of the economy has grown by about 6 percent in real terms. Moreover, the benefits of oil wealth and GDP growth have accrued to Azerbaijan's population in a highly uneven manner, as both the incidence of poverty and income inequality have increased in recent years.

Azerbaijan's domestic energy sector remains characterized by a high degree of vertical integration and government control. The major energy companies—the State Oil Company of Azerbaijan Republic (SOCAR), the power company (Azerenergy), and the gas distribution enterprise (Azerigaz)—are still government-owned and used as instruments of government policy. Oil output rose substantially in the second half of the 1990s, from around 65 million barrels per year during 1994–98 to 100 million barrels in 2000. About half the output (55 million barrels in 2000) is consumed domestically.[20] A number of production-sharing agreements (PSAs) with major international oil companies have been signed, but oil sector operations remain dominated by SOCAR, although this is expected to change in the next few years.

SOCAR is also Azerbaijan's major producer of gas. To a much smaller extent, gas is also produced by the Azerbaijan International Operating Company (AIOC), a British Petroleum (BP)-led consortium. During 1993–1999, SOCAR produced around 6 billion cubic meters of gas annually, most of which was consumed domestically. Recently Azerbaijan started importing gas to substitute for crude that is now exported instead of being refined into fuel oil for electricity generation. The state-owned company Azerigaz dominates natural gas transmission, distribution, and retail sale. It purchases gas from SOCAR at a very low price (see below). At the retail level, gas is sold to consumers at an even lower price (US$8 per tcm in 2000). The largest consumers

---

[19]In large part, high external current account deficits in Azerbaijan reflect imports for oil investment projects, financed by foreign direct investment inflows in the capital account.

[20]The country has estimated recoverable crude and condensate reserves of 10 billion barrels, equivalent to about 100 years of production, concentrated in 61 fields targeted for commercial development.

of gas are households (40 percent), the electricity company Azerenergy (30 percent), and other public utilities and budget organizations (20 percent).

The electricity sector has remained almost completely government-owned and is dominated by Azerenergy, which owns the thermal and hydroelectric generating companies, the transmission network, and almost all of the distribution network.[21] Around 16 GWh of electricity are produced annually. The thermal generating stations use heavy fuel (mazut) and natural gas, which is supplied mostly free of charge by SOCAR. The largest consumers of electricity are households (40 percent), wholesalers, including the regional joint stock distribution companies (30 percent), and industry (16 percent).

Energy QFAs

Since Azerbaijan's energy sector still resembles the centralized and government-owned complex of the Soviet era, with economic relations between the energy companies dominated by special arrangements and public policy considerations, it appears appropriate to consider all three energy subsectors jointly.[22] Using consolidated financial data (i.e., revenue, expenditure, and profit/loss accounts) for the major energy sector companies, it is possible to adjust actual data by revaluing input purchases, intrasectoral volume transactions, and sales to end users with appropriate benchmark prices to compute QFAs related to mispricing, arrears, and excessive losses.[23]

Mispricing

Most of the energy in Azerbaijan is purchased and sold at inappropriately low prices. In addition to generally low domestic energy prices, the government provides additional implicit subsidies through preferential tariffs or exemptions on energy products for a significant

---

[21]However, in 2001, the Baku electricity distribution network was formally separated from Azerenergy and a long-term contract was signed with a foreign private company to manage it.

[22]Such consolidation is commonly applied when calculating financial results of large corporations.

[23]Our methodology and data draw on previous studies of energy QFAs in Azerbaijan. See Mamedov and Huseynov (2000) and Nell (2001a and 2001b).

share of the population (estimated at 20 percent in 1999). Households pay lower tariffs than enterprises, giving rise to cross-subsidization. Although privileges for major groups (e.g., teachers) have been eliminated, other special groups (e.g., war veterans, refugees, and single elderly) still remain either exempt from paying for electricity or receive a 50 percent discount on the already low tariffs.[24]

Within the energy sector, SOCAR supplies gas (to Azerigaz), heavy fuel (to Azerenergy), and oil and oil products (to end consumers) at prices that are significantly below market-related prices. The total quasi-fiscal subsidy provided through SOCAR's domestic sales to other energy companies amounted to manat 2,400 billion (US$550 million), equivalent to at least 14 percent of GDP in 1999. In 2000, the quasi-fiscal subsidy on account of mispricing for various types of energy transactions rose, conservatively estimated, to over 20 percent of GDP, primarily reflecting that domestic prices were not raised in line with international prices.[25] As discussed in Section II, these results depend crucially on key assumptions regarding demand elasticities and benchmark prices. However, the magnitude of the result suggests that, regardless of which benchmark price or demand elasticity assumption is chosen, energy QFAs on account of mispricing reached very large proportions in recent years.

Arrears

Even at low actual prices Azerbaijan's energy companies do not get paid fully, and in a timely manner, by end consumers. Collection rates of Azerigaz dropped from 50 percent in 1995 to around 35 percent during 1996–99, before plunging to 13 percent in 2000. Those of Azerenergy fell from 35 percent in 1998 to 13 percent in 2000.[26] The most important nonpayer for Azerigaz has been Azerenergy, while for Azerenergy the main nonpayers have been households, which on average pay only 10 percent of their bills. After subtracting intrasectoral arrears, the quasi-fiscal subsidy provided to end users on account of arrears amounted to 7 percent of GDP in 1999 (Table 18.5). This is likely an underestimate of

---

[24]Preferential tariffs have reportedly been eliminated as of January 2002.

[25]For details on the estimates for the year 2000, see Nell (2001a and 2001b) and Petri, Taube, and Tsyvinski (2002).

[26]No distinction is made between cash and noncash collections due to the unavailability of data. Collection rates for 2000 are for the first nine months of the year.

Table 18.5. *Azerbaijan: Energy Quasi-Fiscal Activities Due to Arrears, 1998–99[1]*

	1998	1999	1998	1999
	(In billions of manat)		(In percent of GDP)	
Arrears of end consumers to Azerenergy and Azerigaz	1,500	1,400	9.0	8.5
Minus arrears of Azerenergy to Azerigaz	170	220	1.0	1.3
Quasi-fiscal activity due to arrears	1,330	1,180	8.0	7.2

Sources: Nell, 2001a and 2001b; World Bank; and IMF staff estimates.
[1]New arrears accrued during the period.

the total quasi-fiscal subsidy provided to energy consumers due to non-payments as arrears to SOCAR for the sale of oil products, for example to the agricultural sector during planting and harvesting seasons, are not captured in our analysis owing to a lack of data.

Excessive losses

The third component of energy sector QFAs in Azerbaijan is excessive losses related to theft, fraud, the lack of metering, and technical problems in transmission and distribution. As these phenomena are tolerated by the government (the owner), they can also be considered a QFA provided to energy sector companies. In principle, these costs would not be incurred to the same extent if the energy sector were privately owned or run on a fully commercial basis with a hard budget constraint. The production and distribution costs for energy products in Azerbaijan are substantially higher than what would normally be expected, even after adjusting for location-specific equipment quality and maintenance needs.[27] Excessive losses are difficult to estimate, but it appears that they are considerably smaller than the QFAs related to mispricing and arrears. According to one World Bank estimate, for example, in 1999 unnecessary losses in the energy sector amounted to manat 150 billion (US$34 million), or 1 percent of GDP.

---

[27]Excessive losses can be computed as the difference between the reported losses and acceptable losses as defined in accordance with international standards and adjusted for the equipment used in Azerbaijan. Note that calculations of energy sector expenditure are sensitive to accounting conventions used; this is particularly relevant for the measurement of capital depreciation.

Table 18.6. *Azerbaijan: Tax and Social Contribution Arrears*
of Energy Companies, 1998–99
(In billions of manat, unless otherwise indcated)

	1998	1999
SOCAR	600	825
Azerigaz	151	77
Azerenergy	54	36
Total	805	939
Total (in percent of GDP)	5.0	5.5

Sources: Nell 2001a and 2001b.

Tax arrears

Mispricing and payment arrears on outputs in the energy sector have in turn triggered tax arrears and noncash settlement of tax liabilities by the energy sector companies. For example, in both 1998 and 1999 energy sector companies amassed tax and social contribution arrears of around 5 percent of GDP, with SOCAR as the largest contributor (Table 18.6). SOCAR's stock of tax arrears rose to 23 percent of GDP at end–1999 (IMF, 2000). In part because of tax arrears from energy companies, total tax arrears in Azerbaijan have increased sharply in recent years, which has complicated budgetary management. If large taxpayers such as SOCAR are allowed to run tax arrears, other taxpayers also have an incentive for noncompliance. At the same time, however, budgetary organizations are running arrears on energy payments to SOCAR and other energy companies, as explained above, thereby contributing to the proliferation of arrears.

Summary

Based on the calculations presented above, it is possible to recalculate the income statement of Azerbaijan's energy sector by adjusting actually received revenues for the mispricing of output and arrears and expenditures for the mispricing and nonpayment of inputs, assuming cost recovery (Table 18.7). For 1999, such recalculations suggest that energy sector revenues would have been higher by 27 percent of GDP (manat 4,500 billion) if implicit subsidies on account of mispricing and arrears on sales of outputs (i.e., electricity and gas) had been taken into account. As explained above, mispricing is the most important implicit

Table 18.7. *Azerbaijan: Adjusted Financial Balance of the Consolidated Energy Sector, 1999*[1]
(In billions of manat, unless otherwise indicated)

	1999
Total costs (adjusted)	5,248
Actual costs (cash basis)[2]	1,909
QFAs due to mispricing of inputs (e.g., oil)	2,400
Tax arrears	939
Arrears on other inputs	...
Underinvestment	...
Total revenue (adjusted)	5,248
Actual revenue from sales of outputs (cash basis)	725
QFAs due to arrears on output sales	1,180
QFAs due to mispricing of outputs (residual)	3,343
Mispricing without excessive losses	3,193
Excessive losses	150
Total QFAs	4,523
Mispricing of outputs	3,343
Arrears on output sales	1,180
Total QFAs (in percent of GDP)	26.7

Sources: World Bank; and authors' calculations.

[1]Follows the financial balance methodology described above, consolidating the domestic financial results of SOCAR, Azerigaz, and Azerenergy and intrasectoral arrears and mispricing. Nonfuel costs of energy enterprises remain unadjusted.

[2]Including manat 150 billion on account of excessive losses.

subsidy element, accounting for almost 75 percent of total energy QFAs.

These results suggest that implicit subsidies provided through low energy prices and arrears were significantly larger than explicitly measured budgetary expenditures, which totaled 21 percent of GDP in 2000.[28] Large energy QFAs thus obfuscate the overall extent as well as the relative focus of the government's involvement in the economy, as, for example, the implicit and untargeted energy subsidies to households and enterprises are more than ten times higher than what the government spends on health through the budget. While the govern-

---

[28]Adjusting nominal GDP upward (by about 20 percent) to take account of energy mispricing would result in somewhat lower, but still large, energy sector QFAs relative to GDP.

ment has provided large and untargeted implicit energy subsidies to the whole population, explicit budgetary spending on social sectors has remained inadequate and characterized by major inefficiencies, causing a deterioration in the quality of social sector service provision, especially for the poor.[29] Against the background of substantial oil wealth and revenues, the government's policies appear to have been highly ineffective with regard to social objectives, since poverty, income inequality, and unemployment increased in the second half of the 1990s.[30]

V. Conclusions and Policy Implications

In the preceding sections, we have analyzed the extent, causes, and implications of energy sector QFAs through two case studies based on two different methodologies. Taken together with the findings of a survey of other FSU countries (Appendix), the key results of our analysis are as follows. First, in most of the former Soviet Union countries QFAs in the energy sector have been large and pervasive in recent years, often accounting for 5 percent of GDP or more. These activities have declined in some of the energy-importing countries (e.g., Armenia, Kyrgyz Republic, and Ukraine), but have risen in energy-rich countries (e.g., Azerbaijan, Russia, and Turkmenistan), largely on account of higher international prices and failure to increase domestic prices accordingly. Azerbaijan appears to have the largest energy sector QFAs among the FSU countries, estimated at more than 20 percent of GDP in 1999 and 2000. Second, the primary sources of energy sector QFAs in these countries are mispricing and the toleration of arrears. Other QFAs, such as excessive losses due to neglect and theft, are quantitatively much less important, although they clearly have adverse implications for future energy sector operations as they lead to capital

---

[29]Budgetary outlays on education and health barely cover wages, with few resources left for supplies and maintenance. In addition, informal user charges have surged and made education and health care less accessible to the poor. For further details see World Bank (1997) and IMF (2000).

[30]According to Azerbaijan's Poverty Reduction Strategy Paper (PRSP), 61 percent of the population lived below the poverty line in 1999. The Gini coefficient for the adult population rose to 0.35 in 1999, and the unemployment rate went up from 10 percent in 1994 to 14 percent in 1999. In 1999, wages in the oil and gas sector were on average ten times higher than in agriculture (Azerbaijan Republic, 2001).

stock depletion. Third, energy sector payment arrears are key in triggering tax and other payment arrears by energy companies and in perpetuating the vicious circle that involves arrears, offsets, netting operations, and noncash payments. Fourth, in addition to quantifiable energy sector QFAs like those related to mispricing and the toleration of arrears, there are others that are more difficult to estimate and integrate into the analysis. These comprise excessive losses, noncash operations, and government guarantees on domestic and external borrowing by energy companies.

With these findings in mind, the following policy conclusions can be drawn.[31]

Reforms should first of all focus on mispricing and the toleration of payment arrears—the main energy sector QFAs. Because of inappropriately low energy tariffs and the toleration of payment arrears, energy consumption and waste have remained high across the FSU even after ten years of transition, particularly in the energy-rich countries where resource rents are dissipated to provide untargeted subsidies to the population as well as (state-owned) enterprises. To reduce or eliminate QFAs in FSU countries, energy prices should be raised, often substantially so, and preferential tariffs or free provision of services for specific consumer groups eliminated as much as possible. These reforms should be combined with the provision of explicit and better-targeted cash transfers to needy population groups. Implicit subsidies to (state-owned) enterprises in the industrial, agricultural, and other sectors should be reduced or eliminated and, if deemed necessary, replaced by explicit subsidies from the budget, with the objective to reduce them over time. Raising energy tariffs will not only improve the efficiency of the energy companies themselves and make them more attractive for privatization, but it will also trigger restructuring in enterprises that are still benefiting from cheap energy. As such restructuring will lead to retrenchment of workers, it will be important to strengthen existing or put in place new safety nets to mitigate the adjustment costs. Energy price increases should also be combined with better enforcement efforts to reduce arrears and improve pay-

---

[31]There is scope for refining the analytical frameworks applied here, for example by differentiating between cash and noncash payments by introducing a discount factor for the latter. For an attempt to analyze implicit subsidies due to offsets in Russia see Pinto, Drebentsov, and Morozov (2000). However, it would be difficult to determine the size of the discount factor, which could vary over time, across countries, and perhaps even from one transaction to another.

ment discipline, including better use of metering for residential and commercial users. In this context, governments need to improve budget planning and management to ensure full payment of utility bills by budgetary organizations, while allowing energy companies to cut off supplies.

As far as fiscal policy is concerned, greater efforts are required in capturing energy sector QFAs as part of the fiscal landscape, through more data dissemination, analysis, and policy reforms focusing on fiscal transparency and accountability. In many FSU countries, there appears to be a need for closer monitoring and public dissemination of data on the financial situation of individual energy sector enterprises and the financial flows between the energy sector and other sectors of the economy. A good example in this regard is Armenia, where quarterly cash flows of energy sector enterprises are monitored closely by the government. Also, in Azerbaijan, Moldova, the Kyrgyz Republic, and Ukraine audits of the large energy companies have been performed, another important avenue for further reforms. To improve fiscal transparency, (energy) QFAs could be included in standard fiscal analysis and reporting, and they could be addressed in the context of fiscal Reports on the Observance of Standards and Codes (ROSCs).[32] For example, it may be useful to augment conventional measures of the government budget deficit to reflect (energy) QFAs. Alternatively, the financial performance of energy enterprises, bank credit to these enterprises, and energy QFAs could be subjected to closer regular scrutiny separately from the budget. In Azerbaijan, the government has begun to address energy sector QFAs through reforms focusing on energy sector financial discipline and fiscal transparency. For instance, some of the energy sector QFAs that have previously been provided by SOCAR to Azerenergy and Azerigaz are now included in quarterly reports on budget implementation, with SOCAR receiving tax credits for the value of these subsidies. Azerbaijan's government has chosen to implement a sequence of reforms that emphasizes gradualism and focuses first on improving payment discipline and establishing greater transparency while tackling the mispricing of domestic energy products only gradually over the medium term.

---

[32]Such reports have been published on the IMF's website (http://www.imf.org) for Armenia, Azerbaijan, the Kyrgyz Republic, and Ukraine. The report on Russia is under preparation.

Appendix. Overview of Quasi-Fiscal Activities in the Former Soviet Union (FSU)[1]

Country	Nonpayments and Arrears	Mispricing	Others	Total
Armenia	Detailed estimates not available.	Low communal tariffs.	Theft and technical losses: 15 percent of electricity generated.	1999: 4.5 percent. 2000: 2.3 percent.
Azerbaijan (1999)	Arrears from end consumers, intrasectoral arrears. Total arrears: 7.2 percent.	Below-market-value pricing of oil and gas; below-cost-recovery tariffs; privileged groups. Total mispricing: 20 percent.	Excessive losses: 0.8 percent.	Total: 28.0 percent.
Belarus	Domestic arrears: 0.8 percent.	Gas is supplied by Russia at a third of world price. Mispricing of imported gas— 12 percent.	Directed credits to agriculture: 1.4 percent (2000); 0.5 percent (2001).	Domestic QFA: 2.2 percent. Total: 14.2 percent.
Georgia	No information available.	No information available.	No information available.	No information available.
Kazakhstan	No information available.	Oil is sold domestically at 25 percent of the world price.	Subsidies and privileges skewed toward the new capital, Astana.	Estimates not available.
Kyrgyz Republic	Collection rates for electricity increased from 70 to 87 percent in 2000.	60 percent of population is privileged; tariffs are below cost recovery; cross-subsidization from exported electricity.	Technical and commercial losses: 2.5 percent.	Agriculture: 0.4 percent. Budget: 0.5 percent. Population: 3.8 percent. Others: 1.3 percent. Total: 6 percent.

Martin Petri, Günther Taube, and Aleh Tsyvinski

Appendix (concluded)

Country	Nonpayments and Arrears	Mispricing	Others	Total
Moldova	Collection rates: Population—88 percent. Energy Company—50 percent.	Implicit subsidies for privileged groups—3.2 percent (in 1999), but since then replaced by cash compensation (1.5 percent).	No estimates available.	Total for 1999: 5 percent, but declining in 2000.
Russia	Electricity end-user arrears: 6 percent (1998).	No estimates available, but sizable QFAs due to mispricing in all energy subsectors.	No estimates available.	No estimates available.
Tajikistan	No detailed estimates available.	Tariffs are below cost recovery and market prices (electricity and natural gas).	Technical losses: 1.5 percent.	Total for electricity and natural gas: 7.3 percent.
Turkmenistan	No information available.	Domestic oil price is 1/20 of the true economic value. Implicit petroleum sector subsidy: US$300 million (6 percent). Below-market pricing of gas: US$180 million (4 percent). Below-cost-recovery pricing of electricity: US$105 million (3 percent).	No information available.	Total: 13 percent.
Ukraine	Arrears are decreasing, but still significant. Gas sector arrears: 4.1 percent (1999); 1.1 percent (2000). Electricity arrears: 0.7 percent.	Below-market pricing in the gas sector: 1.5 percent (1999); 3.3 percent (2000). Below-cost recovery for electricity: gross, 1.4 percent; net, 1.1 percent.	Excessive technical losses and theft.	Arrears: 1.8 percent. Underpricing: 4.7 percent. Total: 6.5 percent.
Uzbekistan	Arrears in the electricity sector.	Below-market-value sales of energy domestically.	Multiple exchange rate system with preferences for energy sector.	Estimates not available.

Source: Survey of IMF economists.
[1] All data are for 2000 and are in percent of GDP, unless otherwise indicated.

Bibliography

Azerbaijan Republic, 2001, *Poverty Reduction Strategy Paper, Interim Report*, available via the Internet at http://www.imf.org/external/np/prsp/2001/aze/01.

European Bank for Reconstruction and Development, 2001, *Transition Report 2001: Energy in Transition* (London).

International Monetary Fund, 1998, *Republic of Uzbekistan: Recent Economic Developments*, IMF Staff Country Report No. 98/116 (Washington).

——, 2000, "Azerbaijan Republic: Report on the Observance of Standards and Codes (ROSC) Fiscal Transparency Module" (Washington). Available via the Internet: http://www.imf.org/external/np/rosc/aze/fiscal.htm.

——, and others, 1991, *A Study of the Soviet Economy*, Vol. 3 (Paris: Organization for Economic Cooperation and Development).

Johnson, Simon, Daniel Kaufmann, and Andrei Shleifer, 1997, "The Unofficial Economy in Transition," *Brookings Papers on Economic Activity*: 2 (Washington: Brookings Institution), pp. 159–239.

Krishnaswamy, V., 1999, "Non-Payment in the Electricity Sector in Eastern Europe and the Former Soviet Union," World Bank Technical Paper No. 423 (Washington: World Bank).

Lovei, Laszlo, 1998, "Electricity Reform in Ukraine—The Impact of Weak Governance and Budget Crises," *Viewpoint*, Report No. 168 (Washington: World Bank). Available on the Internet: http://rru.worldbank.org/viewpoint/HTML/Notes/168/168summary.html.

Mackenzie, George A., and Peter Stella, 1996, *Quasi-Fiscal Operations of Public Financial Institutions*, IMF Occasional Paper No. 142 (Washington: International Monetary Fund).

Mamedov, F., and E. Huseynov, 2000, "Azerbaijan Republic Energy Sector Quasi-Fiscal Deficit Assessment" (unpublished; Washington: World Bank).

Nell, Jacob, 2001a, "Fiscal Implications of Low Utility Collection Rates" (unpublished; Baku: Macroeconomic Policy Group).

——, 2001b, "SOCAR Taxation and Energy Sector Subsidies" (unpublished; Baku: Macroeconomic Policy Group).

Oxford Analytica, various issues.

Petri, Martin, Günther Taube, and Aleh Tsyvinski, 2002, "Energy Sector Quasi-Fiscal Activities in the Countries of the Former Soviet Union," IMF Working Paper 02/60 (Washington: International Monetary Fund).

Pinto, Brian, Vladimir Drebentsov, and Alexander Morozov, 2000, "Dismantling Russia's Nonpayments System—Creating Conditions for Growth," World Bank Technical Paper No. 471 (Washington: World Bank).

Rosenberg, Christoph B., and Maarten de Zeeuw, 2000, "Welfare Effects of Uzbekistan's Foreign Exchange Regime," IMF Working Paper 00/61 (Washington: International Monetary Fund).

Tanzi, Vito, 1993, "The Budget Deficit in Transition: A Cautionary Note," *Staff Papers*, International Monetary Fund, Vol. 40 (September), pp. 697–707.

Taube, Günther, 2001, "Fiscal Policy and Quasi-Fiscal Activities in the Islamic Republic of Iran," paper presented at the conference of the Central Bank of the Islamic Republic of Iran on "Structural Reforms in the Real and Financial Sector of the Iranian Economy," Tehran, May.

United States & Foreign Commercial Service and United States Department of State, 2000, "Oil and Gas Services in Ukraine." Available via the Internet: http://www.bisnis.doc.gov/bisnis/country/000203oil-ua.htm.

World Bank, 1997, "Central and Eastern Europe: Power Sector Reform in Selected Countries," Energy Sector Management Assistance Program Paper No. 196/97 (Washington).

———, 1998, "Profile of Energy Sector Activities of the World Bank in Europe and Central Asia Region," World Bank Working Paper No. 18891 (Washington).

———, 2001, "Towards a New Role for State in Infrastructure and Utilities," in *Kyrgyz Republic: Fiscal Sustainability Study*, World Bank Country Study No. 23404 (Washington).

Contributors

Ehtisham Ahmad, Division Chief, Fiscal Affairs Department, IMF

Steven Barnett, Resident Representative in Thailand, Asia and Pacific Department, IMF

Thomas Baunsgaard, Economist, Fiscal Affairs Department, IMF

Benedict Bingham, Deputy Division Chief, Asia and Pacific Department, IMF

Giorgio Brosio, Professor of Public Finance and Local Government, Department of Economics, University of Turin, Italy

Benedict Clements, Deputy Division Chief, Fiscal Affairs Department, IMF

James A. Daniel, Deputy Division Chief, Fiscal Affairs Department, IMF

Jeffrey Davis, Senior Advisor, Fiscal Affairs Department, IMF

Benn Eifert, Department of Economics, Stanford University

Ramón Espinasa, Consultant, Integration and Regional Programs Department, Inter-American Development Bank

Annalisa Fedelino, Senior Economist, Fiscal Affairs Department, IMF

Giulio Federico, Formerly Summer Intern, Fiscal Affairs Department, IMF

Kevin Fletcher, Economist, Fiscal Affairs Department, IMF

Alan Gelb, Chief Economist, Africa Regional Office, World Bank

Sanjeev Gupta, Assistant Director, Fiscal Affairs Department, IMF

Ricardo Hausmann, Professor, Kennedy School of Government, Harvard University

Gabriela Inchauste, Economist, Fiscal Affairs Department, IMF

Paul Mathieu, Senior Economist, European II Department, IMF

Charles E. McLure, Jr., Senior Fellow, Hoover Institution, Stanford University

Charles McPherson, Senior Advisor, Oil, Gas, Chemicals, and Mining Department, World Bank

Eric Mottu, Economist, Middle Eastern Department, IMF

Rolando Ossowski, Division Chief, Fiscal Affairs Department, IMF

Martin Petri, Economist, Fiscal Affairs Department, IMF

Roberto Rigobon, Professor, Sloan School of Management, Massachusetts Institute of Technology

Dominque Simard, Economist, Fiscal Affairs Department, IMF

Martin Skancke, Director General, Office of the Prime Minister, Norway

Emil M. Sunley, Assistant Director, Fiscal Affairs Department, IMF

Nils Borje Tallroth, Senior Economist, Africa Regional Office, World Bank

Günther Taube, Senior Economist, Fiscal Affairs Department, IMF

Aleh Tsyvinski, Formerly Summer Intern, Fiscal Affairs Department, IMF

Bert van Selm, Economist, European II Department, IMF

Alvaro Vivanco, Formerly Research Assistant, Fiscal Affairs Department, IMF

John Wakeman-Linn, Deputy Division Chief, European II Department, IMF